# UNHOLY ALLIANCE

# Unholy Alliance

## Russian-German Relations
## from the Treaty of Brest-Litovsk to the
## Treaty of Berlin

## GERALD FREUND

\*

*With an Introduction by*
## J. W. WHEELER-BENNETT

### HARCOURT, BRACE AND COMPANY
### NEW YORK

© 1957 BY

Gerald Freund

*first American edition*

PRINTED IN GREAT BRITAIN

*To*
GILBERT FOWLER WHITE
*and*
JOHN W. WHEELER-BENNETT
*for their*
*Friendship and Inspiration*

# CONTENTS

# CONTENTS

# FOREWORD

IN the writing of this book I have received help and criticism from a number of friends and scholars to whom I wish to express my deepest gratitude.

First of all, I am immensely grateful to Mr John W. Wheeler-Bennett and to Mr James Joll of St Antony's College, Oxford, for their good counsel and constant encouragement without which this book could not have been written. I am indebted to the President and Fellows of St John's College, Oxford, for the pleasant two years I spent there as a Fulbright Scholar. To the Warden, Mr F. W. D. Deakin, and Fellows of St Antony's College, Oxford, also to the Rockefeller Foundation of New York, who made it possible for me to remain at Oxford University as a scholar and then as a Research Fellow, I am sincerely grateful not only for their generous support, but also for making these two years among the most enjoyable and profitable ones of my academic career.

For their kind assistance in my research into the German Foreign Office and German Army Archives I am especially indebted to the Hon. Margaret Lambert and members of her staff, Miss A. C. Johnston and Mr M. H. Fischer in particular, in the German Documents Section of the Foreign Office Library, and also to Mr Paul Sweet of the Department of State, as well as to Mr Elbert Huber and Mr Robert Krauskopf of the National Archives. I am also grateful to the staffs of the Wiener Library, the Public Record Office, and the Library of the Royal Institute of International Affairs for their courteous and efficient attention at all times.

I wish to express my gratitude to the authors, editors, publishers, and agents concerned for permission to quote from the following books: *Soviet Documents on Foreign Policy* edited by J. Degras, Oxford University Press for the Royal Institute of International Affairs; *Vanguard of Nazism* by R. G. L. Waite, Harvard University Press; *Stalin and German Communism* by R. Fischer, Harvard University Press; 'Reichswehr und Rote Armee' by H. Speidel, 'Deutsch-Russische Beziehungen im Sommer 1918' by H. W. Gatzke, 'Von Rapallo nach Berlin: Stresemann und die deutsche

Russlandpolitik' by H. W. Gatzke, *Vierteljahrshefte für Zeit-geschichte*; Deutsche Verlags-Anstalt Gmbh. for the Institut für Zeitgeschichte; *Deutschlands Weg nach Rapallo* by W. v. Blücher, Limes Verlag; *Russia and the Weimar Republic* by L. Kochan, Bowes and Bowes; *The Soviets in World Affairs* by L. Fischer, Princeton University Press; *The Incompatible Allies* by G. Hilger and A. G. Meyer, The Macmillan Company; *The Bolshevik Revolution 1917-1923* and *The Interregnum 1923-1924* by E. H. Carr, Curtis Brown Ltd and Macmillan and Company Ltd; *Hindenburg: The Wooden Titan, Brest-Litovsk: The Forgotten Peace, The Nemesis of Power* by J. W. Wheeler-Bennett, Macmillan and Company Ltd.

I am indebted to many in America, Britain, and Germany who assisted me in locating sources and who gave me much important information in the course of my research work. Of these I would like to mention with especial gratitude Major-General Telford Taylor of New York City; Professor Fritz Epstein of the Library of Congress; Professor Gordon Craig of Princeton University; Professor E. H. Carr of Trinity College, Cambridge; Mr Alan Bullock, Censor of St Catherine's Society, Oxford; Mr Richard Taylor, formerly of the U.S. Educational Commission in the U.K., London; Mr Gustav Hilger of the Auswärtiges Amt, Bonn; and Dr Herbert Helbig of the Freie Universität, Berlin. I also wish to thank the following: Mr Lionel Kochan for letting me read the manuscript of his valuable book on Russo-German relations before its publication; Mr Jackson Piotrow of Haverford College and Christ Church, Oxford, for his help with the translations; Mr Peter Calvocoressi of Chatto and Windus Ltd, who has been more helpful and tolerant than any new author has the right to expect of a publisher; Miss Jane Trask of Radcliffe College and Lady Margaret Hall, Oxford, whose assiduous labours in correcting and checking the manuscript have made an invaluable contribution to this work. Finally, I wish to thank my parents for their encourage-ment and understanding at all times, and especially for their endurance during the last four years while this book was in the making.

GERALD FREUND

# INTRODUCTION

I GLADLY accept the invitation of Mr Gerald Freund, and his publishers, to write an introduction to this book, because in a sense I feel an indirect responsibility for it in that I encouraged the Author, when at Oxford, to expand his excellent doctorate thesis into book form. The result is a work of significance. Much has been told and written of the degree of German-Russian collaboration during the second decade of this century, but it has remained for Mr Freund to produce fresh evidence from his researches into the documentary material which has become available since the conclusion of the Second World War and, hence, to throw new light on certain of the hitherto obscure aspects of the subject. His book, therefore, constitutes an important addition to the literature of this period of history.

There is, I think, something of particular interest—and of a certain sinister import—in the fact that the story which Mr Freund has told in these pages follows a pattern in German-Russian relations which has persisted for nearly two hundred years, resulting in a series of estrangements, distinguished for their bitterness, and of *rapprochements*, remarkable for their warmth.

Who, for example, could have foreseen in 1761, when Russian troops had overrun Prussia, occupied Berlin and humbled Frederick the Great, that the sudden death of the Tzarina Elizabeth would bring to the Russian throne Peter III, the inveterate admirer of Frederick and of Prussia, and that he would promptly make peace with his hero? Or that, nine years after this reprieve, Prussia would join with Russia and Austria—in Frederick's own blasphemous phrase—'in taking Communion in the one Eucharistic body which is Poland'?

A cardinal factor in this Russo-German relationship has been the existence of an independent Poland; for, in general, it has been true that, when separated by a buffer state, the two great Powers of Eastern Europe have been more or less friendly, whereas a contiguity of frontiers has bred hostility. In the period between the first and third partitions of Poland (1772-1795), Russia and

Prussia were in the position of two gangsters, who with a weaker confederate—Austria—were dividing up a rich haul of loot. While the division was in process, relations between the partners remained amicable, save for the growlings which arose if one or the other took rather too much for his share. But when Poland had vanished from the map of Europe Russia and Prussia confronted one another with nothing more to consume than each other.

The outbreak of the French Revolution and the rise of the common enemy of egalitarianism averted any major clash, and Napoleon's creation of the Grand Duchy of Warsaw, under French protection, still further improved Russo-Prussian relations. But the bond, forged in the common task of freeing Europe from the Napoleonic hegemony, was very much a one-sided partnership, with Russia as the dominant partner. Nor was it without its strains and rifts. The Napoleonic wars carried both Russian and Prussian troops on to each other's soil as invaders. And though, by the Convention of Tauroggen (1812), Yorck paved the way for Prussia to join the Tsar as an ally in harrying the retreating French armies, it was through Prussia and other parts of Germany that the Russians had to fight their way before reaching France. From 1815 to 1860, Prussia was virtually a vassal of Muscovy. After grovelling to Napoleon for 15 years she now grovelled to Russia for 45, and indeed to Austria also. Nor was Prussia alone in her Russian subservience. The omnipotent presence of the Tsar was felt in every princely German Court. 'If,' Prince Bülow has written of his childhood days at the Court of Strelitz, 'if the Grand Duke of Mechlenburg-Strelitz said that the Tsar would have wished this or that, it was as if God himself had spoken.'

Bismarck's creation of a unified Germany was effected as much in reaction against this Russian and Austrian tutelage as it was stimulated by rivalry with France. It was the emergence of this new force in Central Europe, and the final extinction of Poland, which exacerbated Russo-Prussian relations in the later 'sixties. Bismarck, however, when he had made Germany independent of both France and Russia, bought the friendship of Russia with the Black Sea Agreement of 1871, and made the maintenance of this friendship a salient objective of his policy, successfully avoiding major controversies with his powerful Eastern neighbour throughout his long term of office. He himself, however, departed temporarily from this policy in concluding the Dual Alliance with Austria-Hungary in 1879, but in the political precepts which he laid down for the guidance of the young Emperor Wilhelm I friendship with Russia transcended all other considerations.

This policy was not prompted merely by a dread of a 'two-front war' but by a sincere belief in the possibilities of Russo-German co-operation. Contrary to common belief, Bismarck was not an advocate of the Pan-German doctrines; on the contrary, he regarded them as fantastic. He did, however, believe in the 'manifest destiny' of Russia and Germany to share *Weltmacht*, and he was confident, not without reason, that together the two Powers could do anything they desired.

Herein lay the germ of the deep-seated conflict of thought which existed in the German Foreign Office and General Staff after Bismarck's departure: that battle for power between the Eastern school, which followed the old Prince's policy of collaboration with Russia, and the 'greater Germany' school, which sought the territorial aggrandizement of the Reich, if necessary at Russia's expense.

The 'greater Germany' school won the day; the erratic policy of Wilhelm II and his avowed preference for Austria-Hungary sapped the foundations of the structure of alliance that Bismarck had built so laboriously, drove Russia into the arms of France, and ultimately made possible the formation of the Triple Entente. The First World War was thereby brought within measurable distance, since Germany had contributed to her own encirclement (*Einkreisung*) and thus produced her own claustrophobic state of mind.

The process of alienation was completed by the humiliation of Russian arms by Germany in 1914-1917, though it is of interest to note that throughout these years there was a strong Peace Party in Petrograd who were vainly endeavouring to persuade the Tsar to come to terms, however humiliating, with Germany, in order to preserve autocracy in Russia. There followed the turmoil of the Bolshevik Revolution, in which the Germans played no insignificant part in facilitating Lenin's return to Russia from Switzerland in the famous 'sealed train,' and the 'Tilsit Peace' of Brest-Litovsk in March 1918, in which the 'greater Germany' school gave free rein to their ambitions.

To many it appeared that in no foreseeable period could Russia and Germany be found in the same camp. But one of the unpredictable *rapprochements* was again to occur.

It is a curious fact that, just as the overvaulting ambition of triumphant German militarism had dictated the Peace of Brest-Litovsk, so now this same German militarism, grown humble and cunning in defeat and concerned only with its own survival, brought about the renewal of amicable relations. In the shifting of power which followed the collapse of the monarchies of Central Europe, Bismarck's tradition again asserted itself; Germany and Russia found themselves drawn together as pariahs and discovered that they had grievances, as well as interests, in common.

It is at this point that Mr Freund's book begins. His pages tell, with a wealth of documentary support, the strange and ever-fascinating story of German-Russian collaboration during the 'twenties, with its enthralling mysteries and its eternal queries.

The genius manifested by General Hans von Seeckt in making bricks without straw and fashioning swords out of ploughshares can never fail to hold the interest of the student of this period and Mr Freund does it full justice. And there is the enigma of Gustav Stresemann's condonation of, and participation in, von Seeckt's clandestine rearmament policies. On this Mr Freund sheds fresh light and poses the question: 'Was Stresemann a patriot or a statesman? How much, after all, is foresight a part of statesmanship?' He wisely refrains from passing a conclusive judgment on the German Foreign Minister, resting his case on the statement that Dr Stresemann's motives 'are still a matter of conjecture.'

No such uncertainty, however, attaches to the impulses of General von Seeckt. Throughout the period of this strange *mariage de convenance* the motives of the German General Staff were those of pure expediency. In no conceivable way were they actuated by a sympathy or an affinity for Bolshevism. Their aim and purpose was collaboration with *Russia*, with her vast resources in manpower and material; they treated with the Soviet Union on a purely technical basis, and maintained a stern watch on any possible infiltration of Communist doctrines into the ranks of the Reichswehr. It was typical of von Seeckt's singleness of purpose that he could use the Reichswehr with equal efficiency to suppress a Communist uprising in Germany or to collaborate with the Red Army in Russia. The Bolsheviks, for their part, were equally undeceived as to the fundamental nature of the cordiality obtaining between themselves and Germany. Both were pursuing a policy of stark *Realpolitik* in which ideology played no part.

With the downfall of the Weimar Republic in January 1933 and the founding of the Third Reich, a change was to be expected in Soviet-German relations, due partly to the fact that under the Nazi regime the clandestine circumvention of the military clauses of the Treaty of Versailles was no longer necessary, and partly to the very definite ideological views of Adolf Hitler towards the Soviet Union.

Politically and doctrinally opposed to Russia, Hitler proclaimed a deathless war against Communism and reverted in his planning to the imperialist designs of Ludendorff and the German General Staff at Brest-Litovsk for a German *Lebensraum* in the strategically important Baltic lands and the rich black soil of the Ukraine. Yet the Führer did not at once completely disrupt the course of German-Russian relations. While the Comintern and the Goebbels propaganda machine spewed forth a reciprocal flow of venom and recrimination, the German Government was careful to maintain the economic agreements with Russia, and went so far, in 1933, as to renew the Pact of Mutual Non-Aggression for a further period of five years.

Moreover, Hitler was either unable or unwilling to break the liaison of the German General Staff with Moscow, and comparatively amicable relations were maintained on this level until the Russian military purge of 1937, when the Chief of the General Staff of the Red Army, Marshal Tukhachevsky, and six other general officers were court-martialled on a charge of high treason and summarily executed. In the drastic reorganization of the Reichswehr which followed the Blomberg-Fritsch crisis of February 1938, the Führer took occasion to dispense with the services of a dozen senior general officers, many of whom had been nurtured in the Seeckt tradition. The liaison was thus brought to an abrupt termination.

One reason for Hitler's circumspection in his early dealings with the Soviet Union was that, until he had firmly established the Nazi regime inside Germany, he dared not alienate the German Army. Another reason was that his first acts of terrorism and threatened aggression had produced an acute tension with the Western Powers and with Italy, and he was anxious not to have all

Europe against him simultaneously. A third reason was that, though undoubtedly hostile to Russia, the Führer also had designs on Poland; yet such was his guile that he wished to lull his destined victim into a state of false security while utilizing her as a cat's-paw against the Soviet Union. Thus, at the signing of a pact of non-aggression with Poland on 26 January 1934, the Führer, and also Göring, impressed upon the Poles the evil which Weimar Germany had consistently worked with Russia against Poland, who, they insisted, had been the intended victim of the Rapallo policy. This, said the Nazi leaders, was all changed now; the Third Reich entertained only the friendliest feelings for Poland and was ready to protect her against Soviet aggression.

In short, beginning in 1935, it became one of the chief objectives of Hitler's foreign policy to exacerbate Soviet-Polish relations and to dazzle the Poles with promises of gigantic territorial aggrandizement. In all their conversations the German leaders were studiously modest in describing their own prospective demands upon Russian territory. These, they said, were confined to annexing the Baltic States and establishing the paramount position of Germany on the Baltic Sea. Germany had not the slightest design upon the Ukraine, not even upon a part of it, and looked upon this fertile land as the perquisite of Poland, to be united to those Ukrainian provinces taken from Russia in 1921 by the Treaty of Riga. With these honeyed words the Nazi leaders pushed Poland forward, first against Czechoslovakia and then against the Soviet Union, while at the same time preparing the destruction of the Polish State.

Indeed, the events of 1936-1939 constitute one of the most outstanding examples of these historic estrangements and reconciliations between Germany and Russia. Beginning with the military and political purges in Moscow and Berlin, official relations between the two States grew progressively worse, and when, in September 1938, Hitler achieved his great diplomatic victory at Munich—not the least of the fruits of which were the exclusion of Russia from the Concert of Europe and the consequent isolation of Poland—it seemed as if the two great Powers in Eastern Europe were permanently alienated. Yet events proved that nothing could be further from the truth. Less than nine months after the Munich Agreement there began those intricate negotiations which reached their conclusion in the Nazi-Soviet

Pact of August 1939. The details and outcome of this infamous agreement are too well known to require repetition. Two important aspects may, however, be noted: first, that this overpowering attraction between Germany and Russia could assert itself under the most adverse circumstances, and that this strange affinity could transcend even the sharpest political divergencies and the most bitter of ideological conflicts; and secondly, the delight and relief with which this new departure in German foreign policy was greeted in many circles in the German Foreign Office and General Staff.

The existence of an independent Poland had once again proved the irresistible magnet which, as in the case of Frederick and Catherine, and of Seeckt and Lenin, had now drawn together Hitler and Stalin, Nazi and Bolshevik, albeit in a Pact of Mutual Suspicion. This suspicion certainly obtained at the highest levels in Berlin and in Moscow, but in the Wilhelmstrasse and the Bendlerstrasse the first signs of the new orientation of German policy towards Russia were hailed as a return to diplomatic sanity. The German Ambassador in Moscow, Count von der Schulenburg—later to be hanged for complicity in the abortive conspiracy of 20 July 1944—conducted the preliminary negotiations with the most genuine warmth and good faith. The General Staff welcomed with relief the banishment of their inherent fear of the threat of a two-front war and applauded in all sincerity this new move which should re-establish the old relationship of 'distant friendship' which von Seeckt had inaugurated. Even General von Fritsch, who, only a little more than a year before, had been summarily dismissed as Commander-in-Chief of the Army by Hitler on a trumped-up charge of homosexuality, now reappeared in Berlin in fervid support of the Führer's new policy.

Once again there opened before the eyes of these professional diplomats and soldiers the alluring prospect of at last achieving their long-cherished dream of allying the genius of Germany with the might of Russia—always, of course, with the ultimate control of policy in German hands.

This gratified day-dreaming received a rude shock when, in the summer of 1940, it became known that the Führer had directed his planners to prepare for an attack upon Russia. The Seeckt tradition died hard in the German High Command and, almost for the last time, there was a minor show of opposition to the Führer's will. Needless to say, it failed to deter him from his objective, but the fact remains that the hesitant support which certain high ranking general officers gave to the conspiracy against Hitler dated from the invasion of the Soviet Union on 22 June 1941, when their hopes of an alliance of power between Germany and Russia were shattered and their dread of a two-front war was realized.

Two points are worth noting here in passing. One is an historical parallel of some interest, which harks back to that other school of thought within the General Staff, the Pan-German expansionists, of whom Ludendorff and Hoffmann had been the leading protagonists in the First World War. The plans for the partitioning of the Soviet Union, which Hitler discussed with his ministers at a conference at the Führerhauptquartier on 16 July 1941, were *mutatis mutandis* almost identical with those urged upon the Imperial Chancellor by Ludendorff in a memorandum of 9 June 1918.

The second point, which underlines the existence of this strange dichotomy of thought, this fantastic ambivalence of attitude, in Germany towards Russia, is the fact that, even within the ranks of the conspiracy against Hitler, there was this same conflict of approach to the problem of how peace should be secured after the Nazi regime had been overthrown. There were those among the conspirators, led by von der Schulenburg, the old Ambassador, and the young leader of the revolt, Claus von Stauffenberg, who favoured an approach to Moscow—not, be it understood, towards Communism—as being of greater probable advantage to Germany, and side by side, in considerable hostility with them, were those more conservative elements, such as Beck and Goerdeler and von Hassell, who desired to negotiate an armistice only with the Western allies to the exclusion of Russia. So deep was the split in opinion that, at the moment of the abortive rising on 20 July 1944, the issue was still unresolved and alternative candidates for the post of Foreign Minister appeared in the list of the members of the provisional government.

In other words, the conspirators against Hitler, who sought to replace the Nazi regime with something more humane and civilized, were themselves entirely capable of playing the traditional German game of East *versus* West and *vice versa* in foreign policy.

So, with the fall of Hitler in 1945, there ends the chronicle of nearly two hundred years of German-Russian relations. It is not proposed to carry the story into the post-war period, but those who wish to make such a projection for themselves cannot do better than take as a starting-point the concluding words of Mr Freund's book:

'The inherent dynamic of relations between Germany and Russia, which prevents the judicious historian from introducing any facile themes or theories into his account of these relations, was that each power served, at least potentially, several equally important functions for the other. This dynamic—the complexity, diversity, and flexibility of Russian and German policies—has subjected relations between them to sudden, and sometimes sweeping, reversals. Yet it is on this relationship that the balance of power and, hence, the peace of Europe depends.'

JOHN W. WHEELER-BENNETT

# CHAPTER I

## FROM BREST-LITOVSK TO THE ARMISTICE

BEGINNING in 1915, the German Government waged an active campaign to provoke a revolution in Russia. For nearly two years official German sources encouraged and financed the activities of Russian revolutionary insurgents, including the Bolsheviks in Russia and in exile. Their plan was to overthrow the Czarist regime and then to break up the Entente by negotiating a separate peace with Russia's new rulers, whoever they might be.[1] The February Revolution ended the Czarist regime, but Kerensky could not make up his mind to negotiate with the Central Powers. The Germans, however, had taken the precaution of continuing to 'support the Bolsheviks . . . through different channels and under various headings,' enabling them 'to enlarge and expand their most important organ, "Pravda," to carry on vigorous agitation, and to broaden significantly the formerly narrow basis of their party.'[2] When the Bolsheviks seized power in November 1917, the Germans were immediately able to capitalize on their investment. In a telegram to Kaiser Wilhelm II dated 3 December 1917, the German Foreign Minister, Richard von Kühlmann, envisaged the possibility of detaching Russia from the enemy coalition in the immediate future:

The Bolsheviks have now taken control; at this time it cannot be estimated how long they will be able to keep themselves in power. To consolidate their own position they need peace. On the other hand, it is in line with all our interests to utilize their time in power, which may be only very short, first of all to bring about an armistice, and then, if possible, to achieve peace.[3]

[1] *Akten der Kaiserlich Deutschen Gesandtschaft in Kopenhagen Betreffend Helphand 1915-1916* (Public Record Office, London), Serial 5013, Frames E286693/8, telegram, 6 December 1915, Brockdorff-Rantzau (Copenhagen) to Chancellor (Berlin); *ibid.*, 5013/E286706/9, Copy A. 23564, 6 August 1915, 'Bericht über den Stand der Arbeiten des Herrn Dr Helphand,' signed Dr M. Zimmer; and *passim*.

[2] *Das Verhältnis Deutschlands zu Russland*, Deutschland 131 secr. (St. Antony's College, Oxford), St. Antony's Film Box Number 33 (hereafter cited: St. A. Nr. 33), telegram, 3 December 1917, Kühlmann (Berlin) to Lersner (High Command).         [3] *Ibid.*

A

An Armistice Agreement was signed on 15 December 1917, and peace negotiations between the Soviet Republic and the Central Powers were scheduled to start in Brest-Litovsk five days later. On the fighting front, Russian and German soldiers alike welcomed the Armistice and hoped for a quick peace settlement, which would spare them the blows and burdens of a most agonizing war and the terrors of another winter campaign on the Eastern Front.

Early in December 1917, before the peace negotiations started, Under-Secretary of State von dem Bussche wrote a memorandum on behalf of Kühlmann and the Chancellor, Hertling, advising the Kaiser to agree to the Bolsheviks' peace proposals. The key sentence of the memorandum declares that Germany should be 'prepared to sign a peace without annexations and indemnities and on the basis of the self-determination of the peoples concerned.'[1] The assumption in Berlin was that the Bolsheviks wanted to sign a separate peace, and Kühlmann was prepared to employ all the genteel manners associated with Nineteenth Century diplomacy to hasten a settlement. But the Bolsheviks had other plans.

Although Lenin willingly accepted German help prior to the Revolution, he made no commitments in return regarding Russian policies in the period following the Bolshevik seizure of power. The Russians had no obligations towards the Germans.[2] Therefore, when the Armistice halted the advance of enemy troops into Russia, the Bolsheviks felt free to use the same brazen revolutionary techniques which had carried them into power against the remaining bourgeois 'militarist' regimes in Europe, whose continued existence was inimical to the revolutionaries' conception of peace. According to their creed, there could be no peace until the revolution begun in Russia had permeated and upset the rest of European society. Germany was first on the list:

> For a separate peace Germany's limit of concessions is quite wide. But we did not go to Brest for that; we went to Brest because we are convinced that our words will reach the German people over the heads

[1] *Die Waffenstillstands- und Friedensverhandlungen von Brest Litowsk* (Archives of the United States of America, Washington), Serial 2112H, 'Leitsätze für einen Sonderfriedensvertrag mit Russland.' The best account of the Brest-Litovsk negotiations is given by J. W. Wheeler-Bennett, *Brest-Litovsk—The Forgotten Peace* (London, 1938).

[2] See G. Katkov, 'German Foreign Office Documents on Financial Support to the Bolsheviks in 1917,' *International Affairs*, vol. 32, No. 2 (London, April 1956).

of the German generals, that our words will strike from the hands of
the German generals the weapons with which they fool their people.[1]

The Bolsheviks went to Brest-Litovsk to talk over the heads of
their enemies, not to sign a peace treaty with them. Karl Radek, a
brilliant and indefatigable propagandist, carried his duties as
director of the section for international propaganda to an extreme.
As the delegates' train neared Brest he was seen throwing leaflets to
German troops, urging them to revolt against their commanders.[2]
Radek's chief occupation at this time was publishing *Die Fackel*, a
German-language newspaper which was distributed to German and
Austrian prisoners and to their compatriots in the trenches on the
Eastern Front.[3] The Germans and Austrians on the staff of *Die
Fackel* were probably recruited by emissaries sent out to prisoner
of war camps throughout Russia, where '10,000 German and
Austrian prisoners were organized and trained for revolutionary
work.'[4] In addition to distributing propaganda on the front lines,
the Bolsheviks encouraged their troops to fraternize with the
Germans, succeeding in making some of them so unreliable that
General Max Hoffmann, the German commander on the Eastern
Front, was afraid to transfer them through Germany to the
Western Front, and later regretted shifting some divisions because
they proved to be unreliable.[5]

If the Communist propaganda campaign were successful, Lenin
hoped that hostilities would end with a revolution in Germany
instead of a peace treaty. From the Bolshevik point of view, the
Peace Resolution adopted by a Reichstag majority of Social

[1] Extract from Kamenev's report to the All-Russian Central Executive
Committee (December 1917-January 1918) in *Protokoly danii VTsIK 2 Sozyva*
(1918), p. 82, quoted by E. H. Carr, *The Bolshevik Revolution 1917-1923* (London,
1953), vol. 3, p. 28.

[2] Samples of Bolshevik propaganda leaflets addressed to German and Austrian
soldiers are in the *Heeresarchiv:* Hans Friederich Leopold von Seeckt, (Archives
of the United States of America, Washington), Karton 15, Stück 210. Also see
L. Fischer, *The Soviets in World Affairs* (London, 1930), vol. 1, p. 43.

[3] Carr, vol. 3, p. 18. Cf. A. L. P. Dennis, *The Foreign Policies of Soviet Russia*
(New York, 1924), p. 24.

[4] Carr, *op. cit.*; also see the letter dated Stockholm, 20 December 1917, from
'Michael' to Herr Goldberg, with a covering letter from M. Erzberger, in
*Waffenstillstands Verhandlungen mit Russland*, Weltkrieg No. 2f, No. 1 (St.
Antony's College, Oxford), St. A. Nr. 5.

[5] Wheeler-Bennett, *Brest-Litovsk*, p. 352.

Democrats, Centrists, and Progressives in July 1917 indicated that the mass of the German people were 'anti-chauvinist' and 'anti-imperialist.' The metal workers' strike in Berlin (28 January-3 February 1918) against annexations and indemnities and for immediate peace with the Soviet Government reassured Lenin that the revolutionary proletariat was growing in strength and would soon overthrow the 'militarists' in Germany.[1] On the assumption that the revolution was spreading to Central Europe, the Bolsheviks' strategy at Brest-Litovsk was to stall for time pending the upheaval, thus preventing a further encroachment of Soviet territory, while simultaneously exacerbating the revolutionary frictions evident in the German society with intense propaganda campaigns.[2]

These Bolshevik manœuvres did not deceive the Germans for long. Intelligence agents warned the Foreign Ministry and the High Command not to allow the negotiations to be prolonged, for if the Bolsheviks persisted in their stalling tactics the revolution might indeed spread beyond Russia's boundaries, leaving German troops dangerously exposed on the Eastern Front. The Central Powers rejected Trotsky's appeal to move the conference to Stockholm or Copenhagen, realizing that the Russians would avail themselves of unrestricted propaganda facilities in a neutral country.[3] In Vienna, where the failure to reach a settlement at Brest-Litovsk was demoralizing the population, the German Ambassador expressed the opinion that 'the Russian negotiators are less representatives of Russia than of the revolution.'[4] This judgment was confirmed by a letter, intercepted by the Germans, from Trotsky to a Swedish collaborator, in which Trotsky asserted 'that a separate peace involving Russia is inconceivable; all that matters is to prolong the negotiations to screen the mobilization of international social-democratic forces promoting a general peace.'[5] From Copenhagen

---

[1] The Peace Resolution and the metal workers' strike are discussed by S. W. Halperin, *Germany Tried Democracy* (New York, 1946), pp. 27, 30, 42-43.

[2] In an interview with *Izvestiya*, 2 March 1922, Joffe admitted that the Soviet delegation at Brest-Litovsk had stalled pending the outbreak of world revolution.

[3] *Die Waffenstillstands- und Friedensverhandlungen von Brest Litowsk*, 2112H, telegram, 12 December 1917, Rantzau (Copenhagen) to Foreign Ministry (Berlin). Also see *Friedensverhandlungen mit Russland in Brest Litowsk*, Russland. Politisches Nr. 1 (Public Record Office, London), 9300H/H256869.

[4] *Die Waffenstillstands- und Friedensverhandlungen von Brest Litowsk*, 2112H, memorandum, 17 January 1918, Wedel (Vienna) to Hertling (Berlin).

[5] *Friedensverhandlungen mit Russland in Brest Litowsk*, 9300H/H257361/2.

Ambassador Brockdorff-Rantzau reported that the Bolshevik delegates who returned to Petrograd during the Christmas recess of the peace conference were talking in warmongering terms of what they would do if the Central Powers did not meet *their* demands. 'By the way,' Rantzau added, 'this is all bluff; the Russians have no army and consequently they cannot seriously contemplate an offensive.'[1]

When the delegations reassembled in the second week of January 1918, Kühlmann and Hoffmann, spurred by insistent telegrams from the Kaiser and Ludendorff, enjoined the Bolsheviks to agree to terms, but to no avail.[2] The Russians continued to procrastinate. German impatience in the face of continued Russian intransigence finally brought the negotiations to their climacteric at the beginning of February. The Kaiser had lost all patience and dispatched an ultimatum:

Today the Bolshevik regime openly incited my army to revolt against its leadership. Neither I nor Hindenburg can tolerate such a state of affairs any longer. An end must come to this immediately. Trotsky has until tomorrow the tenth at eight o'clock to sign the peace in accordance with our demands.[3]

The Russians had no intention of submitting to the German demands, which, at Ludendorff's insistence and with the Kaiser's approval, now included all the Baltic territory to the line Narva-Pleskau-Dünaburg, a far cry from a 'peace without annexations.' However, Trotsky's brilliant speech on 10 February, which broke off the negotiations, was made without prior knowledge of the Kaiser's ultimatum.[4] Trotsky's indictment of 'militarists' and

[1] *Ibid.*, 9300H/H256914/5.

[2] *Ibid.*, 9300H/H257665/7, H257682, and *passim.* Also see the 'Stenographischer Bericht über die Konferenz mit den Vertretern der Parteien des Reichstags' on 23 January 1918, *ibid.*, Russland. Politisches Nr. 1, adh. 2, 9344H/I. H263363-H263449.

[3] *Die Waffenstillstands- und Friedensverhandlungen von Brest Litowsk*, 2112H, copy of a telegram, 9 February 1918, Kaiser Wilhelm (Homburg) to Hoffmann and Kühlmann (Brest-Litovsk), sent to Hertling (Berlin). Cf. *Friedensverhandlungen mit Russland in Brest Litowsk*, 9300H/H257952/3.

[4] Wheeler-Bennett, *Brest-Litowsk*, pp. 225 f.; *Friedensverhandlungen mit Russland in Brest Litowsk*, 9300H/H257688/91. According to one report the Germans received, 'Trotsky would be killed if he returned to Russia without signing a peace,' *Die Waffenstillstands- und Friedensverhandlungen von Brest Litowsk*, 2112H, telegram, 14 January 1918, Lersner (High Command) to Foreign Ministry (Berlin).

'imperialists' at the outset of his speech followed the pattern of vilification to which the delegates had been subjected by the Bolsheviks since the first session at Brest. He charged the Germans and their allies with bad faith; accusing them of first accepting the principle of a peace without annexations and indemnities, and then imposing 'conditions which bring with them oppression, misery and hate to millions of human beings.'[1] Kühlmann and Hoffmann had grown immune to the stream of invective. They were waiting for the policy statement Trotsky had promised to make. When Trotsky stopped gesticulating to pause briefly before reading the important paragraphs, General Hoffmann, who thought the Russians were about to capitulate to the German terms, looked up, and, to his chagrin, saw facing him—not a remorseful diplomat about to sign a humiliating peace—but a defiant revolutionary. Trotsky continued:

We cannot approve violence. We are going out of the war, but we feel ourselves compelled to refuse to sign the peace treaty.[2]

'No war, no peace.' The announcement stunned the delegates into complete silence. At last Hoffmann could contain himself no longer. 'Unerhört!' (Unheard of!) he ejaculated. 'Unerhört!' he repeated, scarcely believing that the Bolsheviks had dared to trick him.

That night, as the Soviet delegates boarded the train to Petrograd, they were still laughing and congratulating themselves on the *coup* which had shocked the Germans. But their elation was short-lived; the Kaiser and his High Command did not enjoy the joke. 'This is international Jewry for whose salvation *Christians must kill* one another,' the Kaiser fumed.[3]

In Homburg, where the Kaiser was staying, Trotsky's 'no war, no peace' declaration provoked a welter of argument between the High Command and the responsible ministers. Hindenburg and Ludendorff, the *de facto* dictators of German policy from 1916 until the end of the war, and General Hoffmann, demanded the

[1] *Proceedings of the Brest Litovsk Conference* (Washington, 1918), p. 172.

[2] Stenographic report of the Political Committee session at Brest-Litovsk on 10 February 1918, *Friedensverhandlungen mit Russland in Brest Litowsk*, 9300H/H257999-H258000, and H258004-H258017.

[3] *Die Waffenstillstands- und Friedensverhandlungen von Brest Litowsk*, I. Anlagen, 2112H, Kaiser's marginal comments on the *Norddeutsche Allgemeine Zeitung*, 7 February 1918.

immediate resumption of hostilities against Russia. Chancellor
Hertling and Kühlmann did not agree with the High Command.
They counselled that Austria-Hungary would not continue to
fight,[1] that the Majority and Independent Socialists would oppose
renewed warfare against Soviet Russia, and they reminded the
Kaiser that Germany's acquisitions of Eastern territories already
outstripped her declared war aims. Despite Ludendorff's angry
abuse, Kühlmann continued to speak out against the military's
annexationist policies. He declared that 'the policy of excluding
Russia from the Baltic ports and the constant threat to her capital
will most certainly lead to incessant German-Russian hostility and
is bound to lead to another war.'[2] The Kaiser could not make up
his mind. He would bluster and fulminate at other times, but when
confronted by important decisions his tongue was stilled.

Finally, Ludendorff bullied Hertling and Vice-Chancellor von
Payer into supporting the military point of view, and, although
Kühlmann remained steadfast in opposition, the Kaiser allowed
Ludendorff to make up his mind for him too. 'We need solid, good
military frontiers despite all this talk!' the Kaiser wrote. 'Estonia,
Livonia, Courland must become German property!'[3] The
announcement that hostilities would be resumed was 'greeted in
Germany with school holidays, street rejoicings, and in some
towns with the ringing of bells.'[4]

A memorandum prepared by the German Foreign Ministry on
12 February stated that Trotsky's unilateral 'no war, no peace'
declaration had not legally abrogated the Armistice of 15 December
1917, and that, therefore, 'Germany can resume hostilities only
after denouncing the Armistice Agreement in accordance with the
procedure specified in Clause One of the Agreement.'[5] This inter-

[1] Count Czernin had informed Kühlmann that Austria-Hungary would
negotiate separately with the Bolsheviks if the Brest-Litovsk negotiations were
broken off because of German demands: *Friedensverhandlungen mit Russland in
Brest Litowsk*, 9300H/H256711 ff.

[2] A concise statement of Kühlmann's views is in his telegram of 9 March 1918
from Bucharest to Hertling (Berlin), *Die Waffenstillstands- und Friedensverhandlungen von Brest Litowsk*, 2112H.

[3] *Ibid.*, I. Anlagen, Kaiser's marginal comments on excerpts from the
*Frankfurter-Zeitung*, 16 January 1918.

[4] George Bernhard in the *Vossische Zeitung*, 18 February 1918, quoted by
Wheeler-Bennett, *Brest-Litovsk*, p. 232.

[5] *Die Waffenstillstands- und Friedensverhandlungen von Brest Litowsk*; 2112H;
*Texts of the Russian 'Peace'* (Washington, 1918), p. 1.

pretation was subsequently overruled by Hertling. General
Ludendorff—who opposed any interpretation of the Armistice
Agreement which would give the Russians time to regroup their
forces—ordered Hoffmann to attack after giving the Soviet
Government less than two of the seven days' notice prescribed in
Clause One of the Agreement.[1] Thus, with one terse order, the
German High Command broke and denounced the Armistice, and
relegated the Bolsheviks' 'no war, no peace' formula to a dubious
place in history, as an audacious and fictitious solution to a nation's
perils.

Lenin and Trotsky were conferring at their headquarters in the
Smolny Institute when they received General Hoffmann's message
denouncing the Armistice Agreement. Until then even Lenin was
caught up in the buoyant optimism exuded by the delegates returned from Brest-Litovsk, the most pessimistic of whom declared
that 'we have made any advance a very embarrassing affair for the
German militarists,' and most of whom believed that the war was
over and the revolution safeguarded.[2] Two members of the
German Foreign Ministry, Count Mirbach in Petrograd and
Counsellor Kriege in Brest, made irresponsible statements which
added to the Soviets' conviction that the German army would not
resume the offensive.[3] Hoffmann's message disabused the revolutionaries of these illusions. The Bolsheviks had disseminated propaganda and effectively immobilized Germany's armies for two
months, but when the peace talks were broken off the Soviet
Republic was still threatened by the German war machine.

Debate in the All-Russian Central Executive Committee now
centred upon the crucial issues of saving the revolution in its
Motherland, and inciting Europe's proletariat, especially Germany's
toiling masses, in the 'revolutionary struggle . . . against the existing governments.'[4] Despite bitter opposition from Left and Right

---

[1] *Waffenstillstands Verhandlungen mit Russland*, St. A. Nr. 5, telegram, 11
February 1918, Hertling (Berlin) to Kaiser (Homburg), and telegram, 13
February 1918, Kühlmann (High Command) to Foreign Ministry (Berlin).

[2] L. Trotsky, *History of the Russian Revolution to Brest-Litovsk* (London, 1919),
p. 142. Cf. Carr, vol. 3, p. 38.

[3] L. Trotsky, *op. cit.*, p. 143.

[4] J. Degras, *Soviet Documents on Foreign Policy* (London, 1951), vol. I, p. 19.
For Trotsky's report on the Brest-Litovsk proceedings to the Central Executive
Committee meeting on 14 February 1918, see *Friedensverhandlungen mit Russland
in Brest Litowsk*, 9300H/H258135/6.

Social Revolutionaries and various disagreements expressed by Trotsky and Stalin, Lenin insisted that Germany's peace terms had to be accepted if the revolution were to be saved in Russia and spread throughout Europe. He recognized that no government could rule the Russian people without satisfying their craving for peace. Kerensky's failure to conclude peace had made him unpopular with the Russian people and hastened the downfall of his government. The Bolsheviks would suffer the same fate if they failed to achieve peace. The wretched workers and peasants were unmoved by slogans; 'Loyalty to our Allies' was as ineffective as 'Wipe out Prussian militarism.' The army was demoralized. The soldiers had been fighting for and against 'imperialists'; they were through doing the dirty work enriching 'financiers' and 'industrialists.'[1] All they wanted was to go home to toil for their own welfare.

At a later date Trotsky conceded that his 'no war, no peace' formula was wrong and that Lenin had been right to demand that the policy of 'revolutionary phrase-making' be replaced by realism, which meant signing the German terms. But Bukharin's faction labelled Lenin's advice 'traitorous' and continued to advocate waging a revolutionary war against the Central Powers, in order to spread the revolution. While the revolutionaries debated in Petrograd, Hoffmann's armies marched virtually unopposed into Dvinsk in the North and Luck in the South, and further to Lake Peipus, Narva, and deep into the Ukraine.[2] Finally, late at night on 18 February the Soviet of People's Commissars sent a radiogram to General Hoffmann accepting the peace terms. Lenin held sway. 'We cannot joke with war,' he said. 'If we meant war, we had no right to demobilize.'

History will condemn us for betraying the Revolution when we had a choice of signing peace. . . . The revolution in Germany has not begun, we know that it takes time for a revolution to triumph.[3]

While their armies were advancing all along the Front, the Germans were in no hurry to honour Russia's capitulation. More-

[1] N. Basseches, *The Unknown Army* (London, 1943), trl. M. Saerchinger, p. 46.

[2] Major-General M. Hoffmann, *War Diaries* (London, 1921), trl. E. Sutton, vol. 1, pp. 204 f. Trotsky's protest against the German advance is in *Waffenstillstands Verhandlungen mit Russland*, St. A. Nr. 5, telegram, 17 February 1918, Schüler (Brest-Litovsk) to Foreign Ministry (Berlin).

[3] Wheeler-Bennett, *Brest-Litovsk*, p. 249; Carr, chap. 21 *passim*.

A *

over, the Germans heard from a 'reliable authority' in Petrograd that Lenin and Trotsky could be overthrown if additional pressure were put on the revolutionary government. 'Lenin is very un-popular, he travels mostly by armoured car and has a stronger personal guard than the Czar ever had. He remains at the Smolny Institute almost all the time and issues decrees which nobody obeys.'[1] With no clear intention of overthrowing the Bolsheviks, but to intensify the strife among the revolutionary factions which would add to the chaos and further weaken Russia, and to assuage their own lust for conquest, the High Command replied to Russia's submission to one set of peace terms with an ultimatum comprising new and even harsher ones.[2]

The new German terms provoked another bitter debate in Petrograd. But Krylenko's simple admission that 'we have no army' lent credence to Lenin's eloquent appeal for a decision to sign 'this shameful peace . . . in order to save the world revolution . . . in its only foothold—the Soviet Republic.' Once again Lenin emerged victorious from the struggle with the Left and Right SRs; the acceptance of the new terms reached the Germans on 24 February, only a few hours before the deadline of the ultimatum.

Upon their arrival in Brest-Litovsk, the Russian delegates com-missioned to sign the peace treaty were a sullen lot compared to the jocular group that departed for Petrograd less than a month earlier. On Sunday, 3 March, the Russians signed away 34 per cent. of their population, 32 per cent. of their agricultural land, 85 per cent. of their beet sugar land, 54 per cent. of all industrial undertakings, and 89 per cent. of their coal mines. It was indeed a violent peace, but sparse in its fruits and ominous in its precedents for the then jubilant victors.[3]

The reaction to the announcement of the treaty terms in the Reichstag was consternation on the Left and general rejoicing on the Right. The Social Democrats sympathized with the revolu-tionary cause in Russia and had advocated a peace without annexa-tions and indemnities. Now they denounced the severity of the

---

[1] *Die Waffenstillstands- und Friedensverhandlungen von Brest Litowsk*, 2112H, memorandum, 20 February 1918, Bussche (Berlin) to Grünau (High Command); *Friedensverhandlungen mit Russland in Brest Litowsk*, 9300H/H258229/31.

[2] *Friedensverhandlungen mit Russland in Brest Litowsk*, 9300H/H258260/3.

[3] For the Treaty of Brest-Litovsk and an explanation of its terms see Wheeler-Bennett, *Brest-Litovsk*, pp. 270 ff., pp. 403 ff.

terms imposed on the Bolsheviks, but in the voting they lacked the moral courage to oppose that which they had publicly declared to be wrong. The Independent Socialist leader Haase attacked the treaty in a dramatic outburst against the High Command, and only his party voted against its ratification.[1] Both the Right-wing and Centre parties acclaimed the treaty. The leader of the National Liberals, Gustav Stresemann, who regarded the war 'as a romantic crusade of Germanism' and who invariably 'preached implicit faith in the leadership of the High Command,' was jubilant:[2]

It is not the negotiations with Trotsky, nor the Reichstag's Peace Resolution, nor the reply to the Pope's Note, but the advance of Germany's incomparable military legions which has brought us peace in the East.[3]

'Cats cannot leave off mousing,' Philip Scheidemann commented, while others cheered.[4]

But the Prussian cat could not digest all that it had swallowed. Germany now dominated Lithuania, Estonia, Courland, Livonia, Poland, and the Ukraine, but Hindenburg's Watch on the Baltic was to give him more trouble than glory. He and Ludendorff planned to deal the Allies a crushing blow with a spring offensive, enabling Germany to plunder the lands detached from the Russian Empire without distraction from the West. Their plans were foiled on both fronts, and even the immediate task of reaping the Ukrainian harvest to feed millions of hungry people in Germany and Austria-Hungary was not accomplished.

German bayonets established and maintained the precarious Rada Government in Kiev, but, despite an occupation force of half a million Germans augmented by troops cajoled and black-mailed from an unwilling Austrian Government, only a fraction of the grain needed was actually transported out of the Ukraine. Neither the puppet dictator Skoropadsky nor the German commanders in the Ukraine, Field-Marshal von Eichhorn and General Wilhelm Groener, could overcome the peasants' passive and active

[1] *Verhandlungen des Reichstags*, 18, 19, 22 March 1918.

[2] G. Scheele, *The Weimar Republic—Overture to the Third Reich* (London, 1945), p. 234.

[3] Wheeler-Bennett, *Brest-Litovsk*, pp. 304 ff.; *Verhandlungen des Reichstags*, 26, 27 February 1918.

[4] P. Scheidemann, *The Makings of New Germany* (New York, 1929), vol. 2, p. 115.

resistance to the invaders. And not even Germans could make bayonets serve as ploughshares.[1]

While Ludendorff meticulously mapped out the plans for a brilliant offensive campaign in the West, the All-Russian Congress of Workmen's, Soldiers' and Peasants' Deputies convened to ratify what Lenin called 'the Tilsit peace.'[2] The affirmative vote (784 to 261, with the Left SRs abstaining) was also a vote of confidence in Lenin's leadership. His policy of 'heroic retreat,' of introducing a 'breathing space' until the international Socialist proletariat was ready to 'start a second Socialist Revolution on a world scale,' was officially adopted. But despite the Communists' self-assurance, the 'second Socialist Revolution' did not materialize. The upheaval in Germany, beginning with the naval mutiny in Kiel, contained seeds of a radical change in the social order, but these were either crushed or allowed to dissipate in a climate of physical and psychological exhaustion. Germany was defeated in battle. Relentless Entente pressure in the West and the deployment of reserve troops to enforce the victor's peace in the East took a heavy toll. Months of heroic fighting drained Germany's energies and human resources until, suddenly, she could fight no more.

The Soviet Government did not become aware of the serious depletion of Germany's military power until late August or early September 1918.[3] From March until the German collapse in the autumn, Russia's policy towards Germany had two facets aimed at the same goal, namely, securing the Soviet Republic—'Motherland of the Revolution.'[4] On the one hand, diplomatic and financial relations as well as trade negotiations were resumed to strengthen the Russian position, while, at the same time, Soviet representatives on official business in Germany used unofficial channels of communication to spread the Communist gospel, in order to undermine the German regime and hasten the 'inevitable' revolution. It was of secondary importance to the Bolsheviks that the political and financial agreements they signed also benefited the German 'imperialists.' All that mattered to them in the immediate

[1] See below, pp. 18-20.
[2] *Pravda*, 16 and 17 March 1918.
[3] Carr, vol. 3, p. 84, n. 2. Also see below, pp. 28, 31.
[4] 'Our task consists in strengthening the Soviet Republic against the capitalist elements which are striving to swallow it up': Lenin in *Izvestiya*, 18 May 1918.

future was the survival of the Soviet Republic. Threatened by the militant opposition of Left and Right SRs and Mensheviks within the country, and especially after the Entente's invasion in the North, South, and East created a new and direct threat from without, the Bolsheviks were anxious to secure the one remaining frontier, that with Germany. They could only do this by placating the High Command and appeasing the rapacious appetite for indemnities of some of the more powerful German leaders.[1]

But the Russians soon discovered that they could not satisfy the German High Command without giving up their national wealth and identity. Hindenburg and Ludendorff wanted to exploit Russia to replenish Germany's granaries and dwindling stockpiles of essential war materials. In a statement of his policy towards Russia, Ludendorff declared that 'it is of decisive importance for us to secure a place for ourselves in Russia's economic life and to monopolize her exports.' Any Russian grain left over after the Germans had taken what they wanted for themselves was to be given to neutral countries, 'in order to wean them away from the Entente.' 'Help for Russia herself is the last concern.' According to Ludendorff's plan, Russia was to be dispossessed of the Ukraine, Georgia, and the Crimea, as well as of the Baltic territories, and her economy was to be bled until she was impoverished and 'forced to bind herself to Germany.' The 'weaker *Randstaaten*, on the other hand, must be strengthened and their economies made dependent on us.' 'Any other policy would seriously undermine our war and postwar economic interests,' Ludendorff concluded.[2]

Kühlmann and his successor, Admiral von Hintze, as well as Chancellor Hertling, were opposed to Ludendorff's violent anti-Russian policy and repeatedly took issue with it. A memorandum of 26 May 1918 reflects their views: 'At least for the time being, our interests can be served only by achieving friendly and trustworthy relations with the current Russian regime, and by helping to prolong and secure it, to the extent we can do this without direct interference in Russia's internal affairs.' In the opinion of the

---

[1] A good summary of Soviet Russia's military position in the summer of 1918 is in L. Kochan, *Russia and the Weimar Republic* (Cambridge, 1954), pp. 11 f.

[2] *Verhältnis Deutschlands zu Russland*, St. A. Nr. 83, telegram, 28 May 1918, Berckheim (High Command) to Foreign Ministry (Berlin); and *ibid.*, St. A. Nr. 84, telegram, 22 June 1918, Berckheim (High Command) to Foreign Ministry (Berlin).

ministers, Germany had no choice but to support the Bolsheviks, because 'any other regime, regardless whether it is monarchical or bourgeois-democratic, would denounce the Brest treaty, and, most probably, move closer to the Entente.'[1] The Kaiser frequently intervened in this policy dispute, but he did not take a decisive stand one way or the other. He agreed with the logic of the Hertling-Hintze position, but his loathing of the Bolsheviks and his new-found sympathy for the ill-fated Russian Monarch more often ranged him with the policy of the High Command.[2] Consequently Germany had several conflicting policies towards Russia until early in August 1918, when the rapid deterioration of the military situation on the Western Front forced Hindenburg and Ludendorff to acquiesce in the Hertling-Hintze policy of seeking more amicable relations with the Bolsheviks.[3] But by then it was too late to save the situation on either Front.

During the summer and autumn of 1918 innumerable reports predicting the early downfall of the Bolshevik regime reached Berlin and the High Command. The question of how long the Bolsheviks could survive, with or without German intervention, provoked endless speculation. It was indeed a crucial question for the Germans, but only the most astute observers realized that the chaos in Russia and failing communications with important parts of the country made it impossible to do more than guess at an answer. Even Hintze, who adopted a realistic wait-and-see attitude, allowed himself to speculate that Lenin could not last long, although he might retain power longer than the most eager participants in the guessing game asserted.[4] Ludendorff was more gullible. He was convinced that 'the Bolsheviks' future is hopeless,'[5] and that only two battalions were required 'to restore order in Moscow, to over-

[1] *Ibid.*, St. A. Nr. 83, telegram, 26 May 1918, Grünau (High Command) to Hertling (Berlin).

[2] *Ibid.* Also see *ibid.*, St. A. Nr. 84, telegram, 5 July 1918, Grünau (High Command) to Hertling (Berlin).

[3] See below, p. 28.

[4] *Verhältnis Deutschlands zu Russland*, St. A. Nr. 83, telegram, 11 May 1918, Mirbach (Moscow) to Foreign Ministry (Berlin); *ibid.*, St. A. Nr. 84, telegram, 1 July 1918, Biermann (Petrograd) to Foreign Ministry (Berlin); *ibid.*, telegram, 17 July 1918, Schubert (Moscow) to Foreign Ministry (Berlin); *ibid.*, St. A. Nr. 85, telegram, 5 August 1918, Hintze (Berlin) to Helfferich (Moscow). Also see below, p. 25.

[5] *Ibid.*, St. A. Nr. 84, summary of a report by Major Henning (Moscow) sent to the War Ministry (Berlin), dated 15 July 1918.

throw the Bolsheviks and establish a new government.'[1] Encouraged by these favourable calculations, alarmed by the spread
of Communist propaganda among his troops, and justifying himself on the grounds that the Bolsheviks were not living up to the
terms of the peace treaty, Ludendorff planned a new military
offensive to sweep Lenin's Government out of office and impose
more stringent German controls on Russia.[2] Hintze's warning, that
a new regime in Russia would be more hostile to Germany than
the Bolsheviks, was not taken seriously by Ludendorff. It did not
matter to him who ruled in Russia; 'the Russians,' he wrote, 'will
never be our friends.'[3] Nevertheless, the High Command did
negotiate with emissaries of some of the many opposition groups
in Russia who prevailed on the German Government to support
their schemes to overthrow the Bolsheviks and establish new
governments. Ludendorff was convinced that the monarchists
would regain power, but the opposition faction of monarchists,
Duma deputies, and Church leaders, which appealed to him most—
although it had no more support in Russia than any of the other
groups that wooed the High Command—asserted that it did 'not
at first want to re-establish the monarchy, rather a kind of dictatorship in close co-operation with the German military, to whom far-
reaching authority would have to be granted for the restoration of
order, and who would also participate in the government.'[4] But
these negotiations came to nought; 'the pace of history was swifter
than the pace of intrigue.'[5]

While the High Command was engaged in abortive schemes for
a military offensive and a new *coup* in Russia, Chancellor Hertling
and the Foreign Ministry were patiently negotiating with the
Bolsheviks for supplementary agreements to the Treaty of Brest-
Litovsk, and for the normalization of relations between the two

[1] *Ibid.*, telegram, 17 July 1918, Schubert (Moscow) to Foreign Ministry
(Berlin). Cf. Wheeler-Bennett, *Brest-Litovsk*, pp. 334-336.

[2] *Verhältnis Deutschlands zu Russland*, St. A. Nr. 84, telegram, 18 July 1918,
Lersner (High Command) to Foreign Ministry (Berlin).

[3] *Ibid.*, St. A. Nr. 83, telegram, 28 May 1918, Berckheim (High Command)
to Foreign Ministry (Berlin).

[4] *Ibid.*, telegram, 20 April 1918, Mumm (Kiev) to Foreign Ministry (Berlin),
and *ibid.*, 24 April 1918, Berckheim (High Command) to Foreign Ministry
(Berlin). Also see *ibid.*, St. A. Nr. 84, telegram, 18 July 1918, Lersner (High
Command) to Foreign Ministry (Berlin).

[5] Wheeler-Bennett, *Brest-Litovsk*, p. 336.

countries. Ambassadors were exchanged in April 1918. The Kaiser appointed Count Wilhelm von Mirbach-Harff, counsellor of the Petrograd Embassy before the war and leader of the German mission to Petrograd during the Armistice,[1] to serve in Moscow. Lenin sent Adolf Joffe as his Ambassador to Berlin. The resumption of diplomatic representation did not, at first, lessen the strain between the powers. Even the minimum formalities were not observed. Lenin refused to receive Mirbach, and Joffe would not present his credentials to the Kaiser. The Germans in Moscow were victims of studied insults in the press[2] and suffered other indignities at the hands of the Russian people, who were embittered by the 'German war,' the victor's peace, and—most recently—by the invasion of the Crimea.[3] Within a week of his arrival in Moscow, Mirbach protested against an infringement of the peace treaty. On May Day he had seen detachments of German prisoners, who had been converted to Communism, parading with banners urging their compatriots to overthrow the Kaiser. Trotsky assured Mirbach that, in future, the terms of the treaty would be observed. But Article 2 of the treaty, which states that 'the contracting parties will refrain from any agitation or propaganda against the Government or the public and military institutions of the other party,' was interpreted in a 'light-hearted spirit' by the Communists.[4] 'Yes, of course, we have violated the treaty,' Lenin admitted in private in March 1918. 'We have already violated it thirty or forty times.'[5]

Although the open provocations of April and May seem to have been avoided, Communist propaganda among prisoners of war and the recruitment of prisoners for the Red Army continued throughout the summer and autumn of 1918. In Berlin, Joffe, even

[1] Details of Mirbach's activities as chief of the German mission in Petrograd during the Armistice are in *Verhältnis Deutschlands zu Russland*, St. A. Nr. 33, and in *Friedensverhandlungen mit Russland in Brest Litowsk*, Russland. Politisches Nr. 1, adh. 1, 9343H/1., and *ibid.*, adh. 2, 9344H/1. and 2., and *ibid.*, 9345H/1., and *ibid.*, Russland. Politisches Nr. 1a, 9345H/2. *passim.*

[2] For example, see Radek's article in *Izvestiya*, 28 April 1918.

[3] *Allgemeine Angelegenheiten der Ukraine*, Die Ukraine Nr. 1 (St. Antony's College, Oxford), St. A. Nr. 36, telegram, 1 April 1918, Lersner (High Command) to Foreign Ministry (Berlin); Wheeler-Bennett, *Brest-Litovsk*, pp. 326, 330.

[4] Degras, *Soviet Documents*, vol. 1, p. 52; Carr, vol. 3, pp. 71 f.

[5] Carr, *op. cit.*

while carrying out his official duties, constantly violated the treaty with revolutionary activity, which included apportioning at least 'several hundred thousand marks' of Soviet largess to Independent Social Democrats and Spartacists for revolutionary-propaganda purposes.[1] This duplicity of Soviet policy followed from Lenin's pledge to the Petrograd Soviet, that 'the Central Executive Committee signs the Peace; the Council of Commissars signs the Peace, but not the Central Committee of the Party, and for the behaviour of the Party the Soviet Government is not responsible.'[2]

Soviet revolutionary activity against Germany continued unabated, but events in April and May 1918 forced Lenin to resort to a new manœuvre in striking a balance between the Entente and the Central Powers and seeking protection against both camps. Until May the threat from Germany, whose troops frequently violated the boundary lines established at Brest-Litovsk, presented the worst external danger to the Bolsheviks. The German threat persisted, but after the Japanese landing at Vladivostok and indications of further hostile Entente action following the Soviet rejection of demands to renew hostilities against the Central Powers, the greatest immediate danger appeared to come from the other side.[3] These developments, coupled with Russia's urgent need to revive her trade and to gain a share of the Ukrainian harvest, caused Lenin to seek a new accommodation with the German Government. Strong opposition to this manœuvre from Left and Right SRs and Mensheviks forced the Bolsheviks to move cautiously, but on 14 May Chicherin, the Soviet Foreign Minister, ordered Joffe to inform the Germans that the Soviet Government wanted to set up a commission in Moscow to discuss all commercial and political questions between the two countries.[4] Because the Germans were

---

[1] See below, p. 31.

[2] Quoted by Wheeler-Bennett, *Brest-Litovsk*, pp. 348 f.

[3] *Verhältnis Deutschlands zu Russland*, St. A. Nr. 83, telegrams, 10, 11, and 14 May 1918, Mirbach (Moscow) to Foreign Ministry (Berlin).

[4] *Ibid.*, telegram, 14 May 1918, Chicherin (Moscow) to Joffe (Berlin). This telegram was sent via the German Embassy in Moscow because Soviet diplomatic communications with Berlin were interrupted by a breakdown on German soil. Cf. J. Sadoul, *Notes sur la Révolution Bolchevique* (Paris, 1920), who heard rumours of a 'German orientation' in Moscow at the end of May. Cf. H. W. Gatzke, 'Zu den Deutsch-Russischen Beziehungen im Sommer 1918,' *Vierteljahrshefte für Zeitgeschichte* (Stuttgart, January 1955), 5. Jhrg., 1. Heft, pp. 71 f.; cf. Carr, vol. 3, pp. 79 f.

alarmed by the threat of renewed warfare on two fronts, and because they wanted to speed the delivery of Russian grain and resources, the Soviet initiative was welcomed in Berlin. Joffe replied on the same day he received Chicherin's message, that the Germans were willing to 'negotiate on all outstanding issues,' but added that Hintze insisted on holding the discussions in Berlin.[1] The Russians accepted this condition. On 7 June their 'delegates to the political commission' arrived in the German capital.[2] Joffe was in charge of the Russian delegation, which also included Krasin, chief adviser on trade matters, Larin, Sokolnikov, and Menzhinsky.[3] For the Germans, Nadolny and Kriege represented the Foreign Ministry, von Prittwitz and Graf Harry Kessler were delegated by the Chancellor, Schlubach acted for the High Command, and Gustav Stresemann represented the interests of German heavy industry. Stresemann was principally involved in the trade talks, but because of his close connexions with the High Command he gained especial stature with the Russians. The sixth member of the German delegation, Paul Litwin, was a key figure in the negotiations. He was born in Russia, spoke the language fluently, and had many contacts there which proved useful in his work for the German Export Organization and on behalf of a German-Bolshevik alliance, which he advocated.[4]

The formal talks started in mid-June.[5] Joffe and Krasin soon made proposals from which practical results might have followed in short order. They told Litwin that 'the Russian Government is willing to work in closest collaboration with the German Government in economic matters,' and made the specific suggestion that Germany 'authorize the Ukrainian Government to deliver 360,000 tons of grain to the Russian Government,' and that the Russians be given a free hand in the Ukraine to see that the agreement were carried out. 'Since the Russian Government only needs 180,000 tons for its own use, it would undertake to deliver the additional

---

[1] Carr, *loc. cit.*

[2] *Verhältnis Deutschlands zu Russland*, St. A. Nr. 83, telegram, 2 June 1918, Mirbach (Moscow) to Foreign Ministry (Berlin); *ibid.*, memorandum, 7 June 1918, signed B? or R? (Berlin) to Kühlmann (Berlin).

[3] Carr, vol. 3, p. 81. Cf. Gatzke, *op. cit.*

[4] *Ibid.*

[5] Informal talks about trade matters may have been held as early as the middle of May when Krasin arrived in Berlin from Sweden: Gatzke, *op. cit.*

180,000 tons to the German Government.'[1] In compensation for its share of the grain, the Soviet Government was willing to make 'textiles, copper and other natural resources available' to Germany. Joffe said that this proposition 'was thought of as a basis for the development of further intimate political and economic relations.' He convinced Litwin that 'the Russian Government looks on the Brest treaty as a *fait accompli* which it has to accept once and for all,' and said that 'now Trotsky as well as Lenin seeks closer relations with Germany.' But 'an open alliance with Germany would meet with difficulties today,' Joffe continued, 'because of the predominant [anti-German] public feeling in Russia.' What the Soviet Government wanted to do, Joffe asserted, was 'to sign an agreement with Germany that would lead to such an alliance in the near future,' and he was of the opinion that 'the delivery of grain to hungry people in the cities' would help to influence public opinion in this direction.[2] The 'open alliance' between Russia and Germany that Joffe envisaged for the future was to be based on the Brest treaty, but, he said, Russia was willing to make concessions beyond the provisions of the treaty. According to Joffe, Russia would grant Estonia and Livonia independence on the single condition that the Germans facilitate Russian trade through the Baltic ports when they annexed the territories.[3] In the course of the conversation, Litwin asked Joffe if Russia would accept German military help against the Entente invaders. Joffe replied that the Soviet Government was perfectly capable of driving the British out of Murmansk and combating the Czech insurgents without Finnish or German military help, if 'the German Government would only protect our back.'[4] This assurance from Germany would give Russia all the strength she needed to deal with the invaders, and in this way, too, 'the danger of a new war in the East could be avoided.'[5]

When the Soviet proposals were forwarded to Ludendorff, he

[1] *Nachlass des Reichsministers Dr Gustav Stresemann* (Public Record Office, London), Serial 6912H, Frame numbers H136131-H136135 (hereafter cited: 6912H/H136131/5), unsigned notes, most probably Stresemann's, dated Berlin, 5 July 1918.

[2] *Stresemann Nachlass*, 6912H/H136131/5.

[3] Stresemann wrote that he was in favour of a German-Russian treaty 'because it would finally secure Estonia and Livonia for us,' *ibid.*, 6911H/H136210.

[4] '. . . wenn ihr von der deutschen Regierung nur der Rücken gedeckt wird' in the original.

[5] *Stresemann Nachlass*, 6912H/136131/5.

immediately rejected them. An agreement to share the Ukrainian grain was unacceptable to the High Command.[1] Ludendorff said he wanted 'deeds' not words from the Soviets to prove that they had really broken away from the Entente and now wanted to live in peace and friendship with Germany. If the Bolsheviks wanted to prove their good faith, he said, they should dismiss Trotsky from office, reach an agreement with Finland for joint action against the British in Murmansk, and deploy the troops stationed on the demarcation line with Germany against the British and Czech forces. 'If the Soviet Government were to give us these proofs unconditionally,' Ludendorff wrote, 'then I would agree that we should make concessions in several less important questions during the course of the German-Russian negotiations, in order to get our way in the remaining questions, which are the most important ones for us: the recognition of Livonian, Estonian, and Georgian independence.'[2] Ludendorff's categorical rejection of the Soviet proposals, and his uncompromising demands, made the task of the Berlin negotiators very difficult. That the negotiations were not broken off altogether was due, in equal measure, to Russia's need of some accommodation with Germany—however temporary it might prove to be—and to the belief shared by all the German negotiators, that an agreement could be reached which would stabilize Germany's frontiers and improve her economic position, and that such an agreement could be made palatable to the High Command.

The talks continued throughout July. On 7 July Stresemann had a long talk with Joffe and Krasin, mostly about economic matters, but political questions were also raised. Joffe wanted a German loan for Russia; without it, he said, Russia could not discharge her treaty obligations. Stresemann could not commit his Government on this point, and merely repeated the demand for six billion marks in gold, bonds, and goods 'as compensation for the loss to Germans caused by the Russian measures'—which is the language in which the indemnity clause of the supplementary treaties was officially obscured. Stresemann did not raise the question of the independence of the Baltic states, but he was of 'the general opinion, that the present regime will not actively resist even these German

[1] See above, pp. 11-12.
[2] *Verhältnis Deutschlands zu Russland*, St. A. Nr. 84, telegram, 22 June 1918, Berckheim (High Command) to Foreign Ministry (Berlin).

demands, if the Russians could be assured that, later on, the Ukraine and the Donets-Basin would be returned to them.' Stresemann believed Joffe's plea that these territories 'are Russia's life-lines which she cannot relinquish.' He drew the conclusion from this conversation that 'a German-Russian understanding . . . seems to be in the offing, if it is handled expertly.'[1]

During the course of their talk, Joffe had asked Stresemann, whom he knew to be very popular in German military circles, if the Russian delegates could have closer contact with the High Command. He said that Krasin's interview with Ludendorff in June had done some good and that more talks could bring about better mutual understanding. But Stresemann was evasive; he wanted to keep the power of his contacts at Spa to himself, and it was not until August that he used these contacts to expedite the negotiations. Because he was convinced that 'the peace largely depends' on Germany's relations with Russia, Stresemann preoccupied himself with the Berlin negotiations throughout the summer.[2] But later on he regretted involving himself as much as he did because, as he wrote, his activities might be misconstrued 'as if I have been working for Russian interests, although our entire effort is, of course, for the German cause.'[3]

In subsequent meetings during July drafts of a 'far reaching commercial pact' and preliminary political agreements were agreed on. The drafts were approved by Hintze and Hertling, but they were not ready for signing because no agreement had been reached on several issues, notably on the future of the Donets-Basin and the important oil centre of Baku. Moreover, neither the Soviet Government nor the German High Command had as yet approved the drafts, and it was known that Ludendorff was certain to reject as inadequate any agreement that did not provide for effective counter-measures against the Entente's intervention in Russia, which was a growing menace to Germany's frontier. The German

---

[1] *Stresemann Nachlass*, 6912H/H136144/58, undated and unsigned notes, but with corrections in Stresemann's handwriting.

[2] *Ibid.*, 6912H/H136167/70, letter to Justizrat Müller, 13 July 1918.

[3] *Ibid.*, 6911H/H135916/8, letter to Graf Kessler, 15 August 1918. Stresemann feared he was 'playing too large a role' in the Russian Embassy's dispatches to Moscow. A year later, Kessler was accused by Karl Helfferich of having been too friendly with the Bolsheviks; see the article entitled 'Joffe und Graf Kessler,' *Kreuz-Zeitung*, 23 November 1919, and Stresemann's letter to Helfferich, 24 November 1919, *Stresemann Nachlass*, 6923H/H138065/6.

negotiators repeatedly pressed Joffe 'to accept German military help,' but the Russians did not trust the High Command's intentions and continued to reject the demand.[1]

Because Germany as well as Russia was imperilled by the Entente's intervention, the Left SR uprising, in which Ambassador Mirbach and the German commander in the Ukraine, Field-Marshal Eichhorn, were assassinated, did not disrupt diplomatic relations and negotiations between the two countries, although the incidents served to increase recriminatory exchanges between sections of both populations, especially in the press.[2] The Germans blamed the Left SRs and the Entente, not the Soviet Government, for these crimes. When he heard that the German military attaché in Moscow, Schubert, wanted the entire legation withdrawn in protest against the assassinations, the Kaiser objected. He said that if this were done, at least part of the Entente's purpose in ordering the murders would be accomplished. 'Right now,' the Kaiser said, 'we have to support the Bolsheviks under any circumstances.'[3] Securing the Eastern Front and obtaining supplies from Russia was more important to the Germans than the lives of an ambassador and a marshal.

General Ludendorff agreed that no retaliatory action should be taken for the assassinations, but he still believed that his demands could be imposed on the Bolsheviks and, therefore, became increasingly impatient with the slow progress of the negotiations in Berlin. Conferences at Spa on 2 July and 15 July between the Government and the High Command, in the presence of the Kaiser, failed to reconcile the different views of a realistic basis for supplementary treaties with the Russians. In addition to his earlier demands, Ludendorff now wanted to support the Don Cossacks and to recognize their independence from Russia.[4] He insisted that

[1] Ibid., 6912H/H136136/8.

[2] Eye-witness accounts of Mirbach's assassination are in Verhältnis Deutschlands zu Russland, St. A. Nr. 84, telegram, 6 July 1918, Riezler (Moscow) to Foreign Ministry (Berlin), and the letters of Riezler and Lt. Müller, 7 July 1918, to the Foreign Ministry. Cf. G. Hilger and A. G. Meyer, The Incompatible Allies (New York, 1953), pp. 2 ff.

[3] Verhältnis Deutschlands zu Russland, St. A. Nr. 84, telegram, 11 July 1918, Lersner (High Command) to Foreign Ministry (Berlin).

[4] Gatzke, 'Deutsch-Russischen Beziehungen im Sommer 1918,' pp. 84 ff.; Verhältnis Deutschlands zu Russland, St. A. Nr. 84, 21 July 1918, Ludendorff (High Command) to Hintze (Berlin).

the Bolsheviks were merely stalling the negotiations, as they had done at Brest-Litovsk, until the Entente would come to their support and renew the war against Germany in the East. Hintze denied this, saying that 'the negotiations with Joffe could be concluded as soon as we can reach an agreement on Article 3 of the draft treaty [non-interference in internal affairs and non-support of separatist movements]. In the event Your Excellency is prepared to stop supporting the Cossacks and ready to give the local authorities orders to this effect, the treaty can be signed in the shortest time.'[1] But Ludendorff refused to compromise and even tried to undermine Hintze's policy by suggesting that a military man be appointed to replace Mirbach in Moscow. Hintze and Hertling were able to prevail on the Kaiser to designate Karl Helfferich instead.[2] Helfferich, however, was an unfortunate choice. He spent only ten days in Moscow, where he secreted himself in the Berg Palace, and sent alarming dispatches to Berlin, also to the High Command and the Kaiser, insisting that the Bolsheviks were doomed, that, moreover, Germany ought to help overthrow them, and that in any event he and his staff should be withdrawn to a safer location.[3]

On 2 August, Chicherin went directly from a meeting in the Kremlin to the Berg Palace to ask Helfferich for German military help against the British forces in Murmansk. Chicherin said that an open German-Bolshevik military alliance was still impossible, and German troops would have to be kept out of Petrograd in whatever action were taken, but the Soviet Government was now in favour of German intervention and wanted a parallel military action against the British to start without delay. Chicherin also wanted Germany to mount 'an offensive against Alexeyev, and to stop supporting Krasnov.'[4] Reporting Chicherin's *démarche* to

[1] *Ibid.*, telegram, undated but most probably 21 or 22 July 1918, Hintze (Berlin) to Ludendorff (High Command). This file also contains a preliminary draft of the supplementary political treaty.

[2] *Ibid.*, letter, 24 July 1918, Ludendorff (High Command) to Hintze (Berlin).

[3] *Ibid.*, St. A. Nr. 85, see Helfferich's reports from Moscow, especially the telegrams dated 31 July and 5 August 1918 to Hintze and Hertling. Cf. Hilger, *Incompatible Allies*, pp. 9 f.

[4] *Verhältnis Deutschlands zu Russland*, St. A. Nr. 85, telegram, 2 August 1918, Helfferich (Moscow) to Foreign Ministry (Berlin). Cf. K. von Bothmer, *Mit Graf Mirbach in Moskau* (Tübingen, 1922), p. 117; cf. Hilger, *op. cit.*, who does not mention this conversation.

Berlin, Helfferich wrote that 'this move' on the part of the Soviet Government leaves no doubt about 'the extremes of the dilemma in which the Bolsheviks find themselves.' He urged the German Government to 'pretend to fall in with the Russian request for intervention and to make all feasible military preparations for it, but at the last moment to form a common front with the Cossack leaders against the Bolsheviks.'[1] Hintze replied that it would be a 'mistake' to overthrow the Bolsheviks. 'All that we have accomplished in the course of the war and through our policy in the East, which aims at the military paralysis of Russia, would be overturned and lead to the birth of a new Russia which would be our enemy.' Since Helfferich's views were incompatible with those of the Foreign Ministry, whose policy directives he refused to carry out, Hintze ordered him to leave Moscow immediately and report to Berlin.[2]

Although Chicherin's request for German military intervention in Murmansk fulfilled one of the major demands the High Command had been making since May, Ludendorff agreed with Helfferich's interpretation of the Soviet request; above all, he believed that the downfall of the Bolsheviks was imminent. Ludendorff was convinced that he had enough troops in the East to drive out the British and overthrow the Bolsheviks at the same time. He informed Hintze that the German army could advance into Russia and establish a new government there 'which would have the people behind it.'[3] Hintze had anticipated this crisis and took immediate action to prevent the complete reversal of his policy, which he believed to be the only policy for Germany in the East as long as the decisive battles of the war were being fought on the Western Front. Hintze's reply to Ludendorff's plan for an anti-Bolshevik

[1] *Verhältnis Deutschlands zu Russland*, St. A. Nr. 85, telegram, 2 August 1918, Helfferich (Moscow) to Foreign Ministry (Berlin).

[2] *Ibid.*, telegram, 5 August 1918, Hintze (Berlin) to Helfferich (Moscow). According to Hilger, *op. cit.*, p. 10, Hintze said in 1922 that Helfferich 'left Moscow on his own initiative' and that his flight was a 'breach of discipline quite unusual in the history of diplomacy; and it was so regarded in the Foreign Ministry.' This assertion is at variance with Hintze's telegram of 5 August, ordering Helfferich 'to come here and report as soon as possible' and to leave the Embassy in Dr Riezler's charge.

[3] *Verhältnis Deutschlands zu Russland*, St. A. Nr. 84, telegram, 18 July 1918, Lersner (High Command) to Foreign Ministry (Berlin), and *ibid.*, St. A. Nr. 85, telegram, 5 August 1918, Ludendorff (High Command) to Hintze (Berlin). Also see above, p. 10.

crusade took the form of a long and brilliant analysis of Germany's relations with Russia. 'A [Russian] Government that has the people behind it does not need our support,' Hintze wrote. The Bolsheviks, he continued, had asked Germany to intervene against the common enemy; 'any other government—we have to be perfectly clear about this—is either immediately or within a short time a friend and ally of the Entente. We do not have any friends worth mentioning in Russia,' Hintze continued; 'whoever informs Your Excellency to the contrary is deceiving himself.' It was true that the Bolsheviks had been losing popular support, Hintze admitted, but there was no indication that they would be deposed in the immediate future. If they are overthrown, the German Government, Hintze wrote, must try to accommodate itself with their successors. But,

in the meantime, we have no reason to wish or to provoke a rapid end to the Bolsheviks' regime. The Bolsheviks are an evil and most anti-pathetic people; but that did not prevent us from forcing the peace of Brest-Litovsk on them and, bit by bit, taking even more of their territory and possessions from them. . . . Whether or not we like the idea of working with them is unimportant as long as it is useful to do so. History shows that to introduce feelings into politics is a costly luxury. . . . To this day and for a long time to come, politics are utilitarian.

Having instructed Ludendorff in the art of conducting foreign policy, Hintze went on to restate his version of Germany's policy in the East:

What, after all, do we want in the East? The military paralysis of Russia. The Bolsheviks are doing a better and more thorough job of this than any other Russian party, and without our devoting a single man or one mark to the task. We cannot expect them or other Russians to love us for milking their country dry. Let us rather be content with Russia's impotence.

The Bolsheviks, Hintze continued, are the only ones in Russia who have taken a stand against the Entente and who recognize the Brest treaty. 'Are we to sacrifice the fruits of four years of battle and triumph in order to absolve ourselves of the odium of having used the Bolsheviks? Because that is what we are doing: we are not working with them, we are exploiting them. That is both politic and politics.' Summarizing his views, Hintze declared that

it is good policy to exploit the Bolsheviks as long as they have something

to give. If they fall, we can observe the chaos which may result with
calm detachment, until we think the country is weak enough for us to
restore order without great loss to ourselves. If no chaos develops, but a
new party takes over right away, then we have to move in under the
heading: no war with Russia nor with the Russian people, no conquests,
rather order and protection for the weak against their being ill-used by
our enemies. The lattermost alternative forces us to act without foreseeable advantages, therefore I prefer the other two.[1]

Within hours of receiving copies of this telegram, Hertling and
the Kaiser informed Hintze that they were 'in complete agreement'
with his policy.[2] Then followed a telegram from the High Command in which Ludendorff retreated as rapidly as he could.

I completely agree with Your Excellency that we are aiming at
Russia's military paralysis, but, on the other hand, I am of the opinion
that we have to prevent Russia, in her helplessness, from falling prey to
the Entente, a danger which is by no means out of the question, even if
we reach an understanding with the Bolsheviks in Berlin. I am prepared
to fight against the British on the Murmansk coast, if we can occupy
Petrograd.

In every other respect Ludendorff said he agreed with Hintze's
policy and disclaimed any intention of attacking or subverting the
Bolshevik Government. However, he suggested that the Soviet
request for a German attack on General Alexeyev should be met
with 'words' rather than action, because honouring the request
would amount to giving 'unilateral support to the Bolsheviks,
which I cannot recommend.'[3]

Ludendorff's reply to Hintze is dated 7 August, one day before
the massive German offensive on the Western Front was stopped
short of its objectives—'the black day in the history of the German
army.' After this, although a Soviet agent in the Berlin Embassy
was able to inform Chicherin that 'the High Command as well as
the Foreign Ministry want nothing other than a complete understanding with Russia,' it was too late for the Germans to move

---

[1] *Ibid.*, St. A. Nr. 85, telegram, 6 August 1918, Hintze (Berlin) to Ludendorff
(High Command). Also see Appendix A.

[2] *Ibid.*, telegram, 6 August 1918, Lersner (High Command) to Foreign
Ministry (Berlin), and *ibid.*, telegram, 7 August 1918, Lersner (High Command)
to Foreign Ministry (Berlin).

[3] *Ibid.*, telegram, 7 August 1918, Ludendorff (High Command) to Hintze
(Berlin).

against the Entente invaders in Russia.[1] Although a preliminary agreement was reached in Berlin, which was later incorporated in the exchange of secret notes on 27 August, to send German troops to Murmansk via Petrograd and Vologda under the nominal command of Russian officers, the crisis on the Western Front forced Ludendorff to transfer the last available reserves from the East, and the Murmansk adventure was too hazardous to risk with the troops remaining on that front.[2]

At the end of the first week in August the successful conclusion of the Berlin negotiations was still thwarted by Ludendorff's insistence on supporting the Cossacks and maintaining German control over the Donets-Basin and Baku. Most of the German press was also resolutely hostile to an accord with Bolshevik Russia. The newspapers changed their tone only after Stresemann lectured to their editors about 'taking a line friendly to the Government's point of view' in an off-the-record conference.[3] Stresemann had interrupted his vacation at the beginning of August to be available in Berlin, where he could use his influence in support of the treaties with the Russians. On 8 August he wrote to Lieutenant-Colonel Bauer at Spa, advising the High Command to withdraw its objections to the draft agreements. It was not a 'pleasant prospect' to go 'arm in arm with the Bolsheviks,' Stresemann admitted—'one does not like to be seen on Unter den Linden with a tramp'—but the only alternative regimes in Russia were Right-wing parties, Miliukov for example, 'who demand revisions of the Brest peace and might join forces with the Entente.' Stresemann repeated Hintze's arguments that Germany had every reason to deal with Lenin's regime, 'which is at least not imperialistic under any circumstances and which could never join forces with the Entente.' But he also had other reasons for supporting the supplementary treaties:

Because we unfortunately neglected immediately to move the boundary lines further [eastward] in the peace treaty, we were in danger

[1] *Stresemann Nachlass*, 6911H/H135986, telegram, 13 August 1918, Solomon (Soviet Embassy) to Chicherin (Moscow). Litwin gave Stresemann a copy of this telegram, but there is no explanation in the file of how Litwin acquired it.

[2] *Ibid.*, undated telegram, Solomon (Soviet Embassy) to Joffe and Chicherin (Moscow). Cf. Wheeler-Bennett, *Brest-Litovsk*, p. 436; cf. Degras, *Soviet Documents*, vol. 1, pp. 96 f.

[3] *Stresemann Nachlass*, 6911H/H135916/8, letter to Graf Kessler, 15 August 1918.

at the outset of our Reichstag discussions—which are more partial to the Russians than to ourselves—of providing an opening for British influence in the Baltic.

The terms of the draft treaties satisfied Stresemann because 'Russia offers to cede Estonia, Livonia, and Georgia, as well as a payment of 6 billion marks in indemnities.' It was clear that Germany had 'every reason to conclude extensive commercial and political agreements with the present [Soviet] government,' and Stresemann hoped that Ludendorff could be made to understand this too.[1] By this time Ludendorff's nerves were frayed. He was beginning to anticipate defeat and was losing his grip on the Government. Perhaps he also realized that the political and com-mercial terms of the treaties were more advantageous to Germany than they would have been had Joffe and the Soviet Government been aware of the weakening of the High Command and its armies. Whatever the reasons, Ludendorff withdrew his objections to the drafts, and therewith the last obstacle to the treaties on the German side was removed.

In the meantime Krasin and Joffe had visited Moscow to report on the progress of the negotiations. When they returned in the middle of August, Joffe alarmed the Germans, who were anxious to sign the treaties as soon as possible, with a number of objections to clauses in the supplementary political treaty. The chief problem seems to have been the Turkish military expedition against Baku, which threatened the settlements reached in Articles 12 and 14 of the political agreement. But the Bolsheviks still failed to realize that the German bargaining position had appreciably weakened since the beginning of August, so when Hintze assured Joffe that the German Government would force the Turks to retreat behind the demarcation line, Joffe agreed to sign the treaties, which he did four days later, on 27 August 1918.[2]

With excessive self-satisfaction Litwin asked Stresemann to help him get an Iron Cross for his part in the negotiations, and added that he thought the negotiations with the Bolsheviks should be continued. 'We must not under any circumstances repeat the

---

[1] *Ibid.*, 6911H/H136261/70.

[2] *Ibid.*, 6911H/H135973/5, letter from Litwin, 23 August 1918. The *Nord-deutsche Allgemeine Zeitung* reported on 28 August 1918 that there had been an exchange of confidential notes, but the notes were not published until 1926, in *Europäischen Gespräche*, Bd. 4, pp. 148 ff.

mistakes we made in the Ukraine.' Litwin believed that Germany should work 'peu à peu towards a military alliance with Russia. This has to be done slowly and carefully and is in my opinion the most important goal.'[1] Stresemann did not disagree, but he had a broader outlook. 'Perhaps,' he wrote in September 1918, 'in the future Germany will turn her gaze somewhat more towards the East, and we shall find some compensation there for what we cannot attain for the time being in competition abroad.'[2]

Together with the supplementary political and financial treaties signed on 27 August, Hintze and Joffe exchanged confidential notes, which amounted to a third agreement expounding the more delicate clauses of the other two. Taken altogether, the agreements marked a notable reversal for the Germans, especially for the High Command, who only three weeks earlier had plotted the forcible overthrow of the Bolsheviks, and now accepted prohibitions against supporting forces, Russian or others, operating against the Soviet Government on Russian soil, and agreed to act in concert with the Bolsheviks against General Alexeyev's 'insurrection' in White Russia.[3] The treaties were a credit to Lenin's policy. With the exception of the indemnity clauses, the supplementary agreements were totally unlike the one-sided peace treaty signed six months earlier, consisting of bargains and compromises between two hard-pressed powers seeking security from a normalization of relations with one another.[4] Until November, when the threat of imminent revolution and a desire to appease the besieging powers required new tactics, the onslaught of Marshal Foch's armies headed the Germans into still better relations with Soviet Russia. This suited the Bolsheviks, because they needed support in combating the intervening forces and sufficient time to establish Soviet institutions while retrenching their revolutionary powers.

While the Imperial German Army was collapsing, the Russians were building up a new Red Army. The exigencies of the national emergency did not allow the Communists to demobilize any more

---

[1] *Stresemann Nachlass*, 6911H/H135973/5. On the Russian side, Lenin's confidential memorandum of May 1918 did not exclude 'military agreements' with an 'imperialist coalition' from Soviet policy; see Carr, vol. 3, p. 70.

[2] Gatzke, 'Deutsch-Russischen Beziehungen im Sommer 1918,' p. 77.

[3] Degras, *Soviet Documents*, vol. 1, p. 97.

[4] Radek's comments on the indemnity clauses are in Dennis, *Foreign Policies*, p. 45. On the supplementary financial treaty see L. Fischer, *Soviets in World Affairs*, vol. 1, p. 130; Wheeler-Bennett, *Brest-Litovsk*, pp. 344 f.

than it allowed Trotsky merely to 'issue some revolutionary proclamations' from the Foreign Commissariat 'and then close up the joint.'[1] The Bolsheviks had to engage in diplomatic relations and they even resorted to secret diplomacy. To carry out their foreign policy they needed an army. The decision to create a Workers' and Peasants' Red Army was taken in January 1918 at a meeting of party leaders, including Lenin and probably also Trotsky. Recruitment began on a large scale with the resumption of the German offensive in February. One day after the Brest treaty was signed, Trotsky was appointed president of the Supreme War Council, and thereafter he devoted his organizing skill to the creation of a new military establishment.[2] Professor Carr has written that 'the formation of organized armies by the "white" generals, and the beginning of something like regular warfare in the Ukraine . . . forced on the new regime the task of building up a military force capable of taking the field against them.'[3] An equally important reason for the decision to create a Red Army was that when the Bolsheviks seized power they had to accept the fact that Russia was a state in a system of states, many of which were hostile to the Soviet Republic, and that they therefore needed an army, not only to drive out the Entente and to crush the 'white' forces, but equally to support and protect the Republic in the future.

On 23 September General Groener visited the High Command at Spa. He asked Ludendorff how long he could hold out in the West. 'I can offer resistance for a few months,' but 'we must have peace before Christmas,' was the reply. Appalled as much by Ludendorff's nervous state as by the deplorable military predicament, Groener returned to Berlin to persuade politicians of the Right that they must anticipate defeat and prevent an upheaval by leading the way towards a parliamentary monarchy. Hugo Stinnes' reaction was typical. He believed in the German army, he said. 'Ludendorff will win!' he thundered. 'Ludendorff will *not* win!' Groener shouted, and slammed the door behind him.[4] Four days

[1] T. H. von Laue, 'Soviet Diplomacy: G. V. Chicherin,' in G. Craig and F. Gilbert, *The Diplomats 1919-1939* (Princeton, 1953), pp. 235, 239.

[2] In April 1918 Trotsky received the additional title of People's Commissar for War. *The Norddeutsche Allgemeine Zeitung* reported on 16 February 1918 that the Russians were 'demobilizing one army and at the same time building a new Red Army.'

[3] Carr, vol. 3, p. 61.

[4] E. Kabisch, *Groener: Männer und Mächte* (Leipzig, 1932), pp. 56-58.

later Ludendorff panicked. He demanded an immediate armistice. Hertling, Hintze, and Hindenburg told the Kaiser the war was lost. On 4 October Prince Max formed a coalition government which presided over the dissolution of the Hohenzollern Empire.

When the Bolshevik leaders finally realized that the war was drawing to an end, they exulted in the misapprehension that the German collapse had begun the second stage of the world revolution. Amidst the chaos and undirected ferment rife in Germany during October and November there was indeed evidence to convince a Bolshevik that the German upheaval was a revolution on the Soviet model. Lenin predicted that 'the time is approaching when circumstances may demand from us help for the German people to liberate itself from its own imperialism against Anglo-French imperialism.' He decreed that there should be 'no relations with the government of Wilhelm nor with the government of Wilhelm II plus Ebert and other scoundrels,' and proposed that once the revolt was under way, German working masses should be given 'brotherly union, *bread*, military help.'[1] Meanwhile the Soviet Government, acting through the Communist Party, redoubled its efforts to intensify the struggles in Germany. Joffe's contributions to the revolutionary fervour in Berlin have been recounted in a number of works and do not require further elaboration.[2] But it is important to emphasize that Soviet money and propaganda were not instrumental in causing the German military defeat and the Kaiser's downfall. Joffe's activities were more disruptive than revolutionary, and although every bit of disruption helped to create general chaos, Joffe himself admitted that he had 'accomplished little or nothing of permanent value.' 'We were too weak to provoke a revolution,' he added.[3] It is true that German troops in Russia were infected with Bolshevism, and some in the West were affected too, but Germany was humbled in battle at the hands of a stronger foe, not by a 'stab in the back.' The social fabric within the country was rent by schisms which were intensified by Communist activity, but the vast majority of Germans rebelled against existing authority out of desperation—from hunger, cold,

[1] Lenin on 1 and 3 October 1918, quoted by Carr, vol. 3, pp. 91 f.

[2] Degras, *Soviet Documents*, vol. 1, pp. 126, 127 f.; Wheeler-Bennett, *Brest-Litovsk*, pp. 348-360; Carr, vol. 3, pp. 71, 76 f.; L. Fischer, *Soviets in World Affairs*, vol. 1, pp. 75 f.

[3] L. Fischer, *Men and Politics* (New York, 1941), p. 31.

complete exhaustion—not from inspiration to emulate the Bolshevik Revolution.

Because they failed to appreciate those factors which might have led them to be more apprehensive, the Bolsheviks convinced themselves that Germany would soon be in the throes of a revolution on the Soviet model. They were not discouraged when Joffe was expelled from Berlin for his revolutionary activities, nor were they surprised when Prince Max's Government, in an effort to persuade the Entente that Germany would not continue friendly relations with the Bolsheviks, revived the issue of Mirbach's assassination, on the pretext that Germany 'cannot tolerate the crime against the ambassador remaining unexpiated.'[1] Even when the Workers' and Soldiers' Councils in Berlin failed to elect Rosa Luxemburg and Karl Liebknecht to the Council of People's Representatives, and when the Independent Socialists Haase and Kautsky voted with the SPD majority on the Council against asking Joffe to return to Berlin, the Bolsheviks remained convinced that the German masses were ready for a Communist revolution. In reality, the Spartacists and other Left extremists who were not reconciled to socialization by the ballot box gained mass support only as long as the popular demands for peace and the Kaiser's abdication remained unfulfilled. The Social Democrat leaders of the Provisional Government that replaced Prince Max's coalition, especially Ebert, Scheidemann, and Landsberg, regarded the extremists on the Left as the deadliest enemies of the working class. Consequently their first concern was not to promote the revolution but to curb it. 'Ebert himself remarked that he hated revolution as he hated sin,' and it is not surprising that he flirted with the idea of replacing Wilhelm II with a regency for the infant son of the Crown Prince, and only resigned himself to a different solution when he realized that the Spartacists and Independent Socialists were gaining mass support at the expense of the Social Democrats, by demanding the creation of a republic as well as abdication.[2]

On 9 November the Kaiser fled to Holland. Thousands of striking workers and rebellious soldiers streamed through the streets of Berlin calling for the establishment of a republic. The splits on the Left were irreparable: Liebknecht proclaimed a 'Soviet

[1] From an unpublished diplomatic note, quoted by Carr, vol. 3, p. 94.
[2] R. D. Butler, *The Roots of National Socialism 1783-1933* (London, 1941), p. 215; Halperin, *Germany Tried Democracy*, pp. 86 f.

republic' from the balcony of the royal palace and at the same time Scheidemann precipitously launched a 'German republic' from a Reichstag balcony. Ebert was appalled. He headed a caretaker government but had no force to establish order; in the streets the Spartacists threatened to fill the power vacuum. The parallel with events in Russia was too terrifying. Late at night on 9 November General Groener called from the High Command to offer Ebert the support of the Officer Corps, on the condition that the authority of the officers and their armies remain inviolable in the new circumstances. Ebert agreed without hesitation, and then immediately discussed with Groener the task that both men considered most urgent, the suppression of 'Bolshevism' in Germany.

This telephone alliance 'between a defeated army and a tottering semi-revolutionary regime' crushed what was left of a proletarian revolution in Germany, and doomed the Weimar Republic at birth.[1] What irony then, that the continued authority and resurgence of a powerful Officer Corps should prove decisive to the Soviet Republic in its future good relations with Germany.

[1] Wheeler-Bennett, *The Nemesis of Power* (London, 1953), pp. 20 f. Cf. Scheele, *The Weimar Republic*, p. 81; cf. R. Fischer, *Stalin and German Communism* (Cambridge, Mass., 1948), pp. 60 ff.

# CHAPTER II

## THE FAILURE OF TWO REVOLUTIONS

DURING the crucial weeks following the Armistice of November 1918, splits within and among the parties of the German Left prevented decisiveness in the counsels of their leaders. The locus of power remained with the mobs in the streets of Berlin. 'Disorder, insecurity, plundering, wild commandeering and house-prowling had become the order of the day. . . . The only masters of Berlin were Disunity, Licentiousness and Chaos. . . . And day and night, senseless shooting—partly from exuberation, partly from fear. Berlin lived, danced, drank and celebrated.'[1]

Only the High Command, now situated at Cassel, and the militant Spartacists had definite plans what to do next: Hindenburg, Groener, and von Schleicher to retain power and the officers' prerogatives as arbiters of the destinies of the state; Liebknecht to seize power on the Soviet model. The *Spartakusbund*, however, was signally unfit to rule. It was a small organization, composed of a handful of intellectuals leading an assortment of semi-intellectual malcontents. The Spartacists had lost most of the meagre popular support which they had aroused by agitating for an end to the war and abdication when these objectives were attained. To invigorate the movement Liebknecht wanted to associate the Spartacists with the revolutionary shop-stewards in Berlin, but Rosa Luxemburg, who realized that most of the workers were satisfied with the *révolution manquée* that had taken place, rejected the proposal and convinced a majority in the newly formed KPD to vote against it.[2] In Luxemburg's opinion it was not possible to extend the revolution. The Provisional Government had taken an unequivocal stand against the Left extremists: 'At this moment there is no danger of a counter-revolution. . . . The danger which threatens the success of the revolution in this hour is anarchy.'[3] Luxemburg contended that if the Spartacists acted against the government they would do

[1] From a contemporary account quoted by R. G. L. Waite, *Vanguard of Nazism* (Cambridge, Mass., 1952), p. 3.

[2] R. Fischer, *Stalin and German Communism*, pp. 73-79.

[3] *Vorwärts*, 24 December 1918.

so without mass support, because 'the German working class is not ready' to 'seize power now.' The workers, she said, must 'fight within factories and on the streets against Ebert and Scheidemann, but they should not aim at the overthrow of the Ebert Government.' A Communist effort to seize power at the turn of the year would have been premature and doomed to failure. Luxemburg said it was 'useless' and 'childish' to overthrow the Ebert regime as long as 'the masses are not ready and able to organize Germany. Our battlefield is within the factories,' she concluded.[1] Following Luxemburg's lead, the KPD adopted a programme at the beginning of January 1919 which was, in effect, 'equivalent to a critical tolera-tion of the Ebert Government, combined with militant propaganda against the army and for socialist aims.' The programme did not mention the Bolsheviks and contained only a vague reference to international co-operation with other Communists.[2]

Of Lenin's five delegates to the German party only Karl Radek eluded the German border guards and made his way to Berlin. He was neither a welcome visitor nor at all influential at the Founding Congress of the KPD. Factional differences in the Polish party before the war divided him from Luxemburg. Furthermore, Luxemburg was critical of the complete 'elimination of democracy' by Lenin and Trotsky in Russia and, as we have noted, she believed that the Communist revolution in Germany, which Radek had come to spur on to victory, had not yet begun.[3] The presence of Radek, who behaved rather like a revolutionary elder statesman at the congress, was a sign of the Bolsheviks' intense interest in the development of the German party. But from Luxemburg's point of view it was unwarranted interference in German Communist affairs. She was, moreover, opposed to the formation of a Third International as long as the German revolution had not succeeded, realizing that until that time a new International was bound to be dominated by the Russians.[4] But Radek was imbued with the

---

[1] *Bericht über den Gründungsparteitag der Kommunistischen Partei Deutschlands (Spartakusbund)* (Berlin, n.d.), p. 34.

[2] *Ibid.*, pp. 33–35; R. Fischer, *op. cit.*, p. 75; Carr, vol. 3, p. 106.

[3] R. Luxemburg, *Die russische Revolution* (Berlin, 1922), ed. P. Levi, pp. 108, 109.

[4] Eberlein, the only KPD representative at the Founding Congress of the Third International, abstained from the vote on the establishment of Comintern on 4 March 1919: O. K. Flechtheim, *Die Kommunistische Partei Deutschlands in der Weimarer Republik* (Offenbach, 1948), p. 57.

revolutionary enthusiasm prevalent in Moscow at that time and could neither justify Luxemburg's criticisms of the Bolshevik party, nor appreciate her keen analysis of the predicament in which the German Communists found themselves in 1918-1919. Unlike Russian delegates to foreign Communist party meetings in subsequent years, Radek could not discipline the Germans into subscribing to Bolshevik policies. He did, however, inflict speeches on the delegates which showed no awareness of the realities of their dilemma at the time. Radek hailed the 'German revolution,' and then, when appeals for 'international revolutionary solidarity' failed to move the delegates, he tried flattery, saying that 'the Russian working class knows well that without the socialist revolution in Germany the Russian workers' revolution would not have sufficient strength to build a new house on the ruins left behind by capitalism.'[1]

According to his own testimony, Radek was rapidly disabused of his illusions concerning the prospects of a proletarian revolution in Germany. In December 1918 he had predicted that by the following May 'all Europe would be Soviet,' but in February, when he was imprisoned at Moabit in Berlin, Radek came out 'against any attempt to seize power' because that 'can be effected only by a majority of the working class, which [is] certainly not on the side of the Communist party.'[2] Unfortunately Liebknecht did not appreciate the significance of these facts. Despite the official KPD programme and Luxemburg's repeated attempts to sever his relations with the shop-stewards, Liebknecht obstinately continued to collaborate with all 'activist' groups who were working for the immediate overthrow of the Provisional Government. This led directly to the Communist catastrophes in January 1919. During that month the threat of Sovietism on German soil was eliminated. The mutinous sailors ensconced in the Marstall were forced to capitulate, and the insurgent shop-stewards were crushed by Gustav Noske and the Free Corps under his direction in the bloodletting of 'Spartacus Week.' At the same time the KPD was

[1] *Akten betreffend: Karl Radek*, Deutschland 131, adh. 3, nr. 2 (St. Antony's College, Oxford), St. A. Nr. 38, unsigned memorandum dated 31 December 1918 reporting Radek's speech of the previous day. Also see K. Radek, *Die russische und die deutsche Revolution und die Weltlage* (Berlin, 1919), p. 31.

[2] *Pravda*, 5 December 1918, quoted by Kochan, *Russia and Weimar*, p. 13; 2(i) *Vsegermanskii S'ezd Rabochikh i Soldatskikh Sovetov* (1935), p. 324, quoted by Carr, vol. 3, pp. 106 f.

emasculated by the loss of its leadership, as both Liebknecht and Luxemburg were murdered by officers of the Guard Cavalry Division.[1]

By destroying the Communist movement the Ebert Government improved its standing both with the High Command and with the Entente powers; it seemed that the government was preserving Germany from disorder, from Bolshevism. Yet every time Ebert had recourse to regular troops or irregular Free Corps formations under the army's control he became more dependent upon their commanders and, ultimately, upon the High Command. In preventing the radicals from achieving their aims the Officer Corps was enabled to impose its will on the Provisional Government. Thus the counter-revolution thrived upon the excesses of the revolutionaries.

To Hindenburg, Groener, and von Schleicher, however, suppressing Bolshevism meant more than eliminating the Spartacists; they wanted to crush every vestige of change and progress that threatened to incapacitate the army. In particular, they wanted to dissolve the Soldiers' and Workers' Councils before these could effect the popular demands 'to disarm the General Staff' and 'dispossess the Officer Corps.' Ebert, who also feared the revolutionary impetus of the Councils, needed the support of the High Command to conduct an orderly transitional government and to withdraw the troops from the Western Front in accordance with the Armistice terms, and therefore refused to heed the Councils' entreaties to disenfranchise the officers. In fact, Ebert moved closer to the opposite extreme when, late in December 1918, he took Groener's advice to reconstruct the Provisional Government without the Independent Socialists. By the beginning of the new year the Ebert-Groener 'telephone alliance' was more secure than ever before.

In Eastern Europe the period following the Armistice of 1918 was turbulent because a final settlement of Germany's eastern boundaries was not made until the diplomats met at Versailles to arrange peace terms. The Armistice invalidated Germany's claims under the Treaty of Brest-Litovsk and the supplementary treaties, thereby encouraging Polish nationalists to take matters into their own hands before the diplomats could meet to decide Poland's fate.

---

[1] Halperin, *Germany Tried Democracy*, pp. 121 f.; R. Fischer, *Stalin and German Communism*, p. 87. Cf. E. H. Carr, *Studies in Revolution* (London, 1950), pp. 183 f.

Treating Wilson's thirteenth point as a legal document, the Poles staged a successful insurrection against their German overlords in Posen. Hindenburg, fuming that Posen—which was his birthplace —had been the 'sacred soil of the Fatherland' for 200 years, ordered General von Bülow's Free Corps to recapture Culmsee in order to save it from the hated Poles. This provoked Paderewski to raise a storm of protest to the Allies, whom he persuaded to deliver an ultimatum for the withdrawal of all German troops from Posen under the threat of an Allied occupation of Westphalia.[1] The Allied governments had resolved to free the Poles from the German yoke, but they were equally determined not to allow German occupation forces in the Baltic territories to withdraw until 'the Allies shall think the moment suitable, having regard to the internal situation of these territories.'[2] The purpose of this injunction was to prevent the Red Army from moving into the Baltic as the German armies withdrew, and before the British could erect a *cordon sanitaire* between Germany and Russia in the form of independent Baltic governments under Western protection. Britain and her allies did not want to incur the expense and hardships of a campaign against the Red Army in the Baltic. Considering the war-weariness of the soldiers and of people on the home front, and appreciating the effectiveness of Communist propaganda, Lloyd George and his colleagues were afraid that another military expedition against the Bolsheviks might have dangerous consequences.[3] Since German troops were already in the Baltic, the Allies thought they could use these to halt the Red advance both cheaply and painlessly. Meanwhile British political influence was exerted in the Baltic to lay the groundwork for independent governments which would control the territories after the Red Army was defeated and German troops were withdrawn.[4] In December 1918 August Winnig, German plenipotentiary in the Baltic, offered to make additional Free Corps legions available to halt the Russian advance. The Allies accepted the offer; it seemed

[1] Waite, *Vanguard of Nazism*, pp. 93 ff.

[2] H. R. Rudin, *Armistice 1918* (New Haven, 1944), pp. 428 f.

[3] See Lloyd George's statement in the Council of Ten on 16 January 1919, *Foreign Relations of the United States: The Paris Peace Conference 1919* (Washington, 1943), vol. 3, pp. 589-593, and the debate in the House of Commons, *The Parliamentary Debates, Official Report, House of Commons*, vol. 118, 5th session, columns 1969-1970, 1980, 2066, 2944.

[4] *The Times*, 27 October 1918.

to provide the perfect solution to their problems in the territories.[1]

The call of the Baltic lured many different types of German
volunteers: idealistic young patriots who went to defend the soil
of the Fatherland from the 'Red peril'; older men to claim 'great
estates' in the 'beautiful Baltic' promised to them by the recruitment officers; men from aristocratic families who could not
stomach the 'miserable socialist rabble' of the post-monarchical
governments at home; and the most common Free Corps type:
young men 'who had learned war and did not want to learn anything else,' who went for adventure and excitement, and to escape
the boredom of civilian life.[2]

When the Free Corps arrived in the Baltic under Count Rudiger
von der Goltz at the beginning of the new year, the situation was
confused by the presence of three groups vying for control. There
were the Baltic barons, who were striving to retain power against
the recently formed native governments, and the Red Army,
which threatened to engulf and reclaim the border states for Russia.
The German military commanders on the spot and at the headquarters of the High Command were agreed that Baltic sovereignty
was not to be tolerated under any circumstances, but they differed
about the measures to be taken to meet the situation. At his new
headquarters in Colberg, General Groener sought a plan to sustain
Germany's military triumphs in the Baltic, the only front where
German forces had not crumbled in November 1918. Groener was
a realist. After studying the alternatives he reached the irrefutable
conclusion that the war was lost on both fronts; there could not be
a German hegemony in the East. Looking towards the future,
Groener said that Germany would have to contend with the
existence of Poland, 'a people who are again registering a mark in
history.'[3] To counterbalance the hostile Poles Germany must
cultivate the 'Russia of the future' as a friend. 'We must do what
is required to secure Russia's friendship in the future,' Groener told

---

[1] Waite, *op. cit.*, pp. 101 f.

[2] *Ibid.*, pp. 97 ff. Cf. General Fürst Awaloff, *Im Kampf gegen den Bolschewismus*
(Glückstadt/Hamburg, 1925), p. 222. On the organization of the Free Corps
also see Wheeler-Bennett, *Nemesis of Power*, p. 41; cf. W. Görlitz, *Der Deutsche
Generalstab* (Frankfurt, 1951), pp. 301 ff.

[3] *Heeresarchiv*: Wilhelm Groener (Archives of the United States of America,
Washington), Karton 16, Stück 213, notes of a discussion in the War Ministry
on 15 May 1919.

the cabinet.[1] But who were the future rulers of Russia? Who could tell how long the Bolsheviks would remain in power? Groener was willing to guess, and his guess was wrong. He thought that the Bolsheviks would soon be overthrown, and he was prepared to hasten the destruction of their regime in a military alliance with the Western powers. In Paris, Marshal Foch had indeed made 'suggestions for a combined operation against Soviet troops,' but these were not adopted.[2] This left Groener without a clear plan for the East. He was entirely out of sympathy with von der Goltz and others who wanted to renew the war on both fronts, and who advocated, as a first step, an all-out military offensive in conjunction with the Russian 'whites' to 'defeat' the Bolsheviks in Russia. Their plan was to fight a simultaneous 'defensive war' against the Allied armies in the West, but Groener knew that this was unendurable. 'A new war,' he wrote, 'would mean foreign troops right up to the capital,' and that spelled 'Finis Germaniae.'[3] What, then, was to be done in the Baltic? 'We need a bridge to Russia,' Groener wrote, and 'for that the best thing would be: to stay in; to wait.'[4]

The commanding officer on the North-Eastern Front responsible for carrying out Groener's simple but crucial plan was General Hans von Seeckt. Seeckt agreed with Groener on the fundamental issue: a land-bridge to Russia was a desirable strategic position for the future, and its existence would strengthen Germany's bargaining power in the negotiations at Versailles. But Seeckt also saw something that Groener had failed to consider, namely, that by defending the Baltic territories Germany was inadvertently participating in the Allied plan to use the border states as a *cordon sanitaire* between Russia and herself. To prevent this from happen-

---

[1] R. H. Phelps, 'Aus den Groener-Dokumenten IV: Das Baltikum 1919,' *Deutsche Rundschau* (Darmstadt, October 1950), 76. Jhrg., pp. 836 f.

[2] *Heeresarchiv*: Groener, Karton 16, Stück 213, notes from a cabinet meeting on 24 April 1919. Also see Groener's letter to Erzberger of 31 March 1919, quoted by R. H. Phelps, 'Aus den Groener-Dokumenten II: Die Aussenpolitik der O. H. L. bis zum Friedensvertrag,' *Deutsche Rundschau* (Darmstadt, August 1950), 76. Jhrg., p. 621, and *The Intimate Papers of Colonel House* (London, 1926), ed. C. Seymour, vol. 4, pp. 358 ff.

[3] *Heeresarchiv*: Draft Autobiography of Wilhelm Groener, p. 77. Also see the interesting discussion of this problem in G. A. Craig, *The Politics of the Prussian Army 1640-1945*, pp. 368 ff.

[4] Phelps, 'Aus den Groener-Dokumenten IV,' p. 837.

ing, Seeckt advocated a retreat to the line Libau-Kovno-Grodno, which could be held to protect East Prussia, thereby allowing the Red Army to advance along the Baltic coast in order to establish the desired land-bridge between the two countries. Already at this time, Seeckt, who later had considerable influence on German policies in the East, 'frequently reiterated the opinion that war should never again be waged against Russia,' and that Germany must have 'a wide, direct surface of contact with Russia' no matter what party ruled in Moscow.[1] In the end, neither Groener's plan nor Seeckt's was carried out. The activities of the ambitious von der Goltz ruined this opportunity of establishing friendly relations with the 'Russia of the future.' Goltz thought he could salvage Germany's war-time triumphs in the East. In open defiance of Seeckt's and the High Command's orders to fight a defensive battle, Goltz mounted an offensive at the beginning of February and continued the advance until his troops captured Riga. Using Riga as a base, Goltz wanted a 'large army' with which to 'crush Bolshevism in Russia' and to install a 'white' government there which, in his opinion, was bound to be friendly to Germany.[2] Although the High Command continued to pay and supply Goltz's Free Corps during the summer and autumn of 1919, Groener stubbornly refused to send Goltz the men and material he needed to invade Russia. Goltz's scheme was ultimately frustrated by the Allies, who were alarmed by the success of the Free Corps and feared that they would destroy the independent governments in the border states along with the little group of ill-equipped, disorganized Russians who constituted the 'Red peril,' leaving the territory to fall under German rule. Seeckt gladly obliged the Allied demand for Goltz's recall.[3]

In failing in the last German attempt before Hitler to overthrow the Bolshevik regime, Goltz had frustrated the first post-war German effort to secure contact with the 'Russia of the future.'

Meanwhile inside Germany a Republic was being erected on the shaky foundation of Weimar and Versailles. The National

[1] *Heeresarchiv*: Seeckt, Karton 19, Stück 290, letter from Major Tschunke to von Rabenau, 13 February 1939. Cf. F. v. Rabenau, *Seeckt—Aus Seinem Leben 1918–1936* (Leipzig, 1940), vol. 2, pp. 120 f.

[2] General Graf R. v. d. Goltz, *Meine Sendung in Finnland und im Baltikum* (Leipzig, 1920), pp. 127, 165.

[3] Waite, *Vanguard of Nazism*, pp. 118 ff.; Rabenau, *op. cit.*, p. 215. Cf. Kochan, *Russia and Weimar*, p. 16.

Assembly which convened at Weimar was composed of a preponderance of the parties of the Left, but the striking feature of the deliberations was the strength and confidence displayed by the rejuvenated parties of the Right: the Conservatives, who now called themselves the National People's Party, and their allies, the former National Liberals, re-christened the German People's Party. The Assembly created a 'superficially decentralized unitary state' whose constitutional life depended upon a continuing interaction of parties.[1] But the multiplicity of parties, and factions within the parties, left no one of them strong enough to act as a responsible majority government. All the admirable devices which contributed to the mechanical perfection of the Weimar Constitution could not insure the success of the democratic process in a society which had little or no experience with free institutions. It was tragic, too, for the Germans that the Weimar experiment with democracy was begun in the shadow of defeat, and that it trailed clouds of memories of defeat throughout its course.

Although the High Command was culpable for the defeat, the officers and other reactionaries advanced the theory that the civilians, the Socialists in particular, were alone responsible. From the beginning, the army dishonoured the Republic and fomented distrust of its leaders. But Ebert, the first President of the Republic, Scheidemann, the first Chancellor, and Noske, the Minister of Defence, had to rely on the army to keep order and to unify the country in conformity with the constitution ratified by the National Assembly. Troops were dispatched to quell outbursts of separatism in Saxony and Brunswick, and the abortive Soviet republic in Bavaria was deposed at the beginning of May. Wherever it was sent, the Free Corps, like Sherman's army in Georgia, wreaked havoc and destruction with the pretence of restoring civil order.

The overthrow of the Munich Soviet was acclaimed by the Allied governments, who convinced themselves that 'Germany constituted Europe's first bastion against Bolshevism.'[2] In Western Europe as in Germany itself the power of the German Communists was vastly overestimated. The Munich Soviet, for instance, had

---

[1] Scheele, *The Weimar Republic*, p. 42. Also see the interesting discussion of the Weimar Constitution in E. K. Barker, *Reflections on Government* (Oxford, 1942), pp. 370 ff.

[2] Wheeler-Bennett, *Nemesis of Power*, p. 40.

only a few Communists attached to it, and although a Red Army was organized for its defence, the KPD gave no active support and not much encouragement to the experiment. After January 1919 the KPD was, in fact, a small, disorganized faction, lacking in leadership and incapable of effective revolutionary action. Because the government exaggerated the strength of the Communists it had to place excessive reliance on the army.[1] The officers, in turn, were enabled to transcend their legitimate status as servants of the government, rising to important positions in the political councils of the Reich and exercising a powerful influence on all policies, including Germany's relations with her neighbours.

The foreign policy of the Weimar Republic was circumscribed almost from the start by the promulgation of the peace terms on 7 May 1919. The severity of the terms came as a shock to the German people, already burdened with the ignominy of defeat and the hardships of the winter that followed hard upon it. In the subsequent crisis, General Groener did not let the impassioned pleas of some officers, to renew the war rather than submit to the *Diktat*, dissuade him from following the hard but reasonable course of action which he knew had to be taken. He persuaded Ebert that the Versailles terms would have to be signed. If the treaty were rejected, a new war would start in which 'Germany would be forever wiped from the tablet which contains the names of the great nations on earth.'[2] At High Command headquarters there were tentative suggestions of a German-Russian alliance to fight the West, but Groener would not even contemplate this. 'An alliance with Russia, that is with Bolshevism,' he said, 'is something for which I cannot take the responsibility.'[3] He made a similar declaration to the cabinet: 'We have told the Entente again and again that we are willing to fight against Bolshevism; if we were now to ally ourselves with the Soviets, the Entente would consider this an act of treachery.'[4] Groener said that even if one could justify an alliance with the Bolsheviks, in the ensuing war Germany would be destroyed and occupied. He could see no reasonable alternative to

[1] Flechtheim, *Die KPD*, pp. 52 ff. Cf. E. O. Volkmann, *Revolution über Deutschland* (Oldenburg, 1930), p. 301.

[2] K. Caro and W. Oehme, *Schleichers Aufstieg: Ein Beitrag zur Geschichte der Gegenrevolution* (Berlin, 1923), p. 79.

[3] Phelps, 'Aus den Groener-Dokumenten II,' p. 624.

[4] *Heeresarchiv*: Groener, Karton 16, Stück 213, notes from a cabinet meeting on 24 April 1919.

signing the peace terms, although he realized that the Versailles treaty had the gravest implications for Germany's policy in the East. The greatest menace, according to Groener, was 'the expansionist impetus of the Poles.' 'One of these fine days,' he continued, 'we may discover that Poland has taken Pomerania and East Prussia, so that the Oder will become our frontier.' But what could the Germans do to prevent this catastrophe? Groener said that, at a later date, they might be able to depend on Russia's support, and perhaps also on a clash between Poland on the one hand and Czechoslovakia and Hungary on the other, but in the meantime 'we must rely on ourselves. We must be firmly resolved and have the means to defend ourselves in the East.'[1]

With this plea Groener joined Seeckt, the military expert on the German delegation at Versailles, and General Reinhardt, the Prussian Minister of War, in protesting to the Scheidemann Government for having accepted the articles of the Versailles treaty which were to render Germany militarily impotent, without first trying to moderate the armament restrictions. Scheidemann had not objected to these articles on the advice of Count Brockdorff-Rantzau, chief of the German peace delegation, who hoped that by accepting the disarmament clauses Germany might be compensated by the Allies 'in other questions.'[2] Seeckt held that military questions were the last ones on which to give way; he was outraged by Brockdorff-Rantzau's decision and dissociated himself from it, declaring that 'the 100,000 man army . . . had been agreed to by the delegation without even consulting him.'[3] Brockdorff-Rantzau retorted with equal passion that 'the catastrophe that had befallen Germany stemmed from the army' and that it deserved to suffer.[4] This was too much for Seeckt. The hurt pride of these two proud men almost brought matters to a duel. Years later Groener recalled the incident in his autobiography:

. . . even if Brockdorff-Rantzau was not able to accomplish much [at Versailles], he nevertheless represented us forthrightly and was listened

[1] *Ibid.*, notes from a meeting in the War Ministry on 15 May 1919.

[2] *Ibid.*, telegram from Groener to Scheidemann, 27 May 1919.

[3] *Heeresarchiv*: Seeckt, Karton 13, Stück 110, notes from a meeting of the German delegation at Versailles, 25 May 1919; and *Heeresarchiv*: Groener, Karton 16, Stück 213, Seeckt's letter to Groener, 26 May 1919.

[4] *Heeresarchiv*: Groener, Karton 16, Stück 213, conversation between Groener and Brockdorff-Rantzau.

to; I doubt that another could have achieved more. But also here the old German misery, the two leading figures, Brockdorff and Seeckt, could not work together: here, too, the lines of thought of statesmen and military men ran far apart.[1]

The enmity between Seeckt and Brockdorff-Rantzau, which started with a dispute during the war, was intensified by their encounter at Versailles, and three years later it threatened to interfere with the conduct of policy towards Russia, in which both men played leading roles.[2] Yet another aspect of Germany's subsequent policy towards Russia had its origin at Versailles: the articles prohibiting the production of military aeroplanes, tanks, and other weapons of offence in Germany forced Seeckt and leaders of German heavy industry to seek a foreign hinterland where weapons could be produced beyond the jurisdiction of the Military Control Commission. Their search ended in Russia.

A week after the Versailles treaty was signed, the German Government appointed Seeckt president of the Preparatory Commission for the Peace Army. Seeckt was so dismayed by the restrictions placed on the new army that he was prepared to quit the job soon after he was appointed. Groener was among those colleagues who persuaded him to stay. The hopes for the future that induced many officers to remain in the services are openly expressed in their letters to Seeckt at this time. One officer wrote at the end of June 1919:

I hope that the Monarchy will be restored in the foreseeable future, and that it will be possible to make war on Poland and perhaps also on France. . . . I consider it my duty to bid you, Herr General, to continue working for these prospects and goals.[3]

Seeckt shared these aspirations, but he took care not to express them publicly. He dedicated himself to rebuilding Germany's military potential, a task which demanded 'much silent heroism and self-control and much quiet endurance.'[4] In a memorandum laying

[1] *Ibid.*, Draft of Autobiography of Wilhelm Groener, p. 687.

[2] See below, pp. 129 ff.

[3] *Heeresarchiv*: Seeckt, Karton 13, Stück 124, letter from Major Oskar von Stülpnagel dated 28 June 1919.

[4] General von Seeckt, *Thoughts of a Soldier* (London, 1930), trl. G. Waterhouse, p. 21. Most of Seeckt's political thought was based on the works of the historian Treitschke, who once wrote: 'The army is not always upon active service, but the silent labour of preparation never ceases': *Politics* (London, 1916), trl. B. Dugdale and T. de Bille, vol. 2, pp. 396 f.

down the 'Basic Principles of the New Army,' Seeckt declared that 'four hard years of war' and the 'Tradition of the Army' were 'the best foundation on which to build a new army.'[1] His goal was to re-establish Germany as a major European power, to liberate her from the isolation and forced neutrality imposed by the Versailles treaty. But Seeckt did not think in conventional military terms; he realized that the army alone could not redress Germany's grievances. The most important step for the country to take on the road towards the abrogation of Versailles was the formation of alliances which would help it to achieve its policy objectives. 'The value of a State as an ally,' Seeckt wrote, 'is most succinctly expressed by the number of its battalions and guns, and, in addition, by its geographical position and in the coincidence of economic or political objectives, ambitions, and aversions.'[2] In 1919 Soviet Russia fitted these criteria best for Germany. By the beginning of the following year Seeckt considered a 'political and economic agreement with Russia' as 'an irrevocable purpose of our policy.' But this did not mean flirting with Communism; on the contrary, Seeckt wanted to build Germany into 'a wall against Bolshevism.'[3] It was chiefly Seeckt's influence which made Groener qualify his aversion to co-operation with the Bolsheviks, for by July 1919 he was ready to agree that there were advantages to be gained from 'supporting the present Russian government.'[4]

During the year 1919 Soviet Russia was almost completely isolated from the outside world. Although he was in jail in Berlin at the time, Karl Radek was probably the only leading Bolshevik who really understood conditions in Germany. While Lenin and others in Moscow believed in an imminent German Communist revolution, and continued to do so until the fiasco of the 'March Action' reduced the whole time-table of world revolution to absurdity, Radek grappled with the real issues and could only be pessimistic about the work of the German party. He was imprisoned in Berlin from February until December 1919 on charges of illegal entry into Germany and inciting revolution. In June the

[1] *Heeresarchiv*: Seeckt, Karton 13, Stück 110; the memorandum is dated 1 March 1919.

[2] General von Seeckt, *The Future of the German Empire* (London, 1930), trl. O. Williams, pp. 152, 157.

[3] Rabenau, *Seeckt*, vol. 2, p. 252.

[4] Phelps, 'Aus den Groener-Dokumenten IV,' p. 835.

cabinet decided to drop the charges and to allow Radek to return to Russia, but the negotiations for his return were not completed until January 1920.[1] On the initiative of the Reichswehr Ministry, possibly due to Seeckt himself, Radek was released from solitary confinement at Moabit and allowed to have visitors. His cell, and later on the apartment of Baron Reibnitz where Radek spent his last eight weeks in Berlin, were turned into a sort of political *salon*. Leading German politicians, including Communists, also industrialists and military figures, obtained passes at the Reichswehr Ministry to visit Radek. The diversity of the political interests among those who went to discuss the future of German-Russian relations with Radek gives some indication of the ferment in political thought in Germany at this time.[2] Although the discussions did not have important political consequences in the immediate future, they showed that Germans in many walks of life were thinking more and more about relations with the Soviet Republic and were wrestling with the inhibitions that still prevented them from adopting a positive attitude towards the Bolsheviks.

Radek's first visitor at Moabit was Seeckt's friend Enver Pasha, an exiled Turkish nationalist. On Radek's suggestion, and with Seeckt's help, Enver set out for Moscow in October 1919 to discuss mutual problems with the Soviet leaders and to make contacts for Seeckt.[3] Other early visitors to Radek's *salon* were leading figures of the extreme Right and Communists who expounded doctrines of German-Soviet collaboration later called National Bolshevism; meaning in the case of Baron Reibnitz and Colonel Max Bauer, both of whom were formerly attached to Ludendorff's staff, an

---

[1] See the *Akten betreffend: Karl Radek*, St. A. Nr. 38 *passim*.

[2] A partial list of those who visited Radek at Moabit includes: Talaat Pasha, a former Prime Minister of Turkey; Enver Pasha, a former Minister of War in Turkey; Baron von Reibnitz and Colonel Max Bauer, both war-time associates of Ludendorff; Admiral von Hintze, formerly German Foreign Minister; Walter Rathenau, of the A.E.G. concern, later Foreign Minister; Felix Deutsch, general manager of the A.E.G.; Maximilien Harden, editor of *Die Zukunft*; Hilferding and others of the USPD; Professor Hoetzsch of the German Nationalists; Heilman and others of the SPD; Ruth Fischer, Zetkin, Levi, Lauffenberg, and Wolfheim of the KPD.

[3] See below, p. 79. Köstring, Seeckt's aide, helped Enver to set out for Russia in a new Junkers aeroplane. Cf. Hilger, *Incompatible Allies*, p. 193 n.

alliance of the German Army and Right extremists with the Soviet Republic to fight against the Entente and Versailles and in the case of the Communists Lauffenberg and Wolfheim, seizure of power by the German Communists at the head of the German bourgeoisie, to be followed by an alliance with Soviet Russia and the repudiation of Versailles. Radek rejected the Lauffenberg-Wolfheim thesis in a message to the KPD congress at Heidelberg in October 1919, on the grounds that it was unworkable because the bourgeoisie would undoubtedly prefer a foreign occupation of Germany to a Soviet republic on German soil.[1] Lenin also dealt severely with the deviation of National Bolshevism when he heard about it, condemning the very idea of a Communist 'bloc with the German bourgeoisie for a war against the Entente.'[2]

Late in 1919 Radek wrote a number of articles which reflected the impact the conversations in Moabit had on him. As long as Soviet Russia remained isolated and the KPD hopelessly weak, Radek knew there would be a delay until the final 'disintegration' of the capitalist states. Therefore,

*the problem of the foreign policy of Soviet Russia, and, unless the world revolution announces itself more quickly than hitherto, of all other countries in which the working class is victorious, consists in arriving at a modus vivendi with the capitalist states.*[3]

For a German-Russian *modus vivendi* to be achieved there would first of all have to be a resumption of diplomatic and commercial relations between the powers. Radek suggested this in conversations with German officials and, going one step further, warned that 'Germany should not miss the right moment to go together with Russia.' He said that Russia needed German help 'in the reconstruction of her industry,' and that for the time being this was more important than trade. German engineers and technicians would be welcome in Russia. 'A clarification of political relations between the two countries is also desirable,' Radek said, 'but this does not necessarily have to precede' the resumption of commercial

---

[1] K. Radek, *Die auswärtige Politik des deutschen Kommunismus und der Hamburger National-Bolschewismus*, p. 16, quoted by Kochan, *Russia and Weimar*, p. 20.

[2] See below, p. 53.

[3] K. Radek, *Zur Taktik des Kommunismus: Ein Schreiben an den Oktober-Parteitag der KPD* (Hamburg, 1919), pp. 11 f.

relations.[1] Radek's policy—and it must be remembered that these were largely his own ideas, because he had no direct contact with Moscow during his imprisonment—was the very antithesis of the National Bolshevism of both the Right and Left extremists. It was a practical policy of mutual aid rather than an ideological line, and it complemented the aspirations of Seeckt, also of the industrialists Walter Rathenau and Felix Deutsch, and those of other visitors to Radek's political *salon*. They, too, were interested in a resumption of commercial relations with Russia, although the interest of all the Germans, including the businessmen, in Radek was, from the first, also coloured by their country's military and political predicament.

Following Radek's lead, Rathenau established a Study Commission for Russia which, a few weeks later, sent 'a young man,' one 'Herr Albrecht,' to Russia to investigate opportunities for employing German industry's surplus skilled labour.[2] 'Relations with Russia have occupied me for many months,' Rathenau wrote to a friend in January 1920. He complained that 'the present government [i.e. the Bauer cabinet] does not as yet share my belief that commercial relations with Russia must be started.' Rathenau himself was convinced of 'the necessity of going together with Russia,' and hoped that closer commercial relations would lead to 'ties in the political sphere.'[3] But it was some time before these hopes were realized. The powerful Social Democratic Party preferred any arrangement with France and Britain to co-operation with Soviet Russia. Others in the government and in the bureaucracy held that Germany must 'sail in the waters' churned by the American ship of state. But the *Diktat* of Versailles also caused some influential officials, Socialists among them, to defect from the dominant Western orientation and look to the East for help in re-establishing Germany as a world power. An official of the Foreign Ministry at this time, Wipert von Blücher, recalls that until

---

[1] *Akten betreffend: Karl Radek*, St. A. Nr. 38, notes dated 10 January 1920 of a conversation between Legation Secretary Hey, R. [?] Deutsch (A.E.G.), bank director Simon (Independent Socialist) with Radek and Kopp; and *ibid.*, notes dated 20 January 1920 of a conversation between Hey and Radek on board the train taking Radek to the German-Polish border.

[2] *Documents on British Foreign Policy* (London, 1949), ed. E. L. Woodward and R. Butler, First Series, vol. 3, p. 511.

[3] W. Rathenau, *Briefe* (Dresden, 1926), vol. 2, pp. 220, 229-230, 233.

Versailles the majority of his colleagues were 'more sympathetic to the West than to the East.' But the treaty made it appear 'that the West was much the more dangerous foe,' and 'consequently we turned away from the West and that naturally led us closer to the East, despite our disdain of Bolshevism and Bolsheviks.'[1] In other government circles, too, the 'Easterners' steadily gained adherents to their point of view from the autumn of 1919 onwards, until their influence very nearly equalled that of the 'Westerners.' There were few chronic supporters of either orientation, but a number of these, Baron Ago von Maltzan for example, held important positions. Radek's appeal for industrial and technical help in January 1920 provoked Maltzan, who was head of the Russian desk, to advise his superiors in the Foreign Ministry that, since 'Bolshevism will be a factor with which we have to contend for at least 3 to 4 years,' the very least the government should do was to stop making difficulties for private commercial venturers in Soviet Russia.[2] Maltzan would have liked the government to take more positive action towards bettering relations with Russia, but it was too early for that. Until diplomatic relations with Russia were resumed, the efforts of the 'Easterners' were trifling compared to the weight of appeals, petitions, and entreaties addressed by the hopeful to the unyielding and revengeful Western governments.

Germany's refusal in October 1919 to join in the Allied blockade against Russia represented her first independent act in foreign affairs after Versailles, and exemplified the attitude of benevolent neutralism spreading amongst the German bourgeoisie towards the Bolsheviks, which was to reach a climax during the Russo-Polish war in the following year. The Germans did not reply to the Allied bid 'with a firm refusal,' as Chicherin had demanded.[3] Rather they based their stand on the continuing Allied blockade of 'German coasts and German ships' and on the Covenant of the League of Nations, according to which, the German note stated, 'circumstances at the present time do not justify a blockade' against Russia.[4] The Reichstag debate regarding the blockade indicates that politicians of the Left, Right, and Centre were considering the possi-

[1] *Deutschlands Weg nach Rapallo* (Wiesbaden, 1951), p. 50.
[2] *Akten betreffend: Karl Radek*, St. A. Nr. 38, Maltzan's marginal comments on Hey's notes dated 10 January 1920 (see above, p. 49 n. 1).
[3] Degras, *Soviet Documents*, vol. 1, pp. 170 f.
[4] *The New York Times*, 30 October 1919.

bility of establishing friendlier relations with Russia, and that many of them disapproved of German participation in the blockade for this reason. Opening the debate, Hermann Müller of the SPD argued 'that Bolshevism will only be encouraged if it is fought by the methods that the Allies now want to apply.' Otto Wels added that a blockade was not conducive to the creation of a world family of nations. Right-wing deputies attacked the blockade in unambiguous terms: Schultz of the German Nationalists said Germany must be unprejudiced towards Russia; Haussmann of the German Democratic Party said participation in the blockade was incompatible with a sympathetic 'wait-and-see' attitude towards the Bolsheviks, which he advocated; and Heinze of the German People's Party, although unenthusiastic about Russia, said his party was also against the blockade. It was left to a Centre Party deputy, Pfeiffer, who did not once mention the blockade in his speech, to take the strongest stand on the real issue of the debate: 'Our path lies Eastward . . . the door to the Western world is bolted against us. To me that seems to impose on us the duty of knocking at the Eastern gate.'[1]

The first knock on the Eastern gate was a barely audible one, but it led directly to the resumption of German-Russian diplomatic relations. In the autumn of 1919 the German Government asked the Soviet Government to exchange representatives in order to arrange for the return of the remaining civilian and military prisoners in the two countries. The Russians complied by sending Victor Kopp to Berlin in November.[2] Although Kopp did not gain official recognition as Soviet plenipotentiary for prisoner of war matters until February 1920, he was regarded as an official spokesman of the Soviet Government from the moment he arrived in Berlin. On 19 April 1920 Kopp signed the first of two agreements in Berlin which established prisoner relief agencies by both governments on the territory of the other, granting the plenipotentiaries personal immunity, the right to maintain courier communications and to use code, and the right to exercise consular functions. Two months after the first agreement was signed, Gustav

---

[1] Kochan, *Russia and Weimar*, pp. 23 f.

[2] *Akten betreffend: Karl Radek*, St. A. Nr. 38, notes of a discussion with Kopp on 22 November 1919 signed 'Müller.' Hilger misdates Kopp's arrival 'in the spring' of 1920 (*Incompatible Allies*, p. 25), and Kochan also gives the wrong date (*op. cit.*, p. 41).

Hilger left Berlin to act as Kopp's opposite number in Moscow.[1]
Credit for taking the initiative in this exchange of diplomatic
personnel, whose powers outstripped those normally accorded
mere plenipotentiaries, belongs to two junior officials, Moritz
Schlesinger and another Social Democrat, Stücklen. These two
used their positions at the head of the Reich Central Office for
Military and Civilian Prisoners 'to regain contact with Moscow,'
for which, according to Hilger, 'the exchange of prisoners of war
furnished a welcome pretext.'[2] In working for a *rapprochement* with
Soviet Russia, Schlesinger and Stücklen evidently received cautious
support from the Foreign Minister, Walter Simons. In conferences
with Hilger, before he went to Moscow, Simons made it perfectly
clear that his chief mission was 'to contribute toward the normalization of general political and economic relations between Germany
and Soviet Russia.'[3] But when Hilger arrived in Moscow during
the summer of 1920 he found it difficult to carry out his instructions. The rapid advance of the Red Army against the Poles at this
time raised to their zenith the prospects of extending the revolution.
Despite the galaxy of hostile forces pitted against them, the Soviet
leaders did not succumb to despair nor to a realistic analysis of the
chances of world revolution. They were in the grips of a revivalist
fervour and faith. Of course, the very fact that no capitalist nation
made a bid to the Soviet Government for more normal relations
undoubtedly contributed to their one-sided and vehement espousal
of the revolutionary cause, for there was nothing to be lost by this
on the diplomatic front. But the Bolsheviks were self-confident as
well as self-righteous: Lenin had said in March 1919 that 'the
victory of the proletarian revolution over the entire world is
assured.' In July he predicted that final victory would come within
a year, while Zinoviev—more popish than the Pope—exclaimed
that within a year Europe would have forgotten that there had been
a struggle for Communism![4]

Looked at from Moscow, a policy of sustained revolutionary
fervour was a means of splitting the hostile foreign powers ranged
against the Soviet Republic, and the optimism about the success of
the revolution a necessary expression of hope amidst a sea of

[1] Hilger, *loc. cit.*; *Reichs-Gesetzblatt*, Nr. 130, 16 June 1920.
[2] Hilger, *op. cit.*, pp. 24 f.
[3] *Ibid.*, p. 49.
[4] Flechtheim, *Die KPD*, pp. 57 f.

troubles. But the policy was also based on profound miscalculations regarding the strength and intentions of the German Communists. There is evidence of this discrepancy in the Soviet reaction to the disclosure of the peace terms at Versailles. Zinoviev issued a proclamation on behalf of Comintern, which stated that 'the proletarian revolution is the only salvation for the oppressed classes of the whole world'; in other words, only a revolution in Germany could destroy Versailles, thus:

> Down with Versailles, down with the new Brest!
> Down with the government of the social traitors!
> Long live the power of the Soviets in the whole world![1]

But there were no Soviets in Germany. After January 1919 the KPD was suppressed and forced to go underground. Moreover, the German Communists had a different outlook on the Versailles treaty than their brethren in Soviet Russia had. The treaty would impose burdens on them as on the rest of the German population, while the revolution promised salvation only in the very distant future. The KPD's 'Theses on Peace' argued that, since the 'military state' had been revived in Germany, 'acceptance or rejection of the peace terms under a bankrupt imperialism would be equally disastrous.' But in a subsequent proclamation the party asserted that accepting the treaty would provide 'a breathing-space for the German counter-revolution,' while rejection would precipitate the German bourgeoisie 'into its last crisis, in which it will finally perish.'[2] The implication of this policy was that, when the Communists had seized power, Soviet Russia would come to Germany's aid against the Versailles powers. However, Lenin considered these notions of 'Left-wing' Communism a confusion about the real ends of Bolshevik policy:

> If Russia [Lenin wrote], by herself, could endure the Brest-Litovsk Peace for several months to the advantage of the revolution, there is nothing impossible in a Soviet Germany, allied with Soviet Russia, enduring the existence of the Versailles Peace for an even longer period to the advantage of the revolution.[3]

[1] *Kommunisticheskii Internatsional*, No. 2 (June 1919), cols. 149-150, quoted by Carr, vol. 3, p. 130. Chicherin's denunciation of Versailles is quoted by Dennis, *Foreign Policies of Soviet Russia*, p. 192.

[2] Flechtheim, *op. cit.*, pp. 55, 56.

[3] Lenin, *'Left-Wing' Communism*, pp. 58 f.

Lenin thereby supported the views of Levi and the KPD majority at Heidelberg against Lauffenberg and Wolfheim and the minority which wanted the Communists to abstain from parliamentary elections and refrain from participation in trade unions, but he opposed Levi's ultimatum which had the effect of expelling from the party those who voted against participation in elections and trade unions. Lenin's declaration, that 'from the international point of view the re-establishment of the unity of the German Communist Party is both possible and essential,' arrived too late to influence the delegates at Heidelberg, and Radek's plea to Levi from prison, begging him to make the issue one of persuasion instead of discipline, was ineffective. The Heidelberg schism resulted in the formation of a new German Communist Workers' Party (KAPD), which took away nearly half the KPD's membership of 50,000, including most of the members in North Germany and in Berlin.[1]

Lenin had supported Levi on the issues at Heidelberg, not on his tactics. It was only later that Lenin realized that Levi's KPD faction had supported the right policy—right from Moscow's point of view—for the wrong reasons. The cautious tone of the 'Theses on Communist Principles and Tactics,' which was drafted by Levi and adopted by the congress, shows that the KPD opposed Moscow's conception of a mass party bent on immediate revolutionary action. The party was, in fact, reverting to Luxemburg's principles, to the idea of a small Communist Party penetrating and indoctrinating the politically immature—and politically unwilling—masses. 'The revolution,' Levi wrote, 'consists not of a single blow but of the long stubborn struggle of a class downtrodden for thousands of years.' He rebuked those who, like the Bolshevik leaders, did not understand that the revolution was a long 'process of rise and fall, of flow and ebb':

> The notion that mass movements can be created on the strength of a particular form of organization, that the revolution is therefore a question of organizational form, is rejected as a lapse into petty-bourgeois utopianism.[2]

These ideas were not based on rigid, deviationist dogma; Levi was facing facts—and not merely the failure of the Munich Soviet

---

[1] Carr, vol. 3, p. 138. Cf. R. Fischer, *Stalin and German Communism*, pp. 118 f.

[2] *Bericht über den 2. Parteitag der Kommunistischen Partei Deutschlands (Spartakusbund)* (Berlin, 1919), p. 61.

and the split in the Communist ranks at Heidelberg. These were significant factors, but only symptoms of the fundamental weakness of the party and the dilemma in which it found itself. The KPD had to face the fact that the Social Democrats in league with the army and the Free Corps were restoring order in Germany. The masses simply could not be rallied to a revolutionary standard; they were supporting the Weimar regime which was bringing about national stability and effecting revisionist policies.

When Radek finally returned to Moscow at the end of January 1920, he must have informed the Soviet leaders of the real scope and development of the German revolutionary movement, above all, that it lacked mass support. But Radek's first-hand information did not change Lenin's outlook; at a moment when the civil war was moving towards a victorious end, 'Lenin would abate nothing of his confidence in the coming of a German and European revolution.' He maintained that Germany's 'politically conscious proletariat' would support the Communist Party, and rebuked Radek for drawing the conclusion that the revolution in Europe was bound to be 'a prolonged process.'[1] At the beginning of February, Comintern invited representatives of the KAPD, the KPD, and of the Independent Socialists (USPD) to Moscow for discussions, in the hope of reconciling these elements of the German revolutionary movement, augmenting their numbers, and welding them into an organized mass unit. The USPD, a growing mass party at the time, was the vital factor in Comintern's calculations. If the USPD could be weaned away from social-democratic revisionism and cajoled into obeisance to the revolutionary alphabet—the Twenty-One Conditions—a mass party promoting Communist revolution would exist in Germany for the first time. 'These proceedings were not at all to the taste of the KPD. Comintern had chosen to negotiate with the USPD, which did not even profess to be a Communist party, and with the KAPD, without regard to what claimed to be the one orthodox German Communist Party.'[2] A unification of these elements would produce precisely the kind of conglomeration the KPD had rejected at Heidelberg. Comintern's interference seemed to bear out Luxemburg's fears of Bolshevik control over the Third International. The morale of the KPD plunged to a new low. A bleak pessimism pervaded the halls of the Third Congress

[1] Carr, vol. 3, pp. 140, 171.
[2] Ibid., p. 170.

at Karlsruhe in February 1920. Heinrich Brandler, leader of the Chemnitz party, which, according to Ruth Fischer, formed 'the strongest organization of the Communist Party' at that time, frankly admitted:

we still have no party. . . . What exists is worse than if we had nothing, so it will not be possible in the near future to put the Communist Party on its feet.[1]

While the Communists were bemoaning the weakness of their party, counter-revolutionary forces on the extreme Right conspired to overthrow the Weimar Republic. Unknown to the KPD, the 'military state' which they imagined to exist was soon to become a reality.

The Kapp *putsch* was engineered by officers of the most powerful Free Corps and by elements of the *Nationale Vereinigung* (National Union), a political club whose avowed purpose it was to overthrow the Republic. The underlying cause of the *putsch* was the violent reaction in nationalist-militarist circles to the signing of the Versailles terms. The immediate cause was the government's attempt to demobilize the Erhardt Free Corps Brigade in accordance with the provisions of the treaty. Although 'the Kapp *putsch* was a triumph of ineptitude, infirmity of purpose, and lack of preparedness,' it had a profound effect on the KPD and was a landmark in the development of the Weimar Republic and its relations with Soviet Russia.[2]

The story of the *putsch* is well known and does not have to be repeated in detail. As the Erhardt Brigade approached Berlin in the early hours of 13 March, Minister of Defence Noske called a hurried conference of military leaders to ask if the 'Republican Army' would defend the government against the counter-revolutionary forces. General Reinhardt, chief of the *Heeresleitung*, and one other officer replied in the affirmative; the majority present supported the unequivocal 'no' answer of the chief of the *Truppenamt*, General von Seeckt: 'Troops do not fire on troops. Do you, Herr Minister, perhaps intend to force a battle before the Brandenburger Tor between troops who a year and a half ago were fighting

---

[1] *Bericht über den 3. Parteitag der Kommunistischen Partei Deutschlands (Spartakusbund)* (Berlin, 1920), p. 14; R. Fischer, *op. cit.*, p. 128.

[2] A complete account of the Kapp *putsch* appears in Wheeler-Bennett, *Nemesis of Power*, pp. 63 ff. Waite adds many interesting details, *Vanguard of Nazism*, chapters 6 and 7 *passim*.

shoulder to shoulder against the enemy?'[1] Abandoned by the army, President Ebert, Chancellor Bauer and his cabinet fled to Stuttgart. Having lost the support of the officers, General Reinhardt resigned. Seeckt retired to his suburban home. Berlin fell without a shot being fired.

Although Seeckt was unwilling to commit the army to the constitutional government, because that would have involved it in internecine strife with rebellious old comrades in arms, he had already warned Kapp that he would not support him either. Kapp tried to 'command' Seeckt to give the army's support to the counter-revolutionary government. But Seeckt, who realized that the army could make or break the *putsch*, coldly declined to obey.[2] He was determined to keep the army—which he called 'the purest and most striking image of the State'—inviolate no matter who governed Germany.[3] Seeckt realized that the *putsch* was bound to fail without his support and prepared himself to 'descend with force and dignity on the side of the winner.'[4] He had good reasons to prefer the republican government to the gang of generals and thugs who made up the short-lived Kapp regime. Foremost of these was his plan for an alliance with Soviet Russia. The National Union and Kapp's other associates were not only anti-Communist —Seeckt was that himself—but also anti-Russian. This, we know, Seeckt was most certainly not. Since a 'political and economic agreement' with Soviet Russia was the 'irrevocable purpose' of Seeckt's policy, a German government composed of anti-Russian Rightists was bound to interfere with his plans.

In Stuttgart, Ebert and the Social Democratic government called a general strike against the Kapp usurpers. The silent hostility of the trade unions paralysed the wheels of government in Berlin and cut off all communications with the rest of the country. Clutching at straws, Kapp turned to the anti-republican conservative parties for support. The National People's Party and Stresemann's German People's Party were not unsympathetic to the counter-revolution when it started. 'For us,' Stresemann told a

---

[1] Rabenau, *Seeckt*, vol. 2, p. 222. Of course Seeckt's Reichswehr could and did fire on the 'Red Army of the Ruhr,' which included many former soldiers; see below, pp. 60-61. Cf. Craig, *Politics of the Prussian Army*, p. 379, n. 2.

[2] Waite, *op. cit.*, p. 161.

[3] Seeckt, *Thoughts of a Soldier*, p. 79.

[4] Wheeler-Bennett, *op. cit.*, p. 76.

caucus of the DVP, 'a split [in the party] would be worse than a civil war. Therefore we must choose a course which, on the one hand, does not make things difficult for the new government, but which leaves the way open for us to mediate between Dresden [*sic*] and Berlin.'[1] The issue of conservative support for the *putsch* hung fire for three days, until 16 March. Then, when it was obvious that the general strike had sapped what little strength the Kappists had been able to muster, those who had flirted with the counter-revolution turned on it and denounced it. On 16 March the National Association of German Industries attacked the Kapp government. The next day Kapp fled to Sweden, and his closest associate, Lüttwitz, to Hungary. The *putsch* was over. Ebert and the Bauer cabinet returned to Berlin. On 18 March Stresemann, who had not supported Kapp but had not come out against him either, released a strong statement condemning the defunct counter-revolution.[2]

When he returned to Berlin Ebert rewarded Seeckt for withholding support from Kapp by appointing him acting chief of the *Heeresleitung*, replacing General Reinhardt—the one general who had been willing to defend the government. The Officer Corps learned from this experience that, 'to achieve their aim of reestablishing Germany as a strong military power, they had to work *through* not *against* the Republic.' For the next six years 'the army achieved its greatest political ascendancy and its maximum of real power' by supporting the legitimate authority in Germany.[3] And as the army became the strongest single power within the Weimar Republic, Seeckt, as its chief, became the strong man behind the scenes of German politics. On a number of occasions he was to exercise decisive power in internal affairs, but he did not manage to gain outright control of German Foreign Policy. Therefore Germany did not adopt the exclusive Eastern orientation that Seeckt advocated. Nevertheless, 'for the next four years German policy

---

[1] *Stresemann Nachlass*, Serial 7011H. This file contains interesting new material on the Kapp *putsch*. Cf. H. W. Gatzke, *Stresemann and the Rearmament of Germany* (Baltimore, 1954), pp. 7, 8, 14, 51; cf. H. Prinz zu Löwenstein, *Stresemann* (Frankfurt/Main, 1952), pp. 147 f.

[2] Cf. Carr, vol. 3, p. 174, who over-simplifies the position of Stresemann and of 'heavy industry' towards the Kappists. Cf. Kochan, *Russia and Weimar*, p. 27, who misinterprets the significance of the *putsch* and Seeckt's attitude towards Kapp and the 'organized workers.'

[3] Wheeler-Bennett, *op. cit.*, p. 82.

towards Soviet Russia was the policy of Seeckt.'[1]

The general strike called by the Social Democratic members of the government against Kapp proved to be a double-edged weapon. The KPD was slow to recognize the possibility of using the strike for its own ends. But Communists in Western Germany, particularly in the Ruhr, unmindful of the general weakness of the party throughout the land, precipitated violent action against 'the military camarilla' and tried to seize power. On 13 March, while the KPD leadership in Berlin contented itself with distributing leaflets announcing that 'the proletariat will not raise a finger for the democratic republic,' the Communists in the Ruhr—on the same day—distributed posters urging the workers to revolt:[2]

## WORKERS! COMRADES!

The Ebert-Noske regime has fallen. The bourgeoisie on whom this government depended, have thrown their tools to the devil. The military camarilla that forced us into the war and then lost it so shamefully has come into power.

Workers! Comrades! Now is the time to act. Now is the time to seize power. . . . We do not fight for the Ebert-Noske Government. Down with the betrayers of Socialism! Down with the tools of the bourgeoisie! On to the Dictatorship of the Proletariat!

Workers! Comrades! To arms!

Communist Party of Germany.[3]

Two days later, on 15 March, the KPD leadership in Berlin went so far as to announce itself 'For the General Strike!' and added, 'Down with the Military Dictatorship!', but refrained from echoing the Ruhr workers' call to arms. In the Ruhr the government had incautiously opened its arsenals not only to the loyal Social Democratic trade unions, but to the Communists as well. On the night of 14 March the 'Red Army of the Ruhr,' composed of an indeterminate number of Social Democratic, Catholic, and Communist workers at this time, attacked Free Corps formations, and by 20 March succeeded in dominating the entire area east of Düsseldorf and Mülheim. For these workers anti-militarism was

[1] Carr, vol. 3, p. 318.
[2] Flechtheim, *Die KPD*, p. 62.
[3] *Zur Geschichte der Kommunistischen Partei Deutschlands* ([East] Berlin, 1955), p. 85.

not merely a slogan; it was a deep-seated hatred that united them in the 'Red Army of the Ruhr' against the Free Corps. But the Communists in their ranks were not to be satisfied with a rout of the Free Corps. They set a more ambitious goal for the victorious workers' army:

> There can be only one salvation for the German people. The red flag must wave victoriously over the whole of Germany. Germany must become a Republic of Soviets and, in unison with Russia, the springboard for the forthcoming victory of the world revolution and world socialism.[1]

The KPD leadership in Berlin not only failed to keep pace with the workers' revolutionary activity in the Ruhr, but on 21 March took a stand against it. In a proclamation the KPD leaders announced that in the event the trade unions under Carl Legien established a workers' government, their attitude would be one of 'loyal opposition.' Legien's project failed, but for weeks afterwards the Communists were engaged in acrimonious debate about the orthodoxy of a policy of conciliation with the SPD and USPD which was implied by the 'loyal opposition' statement.[2] Meanwhile the fate of the 'Red Army of the Ruhr,' now 50,000 strong, was being decided by less academically-minded and more ruthless people in Berlin. On 16 March Noske informed the army command that the government had neither called the general strike nor approved of it, and urged that immediate action be taken against the Communists in the Ruhr.[3] A truce was negotiated between the government and the leaders of the workers' 'army,' but this only gave each side time to strengthen its forces and led to a still greater loss of life in the final battle. By 3 April Seeckt had convinced Ebert and Herman Müller, leader of the new coalition government, that the army should be given a free hand to deal with the

[1] Quoted by Waite, *Vanguard of Nazism*, p. 177. Cf. R. Fischer, *Stalin and German Communism*, pp. 126 ff.; cf. Carr, *Studies in Revolution*, p. 186. Also see the 'Operationsplan der Roten Ruhrarmee' in *Zur Geschichte der KPD*, p. 89.

[2] Flechtheim, *Die KPD*, p. 64; Carr, vol. 3, p. 173; R. Fischer, *op. cit.*, pp. 125 ff.

[3] Noske was distorting the facts. Strictly speaking, Noske, Ebert, and Bauer called the general strike as leaders of the SPD—not as the government. Theirs was nevertheless the first strike order. See Waite, *op. cit.*, pp. 174-176 n. and *The Times*, 15 March 1920. Cf. R. Fischer, *op. cit.*, p. 123, and Carr, vol. 3, p. 172. Both authors accept the version that Carl Legien called the strike. Noske himself prudently left out the entire episode in *Von Kiel bis Kapp* (Berlin, 1920).

rebellious workers. 'Help us to protect our people from a horrible tragedy,' Ebert implored the Erhardt Brigade—the very force that had effected the Kapp *putsch* and which Seeckt now unleashed against the workers.[1] 'The Free Corps saved the Republic,' is the fallacious epitome applied by one post-Nazi historian to these sordid events.[2]

While the slaughter in the Ruhr was going on, one of the KPD leaders, Wilhelm Pieck, speaking in the Prussian Diet, disclaimed all responsibility for the 'Red Army of the Ruhr,' characterizing it as the 'petty bourgeois gone wild.'[3] Thus, the aftermath to the counter-revolution was marked by the emergence of Seeckt and the eclipse of the KPD.

[1] F. Ebert, *Schriften, Aufzeichnungen, Reden* (Dresden, 1926), vol. 2, p. 196.
[2] Görlitz, *Der Deutsche Generalstab*, p. 303.
[3] R. Fischer, *op. cit.*, p. 133.

# CHAPTER III

## GERMANY AND RUSSIA AGAINST VERSAILLES

ON Lenin's calendar of revolution the Kapp *putsch* was marked down as the 'German Kornilov-Affair.' Addressing the Ninth Party Congress in Moscow at the end of March 1920, at about the same time as Seeckt was ordering the Free Corps to march against the workers' army in the Ruhr, Lenin hailed the counter-revolution as an important milestone on the road to a successful German Communist revolution:

> The German Kornilov-Affair has played the same role in Germany as in Russia. After the Kornilov-Affair began the swing-over to prole-tarian power not only amongst the masses of the town workers but also amongst the agricultural proletariat of Germany, and this swing-over has a world historical significance. It gives us not only again and again the absolute conviction of the correctness of our path; it gives us the certainty that the time is not far off when we shall march hand in hand with a German Soviet Government.[1]

According to the Bolsheviks' time-table the revolution in Germany had reached August 1917; they awaited 'October' with eager anticipation. The German workers seemed to be 'becoming more and more inflamed' and were 'forming red armies.' All the Soviet leaders joined in acclaiming the 'proletarian uprising' in the Ruhr, although some, like Radek, ridiculed the 'loyal opposition' formula of the KPD leadership as 'a castration of Communism.' However, Lenin was conciliatory. His judgment was that these 'tactics were beyond doubt fundamentally correct,' for it was necessary to spread and strengthen the revolutionary movement, even if that meant co-operating temporarily with revisionist elements.[2] Until March 1921 Comintern's relations with the

---

[1] *Devyati Syezd R.K.P. (b) (9th Congress of the Russian Communist Party (b))*, ed. Meshcheryakov (Moscow, 1934), p. 5, quoted by Kochan, *Russia and Weimar*, p. 26. Kochan's remark that 'the Putsch marked the last attempt, until 1933, by the anti-Russian German Right to seize power' (*ibid.*, p. 27) fails to consider the Hitler-Ludendorff and Küstrin *putsches* which were also attempts by the anti-Russian German Right to seize power.

[2] Carr, vol. 3, p. 175 n.

German party continued to be based on the belief that there was
sufficient mass support for the overthrow of the bourgeois government, and that the masses would assert themselves as soon as the
proletarian forces were properly organized. Zinoviev travelled to
Germany in the autumn of 1920 for the purpose of expediting the
reorganization of the extreme Left-wing factions into a single mass
party. At the USPD congress at Halle in October he tried to
persuade the delegates to link their party to Comintern and to help
create a united German Communist party. The USPD was split
over these issues. Its Right wing leaned towards the revisionist
policies of the SPD, the Left wing believed in the dictatorship of
the proletariat and wanted to follow Zinoviev. Because of this split
in the ranks the USPD could not wield much political power nor
frame a truly independent policy, despite the large vote it amassed
in the Reichstag election of June 1920.[1] Zinoviev and Hilferding
were the chief protagonists in the long and acrimonious debate
between the factions at Halle. The argument centred on Lenin's
Twenty-One Conditions, which one revisionist assailed as con-
stituting 'Moscow dictatorship,' but the basic issue for most of the
delegates was the prospect of world revolution in the near future.[2]
All the workers wanted to keep in step with the revolution, but
they had different opinions about how and when it would come
about. Zinoviev ridiculed the revisionists for believing that the
world was 'in a situation similar to that after the 1848 revolution'
and accused them of being afraid of the revolution. Disposing of
the Rightists—he called them 'the last of the Mohicans'—Zinoviev
went on to paint a rosy picture of the chances of world revolution
in the immediate future.[3] 'The delegates,' says Ruth Fischer, 'fell
under Zinoviev's spell.'[4] Zinoviev was indeed an eloquent preacher,
and his gibes and taunts were merciless. But his speech was not
decisive, it was only the climax to a series of events which drove a
majority of the USPD to vote for joining Comintern and for

---

[1] In June 1920 the USPD polled 4,900,000 votes for 81 seats, the SPD
5,600,000 for 113 seats, and the KPD 446,000 for 2 seats in the Reichstag. See the
table in Scheele, *The Weimar Republic*, p. 149, and Flechtheim, *Die KPD*, pp.
69 f. Cf. R. Fischer, *Stalin and German Communism*, p. 147, who gives the wrong
figures.

[2] Carr, vol. 3, p. 218.

[3] Zinoviev, *All Power to the Workers* (Petrograd, n.d.).

[4] R. Fischer, *op. cit.*, p. 145.

negotiating with the KPD and KAPD.[1]

Two months after the Halle congress, in December 1920, 349 USPD and 136 KPD delegates met in the founding congress of the United German Communist Party (VKPD). This was the first mass Communist party in Germany, with a membership of approximately 350,000, of whom 300,000 stemmed from the USPD. The KAPD remained dissident and entombed in its own brand of orthodoxy, despite Comintern's ultimatum to join the new organization.[2]

The VKPD was expected to discard the Spartacist tactics of a revolutionary *élite* educating the workers for political action in the distant future. Its job was to lead the workers to a position of primary importance on the immediate political scene. All the leading figures of the VKPD were agreed on this, but there were disagreements about what new policies were to be introduced. Ruth Fischer and others on the Left wing of the new party wanted to pursue an active revolutionary policy in the tradition of Liebknecht and in the wake of Zinoviev's exhortations at Halle. The leaders of the Right wing, chiefly Levi, Zetkin, and Däumig, were more realistic, and, therefore, sceptical of what an active policy could accomplish. They agreed that Luxemburg's tactics of political abstentionism would have to be shelved, because a mass movement could not be limited to practices designed for a small sect. But they were also against provoking revolutionary action, because they doubted that the German masses would follow the VKPD. In January 1921 Levi, who led the party from the congress in December 1920 until February 1921, introduced a compromise policy. This 'united front' policy, heralded by the famous 'open letter' in the *Rote Fahne* of 8 January, was supposed to involve the Communists with the trade unions and the political parties of the Left, including the SPD and remnants of the USPD and KAPD, in a joint struggle to free the German workers from their 'intolerable position' as a result of the economic crisis. The VKPD asserted that it was not renouncing 'for one moment the struggle for the proletarian dictatorship,' but it was willing to work for the welfare of all the German workers in concert with the bourgeois Left. The

[1] The majority in the vote at Halle was 236 to 156. For the history of the minority group of the USPD see Flechtheim, *Die KPD*, p. 71. Cf. R. Fischer, *op. cit.*, p. 146.

[2] Carr, vol. 3, p. 223.

'united front' policy, like the 'loyal opposition' formula following
the Kapp *putsch*, was not put into effect. All the important political
organizations to whom it was extended emphatically rejected the
offer of co-operation with the Communists.[1]

Levi's 'open letter' caused a stir in Moscow. Zinoviev and
Bukharin denounced the 'united front' policy; they would not countenance a German Communist programme based upon a sceptical
evaluation of the prospects of revolution in Western Europe.
Radek, on the other hand, was enthusiastic about the new line. In
fact, there is some reason to believe he had a hand in drafting the
'open letter.' The new tactics were in complete accord with the
policy Radek had been advocating ever since his imprisonment in
Berlin. In his view it was necessary to recognize that there was no
immediate chance for revolution. Radek was not as pessimistic as
Levi, for he believed that the prospects might become better in the
near future. 'Everything,' he wrote, 'depends on the world political
situation.' In January and February 1921 Radek saw no real possibilities for extending the revolution and therefore opposed
Zinoviev's schemes of precipitate action, although he also advised
Levi that, because the situation may change rapidly, 'you must do
everything to mobilize the party.'[2] Lenin intervened at the Third
Congress of Comintern to support Radek and Levi's policy
against Zinoviev and Bukharin. He endorsed the 'open letter' as a
'model political move' in the new tactics of seeking a temporary
accommodation with the capitalist world, which the Soviet
Republic itself was just then starting to put into practice.

Undoubtedly Zinoviev was pleased that Levi's 'model political
move' was rebuffed by the bourgeois Left in Germany. A few
weeks later Levi resigned from the leadership of the VKPD, which
was then taken over by Brandler, Thalheimer, Fröhlich, Ruth
Fischer, and others of the Left-wing faction that opposed the
'united front' policy. According to the 'theory of the offensive' of
the new leaders, the time for revolutionary action was at hand. To
spur them on Zinoviev sent Bela Kun and two other emissaries to

[1] Accounts of the VKPD's activities until March 1921 are in *ibid.*, pp. 332 ff.,
and Flechtheim, *op. cit.*, pp. 71 ff. Cf. R. Fischer, *op. cit.*, chap. 2, *passim*.

[2] See Radek's letter to Levi in *Unser Weg*, vol. 3, Nos. 8–9, August–September
1921, pp. 248 f., and Carr, vol. 3, pp. 333 ff. Cf. Flechtheim, *op. cit.*, pp. 71 ff.
Radek was notoriously volatile; it is a mistake to ascribe logical patterns of
thought and consistent opinions to him. Only reliable quotations tell us what his
opinion was at any one time.

the VKPD central committee meeting at the beginning of March.
The emissaries arrived at about the time the Kronstadt revolt began
and apparently used the rising as an additional argument to
galvanize the German Communists into immediate action.[1] Plans
were laid to 'force the revolution ahead' soon after Easter. At this
time the critical political situation in Germany was complicated by
unrest in the industrial region in the centre of the country around
Mansfeld, Merseburg, and Halle, which was a Communist stronghold. On 16 March police and army detachments were sent to
disarm the striking coal workers in Mansfeld, a provocation to
violence wherever government forces encountered armed workers.
The leaders of the VKPD thought this an ideal opportunity to put
their 'theory of the offensive' into practice, believing that 'two to
three million non-Communist workers' would fight on their side.[2]
On 17 March Brandler called the workers to arms and proclaimed
an insurrection against the government. It was a bold challenge,
but the results were uninspiring. There were sporadic clashes
between bands of workers and government detachments near
Halle and elsewhere in the country; bombs were set off in Breslau
and Halle, but civil strife did not reach revolutionary proportions.
The Communists were dissatisfied but not dismayed. Their next
move was to call a general strike. This was the greatest folly. The
strike back-fired and spelled disaster for the VKPD. No more than
300,000 workers supported the strike and they had to fight not only
the police but also the mass of the workers who preferred to stick
to their jobs.[3] What was to have been an April revolution turned
into a disastrous 'March Action.' Within a period of little more
than two months Levi's 'united action' policy was rebuffed by the
bourgeois Left and the VKPD's Left-wing 'theory of the offensive'
had plunged the party into violent conflict with the mass of the
workers.

The March fiasco had immediate repercussions in the German
Communist movement and also in Moscow. The VKPD membership dropped to 180,000, about half its previous size, and a storm

[1] Whether or not Lenin, Trotsky and other principal Russian leaders were
informed of the instructions Zinoviev gave Bela Kun, the Politbureau is partly
responsible for the March débâcle in any event, either for failing to curb
Zinoviev's activities or for endorsing them. Cf. Carr, vol. 3, pp. 335, 338; cf.
R. Fischer, op. cit., p. 175; cf. Flechtheim, op. cit., pp. 73 f.

[2] Flechtheim, op. cit., pp. 73 f.

[3] Ibid.

of recrimination served to intensify and prolong the split within the party. In Moscow the German disaster was taken as a clear sign that the masses were unwilling to support revolutionary action. The calendar of revolution lost its oracular magic and was discarded at last. The effect on Soviet Russia's policy was to enforce 'a new and well-grounded pessimism about the prospects of European revolution,' for where a relatively large party had failed no Communist party in any other country could hope to succeed for some time to come.[1] The Russian drive towards a temporary accommodation with the capitalist world, which had started some time before these events in the late winter of 1921, was therefore reinforced. It was early in 1920, when the external policy of the Soviet Government was still characterized by revolutionary exhortations, that Lenin first realized it was essential for Russia to break out of the isolation to which European disapproval had condemned her. He took the first hesitant steps towards engaging friendlier relations with the capitalist powers in the economic sphere, recognizing that trade relations were mutually profitable and hence most likely to succeed. In February 1920 Lenin sounded an optimistic note about the new policy:

We have already opened a window on Europe which we shall try to utilize as extensively as possible.[2]

But before what was later called the NEP policy could really get under way, Russia was involved in yet another war, this time with Poland. As early as 22 January 1920 Trotsky informed the Politbureau of his apprehension 'that Pilsudski was preparing for war.' On the same day Radek wrote to the leaders of the Polish Socialist Party pleading with them to oppose Pilsudski's aggressive aims.[3] Sporadic forays between Polish and Russian troops across the frontier had been going on for some time. Russia made several efforts to avoid a full-scale conflict by suggesting negotiations and

[1] Carr, vol. 3, pp. 337 f.

[2] Lenin, *Sochineniya*, vol. 25, p. 27, quoted by Carr, vol. 3, p. 157. In calling Tallinn, the Estonian capital, the 'window' through which Russian trade with Europe might pass, Lenin imitated Peter the Great, who 'always came back to the traditional aim of his forefathers—access to the sea, a Baltic port, "a window open upon Europe"': K. Waliszewski, *Peter the Great*, trl. Lady Mary Loyd (London, 1898), p. 294.

[3] I. Deutscher, *The Prophet Armed* (London, 1954), p. 459; Carr, vol. 3, pp. 158 f.

mutual concessions, but these were rejected.[1] On 28 April Pilsudski declared that he would invade the Ukraine, and several days later Polish troops attacked. They encountered little resistance at first and managed to capture Kiev at the beginning of May. But in the ensuing campaign the Red Army, although poorly equipped, proved the stronger force. The Soviet Government pressed five million men into service and aroused the patriotism of the people in the defence of their native land against the invader.[2] In June the Red Army recaptured Kiev and hurled the Poles back to the frontier. Lenin imagined that the Red advance would provoke a revolution in Poland and persuaded a majority of the Politbureau to sanction carrying the offensive into Poland and beyond, to within striking distance of Germany. Thus, as the fortunes of war changed the Red Army was cast in a new role. The army was no longer engaged in a patriotic struggle as it had been when the Poles first attacked, it was now the spearhead of European revolution.

However, it was soon evident that Poland could not be revolutionized at the point of a bayonet. 'The Polish workers and peasants met the invaders as conquerors, not liberators.' Poland was united by the Red advance as it had never been united before, and on 12 August the Polish Army, with the help of an Anglo-French military mission headed by General Weygand, counter-attacked and routed the Red Army at the gates of Warsaw.[3] This cut short the Communist military threat. But until the 'Wunder an der Weichsel' saved the Polish capital, the spectre of Red hordes driving into the heart of Europe, blazing a trail for Bolshevism, loomed up before all the peoples of Western Europe. The French and British were confronted with a threat to their plans for a stable peace in Europe which they had painstakingly worked out at Versailles. The Germans, the victims of the Versailles peace, reacted to the news of successive Russian military victories with mixed feelings. They knew they would be the first to suffer if the Red Army crashed through the gateway to Western Europe, but they realized, too,

[1] Degras, *Soviet Documents*, vol. 1, p. 180.

[2] Deutscher, *op. cit.*, p. 461.

[3] *Ibid.*, p. 466. In a speech to the Tenth Party Congress (*Desyati Syezd R.K.P. (b)* (Moscow, 1921), p. 14), Lenin admitted that the advance on Warsaw had been a mistake and that he should have listened to Trotsky, and to Radek—'who knows the situation in the West better than we do.' Also see C. Zetkin, *Lenin* (Moscow, 1925), and L. Fischer, *The Soviets in World Affairs*, vol. 1, pp. 270-272.

that the destruction of 'that monstrous bastard of the Versailles Treaty,' the Polish state, would work to their advantage.[1] The creation of a common frontier between Germany and Soviet Russia would have shattered the Versailles system and precluded an encirclement of Germany by means of an Allied *Randstaaten-politik*. No German could fail to understand these implications of the Red advance during the summer of 1920, but there were many who feared that the Russians would not be content with the destruction of Poland. Stresemann was one of those who thought the Red Army would roll on to invade Germany. 'Our military leaders believe the Russians can reach our borders by the end of August,' he informed a friend in July. 'Can one really believe that Lenin, who has been preaching revolution all this time, will stop when he reaches this frontier? But what will happen then?'[2]

Indeed, what would have happened if the Red Army had conquered Poland and stood poised on the German frontier in 1920? There were some Germans, Seeckt among them, who thought the only way to guard against a Red invasion was to negotiate with Russia and to sign an alliance with her. In July 1920, at the height of the Russian advance, they argued that although an alliance should have been signed the previous winter it was still not too late to start negotiations. They argued that an alliance with Russia would safeguard Germany from a Red invasion and gain her Soviet support against the Allies. Among those who put forward these arguments was a German who, although he remains unidentified, apparently had considerable political standing as well as cunning and insight. In a letter to Stresemann in July 1920 he wrote:

... however paradoxical it may sound, our salvation lies in the Russian danger.... The Russians have let it be known again and again that they would welcome German negotiators.... Now we must send them right away. We should sign an alliance with the Russians on the following basis: re-establishment of the old frontiers in the East; a trade agreement which would enable us to procure all our natural resources in Russia and to employ our *Intelligenz* ... and our labour force in Russia.

---

[1] S. Mikolajizyk, *The Rape of Poland* (New York, 1948), p. 6. This epithet is credited to Molotov in September 1939, but it was in common use in Germany long before then.

[2] *Stresemann Nachlass*, 6930H/H139314/5, letter to Generaldirektor Vögler, 10 July 1920.

The letter ended with a comprehensive statement of the alternatives confronting the German Government:

The world needs us, the Russians to get to the West to destroy the Entente together with us; the Entente because they want Germany to be a protective wall to hold back the Russian flood. Depending on the way the situation develops we shall have to choose on which road we shall travel.[1]

Some of the same ideas were taking hold in the Reichstag. In foreign affairs debates during the early summer of 1920 all the parties expressed sympathy with the Russians in their war against Poland. At the time of the Spa Conference in July a special debate was held. It is noteworthy that almost all the deputies who spoke linked the Spa Conference—where the schedules of German reparation payments and disarmament were to be worked out—with the future of Russo-German relations. One of the two KPD deputies, Klara Zetkin, said the precedent for Spa 'was established by German imperialism . . . in the peace of Brest-Litovsk.' Because of Spa, Zetkin continued, Germany's future was bleak, and it could 'only be brightened by one other word: Moscow.' Other speakers advocated resuming diplomatic relations and negotiating agreements with the Soviet Government. They pointed out that Germany had always found good markets in Russia and that these markets were especially important now that Germany had to pay vast sums in reparations to the Western powers.[2] The least enthusiastic proponent of a resumption of commercial relations with Russia was Stresemann. He doubted that 'grandiose' business opportunities were to be found in the Soviet Republic. Unlike other leading figures in the DVP, Stresemann was not prepared to negotiate with Soviet Russia at this juncture. Instead he attacked

---

[1] *Ibid.*, 6938H/H140431/57. It may never be possible to identify the author of this 26-page memorandum, which is entitled 'Richtlinien.' He writes about himself that he worked with Count Rantzau in Copenhagen and Stockholm in 1917 for a separate peace with Russia, and that since the war he and Felix Deutsch, August Müller, and Walter Rathenau have been trying to get the government to negotiate with Soviet Russia. These facts allow one to guess that the author of the memorandum was the infamous Dr Helphand, alias Parvus, who had been the vital link between the Germans and the Bolsheviks before the November Revolution (see above, p. 1 n. 1). But there is not enough evidence to make a positive identification.

[2] *Verhandlungen des Reichstags 1920* (Berlin, 1921), Band 344, pp. 161 ff.

the Allied reparations policies for weakening Germany and making her more susceptible to Communist pressures. Stresemann was afraid of a Communist revolution, or at least found it expedient to say he was. The Allies, he said, should realize that they need Germany: 'We are holding the fort against Bolshevism.'[1] Speaking for the government in the debate, Foreign Minister Walter Simons announced in veiled terms that he was prepared to resume diplomatic relations with Russia. 'We do not intend treating the Soviet Republic as a pariah because we do not like her methods of government. We ourselves have been treated as a pariah and suffered too much from it to consider inflicting the same treatment on others now.' Simons declared that Germany would remain strictly neutral in the Russo-Polish conflict.[2] This announcement met with general approval in the chamber, for German neutrality was, of course, to Russia's advantage.[3] The government forbade the transport of French munitions for the Poles across German territory, and in Danzig German dock workers refused to unload French weapons in transhipment to the fighting front. With this policy the Germans showed once again that they would not co-operate in Allied policies which they considered detrimental to their best interests in the East and harmful to their relations with Soviet Russia.

Soon after his Reichstag speech in July, Simons wrote to Chicherin to ask if a German liaison officer could be attached to the right flank of the Red Army, which was then rolling unchecked into Poland and heading for the German frontier. The liaison officer was to help prevent untoward incidents when the Russians approached the old German border. In the same letter Simons confided that his government wanted to resume diplomatic relations with Russia in the near future. He blamed the break in 1918 on the Soviet Government for having refused to make amends for the assassination of Ambassador Mirbach, and said that relations might be resumed if Chicherin consented to have a simple ceremony performed in Moscow in honour of the former German minister, at

---

[1] *Ibid.* These themes appear again and again in Stresemann's speeches in 1920. See the volume entitled 'Politische Reden' (1920) in the *Stresemann Nachlass* (6937H), especially the notes for his speech of 11 April. Cf. above, p. 27.

[2] *Verhandlungen des Reichstags 1920*, Band 344, pp. 255-266.

[3] German neutrality is 'not without benevolence on the side of Lenin' wrote the Stinnes-owned *Kölnische Zeitung*; cited by Kochan, *Russia and Weimar*, p. 30.

which the German flag would be raised over the Berg Palace while a company of Russian soldiers paraded in front of the building.[1] Chicherin sent a verbal reply through Victor Kopp, the Soviet plenipotentiary in Berlin, who told Maltzan that 'the Red Army would not cross the German frontier.'[2] This was not enough to satisfy the Germans. Maltzan repeated that a German officer should be attached to the staff of the advancing Red Army, and also asked Kopp for a guarantee that Russia would respect Germany's frontiers. No guarantee was forthcoming from Moscow, but the talks between Kopp and Maltzan continued. The chief topic of conversation was the possibility of resuming official diplomatic relations, to replace the unofficial relations which these very talks exemplified. Kopp's stature in Berlin rose with every mile of the Soviet advance into Poland, but he was not empowered to negotiate about the resumption of diplomatic relations. Chicherin gave the Soviet Government's views on this matter in a long handwritten reply to Simons. He wrote that he was glad to consider establishing official relations between the two countries, adding that his government had long wondered why the German Government had not made this obviously desirable change in its policy before. 'After all, two underprivileged nations [are] natural partners, given good will and mutual understanding.' The letter continued with a 'short ideological discourse' with which Chicherin endeavoured to prove that the Bolsheviks were 'far too realistic to make any foolish attempts to foster . . . ideas of social organization on an unwilling nation by force of arms,' a theory ill-befitting the events that were then transpiring in Poland, although Chicherin may have been completely sincere in stating his views.[3] At one and the same time, Chicherin refused to give a written guarantee of Germany's frontiers and tried to convince the German Government that it had nothing to fear from the Soviet Republic. Performing a ceremony of atonement for the criminal act against Mirbach, which Simons proposed in his letter, would have been an effective demonstration of Russia's good intentions. But Chicherin was not prepared to allow the ceremony to take place. He had two reasons for this, one of which he stated in his letter. He informed Simons that the

---

[1] Hilger paraphrases Simons' letter in *Incompatible Allies* p. 50.

[2] Blücher, *Deutschlands Weg nach Rapallo*, p. 100.

[3] Hilger also paraphrases Chicherin's 'handwritten reply,' which was 'several pages long, in faultless German': *Incompatible Allies*, p. 51.

ceremony was degrading; the honour and prestige of the proletarian state would suffer too much from it. Sacred national honour
is a commonly accepted reason or excuse for a nation's actions in
international affairs, and Chicherin undoubtedly meant what he
said. But he also had a better reason for rejecting the German
proposal, which he did not mention in his letter. Prior to the
crucial battle at Warsaw, Chicherin and his superiors were convinced that the continuing rapid advance of the Red Army would
lead either to a revolution in Germany, or to a resumption of
diplomatic relations with the existing German Government without Russia first having to submit herself to humiliating pre-
conditions.

Simons was not a brilliant Foreign Minister, but he acted
deliberately and was shrewd enough to have anticipated Chicherin's
rejection of his proposals. Why, then, did he insist on an expiation
of the former ambassador's assassination as a preliminary condition
for the resumption of official relations, especially after Germany
had accepted Lenin's apologies at the time of the killing and had
merely revived the issue in November 1918 to have a pretext for
severing relations with the Communists?[1] Why was this ancient
affair revived in 1920? One explanation is that Simons was reluctant
to approach the Soviet Government openly for fear of incurring
the active displeasure of Britain and France as long as the reparations and disarmament questions remained unsettled, and before
the Upper Silesian plebiscite had taken place. By stating the same
condition for the resumption of relations, the non-fulfilment of
which was used as a pretext for breaking them off, the German
Government was preparing to justify its dealings with the Bolsheviks to the hostile West. A second explanation has to do with
differences of opinion within the German Foreign Ministry. We
know that counterbalancing the so-called Easterners, such as
Maltzan, there were also powerful anti-Russian figures in the
ministry who were actively opposed to a resumption of relations
with Russia. Berend, the head of the Eastern Department, along
with others who shared his opinions, may have cajoled or forced
Simons to pose a condition for diplomatic relations which the
Soviet Government was likely to reject. According to Wipert von
Blücher, the Legal Department of the Foreign Ministry insisted on

_____
[1] See above, p. 32.

'an atonement for the murder of Ambassador Mirbach.'[1] Perhaps the legal experts did press the demand, but it is doubtful if even lawyers would go to such lengths to make a point unless political interests were bound up with it. Chicherin was undoubtedly aware of these differences of opinion in the ministry. They were to be expected, and, furthermore, he received information from Communist agents who were unwittingly employed by the ministry, or who had access to its secrets.[2]

Although the advance of the Red Army into Poland provoked feverish political activity in both Berlin and Moscow, no important change in the relations between the two countries took place at this time. Had the Red Army won the battle of the Vistula there would have been a rapid and perhaps decisive change in Russo-German affairs. But the Polish victory prevented this. Two years were to pass before political relations between the two powers were to be put on a normal footing. But during those two years the German Army, undeterred by the failure of the politicians to bridge the gulf keeping the two countries apart, continued its own policy of *rapprochement* with the Soviet Republic. Russia's defeat struck a blow at Seeckt's hopes and plans, but it did not stop him from pursuing his own foreign policy, in which, as we know, the creation of a common Russo-German frontier played a crucial part. Unlike the country's political leaders, to whom he was theoretically accountable, Seeckt was not concerned with balancing interests and political forces. He presumed to know which policies were correct and did what he could to put them into effect. Simons had to consider all the possible consequences of alternative policies towards the Russo-Polish war before finally choosing a neutral course, but Seeckt was never uncertain what the government's attitude towards the conflict should be. As early as January 1920 he had anticipated the outbreak of war between Russia and Poland. At that time Seeckt said he was 'against supporting Poland, even in the face of the danger that Poland is eaten up.' He thought that Russia would be the aggressor and hoped that she would win the war: 'Although we cannot help Russia to re-establish her old national boundaries, we should at least not prevent her from

---

[1] *Deutschlands Weg nach Rapallo*, p. 101. Cf. E. Eyck, *Geschichte der Weimarer Republik*, 1. Band (Erlenbach-Zürich, 1954), p. 231.

[2] *Stresemann Nachlass*, 6929H/H139062/4 and H139065/6. Also see Carr, vol. 3, pp. 363 f.

trying.'[1] Like all *Realpolitik* this was a sanguinary policy; it was cruel—and also dangerous. Seeckt could not know what the Red Army would do when it reached the old German frontier. He hoped that it would halt, and envisaged Russo-German negotiations leading to the *status quo ante bellum* in the East, meaning a partition of Poland by Germany and Russia as part of a settlement re-establishing the pre-World-War frontiers. Seeckt realized, however, that Russia might try to invade Germany. In that event he said 'we must resist them at our frontier.'[2] But could the German Army and the Free Corps stop the Red Army? In February 1920 the *Landeskammer* of Silesia sent a memorandum to Seeckt asking what action would be taken in the event of a Russian invasion of the eastern territories—could and would Germany defend the territories? Seeckt replied that the Reichswehr could not effectively withstand the Red Army whether it had the 100,000 men stipulated by the Versailles treaty or the 200,000 men Germany had asked for. Although it stated the hard facts, the tone of Seeckt's letter was not pessimistic. He pointed out that the probable defeat of Poland by Soviet Russia coupled with Germany's inability to halt the Red Army constituted an attack on the 'narrow military decrees of the Versailles treaty.'[3] Britain and France, Seeckt continued, would be forced to scale down their reparations and disarmament demands if they wanted to count on Germany as a bulwark against Communism. And if Russia occupied Poland, Germany would no longer be bound by the Versailles treaty in any way. Germany, he said, would benefit from Russia's military victories east of the German frontier. Silesia's suffering under the Polish or the Bolshevik yoke would strengthen Germany in the long run; at least the Versailles treaty would become meaningless. Thus, more than a month before the outbreak of the Russo-Polish war, Seeckt saw clearer than any other German what the consequences of a Russian victory would be. How much comfort the loyal Silesians drew from these explanations is another matter.

[1] Rabenau, *Seeckt*, vol. 2, p. 252.      [2] *Ibid.*

[3] *Heeresarchiv*: Seeckt, Stück 130, Karton 13. The Silesian memorandum is dated 14 February 1920, Seeckt's reply 26 February 1920. Lord D'Abernon describes the dramatic scene at Spa when Seeckt signed the disarmament protocol on 10 July 1920 in *An Ambassador of Peace* (London, 1929), vol. 1, p. 63. Hugo Stinnes, a delegate to the Spa Conference, had falsely predicted to Stresemann that the Allies would allow Germany to have an army of 200,000 men: *Stresemann Nachlass*, 6930H/H139314/5.

Some writers have suggested that Seeckt not only tried to under-mine the Versailles treaty—which he certainly did—but that he had plans in 1920 to unite the Reichswehr with the Red Army to fight a war of revenge against the powers that had inflicted the treaty. This is improbable. The charge was first made by Erich Wollenberg, a former official of the KPD, who claims that Seeckt approached the Soviet Government in July 1920 through Kopp with suggestions for co-operation 'against Versailles.'[1] Seeckt was indeed trying to make contacts in Moscow through Radek, Enver Pasha, and a journalist by the name of Waurick.[2] He may also have talked to Kopp in Berlin, but there is no evidence to suggest that he proposed a joint war of revenge against the Allies in 1920. On the contrary, all the available evidence indicates that he was against involving Germany in any war, and he invariably rebuked those of his officers who wanted to take precipitate action. Seeckt did prepare a plan of attack against Poland in 1920 which was always kept up to date, but the military campaign according to this plan did not have Poland fighting on two fronts, so it was obviously not a plan for intervening in the Russo-Polish conflict.[3] Moreover, in a memorandum Seeckt drafted on 31 July, by which time the Red Army had advanced to within 100 kilometres of East Prussia, he deals with the problems that would arise if Russian troops penetrated into Posen and East Prussia, and declares that he will not send German troops to defend these territories nor take any other action contravening the Versailles treaty.[4] Evidently Seeckt had not made any secret agreements with the Red Army by 31 July. The next day he prudently decided to go on holiday, without giving orders to his subordinates that might lead one to suppose he anticipated a link up or co-operation with the Red Army.[5] During the first week in August Russian troops actually crossed the East

[1] E. Wollenberg, *The Red Army* (London, 1938), p. 236. Wollenberg's allega-tions are supported by, among others, Wheeler-Bennett, in *Nemesis of Power*, p. 126. Cf. the comments of the anonymous reviewer of *Nemesis of Power* in *The Times Literary Supplement* (London, 8 January 1954), p. 18.

[2] For Waurick's later activities in Soviet Russia see H. Helbig, 'Die Moskauer Mission des Grafen Brockdorff-Rantzau,' *Forschungen zur Osteuropäischen Geschichte*, Band 2 (Berlin, 1955), p. 309 n.

[3] Rabenau, *Seeckt*, vol. 2, p. 297.

[4] *Heeresarchiv*: Seeckt, Stück 130, Karton 13. The memorandum is entitled: 'Die militärisch-politische Lage im Osten und Schlussfolgerungen.'

[5] Rabenau, *op. cit.*, p. 253.

Prussian frontier and established Soviet regimes in two German border towns, but when the German Government protested they immediately withdrew.[1] This evidence does not support Wollenberg's allegations. But if Seeckt nevertheless offered the Russians a military alliance against Poland and the West, it is certain that neither the Soviet Government nor Trotsky on his own authority were prepared to accept his proposals at this stage. If secret negotiations for a dramatic German-Russian *rapprochement* at the expense of Poland were going on during the summer of 1920, these were abruptly halted following the defeat of the Red Army at Warsaw. The peace of Versailles remained intact.

The Germans were now again forced to concentrate their hopes on efforts to mitigate the terms of the peace treaty. In the autumn of 1920 there were still reasons to be optimistic about the chances of reaching some accommodation with the West. The Allies had not yet presented their final reparations bill, and in Germany itself the spiral of inflation had been temporarily stayed. Furthermore, the results of the East and West Prussian plebiscites favoured Germany, and there seemed to be a good chance that the plebiscite in Upper Silesia, which was arranged by the Allies despite strong Polish objections, would also turn out to Germany's advantage. And while the hopes that some accommodation with the West could be reached were revived in Berlin, the Germans became increasingly sceptical of the support Russia might give them following her defeat in Poland. Even the Bolsheviks' ability to remain in power was once more seriously in doubt, and what relations there were between the two countries were conducted in a distinctly cool atmosphere.[2] In Moscow Hilger became aware of Berlin's growing disinterest in his activities. Without support from the German Government he felt he could not serve a useful purpose in the Russian capital. In despair he wrote to officials in Berlin that 'in spite of hunger, cold, and bitter feelings among the broad masses of the people, the Soviet Government has so far emerged stronger and more consolidated from every crisis.' The Bolsheviks, Hilger concluded, are 'firmly in the saddle' and Germany cannot afford to ignore them.[3] Hilger convinced his friends in Berlin, but the leading officials of the Foreign Ministry did not believe his

---

[1] Hilger, *Incompatible Allies*, p. 50.
[2] *Ibid.*, p. 54; Blücher, *Deutschlands Weg nach Rapallo*, p. 144.
[3] Hilger, *op. cit.*, p. 55.

story. Some distrusted his judgment, others doubted his loyalty. And, regardless of the facts of what was going on in Moscow, there were those who, like Berend, remained resolutely hostile to the Russians at all times. For several weeks after the Red military defeat, until the beginning of the winter of 1920, even Simons hesitated to take additional measures in the direction of normalizing relations with the Soviet Republic. Simons, too, doubted that the Soviet regime would last. He introduced a new note of caution into the government's policy towards the East, assuring the world of Germany's friendship for the Russian people, but noticeably not for their government.[1] There was a similar reaction in the political parties. Only a handful of Reichstag deputies were fully convinced that Russia could prove useful to Germany, and even these few preferred to keep silent lest they arouse the suspicions of Western statesmen and be blamed for the failure of appeals to moderate the reparations demands. There was no vocal opposition when Chancellor Fehrenbach, a member of the Centre Party, upbraided those who had greeted the advance of the Red Army 'with feverish sympathy.' The Chancellor spoke for the vast majority of the deputies when he said the German people should be grateful that the country was not 'misled into intervening in the Russo-Polish war.'[2]

One consequence of the renewed scepticism about the Bolshevik regime was that Kopp's status in Berlin was again reduced to that of a minor official. While Kopp was ignored, 'white' Russian expatriates, of whom there were many in Berlin, regained sympathy and were consulted as experts on the situation in their homeland. The political negotiations between Russia and Germany, which seemed to be leading to agreements in July, had stopped by September.

Nevertheless, the forces in both countries which in spite of every obstacle were making for a *rapprochement* continued to ripen. It was clear, however, that the road to agreement had to be one of slow and precarious negotiations, a far cry from the sudden creation of a common frontier at the expense of Poland, which had seemed to be in the offing only a short time before. Seeckt's disappointment over Russia's defeat did not deter him from seeking an alliance with her. Poland was now more than ever a menace to

[1] *Verhandlungen des Reichstags 1920*, Band 345, pp. 762 f.
[2] *Ibid.*, pp. 786 f.

German security, and for Seeckt Russia was 'a means both of counteracting this menace and of building up a bargaining power in the relations of Germany with the Western powers.'[1] He wanted to combine his policy of *rapprochement* with Russia with the plans to circumvent the restrictive disarmament terms he had been forced to sign at Spa. Seeckt's plan was to persuade the Soviet Government to sanction co-operation between the military establishments of the two countries, allowing the German armaments industry to rebuild on Russian soil. Russia was to be repaid with a share in the production of the industry. Seeckt hoped that the entire arrangement would create a close tie between the two countries.

When Enver Pasha arrived in Moscow he informed the Soviet leaders of Seeckt's intentions.[2] At least a number of the Russian leaders were interested in Seeckt's proposals and welcomed the opportunity of communicating with him through Enver Pasha. On 26 August 1920 Enver wrote to Seeckt from Moscow (in very poor German) that 'there is a party here which has real power, to which Trotsky also belongs, which favours an understanding with Germany.' The letter goes on to say that Trotsky and his associates —Sklyansky, Deputy Commissar for War, is the only other name Enver mentions—were prepared to negotiate a Russo-German-Turkish alliance based on the German frontiers of 1914. Enver's letter was delivered to Seeckt by an unidentified emissary who, according to the letter, had 'full authority' to negotiate with Seeckt 'in complete secrecy.'[3] If Seeckt negotiated with this emissary, which is not known, no agreement was reached, not even concerning the preliminary arrangements for the projected joint rearmament effort. Enver Pasha himself reappeared in Berlin in October under the pseudonym of Professor Ali-Bey and took up residence within walking distance of Seeckt's villa in the Grünewald.[4] Since

[1] Wheeler-Bennett, *Nemesis of Power*, p. 125.

[2] Enver Pasha left Berlin for Moscow in October 1919 (see above, p. 47), but because of several mishaps it took him almost a year to get to his destination; see *Documents on British Foreign Policy* (London, 1948), ed. E. L. Woodward and R. Butler, First Series, vol. 2, pp. 43 f., and C. Okay, *Enver Pasha—der grosse Freund Deutschlands* (Leipzig, 1935), pp. 334-345.

[3] *Heeresarchiv*: Seeckt, Stück 202, Karton 15. This letter and a second one that Enver Pasha wrote to Seeckt from Moscow were edited by Rabenau before their publication in *Seeckt*, vol. 2, p. 307.

[4] Blücher, *Deutschlands Weg nach Rapallo*, p. 133.

he had come away from Moscow convinced that the Bolsheviks were firmly entrenched in power, Enver undoubtedly continued to urge Seeckt and other German leaders to negotiate an alliance with them. However, even if Seeckt wanted to act fast and resolutely, he was, it must be remembered, going beyond the rightful province of a military commander in working out a policy of his own towards Russia, and, therefore, had to move carefully and quietly. The responsible ministers in Fehrenbach's Government did not know of Seeckt's plans, and would have disapproved had they found out about them. It was only late in the winter of 1920-1921, after the Allies had again stiffened their attitude and demands against Germany, that some of the Social Democratic and Centre Party leaders decided to support the plans for a resumption of diplomatic and, above all, commercial relations with Russia. But even at that time most of these men, who included Gustav Bauer, Otto Braun, Hermann Müller, Philip Scheidemann, Otto Wels, and Joseph Wirth, were against military co-operation or an out-right alliance with Soviet Russia.[1] Had Seeckt revealed his plans or negotiated openly with the Russians he would not only have compromised his own position, but also effectively frustrated the Russo-German *rapprochement* he was aiming for, while giving the French a good excuse to occupy the Ruhr. For these reasons Seeckt had to be cautious and patient, and he exercised consummate skill in all the secret negotiations with the Russians.

In Moscow, too, the fact that contact had been made with Seeckt and the secret military negotiations that followed received no public attention. But by the end of 1920 it was no secret that the Soviet Government was seeking a *modus vivendi* with Germany along the lines Radek had envisaged, prematurely, in 1919. Although it may have been the case, as reported by Enver Pasha, that during the summer of 1920 this policy was advocated only by Trotsky and a few others, Lenin's speeches in the autumn and early winter leave no doubt that the development of an alignment with Germany had become official Soviet policy. In a speech in September, Lenin said he had been amazed by the phenomenon of a pro-Bolshevik—of course it was chiefly a pro-Russian—Right wing emerging in Germany during the Polish conflict. 'As our troops approached Warsaw all Germany began to ferment,' he said.

[1] Helbig, 'Die Moskauer Mission des Grafen Brockdorff-Rantzau,' p. 295

'There appeared a strange type of reactionary-revolutionary.'[1] This was a reference to the so-called National Bolsheviks of the Right, of whom Count Reventlow was the most outspoken if not the most important representative. But pro-Russian enthusiasm in Germany at the height of the Red advance into Poland was not limited to extremists, and Lenin knew it. 'Everyone in Germany,' he noted, 'said that the Bolsheviks would save us, when they saw the Versailles peace was splitting at all its seams.'[2] Several months passed before Lenin appreciated the full significance of these events in Germany from the angle of Soviet Foreign Policy. Speaking in December 1920, he said that since the Soviet Republic owed its survival to the divisions among the capitalist powers, Soviet Foreign Policy must aim to perpetuate and intensify the splits in the capitalist camp and to use them to Russia's advantage. One of the two principal means of carrying out this policy, according to Lenin, was to permit foreign investments and concessions to foreign investors on Soviet territory. In this way the Communists would derive economic benefits from the capitalist powers, and, in the event Russia were involved in another war, the capitalist nations with investments in Russia would tend to side with her to protect their own interests. Although he did not restrict the offer of concessions to German capital, Lenin knew that the offer would appeal especially to the German business community, which was anxious to resume previously lucrative commercial relations with Russia. But Lenin saw that Germany could be made to serve Soviet Foreign Policy in other and more direct ways. 'The Versailles peace,' Lenin continued, 'has created a position such that Germany cannot dream of breathing-space, cannot dream of not being plundered, of not being deprived of the means of life, of her population not being condemned to hunger and starvation.' In her desperate situation, Lenin said, Germany's 'only means of saving herself is by an alliance with Soviet Russia.' There was no doubt in his mind that although the German bourgeoisie attacked the Soviet Government and hated Bolshevism, 'the interests of its international position impel it towards peace with Soviet Russia.'[3] From this brilliant analysis of the geographic, economic, political, and military factors which were causing the Germans to seek better

---

[1] Lenin, *Sochineniya*, vol. 25, p. 378; cited by Kochan, *Russia and Weimar*, p. 37.
[2] Lenin, *op. cit.*, p. 148.
[3] *Ibid.*, vol. 26, pp. 7-9, 14-16.

relations with Soviet Russia, Lenin drew a peculiarly Marxist conclusion. He said that the Soviet Republic must welcome the overtures of a bourgeois German Government because it was a cornerstone of Soviet international and foreign policy 'to prove to those peoples conscious of the bourgeois yoke, that there is no salvation for them outside the Soviet Republic.' The twin pillars of the new policy Lenin was proclaiming, fostering capitalist competition in Russia and creating an alliance with Germany, would, he said, work to 'hamper a crusade of the imperialist powers against us.'[1]

If it occurred to Lenin that this policy was wholly contrary to and irreconcilable with the one Zinoviev was pursuing through Comintern at the same time, he neither said so nor made any effort to sacrifice one policy to the other. Despite the fact that Lenin said the Soviet Government would welcome any overtures from Germany that might lead to better relations, Zinoviev continued to work throughout the winter of 1920-1921, without interference it seems, to provoke a revolution in Germany.[2] The VKPD was created and urged into violent revolutionary action at the very time Soviet commissariats were encouraging closer political and economic relations with the German Government. In effect, the Bolsheviks were trying to create a *rapprochement* with the German bourgeoisie and to win the support of the German workers at the same time. Both policies could, of course, be directed 'to exploit the contradictions and oppositions amongst the imperialists,' as Lenin had advised, but whether this ambiguity was purposeful or developed because the attention of the leaders was absorbed by the growth of opposition within the party and by the economic crisis, remains a problem. Whatever the cause of the ambiguity in Communist policy may have been, Lenin's pronouncements were heard and taken seriously in Germany despite the revolutionary activities of the native Communists in the VKPD, and these pronouncements started both countries on the road that was to lead them to Genoa and Rapallo.

In an especially candid and enlightening passage of his speech in December 1920, Lenin correctly identified the essential struggle in the arena of European politics for the next two and a half decades. 'I am not fond of the Germans by any means; but at the present time it is more advantageous to use them than to challenge them . . .

---

[1] *Ibid.*                              [2] See above, pp. 64-66.

Germany wants revenge, and we want revolution. For the moment our aims are the same, but when our ways part, they will be our most ferocious and greatest enemies. Time will tell whether a German hegemony or a Communist federation is to arise out of the ruins of Europe.'[1]

[1] Dennis, *The Foreign Policies of Soviet Russia*, pp. 154 f.

# CHAPTER IV

# TO GENOA AND RAPALLO:
# WALTER RATHENAU

LENIN'S speeches during the last months of 1920 did not fall on deaf ears in Berlin. But the Germans were forced to tread warily. Allied pressure was very strong; the government was not yet in a position to take an independent line in foreign policy. Simons had to warn responsible officials not to make callous or other untoward statements in open debates that might prejudice the Western powers in the decisions regarding reparations payments and the future of Upper Silesia. At the same time, Simons was determined to preserve his freedom of action for the future, in the event the Allies refused to modify the peace terms. If he were forced to 'knock on the Eastern gate' after all, Simons wanted to be sure that he would still be accorded an answer. To reassure German businessmen, especially the leaders of heavy industry, that they would be able to compete for the economic opportunities opening up in Soviet Russia, Simons told the Reichstag in January 1921 that the government would not stand in the way of commercial relations between the two countries. 'Communism as such,' he said, 'is no reason why a German republican and bourgeois government should not trade with the Soviet Government.'[1] In retrospect this sounds like mere common sense, but it was more than that at the time; common-sense attitudes towards the Bolsheviks were by no means prevalent in the West.

Later in January Simons sent Moritz Schlesinger to Moscow to help Hilger find a basis for the resumption of diplomatic relations, and also to begin negotiations for commercial relations. Just how obscure and fluid relations between Soviet Russia and Germany were at this time is illustrated by Simons' final instructions to Schlesinger on the eve of his departure: 'See what you can do,' the Foreign Minister said.[2] Schlesinger's journey to Moscow was no secret, but his mission was. All negotiations for commercial relations had to be conducted under the cover of prisoner exchange negotiations.

[1] *Verhandlungen des Reichstags 1921* (Berlin, 1922), Band 346, p. 1994.
[2] Hilger, *Incompatible Allies*, pp. 65 f.

Shortly before Schlesinger left Berlin Seeckt sent a representative of his own to Moscow, undoubtedly without informing the Foreign Ministry that he was doing so. Colonel Nicolai, who had been chief of the German secret service during the World War, had orders from Seeckt 'to set the stage' for further military talks. His job was to impress on the Soviet Government the necessity of strict secrecy in regard to all contacts with the Reichswehr, and to make the arrangements for subsequent talks about which not only all foreign powers but also the civilian heads of the German Government itself were to be kept in the dark.[1] Even before Nicolai left Berlin, Seeckt had informed Kopp that German military and industrial circles were definitely interested in Lenin's offer of concessions on Russian soil, namely those for the production of armaments. Soon after Nicolai arrived, Kopp was recalled to Moscow for consultation. Thus in January and February 1921 talks concerning diplomatic, commercial, and military affairs were going on side by side in the Russian capital.[2]

Kopp soon returned to Berlin with instructions from Trotsky to continue exploratory discussions with German military and industrial leaders.[3] Meanwhile, Hilger and Schlesinger were making good progress in working out a Provisional Agreement for the 'extension of the sphere of activities of the mutual prisoner of war aid delegations,' which was to give the plenipotentiaries new powers and gradually transform their offices into diplomatic missions.[4] A draft of the Provisional Agreement was dispatched to Berlin on 19 February, but the Kronstadt rebellion and the 'March Action' intervened before it could be fully studied and initialled. Chancellor Fehrenbach and Simons were convinced that the VKPD's revolutionary outburst was inspired by Moscow and angrily refused to so much as discuss the draft.[5] They suspected,

---

[1] C. F. Melville, *The Russian Face of Germany* (London, 1932), pp. 54, 68; Wheeler-Bennett, 'Twenty Years of Russo-German Relations 1919-1939,' *Foreign Affairs* (New York, October 1946), vol. 25, No. 1; H. R. Berndorff, *General zwischen Ost und West* (Hamburg, 1951), pp. 91-94; P. Scheffer, 'Die Lehren von Rapallo,' Sonderdruck aus *Merkur*, April 1953, p. 10.

[2] Carr, vol. 3, p. 362.

[3] *Ibid.*

[4] Hilger, *Incompatible Allies*, p. 67.

[5] Stresemann, on the other hand, commented on the 'March Action': 'What a splendid opportunity to make German foreign policy'; quoted by H. L. Bretton, *Stresemann and the Revision of Versailles* (Stanford, 1953), p. 40.

moreover, that the Kronstadt rebellion was the beginning of the end of Lenin's regime, and that they would soon be dealing with a new Russian government. As long as the struggle raged, for the better part of a month, contacts between Berlin and Moscow were suspended. But at the end of March, after the Kronstadt rebellion collapsed and the German Communists had been suppressed, Berlin's interest in the Provisional Agreement suddenly revived. In surviving intervention, civil war, and now a dangerous rebellion, the Soviet Government proved that it was in firm control of Russia. The myth that it was merely a transitional government was finally dispelled; even some of the militant anti-Bolsheviks in Germany were beginning to face up to this fact. Furthermore, in suppressing the 'March Action' the German Government proved to itself that the Communist menace within the country could be controlled and need not interfere with a normalization of relations with Moscow. Just as Lenin encouraged the capitalist countries to invest in the Soviet economy in order to prevent a united anti-Bolshevik crusade, the Germans now believed they could cool the Bolsheviks' ardour for revolution by making trade with the bourgeoisie profitable to the Soviet Republic. Britain had already set a precedent by signing a trade agreement with the Soviet Government, and Lenin's proclamation of the New Economic Policy induced the Germans to follow the same course.[1]

But the chief reason Fehrenbach and Simons decided to make new and more energetic efforts to establish friendly relations with Russia was that by the end of March the last hope of reaching a satisfactory accommodation with the Allies had faded away. Earlier that month the final reparations bill had been published, and the Germans were given every reason to believe that the severe terms of payment which were outlined at the Paris Conference in January would be imposed on them without amendment at the coming London Conference. The French had already occupied three Ruhr towns in retribution for Germany's failure to comply with certain reparations and disarmament demands, and there were constant threats of additional sanctions.[2] The German people were duly alarmed. Simons toured the country making

---

[1] The Anglo-Soviet Trade Agreement was signed on 16 March 1921.

[2] Duisburg, Ruhrort, and Düsseldorf were occupied on 8 March 1921. The phases of the military occupation of German territory are outlined by Bretton, *op. cit.*, chap. 6, *passim.*

inflammatory speeches railing against Allied demands and disclaiming Germany's 'war guilt.' His speeches were widely acclaimed and there were public demonstrations against the Allied demands which led the government to believe it would have mass support for a policy of non-compliance.[1] A natural concomitant of defiance towards the West was a policy of friendship, if not actual alliance, with Russia in the East. Therefore, at the end of March Simons instructed Berend not to let the Moscow discussions which Hilger and Schlesinger were conducting be disrupted under any circumstances. By the beginning of April the atmosphere in which these talks were held was notably cordial; earlier German demands, including those for an expiation of Mirbach's assassination, were dropped.[2]

While those articles of the Provisional Agreement transforming the prisoner of war agencies into political and consular missions were dealt with in Moscow, the basic points of the articles governing future economic relations were agreed upon in discussions between Maltzan and the economist Aaron Scheinmann in Berlin. Scheinmann, who was sent by the Soviet Government to help Kopp, had instructions to insist that a declaration be incorporated in the Provisional Agreement by which the German Government would be bound not to recognize any agency as representing the Russian state on German territory other than the consular and trade missions which were to be established by the terms of the agreement.[3] In assenting to this provision Maltzan and Simons reaffirmed the *de jure* recognition of the Soviet Government which was first given by the Imperial German Government in the Treaty of Brest-Litovsk. The informal recognition granted 'white' Russian organizations in Berlin had to be withdrawn, and the German Government promised to deal directly with the Soviet Government in the future and not to participate in crusades against it. Closely associated with this provision was an article of the agreement in which both governments pledged themselves to refrain from agitation and propaganda against the government and institutions of the other. A similar undertaking had been signed at Brest-Litovsk, but this time at least one of the parties to the agreement, the German Government, assumed that the declaration was to be

---

[1] Eyck, *Geschichte der Weimarer Republik*, p. 236.
[2] Hilger, *Incompatible Allies*, pp. 66 f.
[3] Blücher, *Deutschlands Weg nach Rapallo*, pp. 147 f.

taken seriously and adhered to.[1] Most of the articles of the Provisional Agreement were devoted to settling the unprecedented practical difficulties of trade between private firms and state monopolies, in anticipation of a rapid increase in the volume of trade between the two countries in the near future.

The entire agreement was ready and could have been signed before the end of April. However, the signing was postponed at the request of Simons, who did not want it to coincide with the crucial negotiations at the London Conference. A Russo-German accord would have doomed Simons' last-minute efforts to modify the Allied reparations demands. But these efforts failed anyway. Then, on 6 May, only one day after the Allies confronted the German delegation with the so-called London Ultimatum, Simons agreed to sign and publish the agreement.[2] The timing was not a matter of chance; it was intended as a protest against the treatment accorded Germany by the Western powers. The agreement did not go unnoticed in London and Paris, but it does not seem to have been taken as a warning of things to come. The Allied statesmen did not realize that the Germans were turning more and more towards the East in search of some escape from the repressive policies of the victor powers; they believed that Moscow and Berlin would compete for the favours of the West.

Under the agreement of 6 May new heads of missions were to be appointed to replace Kopp and Hilger in Berlin and Moscow. Kopp and Maltzan met informally in Berlin to discuss the candidates of their respective governments for these posts. The Soviet Government wanted Joffe to go back to Berlin, but Maltzan told Kopp that, considering the circumstances in which Joffe was dismissed three years before, the suggestion was nothing less than an affront to the German Government. Joffe's name was subsequently withdrawn in favour of Nicolai Krestinski. The Germans had reservations about Krestinski, too, but none important enough to prevent them accepting him.[3] The choice of a German to lead

[1] See above, p. 16.

[2] The agreement is published in the *Reichs-Gesetzblatt*, Jhrg. 1920, 16 Juni 1920, Nr. 130. The London Ultimatum is in *Dokumente der Deutschen Politik und Geschichte* (Berlin, n.d.), vol. 3, pp. 115 f.

[3] Blücher, *op. cit.*, pp. 149 ff. Kopp also suggested that the Russian Brodowski be accepted to head the Soviet trade delegation in Berlin. According to Blücher, Brodowski was on the German 'black list,' so Kopp proposed that one Herr Bratman be accepted instead. When Bratman appeared in Berlin the Germans

the mission in Moscow also presented problems. Simons wanted to appoint Count Brockdorff-Rantzau, who was a personal friend of his and of President Ebert. Brockdorff-Rantzau would have been acceptable to the Soviet Government, but Simons and Maltzan finally decided not to nominate him because they considered it unwise to send a man to Moscow with a higher rank than that of the British representative, a consul, and Brockdorff-Rantzau would have been insulted by the mere suggestion that he accept such lowly status. Discussing the problem with Kopp, Maltzan said, 'we have several fitting candidates. I think the best choice would be a parliamentarian. From among these we could send you a Social Democrat or a Democrat. The alternative is to send a professional diplomat; but he,' Maltzan warned, 'would probably stand further Right.' Kopp picked up a flexible ruler from Maltzan's desk and proceeded to demonstrate his preference: 'Look, Herr Baron, we, the Bolsheviks, are here, on the extreme Left; then come the Social Democrats and on the other end the people of the Right. Now, you cannot bring us together with the Social Democrats and the Democrats, but you do not have to apply much pressure'—at this point Kopp bent the ruler until the two ends touched—'and we come very close to the Right. So do not send us a parliamentarian, rather a professional diplomat.'[1] Taking Kopp's advice, the Germans looked for a suitable Right-wing diplomat only to come up with Kurt Wiedenfeld, a Right-wing professor of economics.

Russo-German trade negotiations were making rapid strides even before Krestinski and Wiedenfeld took up their posts in the autumn of 1921. The Russian railway expert, Lomonosov, placed extensive orders for locomotives with firms in the Ruhr, and Krasin spent May and June in Berlin having 'meetings and luncheons and dinners with various German industrialists.' The British Ambassador in Berlin, Lord D'Abernon, followed Krasin's round of interviews with interest. Krasin, he noted in his diary, 'appears to have won their ear,' but he was quite sure that 'nothing very definite' was being arranged.[2] As a matter of fact, Krasin was winning more than interested audiences; he was gaining the

recognized him as the objectionable Brodowski. Asked to explain himself, the new chief of the Soviet trade delegation said he carried the double name, Bratman-Brodowski!

[1] *Ibid.*
[2] *An Ambassador of Peace*, vol. 1, p. 176.

confidence of German industrialists and laying the groundwork for joint Russo-German enterprises. Some of the capitalists who met Krasin did not trust him and would not consider investing in Communist Russia. But most German businessmen knew Krasin as an honest and able trade expert, and the economic opportunities he offered made them believe more firmly in the slogan which the business community itself had popularized: 'The Bolsheviks must save us from Bolshevism.' German industry could see no future for itself in dealing with the West; only commercial relations with Russia could save the German economy from ruin and the society from Communist revolution.[1]

Krasin's sales techniques soon showed results. In the autumn of 1921 the first of the so-called mixed companies were set up. *Derutra*, an organization created by the Soviet Government and the Hamburg-Amerika Line, was to handle all future cargo transport between Germany and Russia across the Baltic Sea. *Deruluft* was the corresponding company for air traffic, and *Derumetall* handled trade in scrap metal between the two countries. The German-Russian trade concern *Russgertorg*, of which the Cologne iron and steel magnate Otto Wolff became the first German director, was also established before the end of the year. A number of German corporations were granted concessions on Soviet soil. The most important of these was a tractor factory and experimental mechanized agricultural station established by Krupps on an extensive tract of land near the Manych River.[2]

Political relations did not keep pace with developments in the economic sphere. The Fehrenbach Government chose to resign rather than accept the London Ultimatum. It was followed by the first Wirth cabinet, in which Dr Friederich Rosen was Foreign Minister. Wirth executed an apparent *volte-face* in German policy by agreeing to meet the Allied demands to the extent the German economy was capable of realizing them. Nationalist elements in Germany attacked Wirth and called his 'fulfilment' policy 'traitorous.' They failed to understand that Wirth had merely adopted tactics which were intended to appease the Allies, in order to prevent an occupation of the Ruhr and to keep Upper Silesia within the Reich. These tactics, to be successful, also required a change of emphasis in relations with Russia. Although Wirth had

---

[1] Blücher, *Deutschlands Weg nach Rapallo*, p. 151.
[2] Kochan, *Russia and Weimar*, p. 42; Hilger, *Incompatible Allies*, pp. 177 f.

been one of the earliest supporters of a resumption of relations with
the Soviet Republic, when he was made Chancellor he felt that he
could not attain his objectives in London and Paris if it were known
that the government was simultaneously developing a close friendship with the Bolsheviks. For this reason, and not because he had
changed his mind about the importance of a link with Moscow,
Wirth decided in April 1921 that the process of *rapprochement* had,
at the very least, to be slowed down. Rosen was an intense anti-
Russian and carried out the Chancellor's directives enthusiastically.
His first act as Foreign Minister was to relieve Maltzan of his post
as chief of the Russian desk and to send him to Athens, where he
would not be able to influence the course of Russo-German affairs.
Hilger and Schlesinger also suffered under Rosen's administration.
Not only were they subordinated to Wiedenfeld, who, according
to Hilger, 'was firmly opposed to any arrangements which
Germany alone might make with Russia,' but their anti-Russian
enemies in Berlin took the opportunity to start a 'typical smear
campaign' against them. Any number of unfounded accusations
were made which Rosen was all too ready to believe. When Hilger
visited Berlin during the summer, Rosen greeted him abruptly with
'Good morning, Hilger, I understand you are a Communist.'
Although Hilger was able to clear himself of this charge, he was
unable to evoke Rosen's interest in relations with Moscow.[1]

But Rosen did not stand in the way for long. When the Allies
decided in October 1921 to detach most of Upper Silesia from
Germany, Wirth reversed the tactics of the 'fulfilment' policy. He
reinforced the drive for an alliance with Soviet Russia, heading
Germany down the same road Simons had followed, and which, a
year later, was to lead to Rapallo. Rosen had carried out Wirth's
instructions to dampen down relations with Russia too enthusiastically to be of any use in directing the new policy. He was forced
to resign, and some other anti-Russian zealots left the Foreign
Ministry with him; Maltzan was called back from Athens to take
over the Eastern Department of the ministry, and other proponents
of an Eastern orientation were also given key positions.

Before examining the political developments following the
Allied decision on the Upper Silesian dispute, we must go back to
find out what progress Seeckt had been making with his own
policy towards Russia since the beginning of 1921.

[1] Hilger, *op. cit.*, pp. 68 f.

While the politicians hesitated, turned East then West and then East again, Seeckt never strayed from the course he had charted for himself. Unlike Fehrenbach and Rosen, and at times Simons and Wirth, Seeckt never believed it possible to exact concessions from the West by means of a policy of pleas, entreaties, and national prostration. He was convinced that the Allies wanted to keep Germany militarily impotent, and was determined to prevent them from achieving their purpose. Seeckt correctly interpreted Wirth's 'fulfilment' tactics as a manœuvre to split Britain from France and to forestall an occupation of the Ruhr. But in his opinion, these tactics could only gain Germany a temporary respite. The nation, Seeckt said, would be vulnerable and at the mercy of Allied whims until it was able to bargain as an equal, which meant bargaining from a position of strength. And the only source of strength available to Germany was Soviet Russia. The fact that Russia's rulers were Communists did not deter Seeckt from seeking to co-operate with them. But, on the other hand, his relations with the Russian Communists did not influence him in favour of their fellow Communists in Germany, who constituted an entirely separate menace which he was prepared to suppress with ruthless vigour.

Seeckt believed it possible to coexist with the Bolsheviks and was even prepared to collaborate with them; but the terms on which he would do so, and did do so, had to be his own. Seeckt's dispassionate realism was understood and equalled in the highest counsels of the Soviet Government. For at the very moment the German Army crushed the Bolshevik-inspired 'March Action,' Kopp was secretly negotiating with German military authorities and industrialists for the rebuilding of the Russian armaments industry under German technical management and control, in return for Soviet aid to the Reichswehr.[1] These talks had started in December 1920 and were interrupted only briefly during Kopp's trip to Moscow.[2] In the middle of March, after the Treaty of Riga was signed to terminate officially the Russo-Polish war, Lenin gave a fillip to the secret talks by formally applying to the German Army for assistance in the reorganization of the Red Army.[3]

[1] Carr, vol. 3, p. 362.          [2] See above, p. 85.
[3] This was revealed by Otto Gessler, Minister of Defence, in his testimony before the Reichstag Foreign Affairs Committee on 24 February 1927; see the *Stresemann Nachlass*, 7128H/H147732.

In anticipation of the development of the army's relations with Moscow, Seeckt created an administrative organization within the War Ministry, called Special Group R, which was to negotiate and sign agreements with the Soviet Government, and to carry out the agreements.[1] Only the most reliable and competent officers and men were assigned to Special Group R, including a number who could speak Russian and had had some experience in the country. Special Group R organized the negotiations with Kopp and invited leaders of German industry to participate in them. The German officers who took part were Colonel Oskar von Niedermayer, who liked to hear himself called 'the German Lawrence' because of his daring adventures in Persia and Afghanistan during the World War; Colonel von Schubert, who had tempered his anti-Bolshevik proclivities since he was military attaché in Moscow;[2] Major Fritz Tschunke, who had helped Enver Pasha to escape to Moscow in 1919; Lieutenant-Colonel Fischer, the first head of Special Group R; and, upon his return from Moscow, Colonel Nicolai. As was his custom, Seeckt remained in the background.[3]

On 7 April, a month before the Russo-German Provisional Agreement governing diplomatic and commercial relations was signed, Kopp reported to Trotsky, sending copies of the report to Lenin and Chicherin, that he had succeeded in working out a project under which aeroplanes, submarines, and guns and shells would be manufactured in Russia by the Albatross Company, Blöhm & Voss, and Krupps. Kopp suggested that a mission of five or six German technicians, to be led by 'Neumann, who is known to you,' should be allowed to go to Moscow to discuss the details of the project. Strict secrecy was to be maintained. Lenin approved the project, and a few weeks later Niedermayer (the

[1] See Tschunke's memorandum entitled 'General v. Seeckt nimmt die Verbindung zur Sowjetunion auf,' which was written for v. Rabenau in February 1939, in the *Heeresarchiv*: Seeckt, Stück 290, Karton 19. The memorandum is reproduced in Julius Epstein's article 'Der Seeckt-Plan,' *Der Monat* (Berlin, November 1948), I. Jhrg., Nr. 2.

[2] See above, p. 14 n. 4.

[3] G. W. F. Hallgarten, 'General Hans von Seeckt and Russia, 1920-1922,' *The Journal of Modern History* (Chicago, March 1949), pp. 28 ff.; Blücher, *Deutschlands Weg nach Rapallo*, p. 153. Cf. Wheeler-Bennett, *Nemesis of Power*, p. 127, who is of the opinion that Colonel Nicolai headed Special Group R.

'Neumann' of Kopp's report), Tschunke, and Schubert arrived in Moscow.[1]

Seeckt was satisfied with the progress of his plans, but he was uneasy about the risks involved. 'The Russian game is not easy and not without dangers,' he wrote to his sister in the spring of 1921. 'But my old commander, General Langenbeck, used to say: in time of war everything is dangerous. And we are, after all, at war, and will remain at war.'[2]

In Moscow the Niedermayer mission was joined by Hilger, Karakhan—the Vice-Commissar for Foreign Affairs—and by the peripatetic Kopp, for an inspection tour of armament works and shipyards in the Petrograd area. The Soviet Government wanted the German War Ministry to provide financial and technical assistance in restoring these war-ravaged facilities, in return for a share of Soviet armament production. However, this project was dropped. Niedermayer reported to Berlin that the plants and docks were utterly devastated and in need of more capital investment than Special Group R had at its disposal.[3] But the mission was not a failure, for contacts were made and other less ambitious projects for collaboration, including those negotiated in Berlin, were worked out in detail. Niedermayer also opened a branch office of Special Group R in Moscow.[4]

Although some German industrialists had shown a willingness to collaborate with the Soviet Government through Special Group R by the summer of 1921, there were others, including armament manufacturers, who were unwilling to participate in the collaboration. They posed as much of a problem to Seeckt as to the Russians, because he wanted a large-scale rearmament programme and needed broad industrial support to finance even a small programme. Evidence of the reluctance in German business circles comes from

[1] Carr, vol. 3, p. 362. The original copy of the report is in the Trotsky Archives in Cambridge, Mass., and bears notations by Lenin approving the project, and by Menzhinsky, deputy chief of the GPU, asking to be kept informed so that security measures could be taken. For the Niedermayer mission see the *Heeresarchiv*: Seeckt, Stück 290, Karton 19, and Hilger, *Incompatible Allies*, p. 195.

[2] Rabenau, *Seeckt*, vol. 2, p. 261. Blücher claims he found out about the secret negotiations in the spring or early summer of 1921 through an indiscretion committed by Niedermayer; see *Deutschlands Weg nach Rapallo*, pp. 152 f.

[3] Hilger, *Incompatible Allies*, p. 195.

[4] The Moscow office was called 'Zentrale Moskau.' See Appendix C.

a dispatch sent by 'one of the German negotiators' to the Polit-bureau meeting of 10 September, just two weeks before Krasin returned to Berlin to conclude the negotiations for mixed com-panies.[1] According to this dispatch, the hesitations in Berlin were due to 'new moves in Western Europe for intervention in Russia,' and to hints by Loucheur that the Allies would make concessions to Germany in their decision on the Upper Silesian plebiscite if Germany refrained from separate agreements with Russia. The informant advised the Politburo to 'play the Polish card,' by which he meant that Russia should exacerbate German fears of Poland and tempt her with the prospect of a combined military operation against Poland in the near future. This was likely to win more Germans for an Eastern orientation. But even at this stage the informant was able to report that some 'concrete positive con-clusions' had been reached in the Berlin talks, presumably meaning the agreements to manufacture aeroplanes, submarines, and muni-tions on Russian soil, but added that these could not be imple-mented until difficulties within the German Government were overcome.[2] What these difficulties were is not specified in the report, but it is almost certain that they were chiefly financial. As we know, Seeckt had not mentioned his Russian connexions to members of the government. Had he been able to get sufficient financial support from private industrial sources he would un-doubtedly never have initiated the politicians and civil servants into his schemes. But since the money cut out of the army budget and the funds pledged by industry did not amount to enough for the rearmament programme, not even for that part of the programme to be carried out in Russia, Seeckt was forced to ask for financial support, which meant he had to ask for approval, too, from official circles. He was on the verge of this in September, but then decided that before he approached the politicians he should have a com-plete list of the opportunities open to German capital and technical specialists, in order to estimate first the total amount of money needed. On Seeckt's initiative the secret military negotiations were resumed in Berlin at the end of September. The Soviet representa-tives at this time were Kopp, who was back in Berlin again, Krestinski, and Krasin and Stomonyakov, both of whom had just arrived from London in order to continue the trade negotiations. Krasin and Stomonyakov spent part of each day in meetings with

[1] See above, p. 90.  [2] Carr, vol. 3, pp. 363 f.

German businessmen about which even the British Ambassador was informed, and a few hours at secret rendezvous with German military leaders, including Colonel Hasse, who was later Chief of the *Truppenamt*; Colonel von der Lieth-Thomsen, senior air officer during the World War; Lieutenant-Colonel Fischer; and Niedermayer.[1]

This combination of military and economic negotiations had Lenin's complete approval. It did not matter to him whether Soviet representatives negotiated with German politicians, generals, or industrialists, as long as the agreements that were reached strengthened the Soviet Republic. He pointed out that German arms factories in Russia could come under the heading of 'concessions.'[2] The most important of the military concessions resulting from the negotiations of September-October 1921 was for the manufacture of Junkers aeroplanes at a factory in Fili, eight miles from Moscow. Junkers had been trying to develop such a project for two years.[3] Now that the Soviet Government had accepted their proposals, the company was only lacking a guarantee from the German Government covering the political risks that were involved and a subsidy to pay for the erection of a costly motor works. Special Group R gave Junkers an unwritten but apparently satisfactory political guarantee and an initial financial outlay totalling 600 million marks.[4]

To finance Junkers and other corporations going into the armaments business in Russia the War Ministry established a holding company with the innocuous-sounding name of Company for the Development of Trade Enterprises, which is usually identified by

[1] Rabenau, *Seeckt*, vol. 2, pp. 307 ff. The private apartment of Major (later General and Chancellor) Schleicher was sometimes used for the secret talks: Hallgarten, 'Seeckt and Russia,' p. 30.

[2] Carr, vol. 3, p. 364.

[3] The aeroplane in which Enver Pasha left Berlin for Moscow on 10 October 1919 was a brand-new Junkers model which also carried two Junkers employees who were in possession of a document enquiring about the legal position of Junkers patents in Russia, the possibility of manufacturing aeroplanes in Russia, and the possibility of developing domestic Russian airlines: *Documents on British Foreign Policy*, ed. Woodward and Butler, First Series, vol. 2, pp. 44 f. Also see Scheele, *The Weimar Republic*, pp. 107-109.

[4] This was to be Junkers' working capital, equal to roughly $3,000,000 at the time. However, inflation reduced the amount to $250,000 by March 1922. See Hilger, *Incompatible Allies*, p. 193, and Melville, *The Russian Face of Germany*, pp. 68 f.

its German initials: GEFU. GEFU was organized in the framework of Special Group R and had offices in Berlin and Moscow which were opened in the autumn of 1921 with Major Tschunke in charge.[1] Its operating capital stemmed from a number of sources. Some funds were taken annually from the army's budget and from Reichstag appropriations camouflaged under other headings, a so-called 'blauer Haushalt.' In later years the Ministry of Transport shunted 27 million marks to GEFU for 'the development of a military air force,' and financial help continued to be solicited and received from private sources.[2] Seeckt, however, was not satisfied with the amount of money available for these purposes, and in September 1921, when there was only just enough money to get the Junkers project started, he made up his mind to inform Chancellor Wirth of the secret negotiations, and to enlist his aid in financing the collaboration with Russia. He had a number of reasons to believe that Wirth would co-operate. In the dual capacity of Chancellor and Finance Minister in his first cabinet, Wirth had proven his willingness to promote the Reichswehr's rearmament programme by giving Krupps enough money to allow the company to preserve 'German armament techniques' for a period of at least ten years.[3] Wirth was, in fact, an experienced conspirator. For at the precise time he secretly released state funds to Krupps he also pledged his government to the 'fulfilment' policy, which included a commitment to carry out the prescribed disarmament programme. If, despite this record, Seeckt still had doubts about Wirth's trustworthiness, the rebuffs to the 'fulfilment' policy in London and Paris, culminating in the Allied decision on Upper Silesia in October, made him certain that Wirth could be won over to the plans for rearmament in Russia and for a *rapprochement* with the Soviet Government. Seeckt decided the right

[1] Hilger, *op. cit.*, p. 194; *Heeresarchiv*: Seeckt, Stück 290, Karton 19.

[2] H. Speidel, 'Reichswehr und Rote Armee,' *Vierteljahrshefte für Zeitgeschichte* (München, January 1953), Heft 1, p. 22. Speidel was a member of Special Group R, attached to the staff of the Luftwaffe. Cf. Görlitz, *Der Deutsche Generalstab*, pp. 365 f. Also see below, p. 206.

[3] *Trials of War Criminals—The Krupp Case* (Washington, 1950), vol. 9, pp. 322 f., Prosecution Exhibit 132, Document NIK-8575: letter from Joseph Wirth to Gustav Krupp, 9 August 1940. Additional proof of Wirth's co-operation in the illegal rearmament programme is in a letter from Lersner to Stresemann in regard to an interview with Seeckt: *Stresemann Nachlass*, 7001H/H142170/1. The letter, which is partly in 'code,' is dated 25 May 1921.

D

moment to approach the Chancellor had come when Wirth formed his second cabinet without Rosen, and after Maltzan had been brought back from Athens. At precisely the same time several members of the SPD got wind of the secret negotiations with the Russians and demanded that Wirth call Seeckt to account for them. Seeckt hurried over to the Chancellory, where he was confronted by Wirth and the Social Democrats who had levelled the charges against him. The Chancellor asked him if it were true that secret talks were going on with the Russians. Pointing to the Social Democrats, Seeckt replied: 'None of *those* gentlemen are ministers and I shall make no explanations in *their* presence.' Thereupon Wirth rose and bade Seeckt into his private study. When they reappeared ten minutes later Wirth dismissed the inquisitive Social Democrats without ceremony: 'Gentlemen, the Chief of the Army Command has told me everything worth knowing. Thank you, gentlemen.'[1]

Shortly after this encounter, Wirth, who was Finance Minister as well as Chancellor until the end of October, saw to it that 150 million marks were made available to Special Group R, the first of a number of payments from the government which were passed on to GEFU.[2] Before the end of October the secret was imparted to a small circle in the Foreign Ministry, perhaps at first only to Maltzan, and a number of other reliable officials were enlisted to help arrange and camouflage the government subsidies, including Finance Minister Dietrich, who took over the ministry from Wirth later in October; Haeckel of the Finance Ministry; State Secretaries von Popitz and Schwering von Krosigk of the Accounting Office; and Ersing of the Centre Party and Stücklen of the SPD, who were both members of the Reichstag's Appropriations Committee.[3]

---

[1] This account is given in a letter from von Selchow, Seeckt's personal adjutant at the time, to von Rabenau: *Heeresarchiv:* Seeckt, Stück 289, Karton -?-. Selchow dates the incident in 1923, which is obviously incorrect since Wirth was no longer Chancellor then. Rabenau is vague about the date of Wirth's initiation, but mentions that he was both Minister of Finance and Chancellor at the time. Wirth relinquished the ministerial portfolio on 26 October, six days after the decision on Upper Silesia was announced. Thus it appears that Selchow's account is of a meeting that took place between 20 and 26 October 1921.

[2] Hallgarten, 'Seeckt and Russia,' p. 31.

[3] Speidel, 'Reichswehr und Rote Armee,' p. 22. Stücklen has already been mentioned for his role at the head of the Reich Central Office for Military and Civilian Prisoners of War; see above p. 52.

From this time onwards, Germany's military, economic, and political relations with Soviet Russia were loosely co-ordinated, but because the military aspects were only known to a few people, they were not fully integrated with the other two.

The secret talks in Berlin with the Russians continued until the beginning of December. Seeckt himself participated in the last session to gratify the Russians, who had always wanted to deal with him personally.[1] A few days later Hasse went to Russia accompanied by Admiral Wülfing von Ditten, Niedermayer, representatives of Junkers, and an unidentified official of the Foreign Ministry.[2] In Moscow Hasse discussed with Lebedev, the Soviet Chief of Staff, what action the countries would take 'in the event of a Polish war.'[3] Hasse made it clear that he personally would welcome a war against Poland at the earliest opportunity. Believing that the Germans still needed to be encouraged to collaborate in the rearmament programme, Lebedev convinced Hasse that the Red Army would attack Poland in the spring of 1922 if Germany made immediate all-out efforts to rebuild Russia's war industry. Hasse was enthusiastic. Until Seeckt set him straight, he seems to have had no idea that Lebedev had merely been playing—unnecessarily on this occasion—one of Russia's Polish cards to attract German interest. Except for Lebedev's statements to Hasse, there is no reason to believe that the Soviet Government was seriously contemplating an attack on Poland at this time, with or without German support.

While Hasse was being schooled in enthusiasm in Moscow, Admiral von Ditten and Niedermayer investigated the possibilities of using Russian bases to train the future German army and naval air arms. They also sought facilities to build submarines. The Russians could not offer them suitable shipyards, but they were willing to lease the Odessa aerodrome, whose location and climate were perfect for training purposes. However, the German Navy subsequently found better facilities for itself in other countries, and when it contracted out of the entire Russian venture the Luftwaffe

[1] Rabenau, Seeckt, vol. 2, p. 308; Hallgarten, op. cit., p. 31.
[2] Heeresarchiv: Seeckt, Stück 290, Karton 19; H. v. Dirksen, Moskau-Tokio-London (Stuttgart, 1949), pp. 45 f. Hilger confirmed the Hasse mission to Carr (vol. 3, p. 364 n.) but failed to mention it in his own book.
[3] Carr, vol. 3, p. 364.

asked for a training centre deeper in Soviet territory than the
Odessa base.[1]

While the military mission investigated facilities in Russia that
could be used for rearmament and training purposes, German
industry was sharply divided in an angry public debate over the
issue of how the greatest profits could be made in Russia. The
dispute was provoked by French and British businessmen who,
with the backing of their governments, proposed that an international consortium be organized to develop and exploit Russian
resources and markets. Most Western *entrepreneurs* believed that
forming a consortium was the only way of effectively negotiating
and trading with the Soviet monolith. If they negotiated as individual capitalists they had to face the disenchanting alternative of
behaving like capitalists: competing for Russian contracts, concessions, and markets; buying at higher prices and selling for lower
ones. Of course this is precisely what Lenin wanted, but the
capitalists were loth to accommodate him. In Germany it was
chiefly, but not exclusively, the light industries which were in
favour of joining a consortium. These were the industries that felt
the post-war shortage of capital most acutely, and they therefore
stood to gain the greatest benefits from an international pool of the
resources that were required to enter into profitable ventures in
Soviet Russia. The light industries, moreover, had traditional
financial connexions with the West and were at pains to restore
them after the war. The consortium proposal offered them an
opportunity to resume harmonious relations with the Western
business community.

The German heavy industries, however, had entirely different
interests. They emphatically rejected the consortium idea on almost
the same grounds upon which the light industries had endorsed it.
The heavy industries were not interested in co-operation with the
West. They were not in dire need of capital and could depend on
the government for supplementary appropriations when they
needed funds. Furthermore, Stinnes, heavy industry's kingpin and
its most illustrious spokesman, Krupp, Wolff, and the other industrial barons were making satisfactory progress in Russia without
support from French and British capital, and they jealously resented
Anglo-French 'interference' in the Eastern markets where they

[1] Speidel, 'Reichswehr und Rote Armee,' p. 18. On the illegal rearmament
of the German Navy see Scheele, *The Weimar Republic*, chap. 7, *passim*.

traditionally made their greatest profits and which they considered their own.[1] The consortium proposal was also a direct threat to the rearmament schemes which were being developed. The production of arms, the heart of the German iron and steel industry, was forbidden by the peace of Versailles. The Allies had even forced the Germans to destroy some of their existing weapon-producing machinery. Seeckt had proposed that the German armament industry be re-created in Russia, but how could heavy industry do this if it had to operate as part of an international trading combine? A Western consortium was certainly not going to help rebuild Germany's military potential on Russian territory!

Although the interests of Stinnes and other industrialists in the secret rearmament accounted for their intractable attitude towards the consortium proposal, they could not, for obvious reasons, give this as a reason or explanation in public discussions of the issue at the time. Instead they heaped abuse on the proponents of the consortium, whipped up hatred against the Allies with patriotic demagoguery calculated to appeal to German public opinion, and even borrowed the Bolshevik propaganda line against the consortium in a massive effort to defeat it. Stinnes himself led the propaganda campaign. Chancellor Wirth also joined in, saying that he would reject 'any policy that wished to consider and treat Russia as a colony.'[2] Opponents of the consortium were also active in the Reichstag and in the bureaucracy. Gustav Stresemann was heavy industry's chief spokesman in the Reichstag. The debate on the consortium took place when personal relations between Stresemann and Stinnes had deteriorated, chiefly because Stinnes was too coarse to appreciate Stresemann's flair for diplomatic methods, and too impatient to admire his skill in implementing them.[3] But the

[1] See the table in J. Kuczynski/G. Wittkowski, *Die deutsch-russischen Handelsbeziehungen in den letzten 150 Jahren* (Berlin, 1947), p. 15. Also the copies of the Rathenau-Stinnes correspondence, which Rathenau sent to Stresemann: *Stresemann Nachlass*, 6992H/H140543/715. According to Dr Fritz Klein, whose unreliable book, *Die diplomatischen Beziehungen Deutschlands zur Sowjetunion 1917-1932*, was published under Communist auspices ([East] Berlin, 1952), at least some of Stinnes' papers are in Eastern Germany (*ibid.*, p. 188).

[2] *Verhandlungen des Reichstags 1921* (Berlin, 1922), Band 352, p. 5562. Wirth's speech echoed 'the very phraseology of Soviet protests against the consortium': Carr, vol. 3, p. 369.

[3] H. W. Gatzke, 'The Stresemann Papers,' *The Journal of Modern History* (Chicago, 1954), vol. 26, Nr. 1, pp. 49 ff. Cf. Bretton, *Stresemann and the Revision of Versailles*, p. 59.

two men agreed on most issues affecting domestic and commercial policies, and on this occasion Stresemann made an excellent speech attacking the consortium idea. He was immediately supported by von Raumer of his own German People's Party and by Professor Hoetzsch of the German Nationalist Party. Both Raumer and Hoetzsch were strong advocates of an Eastern orientation in German Foreign Policy.[1] Following Moscow's lead, the Communist deputies also attacked the consortium idea and specifically endorsed the speeches of the Nationalists.

Maltzan headed the opposition to the consortium within the Foreign Ministry.[2] Wirth and members of his cabinet not only opposed the consortium, but privately encouraged German capitalists to explore and enter the Russian markets as quickly as possible to subvert the proposal.[3]

In the ranks of those who favoured the consortium there were none as talented and powerful as Stinnes, Stresemann, Maltzan, and Wirth. The AEG (Allgemeine Elektrizitäts Gesellschaft) was the most important corporation in the light industry group, but its manager, Walter Rathenau, was not given to blunt assertions of self-interest. He was Foreign Minister for part of the time that the consortium controversy raged in Germany and might have exercised an almost decisive influence in opposition to Stinnes. But although Rathenau thought that Germany would benefit if she joined the consortium he did not speak out for the proposal. Rathenau had been aware of the opportunities open to German free enterprise in Soviet Russia long before Wirth asked him to take over the Foreign Ministry at the end of January 1922, but he had never advocated a policy in the East that would divorce Germany from the West. He had, in fact, come a long way from his standpoint in 1919, when he wanted immediate and close commercial and political ties with the Soviet Republic.[4] Even before he took over the Foreign Ministry Rathenau must have known about Stinnes' plans, and he may also have heard about

---

[1] *Verhandlungen des Reichstags 1922* (Berlin, 1923), Band 354, pp. 6655 ff. For comments on von Raumer and Professor Hoetzsch see v. Dirksen, *Moskau-Tokio-London*, p. 63, and Scheffer, 'Die Lehren Von Rapallo,' p. 10.

[2] D'Abernon, *An Ambassador of Peace*, vol. 1, p. 238.

[3] Dirksen, *op. cit.*, pp. 63 f.; Kochan, *Russia and Weimar*, p. 47. Ernst Koerner, who in 1922 was a lumber operator in Germany, has related to the present writer that Wirth tried to persuade him to negotiate for concessions in Russia.

[4] See above, p. 49.

Seeckt's secret agreements with the Russians.[1] Intellectually Rathenau understood that Germany would derive benefits from closer commercial ties and rearmament collaboration with Russia, but emotionally he seems to have been opposed to everything that was involved in the multifold *rapprochement* with the Bolsheviks that was slowly progressing behind the scenes.

Although there is still insufficient factual evidence to sustain any of the numerous opinions about Rathenau's conception of German Foreign Policy, it is apparent that his feverish negotiations at London, Paris, Cannes, and finally at Geneva, from the last months of 1921 until the early spring of 1922, were inspired by the belief that he could arrange to free Germany from the severest economic fetters imposed by the Allies within the framework of a broader accommodation with the West. Rathenau rightly believed that the tendencies towards a *rapprochement* with Soviet Russia, which were gathering strength in certain circles, were a clear and constant danger to the success of the negotiations he was carrying on in London and Paris. But while Rathenau's cultural and emotional proclivities ranged him with Westward-looking Germans, he was perceptive and honest enough to realize that, if he failed to win Germany an equal place with the Allies at Western conference tables, the country would inevitably turn to Russia for political and also military support. He dreaded this prospect as he dreaded all decisiveness. Therefore he made it his mission, and passionately held that it should also be the West's cause, to save Germany from throwing in her lot with Bolshevik Russia.

The Allies were not unaware of the dangers of a German-Soviet *rapprochement*, but they did not think it an imminent danger, and Rathenau failed to convince them that it would be a likely consequence if a more lenient Allied policy towards Germany were not adopted. Had Rathenau told Allied statesmen about Seeckt's negotiations and Stinnes' activities he might have made his point. But he was too much of a patriot to take such desperate measures, and besides, there was always the threat that the French would react to the information by occupying the Ruhr. Rathenau considered his

[1] Eric Kollmann, who has made a study of Rathenau, writes that 'the question of whether Rathenau knew of these [Seeckt's] negotiations cannot be answered with absolute certainty at the moment; but from internal evidence it seems very probable that he did': 'Walter Rathenau and German Foreign Policy,' *The Journal of Modern History* (Chicago, 1952), p. 138.

own predicament at the conference table to be a part of what he imagined to be Germany's tragic middle position between East and West, with which he became more obsessed day by day.

In short, Rathenau was an egotist and a fatalist. He did not seem to realize that Germany's inherent political strength in a Europe divided between a capitalist West and a Communist East lay in her geographic position in between both camps. In spite of her defeat and the chaos that followed the hostilities, Germany was not impotent. Instead of pleas and entreaties Rathenau might have used the power of a connexion with Russia, or the threat of such a connexion, to cajole concessions and a more lenient policy from the West. He pleaded for reasonableness and a charitable attitude in an international atmosphere that, for the time being at least, was devoid of both virtues. His failure to achieve any of the objectives of his Western policy left him without bargaining power when he finally had to deal with the Bolsheviks.

Rathenau's mistakes loom too large for any but a harsh judgment to be made of his term as Foreign Minister. In the matter of the consortium, for example, he could not bring himself to face the issue squarely. He hinted to French and British leaders that German businessmen might be persuaded to participate in the consortium if they were offered concessions on disputed reparations questions. But when the debate on the consortium took place in the Reichstag he did not take a position either way; he prevaricated.[1] Those who had looked to Rathenau for leadership against heavy industry's alignment were disappointed. Without strong opposition the forces of Stinnes, Stresemann, and the Communists easily prevailed.

Throughout his career as a diplomat Rathenau was handicapped by all the shortcomings one expects to find in an intellectual trespassing into the political arena. Yet Rathenau was not a typical intellectual. He was a man of high intellectual calibre but also of principles, perhaps a man of genius. For all his intelligence and culture, however, Rathenau was tragically incapable of applying his skill to the unique business of politics. His opinions were rarely consistent and often contradictory; he seemed to be suffering from a split personality. Foremost of the inner conflicts which impinged on his public career was a clash between his Jewish heritage, which may account for the messianic drive in him, and an ardent patriotism, which was somehow corrupted into boundless admira-

---

[1] *Verhandlungen des Reichstags 1922*, Band 354, pp. 6655 f.

tion for the Prussians, to whom he felt inferior. It is indeed difficult to understand how this gifted and in some ways great man could respect the Prussians as a superior race!

Although he idealized the Prussians, 'there was no Teutonic obstinacy or dourness' in Rathenau. 'If he assented, it was with grace; if he differed, it was with urbanity.'[1] But his personal short-comings rather than his grace and other virtues counted most in his career as Foreign Minister; and the most damaging of his im-perfections was a propensity to fits of depression in which he would imagine that all was lost. Whenever Rathenau was in one of these fatalistic moods he was entirely ineffective and prey to lesser men with smaller minds, fewer scruples, and none of his altruism, like those who panicked him into signing the Treaty of Rapallo.

[1] D'Abernon, *Portraits and Appreciations* (London, 1931), p. 171.

# CHAPTER V

## THE RAPALLO ALLIANCE

THE fascinating story of the signing of the Treaty of Rapallo during the Genoa Conference is related in detail by Count Harry Kessler in his biography of Walter Rathenau.[1] However, fresh evidence has been uncovered since Kessler's book was published which sheds new light on the events leading up to the signing and on Rathenau's attitude to the treaty.

During the latter part of 1921 French and British businessmen obtained the support of their governments for a proposal to convene an international conference in the following spring, to which Germany and Russia would also be invited, at which the Bolsheviks were to be confronted with a Western consortium and told that only through this medium could Soviet Russia hope to engage in commercial relations with the rest of Europe. The Soviet Government took note of the Allied plan and made a counter-proposal for a different kind of conference 'at which all peoples and powers will be represented.' On 28 October Chicherin sent a note to the Allied powers proposing that the purpose of the conference be 'to consider the claims of the [Western] powers against Russia and of Russia against the powers, and to draw up a definite treaty of peace between them.'[2] Lloyd George saw an opportunity to combine the Russian proposal and the Western one within the framework of a single conference. On the strength of his recommendation the Supreme Council meeting at Cannes on 6 January 1922 decided to convene 'an economic and financial conference' to which all European powers, including Russia and Germany, would be invited for what was euphemistically called 'a united effort . . . to remedy the paralysis of the European system.'[3]

Chicherin accepted the invitation to the conference, which was to be held at Genoa, even before it was formally extended.[4] The

[1] *Walter Rathenau* (London, 1929), pp. 319-359.

[2] Degras, *Soviet Documents*, vol. 1, pp. 270-272. Also see Radek's article in *Pravda*, 30 November 1921.

[3] *Resolutions Adopted by the Supreme Council at Cannes, January 1922, as the Basis of the Genoa Conference*, Cmd. 1621 (London, 1922).

[4] Dennis, *Foreign Policies of Soviet Russia*, pp. 418, 419-420.

haste with which he accepted indicates that the Russians had misinterpreted Lloyd George's proposal. They were convinced, it
seems, that they could use the conference to acquire foreign capital
investments and to develop trade in accordance with the principles
of the NEP. In other words, they thought that the consortium idea
had been dropped and that, instead of being confronted with
proposals that would 'take the form of economic domination' and
infringements of 'the sovereign rights of the Russian Government,'
they were being given an opportunity to bargain and sign contracts
with competing Western capitalists.[1] To impress the world with
the Soviet Government's serious intentions in sending a delegation
to Genoa, Joffe was selected to give a candid interview to *Izvestiya*
in which he first admitted that Soviet policy in the Brest-Litovsk
negotiations of 1917-1918 had been to stall for time pending the
outbreak of world revolution, and then asserted that the Soviet
attitude to the forthcoming talks was completely different: the
government, Joffe said, was now honestly seeking genuine agreements.[2] On 27 January the Central Executive Committee
announced the names of an unusually large delegation for the
conference, headed by Lenin—who was not to attend but whose
position as President of the delegation added to its prestige—with
Chicherin as the effective leader.

Moscow's optimistic outlook on the Genoa Conference lasted
less than two months. It was encouraged by the misconceptions
about Western intentions and emboldened by a false sense of
accomplishment. This is evidenced by a *Pravda* leader of 12
January 1922.

> The inviting of Soviet Russia to an international conference is the
> victory of our revolution. . . . The sickle and hammer triumphed at the
> conference at Cannes, although there was not a single representative of
> Soviet power at this conference.[3]

During the latter part of February Lenin made a more realistic
appraisal of the prospects from the Soviet point of view, and thereafter he was more cautious in predicting the outcome of the
conference. But it was not until the beginning of March, barely a

[1] Degras, *Soviet Documents*, vol. 1, pp. 287 ff. Cf. A. U. Pope, *Maxim Litvinoff*
(New York, 1943), p. 181, for another interpretation of Chicherin's reaction.
[2] *Izvestiya*, 2 March 1922, cited by Kochan, *Russia and Weimar*, p. 49.
[3] Cf. Carr, vol. 3, p. 359.

month before the conference was scheduled to begin, that Lenin publicly expressed a measure of his new pessimistic attitude. Shortly thereafter, at the Eleventh Congress of the Russian Communist Party, Lenin spoke contemptuously of the excessive space given by the press to the Genoa Conference. 'It was as though he wished to warn Russia to expect defeat.'[1] There was now ample proof that the Allies were going to impose unacceptable conditions on the Soviet Government, and that they would continue to demand re-payment of Czarist debts. On 15 March Chicherin sent a stiff note to the British, French, and Italian governments in which he de-nounced the preliminary discussions that were going on in the West. The Soviet Government interpreted these discussions as attempts on the part of some nations 'to enter the conference with their decisions on the Russian question already completely made.' This meant that, 'instead of a free exchange of views, Russia is threatened with a new form of boycott.'[2] Although they protested against Western tactics the Russians did not give the faintest hint that they might reconsider their decision to attend at Genoa. No matter how poor the prospects were, the Bolsheviks were not going to give up their first opportunity to appear as a recognized government in the counsels of Europe. They were still going to go to Genoa 'not as Communists but as merchants,' but they had to assume that they would return empty-handed.[3] The darkened out-look on the Genoa Conference turned Lenin's immediate attention once again towards Germany. He was determined to lead the Soviet Republic out of its enforced isolation, and if the victorious powers were not prepared to accept Russia as an equal, then the only alternative was a partnership with defeated Germany.

Late in January 1922 Karl Radek reappeared in Berlin for the first time since his imprisonment at Moabit. Radek always left a turbulent political atmosphere in the wake of his travels, but on this occasion he surpassed even his own record of stirring up trouble. Any clear and logical exposition of Radek's activities is almost certainly unreliable, for he invariably contradicted himself both in word and deed. Thus, an accurate account of his activities is also likely to be a woefully confusing one.

Radek travelled to Berlin, legally this time, in Niedermayer's

[1] Dennis, *op. cit.*, p. 425.
[2] Degras, *Soviet Documents*, vol. 1, pp. 293 f.
[3] Lenin in *Pravda* on 28 and 29 March 1922, quoted by Dennis, *loc. cit.*

company for the ostensible purpose of talking to Seeckt about German aid in reconstructing Russia's war industry; but, as might have been anticipated, he did not limit himself to this project. He remained in Berlin until April, and during that time injected a liberal dose of volatile new ideas into the minds of Germans of every political stripe who were in a position to influence relations with Soviet Russia. Maltzan was one of his first victims. In a long private conversation Radek told him that the French Government had offered *de jure* recognition and commercial credits to the Soviet Government on the condition that the Soviet Government officially declare the Treaty of Versailles to be binding on Germany and avail itself of the reparations demands under Article 116 of the treaty.[1] Maltzan was thunderstruck, but Radek would not let him go until he had pushed the knife edge in still deeper. The French, Radek added, were even prepared 'to drop the Poles' if Russia would help France to hold Germany down. Maltzan may have doubted Radek's story, but he could not afford to ignore it. He immediately informed Chancellor Wirth, Foreign Minister Rathenau, Seeckt, Wiedenfeld, Stinnes, and officials of Krupps and the AEG All except Rathenau and Seeckt, who were not in Berlin at the time, met a day later at the Chancellory together with Radek. There is no record of what transpired at this meeting, but it is known that Radek repeated the substance of his earlier remarks to Maltzan and then linked his story of French overtures to Moscow with suggestions for closer Russo-German relations, emphasizing economic co-operation.[2] The Germans were led to believe that they would have to act quickly to discourage the Soviet Government from coming to terms with the French. France, they believed, sought their economic ruin and political enfeeblement, and Lloyd George was unwilling to take a stand strong enough to counteract French policies effectively. The Bolsheviks, taking advantage of this situation, were trying to win Germany from the 'capitalist united front' by beckoning with a plethora of economic oppor-

[1] Paragraph 2 of Article 116 of the Treaty of Versailles specified that Russia might demand reconstruction and reparations payments from Germany; see *Dokumente der deutschen Politik und Geschichte von 1848 bis zur Gegenwart*, vol. 3 (Berlin, 1952), p. 45. Also see the discussion in Blücher, *Deutschlands Weg nach Rapallo*, pp. 154-156. Cf. F. von Papen, *Memoirs* (New York, 1953), trl. B. Connell, p. 119.

[2] Blücher, *op. cit.*, pp. 154 f.; D'Abernon, *Ambassador of Peace*, vol. 1, p. 254. Berlin newspapers did not carry reports of these meetings.

tunities, offering the Germans a chance to employ their industrial techniques and experience, while earning handsome profits. Radek hinted that, in addition, the Soviet Government might be willing to forge a new political bond to support Germany's stand against Versailles. The Bolsheviks' outspoken opposition to the Versailles peace had already established a link with Germany, a link which, although chiefly sentimental, also had both political and economic implications. This link now took on new significance in the light of Radek's offer to extend it, while making simultaneous barely veiled threats that the Soviet Government could, if it wanted to, reverse its stand against the treaty and take advantage of Article 116.

For Radek this was a splendid opportunity to play an old game. He had advocated a Russo-German alliance as far back as 1919 and had probably never ceased working for it. But, while his efforts in 1919 were independent and premature, by 1922 he had considerable support for them in Moscow. In February, as Lenin realized that the Allies had not dropped the consortium proposal and would continue to press for repayment of the Czarist debts, Radek, whose first job in Berlin was to sound out the Germans and to intensify the struggle between them and the Versailles powers, became the key figure in 'the work of *rapprochement*' which 'was being quietly pursued' in the German capital.[1] In the middle of February he was joined in Berlin by Krasin, Rakovsky, 'and one or two others.'[2] They also moved around in various political and business circles, spreading the story of French overtures to the Soviet Government and enticing the Germans with prospects of Russian trade.[3] All this was groundwork for the proposal of a political pact which came directly from Moscow a month later.

During February Radek had successive interviews with Rathenau and Seeckt. His conversation with Rathenau was their first since they expounded respective world philosophies to one another in Moabit. This time they discussed more practical matters, covering the whole range of Russo-German relations including the various rearmament ventures that had been agreed on and others

---

[1] Lubov Krassin, *Leonid Krassin* (London, 1929), p. 174. Madame Krassin intimates that Rathenau hastened the *rapprochement* culminating at Rapallo (*ibid.*, pp. 168 ff.). But cf. D'Abernon, *op. cit.*, vol. 1, p. 269, and Carr, vol. 3, p. 370. Also see below, pp. 110 ff.

[2] D'Abernon, *op. cit.*, vol. 1, pp. 261-263.

[3] Blücher, *Deutschlands Weg nach Rapallo*, p. 156.

that were still under consideration. The following day Rathenau freely admitted to Lord D'Abernon that he had talked to Radek, but limited his comments to a few acid remarks. Radek, he said, 'is, of course, very clever and witty, but very dirty. The real type of low-Jew boy.'[1] Indeed, Radek's back-room politics were noted for their pungency; he was not the smooth diplomatic type.[2] On 21 February Rathenau gave a report on the international scene, with special reference to German-Russian relations, to the Foreign Affairs Committee of the Reichstag meeting in closed session. The only available records of this meeting are fragments of handwritten notes taken by Gustav Stresemann, a leading member of the committee. According to these notes, Rathenau made several references to his conversation with Radek and accepted as factual the story of French overtures to the Soviet Government. 'Poincaré is prepared to go along with Russia, Millerand is against this,' Stresemann wrote down, and then scribbled a pertinent comment of his own: 'As a Russian I would not go along with Britai rather with France.' Rathenau also talked about the proposed 'Russian Reconstruction Syndicate' and said that 'Radek is against a consortium.' Other notations confirm that Radek had offered lucrative business opportunities to German enterprises operating on a national basis. The Soviet Government, Rathenau said, was offering 'economic deals in order to conduct political relations'; Lenin wanted Germany to adopt a 'definite Eastern orientation.'[3] Taken by themselves, these notes do not give a clear indication of a trend of thought in Berlin in regard to an alliance with Russia. But it is significant that the only meeting of the Foreign Affairs Committee in February 1922 important enough to require the Foreign Minister's attendance was chiefly if not exclusively concerned with policies towards Soviet Russia. No doubt the activities of Radek, Krasin, and Rakovsky were having their desired effect.

Radek's talk with Seeckt on 10 February remains something of

[1] D'Abernon, *op. cit.*, p. 258.

[2] Radek's witty and callous tongue frequently got him into trouble. In February 1922 he openly criticized the Germans for a lack of national pride: 'We may think internationally in Soviet Russia, but at least we do not attend the British Ambassador's masked ball' (*Stresemann Nachlass*, 7008H/H143190). Also see Ernst Troeltsch's interesting article 'Radek und Deutschnationalismus' in *Spektator-Briefe* (Tübingen, 1924), pp. 269 f., and Wheeler-Bennett, *Brest-Litovsk*, pp. 218 f.

[3] *Stresemann Nachlass*, 7008H/H143197/9.

an enigma. All that is known about it stems from Hasse's diary, but this is unfortunately not a very reliable document.[1] According to Hasse, Radek 'urged Seeckt to arrange for conferences between the Russian and German general staffs and for the delivery to the Russians of German military literature to train the Russian officer corps, whose standard Radek described as low.'[2] Radek also proposed that Reichswehr officers be sent to Russia to train Red Army officers in the use of modern weapons. Prospective German officers could be instructed at the same time. According to Hasse, Radek made these proposals on a note of urgency because 'the essential point for the Russians . . . was their wish to launch an attack on Poland in the spring.' Since aeroplanes were needed for the attack, Radek wanted Junkers to begin operations 'in Russia in April.' This account of Radek's statements must be treated circumspectly. If Radek said that Soviet Russia, equipped with German weapons, would join Germany in an attack on Poland—or would fight Poland alone—in the spring of 1922, then he was hardly representing the serious intentions of the Soviet Government. The Russians were weary from three and a half years of world war, two and a half years of civil war, two years of a crippling blockade, and now famine. Lenin was in no position to provoke war against Poland, even if the Russian people could have endured all the hardships another war would have entailed. Furthermore, it should have been obvious to Hasse that the production of Junkers aeroplanes, starting in April, could not have significantly increased Russia's military potential for an attack in the spring. The immediate use for the aeroplanes and for the other arms the Bolsheviks wanted was to buttress Russia's defences, especially those on the Polish frontier, where Pilsudski might start another offensive into the Ukraine—'an eventuality that obsessed the Bolshevik brain.'[3] If Hasse's account of Radek's statements is accurate, then the only feasible explanation is that Radek was applying with customary irrespon-

[1] The following account of the Seeckt-Radek conversation is based on Hallgarten, 'Seeckt and Russia,' p. 31, who used Hasse's diary, and on Rabenau, *Seeckt*, vol. 2, p. 309, whose longer account is presumably also based on the diary. Hasse's diary was available for research at the National Archives, but was put back on the restricted list before the present writer could use it.

[2] Cf. General Groener's disparaging report on the state of the Red Army officer corps in 1919: *Heeresarchiv*: Groener, Karton 16, Stück 213, *Niederschrift über die Verhandlungen in der Sitzung des Reichsministeriums vom 24 April 1919.*

[3] L. Fischer, *Soviets in World Affairs*, vol. 1, pp. 320, 331.

sibility the injunction 'to play the Polish card,' in the hope of impelling the Germans into a series of agreements with Moscow. Radek apparently fooled Hasse, but not the older and more patient Seeckt. He did not let a desire for revenge against Poland subordinate his good sense. This is evident from the record of the rest of the conversation. For when Radek complained that Germany was co-operating with Britain, Seeckt replied that for the time being Germany 'had to flirt with the British in order to check France,' but that this should in no way adversely affect 'Russo-German co-operation in international affairs' since this 'was a matter for the future.' Although it is possible that tacit agreements were reached in defining Russo-German relations 'for the future' during the course of this talk, nothing definite was decided. The contention that Seeckt assured Radek that the Reichswehr would fight with the Red Army against Britain and France is spurious.[1] However, Seeckt did urge Junkers to begin reconditioning the factory in Fili as soon as possible. Junkers did not actually sign a contract with the Russians until 1923, but a preliminary agreement was reached on 15 March 1922 and German engineers and technicians were working at Fili before the end of April.

When the Soviet delegation to the Genoa Conference arrived in Berlin at the beginning of April the pace of the negotiations quickened. Until this time German trade and other forms of economic co-operation were at the heart of all the talks; economic gains were the real inducements for an agreement, although political and military factors also weighed heavily in the discussions. In the weeks immediately preceding Chicherin's arrival with the rest of the delegation, Radek, Krasin, and Rakovsky made increasingly blunt statements of the Bolsheviks' interest in the negotiations. All they wanted was 'an independent German economic policy in Russia' they said, no more than that. Such a policy 'will open the road to a national employment of German capital, not only in Russia itself, but further to the East, the road towards which lies through Russia.'[2] But no sooner had Chicherin

---

[1] Rabenau, *Seeckt*, vol. 2, p. 309; Hallgarten, 'Seeckt and Russia,' p. 31; Melville, *Russian Face of Germany*, pp. 68, 78 f. Also see the introduction by Hans Rothfels to Speidel's article 'Reichswehr und Rote Armee,' p. 15, especially n. 19.

[2] *Economic Life*, 29 March 1922, quoted by Dennis, *Foreign Policies of Soviet Russia*, p. 422.

arrived in Berlin than he started to bargain for more than simply an economic agreement. By this time the Soviet Government 'despaired of reaching an understanding with the Allies'; the delegation was going to Genoa only 'to assert Russia's natural position on the international stage,' but on his way Chicherin had decided to press the German Government for an immediate political as well as economic treaty which would confront the Allied powers with a *fait accompli* on the very eve of the conference.[1] It was an auspicious moment to put pressure on the German Government and Chicherin knew how to take advantage of the situation. There was widespread frustration with the reparations problems to which there seemed no satisfactory solution, and German public opinion was highly incensed by the policies of the Allied Military Control Commission. Rathenau was one of the very few who reasoned that Genoa might herald a change for the better in Germany's fortunes. Chancellor Wirth, on the other hand, was deeply pessimistic, and the population as a whole was exasperated and infuriated by the abounding ultimata.[2] Chicherin thought the time was ripe to negotiate a treaty with the Germans. Before the delegation left Moscow Lenin had said that 'if Germany were ready to sign a genuine treaty' it would have his blessing, and they 'should go ahead' and sign.[3]

Both Lenin and Chicherin knew that a German-Soviet treaty would wreck the Genoa Conference, but they did not care. Rathenau did care. He held that Germany could not sign a treaty with Russia until after she had re-established her own position in Western society, or exhausted every possibility of doing so. He clung to the hope of reaching agreements at the Genoa conference tables; he did not want to scuttle the conference, he did not want to negotiate with Chicherin—certainly not in Berlin just before the start of the conference. What would Lloyd George think? More to the point: what would Poincaré do? But Rathenau's advice was rejected by a formidable array of powerful individuals in the government, including senior members of the Foreign Ministry.

---

[1] Taken from Chicherin's pronouncements to Louis Fischer in Moscow some weeks later, *Soviets in World Affairs*, vol. 1, pp. 332 f. Although Chicherin was speaking *ex post facto*, his remarks do not appear to be highly coloured by what happened at the conference and afterwards.

[2] Eyck, *Geschichte der Weimarer Republik*, pp. 271-273.

[3] Pope, *Litvinoff*, p. 183.

Maltzan had the unanimous support of the Eastern Department behind him in pressing for immediate negotiations with the Soviet delegation, and, if possible, for the conclusion of a treaty. Chancellor Wirth also put pressure on Rathenau. The Chancellor paid tribute to his Foreign Minister in public and expressed complete confidence in him in private, but at this crucial juncture Wirth turned against him and supported Maltzan's demand for immediate negotiations. Rathenau yielded reluctantly, but he yielded.[1]

It is not surprising that once the negotiations started they moved ahead rapidly. Within a few days Russian and German legal experts were polishing the texts of the major paragraphs of what later became the Treaty of Rapallo. Only two minor clauses were not immediately agreed on. But these were not the reason that the treaty was not signed in Berlin. That was entirely due to Rathenau. Despite the insistence of the Russians, and of Maltzan, too, he stubbornly refused to sign. Not that Rathenau was opposed in principle to normalizing relations with Soviet Russia, or that he objected to the development of trade between the two countries: he simply—and rightly—feared the repercussions and reactions in Paris and London. In fact he felt so strongly about this that, had Wirth interfered again, it seems likely that the Foreign Minister would have resigned. But this time Rathenau had it his way. The treaty was to be held up at least until after the Genoa Conference.[2]

Referring to the events in Berlin before the Genoa Conference in an address to the Central Executive Committee several weeks later, Joffe said:

Evidently the European atmosphere and, so to speak, the specific gravity of Russia had at that time still not sufficiently defined themselves for Germany to venture on such an important step.[3]

In fact, neither the European atmosphere nor 'the specific gravity of Russia' had changed when Rathenau signed the treaty ten days later. Bizarre conditions and unpredictable circumstances at Genoa made the whole difference. The statesmen who gathered at Genoa

[1] Scheffer, 'Die Lehren von Rapallo,' pp. 6 f. Cf. M. Boveri, 'Rapallo: Geheimnis—Wunschtraum—Gespenst,' Sonderdruck aus *Merkur*, September 1952, p. 883.

[2] Fischer, *op. cit.*, vol. 1, p. 332. Cf. Scheffer, *loc. cit.*

[3] A. Joffe, *Ot Genui do Gaagi* (Moscow and Petrograd, 1923), p. 16, quoted by Kochan, *Russia and Weimar*, p. 50.

came without ideals, without a clear purpose, and, after excluding the really crucial world problems right at the start, remained to see 'a web of intrigues spun in the main by very small men.'[1] The only tangible result of the conference was the Treaty of Rapallo, and that only served to accentuate the suspicion and distrust amongst the European powers.

Rathenau held out for seven days at Genoa. During that time Lloyd George, who had denied that Russia was his 'pet child' and only interest at the conference, bitterly disappointed Rathenau by forcing him to sit on the sidelines while the British delegation invited the Russians to one secret conclave after another at the Villa d'Albertis. Rumours reached the German delegates in their seclusion that Britain and France were about to make a bargain with the Soviet Government on terms similar to those Radek had threatened several months before, including a revival of Russian claims to reparations under Article 116. The rumours were false, but the bogy of Article 116 had no less of an effect on the Germans than the real thing. Chicherin actually cultivated the fears of the German delegates in order to prepare the way for the final negotiation of the treaty.[2]

The Germans were understandably depressed. They were also divided in their own counsel. Wirth and Maltzan were bent on finding a way to re-engage the negotiations on which such a promising start had been made in Berlin. Rathenau was as eager as they were to break up the private sessions at the Villa d'Albertis, but for different reasons. He still hoped that a *modus vivendi* in reparations could be reached in the discussions between Carl Bergmann and Seydoux, and that at the appropriate moment he would be invited to the Villa d'Albertis to participate in a general Russo-European settlement. But this was a forlorn hope. The German delegates all agreed on only one thing: any bargain between Russia and the Allies would spell disaster for themselves. On the Saturday evening before Easter they were gloomier than ever. Lloyd George had refused to grant Rathenau an audience and rumour had it that the talks with the Russians were on the verge of

---

[1] Oswald Garrison Villard quoted by Löwenstein, *Stresemann: Das deutsche Schicksal im Spiegel seines Lebens*, p. 163.

[2] '. . . Chicherin and Litvinov saw Wirth frequently and gave him an impression of pleasure with the way the pourparlers in the Villa d'Albertis were proceeding': Fischer, *Soviets in World Affairs*, vol. 1, p. 339.

a successful conclusion. It was a most propitious moment for the Russians to finish the work they had started in Berlin. Late at night Rakovsky called Maltzan from Rapallo and suggested that the two delegations meet to negotiate on the following day. Maltzan replied that there was no sense in negotiating since the Soviet delegation had 'already signed with England and France.' 'No, that is not true,' Rakovsky retorted, 'the negotiations are proceeding satisfactorily but no agreement has yet been reached.'[1] It is entirely possible that by this time Maltzan knew that the negotiations at the Villa d'Albertis were not as advanced as the Russians made out, but if he did know he played along with their ruse in order to achieve the goal he shared with them: a Russo-German treaty.[2] Immediately after Rakovsky's call Maltzan informed Rathenau and roused the entire sleeping German delegation, which then convened for what has since become known as the famous 'pyjama party.' Rathenau was elated to hear the Russian offer, but not for the same reason Maltzan was. 'So, now I shall go to Lloyd George and manœuvre the Russians out of the way,' Rathenau said. Perhaps Maltzan had anticipated this reaction. He was Rathenau's subordinate, but he made up with drive and determination what he lacked in rank. The conflict between himself and Rathenau, between the 'Easterners' and the 'Westerners,' now reached a climax: 'Herr Minister,' Maltzan began, 'if you do that I shall immediately hand in my resignation.' Rathenau might have let Maltzan resign if, at that moment, Wirth had not interjected to speak for Maltzan and in favour of meeting the Russians to sign the treaty on the following morning. An argument lasting several hours ensued, but the outcome was in sight right from the start.[3] By dawn Rathenau had been hammered into submission, and at 6.30 that same evening, Easter Sunday, he signed the treaty with the Russians at the Hotel St Margherita in Rapallo.

[1] W. F. von Rheinbaben, 'Deutsche Ostpolitik in Locarno,' *Aussenpolitik* (Stuttgart, January 1953), vol. 4, No. 1, p. 36. Rheinbaben claims that his account of Rapallo is based on private correspondence with Maltzan. Cf. Kessler, *Rathenau*, pp. 319-359, who is said to have written his account from Maltzan's notes. Also cf. Scheffer, 'Die Lehren von Rapallo,' pp. 7 ff. Scheffer was a newspaper correspondent at the Genoa Conference.

[2] See Fischer, *op. cit.*, vol. 1, pp. 339 f.; Wheeler-Bennett, *Nemesis of Power*, p. 125. Cf. the anonymous review of *Nemesis of Power* in *The Times Literary Supplement* (London, 8 January 1954), p. 18.

[3] Rheinbaben, *loc. cit.* Cf. *Stresemann Nachlass*, 7012H/H143749/55.

With this treaty Russia and Germany cleaned the slate of all the claims and counter-claims that had accumulated since Brest-Litovsk. The Damoclean sword of Article 116 was swept away from above the heads of the Germans by Article 1 of the treaty, in which both countries renounced all claims for debt and damage compensation, with the single proviso (Article 2) that Germany could bring up the question of Russian debts if the Soviet Government satisfied similar claims of other states. The treaty also provided for the immediate resumption of diplomatic and consular relations on a normal footing (Article 3) to replace the exchange of representatives under the agreement of 6 May 1921, and guaranteed preferential treatment by both countries of the citizens of the other country, especially in regard 'to trade and other economic matters' in which each country granted the other treatment as the most favoured nation (Articles 3 and 4). Article 5 was crucial from the Soviet viewpoint. By it both governments agreed 'to meet the economic requirements of both countries in a spirit of goodwill,' which meant that 'in the event of this question being settled in principle on an international basis, they will enter into a previous exchange of opinions with each other.' The German Government also promised to 'support and facilitate' the work of private firms that signed contracts with the Soviet Government.[1]

The Treaty of Rapallo was not a grand alliance. But it was a major accomplishment for both countries. Russia was assured that Germany would not be a party to any international consortium to exploit the Soviet economy, while the reaffirmation of *de jure* recognition of the Soviet Government coupled with a promise of closer economic relations constituted a breach in the wall of economic and political ostracism which had heretofore isolated the Soviet Republic. Russia gained in Germany a *point d'appui*, a foothold in the enemy's camp. Germany, on the other hand, was assured of advantages in commercial relations with Russia, escaped from the threats of Article 116 and complete encirclement, and gained an alliance against the Versailles powers which held out hope for a revision of the Eastern frontiers.

More important than the formal contents of the treaty was the fact that Germany and Russia had dared to sign it. Although the German Government later claimed that it had kept London in-

---

[1] For the Treaty of Rapallo see *Dokumente der deutschen Politik und Geschichte*, vol. 3, pp. 126 f.

formed of the negotiations right up to the last moment, the treaty came as a complete surprise to all the nations gathered at Genoa.[1] Lloyd George was beside himself with agitation. The Germans had copied his own methods and had effectively frustrated his attempts to come to terms with Russia behind Germany's back. Seen from London and Paris this was more than an exhibition of bad international manners; it was a bold and immoral move, bolder and more immoral than the Germans had any right to be so soon after suffering defeat. On Easter Sunday night, only hours after the treaty was signed, Lord Hankey registered an official British protest, and for weeks afterwards the Germans were made to suffer the indignant wrath of outwitted statesmen. Accusations of bad faith were more than Rathenau could bear. At first he was despondent. To his mother he wrote: 'Today, on Easter Sunday I made an excursion to Rapallo. The details are in the newspaper.'[2] As more and more criticism was levelled at him Rathenau became almost frantic and inflicted himself with unusual sarcasm and passionate vindictiveness on those around him. Maltzan, who on later occasions admitted he 'raped' Rathenau at Rapallo, was the chief victim of his choler. But Rathenau's sarcasm was lost on the phlegmatic Hasse, who was in Genoa as Seeckt's observer. When Rathenau said he hoped his Eastern policy would please Seeckt, Hasse took the gibe literally and, by recording it in his diary, gave rise to the myth that Rathenau had fallen under the spell of the Maltzan-Seeckt policies and expected salvation from the East.[3] Far from expecting a happy deliverance, Rathenau was so completely terrified by the possible consequences of what he had signed that he actually approached Chicherin to ask if the Bolsheviks would agree to annul the treaty. Chicherin was unwilling, of course, but he offered to help Rathenau by drawing the Allied wrath on to the Soviet delegation—a difficult project which Chicherin failed to carry out.[4]

In Berlin as elsewhere in Germany the treaty had a generally favourable reception. People were relieved that the threat of Article

[1] Scheffer, 'Die Lehren von Rapallo,' p. 6.
[2] *Walter Rathenau Briefe*, vol. 2, p. 348. The letter is misdated 19.4.1922 instead of 16.4.1922.
[3] Hallgarten accepts this allegation against Rathenau. See 'Seeckt and Russia,' p. 32.
[4] Fischer, *Soviets in World Affairs*, vol. 2, p. 591.

116 had been removed, and they were proud that Germany had successfully completed an important and independent act of foreign policy. This treaty, the first Germany entered into after Versailles, gave promise of a more active foreign policy in the future. The distress of the Allies only added spice to the success, although there was widespread fear of reprisals, especially from France. Some people had other reservations, among them President Ebert. Ebert had been kept in the dark about the negotiations until the last moment, and then only reluctantly assented to the treaty when Wirth consulted him by long-distance telephone from Genoa. He was surprised and embittered by Wirth, who, in Ebert's opinion, had overstepped the bounds of his authority by not consulting the President before agreeing to meet the Russians at Rapallo.[1] Furthermore, Ebert distrusted the Russians and felt that it was a mistake to anger the Allied powers when Germany's future largely depended on their goodwill, even if one was sceptical of it.

Ebert fell in with those critics of Rapallo who were of the opinion that it should either not have been signed at all, or that it was at least a year premature. There were other critics who said that the treaty had come three and a half years too late, 'a similar agreement signed in December 1918 would have given Germany's domestic and foreign policies a different complexion.'[2] The dissenters were mostly on the Left wing of German politics. In the Reichstag debate on the Genoa Conference the USPD attacked the Rapallo treaty as 'capitalist orientated policy,' a betrayal of socialism. The SPD was less critical. Its spokesman welcomed the 'new active German policy,' but the party was uneasy about a one-sided orientation and urged the government to make new efforts to reach agreements with the West. Most of the deputies agreed with Wirth when he said that, by 'inserting Article 116 in the Versailles treaty, the Entente made it necessary for us to reach a direct settlement with Russia.'[3] The German Communists, however, did not know what line to adopt; they had apparently not

---

[1] F. Stampfer, *Die vierzehn Jahre der ersten deutschen Republik* (Karlsbad, 1936), p. 270; H. Holborn, 'Diplomats and Diplomacy in the Early Weimar Republic' in *The Diplomats*, p. 170; Eyck, *Geschichte der Weimarer Republik*, p. 282.

[2] A. Rosenberg, *Geschichte der Deutschen Republik* (Karlsbad, 1935), p. 130.

[3] Speech in the Reichstag on 29 May 1922, *Joseph Wirth: Reden Wahrend der Kanzlerschaft* (Berlin, 1925), pp. 337 ff.

been told. The independent KAPD attacked the treaty as a Bolshevik capitulation to German counter-revolution, while Paul Fröhlich, speaking for the KPD, minimized the importance of Rapallo and then levelled a bitter attack on the USPD and SPD for following policies which, he insisted, compelled the Russians to sign a treaty with a bourgeois state.[1] The Right-wing parties unanimously acclaimed the accomplishments of the Genoa delegation. Nothing said in open debate substantiates Lord D'Abernon's assertion: 'It is generally acknowledged that the German delegation . . . committed a serious blunder.' D'Abernon's closest contacts on the Right were members of Stresemann's DVP, but it is doubtful indeed that conversations with these nationalists could have led him to conclude: 'Rapallo is not regarded with much favour here.'[2] Stresemann himself was certainly for the treaty. He had taken the precaution of sending von Raumer, one of the ablest and cleverest members of the DVP, to Genoa. Although von Raumer was not an official delegate, he played a key role in supporting Maltzan and the treaty.[3] On the day the treaty was signed von Raumer cabled to Stresemann:

In accordance with your last speech in the Reichstag I decided to use my influence in favour of a treaty with the Russians which cancels out Article 116 of the peace treaty and gives us preference over all other powers in Russia. Please influence our press to approve the treaty.[4]

Stresemann himself came out in favour of the treaty, principally because it removed the threat of Article 116 and precluded an encirclement of Germany.[5]

The treaty came as a shock to Seeckt. He had not expected it. In fact, when the Genoa Conference began he thought there was a

---

[1] *Verhandlungen des Reichstags 1922* (Berlin, 1923), vol. 355, pp. 7675 ff. For the KAPD and the VKPD reactions to the treaty also see Carr, vol. 3, pp. 414 f. Cf. R. Fischer, *Stalin and German Communism*, p. 193.

[2] D'Abernon, *Ambassador of Peace*, vol. 1, p. 298.

[3] Dirksen, *Moskau-Tokio-London*, p. 46; Scheffer, 'Die Lehren von Rapallo,' p. 10.

[4] *Stresemann Nachlass*, 7009H/H143326. Stresemann and the DVP had a controlling influence over the editorial policies of at least ten major German newspapers; see Bretton, *Stresemann and Versailles*, pp. 32 ff.

[5] See the correspondence in the *Stresemann Nachlass*, 7900H/H143275-H143411 *passim*. Ludendorff wrote to Stresemann that he was against the treaty: 'Through this Rapallo [*sic*] Treaty we are becoming ever more Russia's domain' (*ibid.*, 7002H/H142427).

good chance that the Russians would sign with the French. Immediately after the signing Hasse rushed to Konstanz, where Seeckt was celebrating his birthday, to tell his chief the good news. Both men realized that Rapallo was a major step in the direction of the foreign policy Seeckt had been working for since 1919. Although the army had nothing to do with negotiating the treaty, Seeckt was instantly aware of the possibilities of exploiting it to achieve his own ends. Only a few hours after the terms of the treaty were announced, even before Hasse arrived at Konstanz, rumours were spreading that a secret military alliance had also been signed at Rapallo. Western statesmen and editors were so badly shaken by the treaty that they completely lost their heads. All sorts of outlandish stories were spread, some going so far as to suggest that a new triple alliance between Russia, Germany, and Turkey had been signed and that war would break out in a matter of weeks.[1] Seeckt's reaction to these wild allegations pays tribute to his daring and shows that he was a master of political opportunism. Instead of hotly denying the allegations, which is what a less discerning man in his position would have done, he shrewdly turned the vapourings of Germany's 'oppressors' to Germany's advantage. 'I do not look to the formal contents of the treaty, but rather at its moral effect,' Seeckt wrote. 'It is the first but a very substantial strengthening of German influence in the world. The reason for this is that more is suspected behind it than is actually justified.' No military agreement was signed, Seeckt continued, 'but the existence of one is believed in. Is it to our interest to destroy this far-fetched illusion?' No, he continued, answering his own question, 'it is far better to have unreasonable people believe in it.' If the Western press wanted to deceive and horrify its readers Seeckt was content to let them continue. But while the spectre of Rapallo was allowed to outgrow the actual contents of the treaty, Seeckt made up his mind to exploit the agreement in order to arrange precisely that alliance with the Russians which would justify Western fears. 'Our aim,' he wrote, 'must certainly be to reach an agreement [with the Russians] that will guarantee us support. I will do anything to achieve this, but until it is accomplished appearances must help us. Our power is small. The eyes of our enemies must magnify it.'[2]

---

[1] Dennis, *Foreign Policies of Soviet Russia*, p. 428; Wheeler-Bennett, *Nemesis of Power*, p. 131.

[2] Rabenau, *Seeckt*, vol. 2, p. 313.

When he met Wirth on 31 May, Seeckt congratulated him on the treaty but bluntly asserted that it was only a first step; Russo-German collaboration in the military field had still to be achieved. Rapallo, Seeckt said, is not enough. Wirth agreed. He was already deeply implicated in the rearmament conspiracy and did not now want to back out of it. But the Chancellor did not possess the indomitable will which drove Seeckt ahead. Moreover, he feared the political consequences that would follow any exposure of the military negotiations. He warned Seeckt that Ebert had found out about Radek's secret talks with Reichswehr officials and that he would undoubtedly oppose them with all the authority vested in the President's office if he heard they were continuing. The military negotiations, Wirth said, should be suspended, at least until after the Reichstag ratified the Rapallo treaty. He recalled that one leak about the talks had already taken place and warned against risking another at such a crucial time, for there was no telling what might happen if the socialists heard that there were plans afoot for a military alliance with Soviet Russia.[1] Wirth asked Seeckt to stop negotiating as long as the Rapallo treaty was in the headlines. In the meantime, if the Reichswehr wanted to serve its own cause it should lobby for the treaty in Right-wing circles, where it could be most effective.

Seeckt was impatient with Wirth's advice. He agreed to air his support of the treaty in nationalist circles, but thought this superfluous since the real danger to the treaty, and to military co-operation with Russia, stemmed from the Left. The Left, he said, would never be reconciled to a strong Reichswehr and would always be on the look-out for ways to discredit it. Since the danger of discovery would not diminish with time, why, Seeckt wanted to know, should they waste time? Whether or not Seeckt persuaded Wirth to his point of view is not clear, but it is not really important either. Seeckt was not dependent on Wirth's approval. On 25 May, six days before he talked to the Chancellor, Hasse had already resumed the negotiations with Krestinski in Berlin. The details of these talks have never been revealed, but their purpose

[1] The leak Wirth referred to occurred on 4 April 1922 when, in a conference between himself and Chicherin, the Soviet Foreign Minister—who should not have assumed that Wirth knew about the collaboration—openly stated that German officers had started to work in Russia: Hallgarten, 'Seeckt and Russia,' pp. 31 f.

was to arrange more German rearmament projects in Russia on the model of the Junkers agreement. The Rapallo treaty had stimulated interest in these ventures among certain Ruhr industrialists, who were now more willing to invest in rearmament.[1] The negotiations proceeded smoothly. At the beginning of July a Russian agent, going by the name of Rosenblatt, was received by Seeckt in Berlin, and on 29 July an agreement was signed 'in deepest secrecy.'[2] Since this document has not been located one can only conjecture about its contents. In all likelihood it covered various industrial undertakings in the rearmament field on Soviet territory, including Junkers, also the joint-stock company *Bersol*, which manufactured poison gases, and Krupps, which manufactured artillery munitions, grenades, and possibly tanks.[3] Shortly afterwards Tschunke started to organize the projects in detail through the Berlin and Moscow offices of GEFU.

A related but separate agreement between the general staffs of the two armies was worked out in Berlin at the same time. On 11 August Seeckt sent either Niedermayer or Nicolai to Moscow to sign the document.[4] It was the product of a series of negotiations, starting with Lenin's request in March 1921 for German officers to train Russian men, which was pressed by Radek when he talked to Seeckt in February 1922.[5] Considerably more is known about this agreement, including the conditions on which the Reichswehr agreed to mutual co-operation between the military establishments. In an outline of their own requirements the Germans said they wanted facilities

(1) to gain a continuous theoretical orientation in regard to tactics, training and the technical sciences for a military force whose development would not be hindered by outside interference;

(2) to engage in practical experimentation and testing in the sphere of forbidden weapons for the purpose of gaining training and tactical experience;

(3) to educate highly qualified personnel in the use of these weapons, with the purpose of training specialists who will both continue the practical development of these weapons and, perhaps later, become a nucleus for the further development and production of the same weapons in Germany;

---

[1] *Ibid.*, p. 32.     [2] *Ibid.*     [3] See below, p. 211.
[4] Hallgarten, *loc. cit.*; H. Rosinski, *The German Army* (London, 1939), p. 194.
[5] See above, pp. 109, 111-113.

(4) to engage in technical testing in order to give new weapons both technical and practical trials under battle conditions, so as to enhance and verify theoretical and technical developments in Germany;

(5) to develop a theoretical foundation on the basis of practical experience with technical and tactical matters, for the purpose of planning modern recruitment and training procedures.[1]

The Germans made three specific requests of the Red Army. First, they wanted military bases put at their disposal for the use of air force, motorized corps (*Panzer*), and gas-warfare units. Second, they wanted permission to use these bases for technical testing and for training purposes. And third, they wanted a free exchange of information and discoveries in the military field. The Soviet Government granted all three requests in the agreement of August 1922. In return the Russians were to receive annual financial compensation for the use of the bases and were to be given every opportunity of benefiting from the theoretical, technical, and tactical knowledge gained by the Germans in the course of their work in Russia. Red Army and Red Air Force personnel were to have free access to the German bases, and German officers and technicians were to be assigned to instruct Red officers and train Red pilots and engineers. In this way the partners hoped to benefit from one another in the fields of their greatest need.[2] At first the agreements were perforce only of a general kind; the ways and means by which the collaboration was to be carried out could only

[1] Speidel, 'Reichswehr und Rote Armee,' p. 18.

[2] Speidel declares that the tempo of negotiations accelerated after Rapallo but denies that a military agreement was signed in 1922 (*ibid.*, p. 17). This assertion contradicts the evidence Hallgarten found in Hasse's diary ('Seeckt and Russia,' p. 32). The truth of the matter may be pointed to by Rosengolts' testimony in the purge trials of 1938. He testified that the military agreement between 'Trotsky' and the Reichswehr was put into effect in 1923 (*Report of Court Proceedings in the Case of the Anti-Soviet 'Bloc of Rights and Trotskyites'* (Moscow, 1938), pp. 259 f., 265). Gessler's statement to the Reichstag in 1926 (see above, p. 92 n. 3) suggests that military agreements were signed and put into effect in the summer of 1922, but not ratified by the Soviet Government until February 1923. In Berlin, Brig.-General J. H. Morgan, of the Military Control Commission, repeatedly told the British Ambassador that German officers were active in Russia, but D'Abernon put no faith in these reports, preferring to believe Maltzan, who 'formally and deliberately' denied the charge. 'The truth is that the military class in Germany is too violently anti-communistic,' D'Abernon concluded without understanding either the German military or the Communists (*Ambassador of Peace*, vol. 1, pp. 303 f., 312).

crystallize as they were put into practice by Special Group R in Berlin and by Niedermayer at the head of the Moscow Central Office, together with responsible officers of the Red Army and Red Air Force, and officials of the Commissariats of War and Foreign Affairs. Although Trotsky and Chicherin did not concern themselves with the details of the organization, both men, as well as other Soviet civilian authorities, including the GPU, kept abreast of the developments. Trotsky was directly involved on a number of occasions when he helped to resolve problems that threatened to disrupt the relationship.[1] On the German side, Seeckt initiated the agreements and also took the responsibility for implementing them, but the ramifications of the work required not only tacit support from reliable civilian authorities, such as Wirth, Maltzan, and officials of the Finance Ministry, but also active co-operation with executive offices of the government, including the Foreign Ministry. The construction and development of bases in Russia, the divisions of responsibility for testing weapons and training men, the domestic and financial provisioning, and, not least important, the working out of a chain of command for the military and civilian personnel involved, required a completely thought-out and detailed plan of operation which the German military could not implement by themselves. The political factors involved and the requirement of maintaining strict secrecy in regard to the entire operation led to 'a complicated and, for the uninitiated, an impenetrable combination of military leadership and civilian camouflage.'[2] At every stage of this delicate and secret operation Seeckt had willing help from civilian authorities. But he wanted the civilians to be docile and silent partners. Instead, as things worked out time and again, the methods and even the plans of the Reichswehr were challenged by obstreperous civilians who refused to abandon their bureaucratic ways and to abdicate their authority to Seeckt and his lieutenants. Needless to say, this experience did nothing to warm Seeckt's feelings for democratic procedures. He never accepted the Weimar Republic as more than a temporary and convenient façade for the reconstruction of a military-monarchical state, and remained implacably opposed to the democratic corollary that military establishments must be subordinate to political control. Seeckt considered his authority to extend to many matters that only a military man would reserve for the

[1] See below, p. 195 and Appendix B.    [2] Speidel, *op. cit.*, p. 19.

military domain and met every challenge to his authority and plans with the instinct and relentless fury of an eagle fighting to protect its young. He never compromised and, significantly, lost only one major battle as long as he headed the army.

That lone battle was fought soon after the Rapallo treaty was ratified, at a moment when the military negotiations of the summer of 1922 were making progress and showing every sign of success. The trouble was entirely of Seeckt's making. He carried a personal grudge against Count Brockdorff-Rantzau to such an extreme that he jeopardized the entire military connexion with Soviet Russia.

It had been agreed at Rapallo that full diplomatic relations should be resumed at the earliest opportunity. Krestinski presented his credentials as Russian Ambassador to Ebert late in August 1922, but the corresponding German appointment was held up by difficulties over the choice of a suitable person. At first there were three candidates. By July two of these, Hintze and Nadolny, were out of the running; the former because the SPD and USPD considered him reactionary, the latter because he was ruled *persona non grata* by the Soviet Government.[1] Only Brockdorff-Rantzau remained as an active candidate, but his nomination was not assured. In the opinion of many people Brockdorff-Rantzau was the right man to serve in Moscow. The Bolsheviks considered him entirely acceptable, both because of his record of support for their activities during the World War and because he came from the circle of the high nobility and would add prestige to the Leninist regime.[2] In Germany the Count had the unswerving support of President Ebert, with whom he had remained in close contact during his retirement after Versailles, and of Maltzan, who had the highest respect for him. Scheidemann and an assortment of socialist leaders, Right-wing adherents, including Gustav Stresemann, and the entire royalist element—not excluding Prinz Heinrich xxxiii Reus j.l.—also supported his candidacy.[3]

---

[1] Blücher, *Deutschlands Weg Nach Rapallo*, pp. 166 f.

[2] Hallgarten, *op. cit.*, p. 32; and see above, p. 89.

[3] Stern-Rubarth, *Graf Brockdorff-Rantzau* (Berlin, 1929), pp. 123, 141; Hilger, *Incompatible Allies*, p. 90. Although Stresemann supported Brockdorff-Rantzau's candidacy, he was unenthusiastic at first because, he wrote, the Count is 'very nervous' and 'incapable of living without nicotine.' He did not object to the Count's drinking as much as he was wont to do, presumably because he himself was given to do the same. See the exchange of letters between Stresemann and Prinz Heinrich in the *Stresemann Nachlass*, 7001H/H141209-H141981 *passim*.

It is clear that Brockdorff-Rantzau wanted the post. German-Russian relations preoccupied his political correspondence long before the Rapallo treaty was signed, and although he was of the opinion that the delegation had acted precipitately and unnecessarily denigrated Germany's reputation with the Allies at Genoa, he was prepared to carry out the treaty to the letter. On 8 July the Count sent a memorandum to Ebert in which he outlined his conception of the job confronting the German Ambassador to Moscow, emphasizing the importance of developing trade relations between the countries.[1] In private conversations with the President, Brockdorff-Rantzau said he would not accept a position subordinate to the Foreign Minister as long as that office was filled by Walter Rathenau. He admitted that Rathenau was brilliant, but considered him erratic and lacking in political sense. The arrogant Count insisted that, if he was appointed Ambassador to Russia, Ebert should make him directly responsible to the President's office instead of to the Foreign Ministry, and he also demanded a free hand in choosing a staff for the Moscow Embassy.[2] These outrageous demands did not make it easier for Ebert to effect his appointment, but the most extraordinary part of the story is that Brockdorff-Rantzau had his way, even though his demands were constitutionally untenable. There were, however, still other obstacles to his appointment and these proved to be the most difficult to overcome. Both Chancellor Wirth and Seeckt were opposed to sending Brockdorff-Rantzau to Moscow. Wirth did not even want to discuss the matter, but upon Ebert's insistence finally had an interview with the Count on 11 July. The former school teacher and the haughty aristocrat did not get along well together. Wirth tried to discourage the Count from seeking the appointment; he did not like the idea of sending someone to Moscow over whom he could exercise no control, and, moreover, knew that Seeckt considered Brockdorff-Rantzau an enemy of an Eastern orientation.[3]

[1] The entire memorandum is quoted by Helbig, 'Moskauer Mission Brockdorff-Rantzaus,' pp. 329 ff.

[2] Hilger, *Incompatible Allies*, pp. 93 f. Brockdorff-Rantzau continued to press these conditions even after Rathenau's assassination, showing that the real motivation of them was his sensitive and towering pride which would not allow him, a former Foreign Minister, to serve under any Foreign Minister—regardless how capable he might be.

[3] Helbig, *op. cit.*, p. 305. Wirth took over the Foreign Minister's portfolio as well after Rathenau's assassination on 24 June 1922.

But the Count could not be discouraged. He took an immediate dislike to Wirth and considered him a schemer in the tradition of Erzberger, the most damning charge Brockdorff-Rantzau could make against any man.

On 24 July, shortly after the Soviet Government had responded to Ebert's informal enquiry that it would gladly welcome the Count as Ambassador, Wirth was forced formally to offer him the post. The Chancellor used the occasion to expound his own foreign policy. While Brockdorff-Rantzau listened in silent amazement Wirth exclaimed that his own policies were often misunderstood, he did not believe in 'fulfilment' at all: 'The only chance I see for us to rise again as a great power is for the German and Russian people to work together as neighbours in friendship and understanding.' For this reason, the Chancellor continued, he signed the Rapallo treaty. He regretted that there were people in Germany —mostly socialists—who opposed the treaty, and who campaigned with the slogan 'No more war.' 'I do not share their viewpoint,' Wirth declared, 'and there is one thing I can tell you point-blank: Poland has to be destroyed. My policy is directed at this goal. . . . On this point I am in complete accord with the military, especially with General von Seeckt.'[1] Wirth's bluntness astounded Brockdorff-Rantzau. In the further course of the discussion he discovered that the Minister of War, Gessler, was uninformed about Wirth's and Seeckt's political plans, but that various members of the nationalist parties—the names of Stinnes, Raumer, and Hoetzsch were mentioned—knew about them and approved. Although a one-sided Eastern orientation did not agree with his own conception of German policy as he had outlined it in his memorandum of 8 July, the Count did not demur and accepted the ambassadorship. It was agreed that the official announcement should be withheld until the completion of the new round of reparations negotiations then going on in London and Paris.[2]

In any case, the appointment of an ambassador to Moscow seemed to be settled. Quite unexpectedly, however, the issue was suddenly complicated anew. Seeckt took advantage of the delay in the official announcement to sabotage Brockdorff-Rantzau's appointment. He urged Wirth to rescind his offer, accusing Brockdorff-Rantzau of having been 'unpatriotic' at Versailles and calling him a 'pacifist' unworthy of the Moscow post.[3] When he

[1] Helbig, *op. cit.*, p. 306.　　　　[2] *Ibid.*　　　　[3] *Ibid.*, p. 307.

E

heard of Seeckt's activities against him Brockdorff-Rantzau reacted
in a number of ways, at times feigning disinterest in the post—at
least until his 'sacrifice' in going to Moscow was generally acknowledged—and at other times sulking like an unwanted child. But he
could also rise to heights of passionate indignation, and in one of
these moods he wrote a furious memorandum attacking what he
thought to be Seeckt's and Wirth's aims in Russia. By the middle
of August he was, in fact, quite sure that Seeckt and Wirth were
plotting a military alliance with Russia to start a war against Poland
and also against the Allies. His anxiety reached a new pitch when,
in another conversation with the Chancellor, he learned of the
secret Reichswehr-Red Army collaboration. To the direct question
of whether Ebert was informed of these schemes, Wirth replied
that he alone was taking the political responsibility; Ebert would
not support an active German policy. For Brockdorff-Rantzau this
was the last straw. He considered the Reichswehr-Red Army
connexion dangerous and the plans for a military alliance foolhardy
—and he attacked both schemes all the more because Seeckt, who
hated him, was behind them—but he would not even countenance
a policy that was being conducted behind Ebert's back. In a state
of great agitation he set down his views in a *Promemoria* which he
intended to submit to Ebert.

Before examining the *Promemoria* itself it is necessary to have a
clear understanding of the circumstances in which it was written,
otherwise one is likely to draw unwarranted conclusions about
Brockdorff-Rantzau's own views. Because it was written in the
heat of a bitter dispute, Brockdorff-Rantzau undoubtedly over-
stated his real opinions, inflating the issues with every pin-prick
administered to his ballooning pride. The *Promemoria* considers
German policies chiefly from the military standpoint. It cannot,
therefore, be interpreted as a considered and balanced statement of
the Count's policy, but rather as a personal attack on Seeckt, and also
on Wirth. After all, the entire episode occurred only because Seeckt
and Brockdorff-Rantzau carried a bitter personal dispute dating
from the war on to the centre of the stage in 1922. Their childish
anxiety to heap vindictive abuse on one another transformed what
was essentially a personal squabble into an immensely interesting
debate of German Foreign Policy, and today this debate is much
more significant than the battle of personalities it once barely
glossed over. This is not to say that there were no genuine differences

of opinion between Seeckt and Brockdorff-Rantzau. These existed, but they were exaggerated by both antagonists and have repeatedly been magnified and overcoloured by historians who have not given adequate consideration to all the relevant sources. Thus, although Brockdorff-Rantzau was not prepared in the summer of 1922 to support a military alliance with Russia, neither was he an advocate of a Western orientation—as at least one noted authority on Weimar has declared.[1]

One of Brockdorff-Rantzau's favourite sayings, which he often repeated in the summer of 1922, was: 'Our debts to the Allies cannot be paid in gold and silver, our account can only be settled with iron.' He was not a warmonger, but, on the other hand, his only reason for opposing a military alliance with Russia was that it would cement relations between Britain and France, while he wanted to split the Allied powers. Brockdorff-Rantzau was, in fact, in that long and growing procession of Germans who during the post-Versailles years had their eyes on Britain and hoped to gain her support against the menacing policies of France. However, there is no reason to believe—although it has become conventional to do so—that Brockdorff-Ranzau any more than Grand Admiral von Tirpitz wanted Germany to ingratiate herself with Britain in the long run; it was a tactical expedient and required no reversal of the Rapallo policy. He was and remained to his dying day a passionate enemy of both Britain and France. In 1922 his fear of a military alignment with Soviet Russia was provoked by the even greater fear that, if a military pact were signed, the Russians could blackmail Germany by threatening to reveal it, and that if it were revealed Germany's chances of taking revenge for the humiliation of Versailles would be ruined. This analysis of the Count's outlook is not contradicted by the views he expressed in the *Promemoria*, from which extensive quotations appear below, and is substantiated by his advice gradually to broaden and improve relations with the Bolsheviks, which we shall consider later:

*Secret!*                                    *Promemoria*[2]

An Eastern orientation and a Western orientation have become abstract concepts for German policy since the defeat in the World War

[1] Cf. Holborn, 'Diplomacy in the Early Weimar Republic' in *The Diplomats*, *passim* but especially pp. 159 f.

[2] The complete *Promemoria*, correctly dated 15 August 1922, was published for the first time by Helbig, *op. cit.*, pp. 331 ff. Helbig also shows (*ibid.*, pp. 302 f.

and are no longer positive alternatives, at least not in the sense of an exclusive attachment in one direction. . . .

It is too early for a German statesman to conduct an active policy of alliances; but he has to consider the possibility of doing so at a later time. . . .

Any appearance of a military alliance on our part with the East would have the most detrimental effect on our relations with the West. We dare not ignore this fact under any circumstances, especially not in regard to England, considering the constricted position in which we find ourselves, and in the face of the obscurity and uncertainty of conditions in Russia.

In view of present-day arms developments England is no longer an island state; for the same reason France is a threat to her. She [England] must therefore seek allies, and one thing is certain: she will always look for allies *against* France as long as no combinations develop which keep England and France together or bring them together again. A German-Russian alliance would represent such a combination. . . . If Germany were to form a military alliance with Russia, the alliance could not become operative until much later on; in the meantime we would run the risk of being crushed ourselves. Therefore, our tactics in the military sphere should have as their aim that England solicits, and must solicit, an alliance with us.

The great drawback of the Rapallo treaty is in the military fears attached to it. Lloyd George expressed these apprehensions in a recent speech in which he said that the peace of the world was seriously endangered by a hungry Russia 'equipped' by a Germany thirsting for vengeance. Therefore, we must reckon with the fact that England suspects us of preparing for revenge together with Russia, and that she [England] is in a position, in the event such agreements have been made or are coming into being, to make us regret them.

The objection that, as a price for deliverance from our desperate situation, we must take this risk, is understandable and would be justified if such action were to vouchsafe success. That, however, is not the case. The enterprise would much more likely be doomed to failure. The reasons for this are to be found both on the German and the Russian side.

Here the socialist parties, and with them large segments of the population, would reject such a policy; an attempt to carry it out would, therefore, inevitably bring about the most serious internal political up-

n. 32) how Julius Epstein's sensationalist article 'Der Seeckt-Plan' (*Der Monat*, 1. Jhrg. (Berlin, November 1948), pp. 42 ff.), which includes a truncated version of the *Promemoria* and Seeckt's reply (see below, p. 135), misdating the former, misled Wheeler-Bennett (*Nemesis of Power*, pp. 133 ff.) and Carr (vol. 3, pp. 438 f.) to misdate the document and to misinterpret Brockdorff-Rantzau's views.

heavals. And as far as Russia is concerned, it is an illusion to believe that it would be possible to engage in a 'Bismarckpolitik' with her today, in the sense given to 'Bismarckpolitik' by the people who utter this slogan at every appropriate and inappropriate opportunity. Russia is no longer the Empire of Czar Alexander I and Nicholas I, and the suppositions on which we have to base our policy with Russia are almost diametrically opposed to those of the Bismarck period. The relations of the two countries are no longer determined by the will of their rulers, rather through the people.

There was a time when Germany and Russia were good neighbours; to the detriment of the interests of both peoples they parted ways. But in the need which fate has bestowed on them they want to come together again to work in common. This work must serve the goals of peace and economic reconstruction. That does not exclude taking precautions in good time, and, in the event of compelling necessity, taking into account still other associations. . . .

A German policy orientated exclusively towards the East would at the present moment be not only precipitate and dangerous, but without prospect and, therefore, a mistake. The policy is precipitate because we are, like the Russians, economically not yet in a position to risk such an experiment. It is dangerous because by agreements which bind us militarily we are giving ourselves into the power of the utterly unscrupulous Soviet Government. . . . The policy is hopeless because, in the event of Russia attacking Poland—and this is the only serious consideration—we would be almost defenceless in the West against a French invasion.

Even if the Russians were to succeed in overrunning Poland, we would be surrendering Germany as a battle ground for the conflict between the East and the West, because we would never be able to protect our Western frontier, and it is sheer utopia to assume that in the face of France's unlimited numerical and technical superiority in the military sphere we could hold the Western frontier until the arrival of the Russians, quite irrespective of the dubious pleasure of having to welcome these Red allies in our own country. They are not coming to our support in the struggle for liberation against the Entente, but to extend the frontiers of Asia to the Rhine. The moment Britain sees us advancing hand in glove with the Bolsheviks, she, too, will certainly intervene.

In my opinion the objective of German policy should be to hold the Russians back from war-like experiments, to which they may easily resort as the only way out if their internal situation deteriorates further for lack of aid from the Entente.

If it should come to war, our leading statesmen will have to labour diligently to keep us out of the conflict. If we succeed in remaining neutral, then, in the event Poland collapses, there is a chance that we shall win back Upper Silesia and perhaps also other territories in the East that were torn away from the Reich. If the Soviet army is defeated —which is by no means out of the question if the Polish forces are led by outstanding French staff officers—then Russia will be faced with further serious internal disruptions which would bring a change of regime well within the bounds of possibility.

In view of both possibilities we have every reason not to bind ourselves militarily at present, especially in view of the likelihood that we shall automatically enjoy the benefits of a formal agreement, because Russia would not stand idly by and watch France and her allies attacking our frontiers, but would in all probability intervene spontaneously, hoping to take advantage of chaos in Germany. . . .

I am not advocating resignation, I am only counselling against haste. The present situation cannot last and demands action. If the Entente remains blind, if it does not decide to change its ways and listen to the voice of reason, if it harasses the German people and drives them into complete despair, then the catastrophe is unavoidable. And this catastrophe must not find us unprepared. Whoever would destroy the German people must realize that he is gambling with his own existence.

Since Versailles I have thought of nothing else than how we can obtain justice or, if necessary, win it. The seeds of revenge were sown at Versailles, and our enemies bear the unexpiable blame if this seed is not extirpated. If the gentlemen in Paris and London really want to challenge fate and destroy Germany, then let them realize that 60 million people will not simply give themselves over to the hangman nor freely commit suicide; then they shall have chaos, and they themselves will be dragged into it.

Brockdorff-Rantzau handed the *Promemoria* to Wirth and said he would accept the post in Moscow only if the Chancellor approved the policy outlined in it and forced Seeckt to give a written undertaking not to carry on independent relations with the Soviet Government. Furthermore, he said he would inform Ebert about the military collaboration with the Bolsheviks, because 'it is out of the question that I should support or carry out a policy which he would consider notorious and damnable.' Wirth was alarmed. 'The President,' he said, 'does not have to be informed,' and the matter had now gone too far for Brockdorff-Rantzau to reject the portfolio.[1] In the end the Count did give a copy of his *Promemoria* to Ebert, but when the latter asked if this polemic was directed

[1] Helbig, *op. cit.*, p. 309.

against a theoretical military policy or against one that was already being effected, Brockdorff-Rantzau answered evasively. He did not betray Wirth's secret. Meanwhile Wirth had sent a copy of the memorandum to Seeckt. Two days later Seeckt sent Wirth a counter-blast totalling twelve handwritten pages, of which the following are important extracts:

### Germany's Attitude to the Russian Problem[1]

Germany must pursue an *active policy*. Every State must do that. The moment it stops pursuing an active policy it ceases to be a State. An active policy must have a goal and a driving force. To carry it out it is essential to assess one's own strength correctly and at the same time to understand the methods and aims of the other powers.

He who bases his political ideas on the weakness of his own country, who sees only dangers, or whose *only* desire is to remain stationary, follows no policy and should be kept far away from the scene of activity. . . .

Have not Germany's first stirrings in active politics, the Treaty of Rapallo, clearly brought her at last nearer to being more respected?

This treaty splits opinions into different camps when the Russian problem is considered. The main point about it is not its economic value, though that is by no means inconsiderable, but its political impact. This association between Germany and Russia is the first and almost the only accretion of power which we have obtained since peace was made. That this association should begin in the field of economics is a natural consequence of the general situation; but its strength lies in the fact that this economic *rapprochement* is preparing the way for the *possibility* of a political and thus also a military association. It cannot be doubted that such a double association strengthens Germany—and also Russia. Now, there are German politicians who fear such an increase of power. They see in the symptoms of a political, military, and economic revival of Germany, and in an active German policy, the danger of renewed and intensified counter-measures on the part of our Western enemies. They are thus confronted with the question, which they prefer not to answer, of whether they should face East or West. This question, however, has in fact not arisen at all. It is best here to avoid misleading parallels with Bismarck's policy, and merely to extract from it for ourselves the principle of at all times following a German policy, that is, to examine on the assumption that every country is pursuing a policy of self-interest, how these interests of the others can be exploited for the benefit of our own

---

[1] *Heeresarchiv*: Seeckt, Stück 213, Karton 15. The memorandum is subtitled: 'Reply to a Pro Memoria from Count Br.-R. to the Reich Chancellor, dated September 11, 1922.'

people for tomorrow and the future. We shall have to see how the interests of the Western powers stand in relation to our own. . . .

French policy is quite indifferent as to whether we ally ourselves with Russia or not, for in either case the complete destruction of Germany, not yet fully brought about, remains her objective, and this aim would be more difficult to achieve if Germany were supported by Russia.

England is drifting towards another historic conflict with France. . . . The British interests in the Dardanelles, Egypt, and India are certainly infinitely more important at the moment than those on the Rhine, and an understanding between Britain and France at Germany's expense, that is, a concession by Britain in return for an immediate advantage, is by no means improbable. Yet even such an understanding would be only temporary. The moment is coming, and must come, when Britain will be looking around for allies on the Continent. When that moment arrives she will prefer the mercenary who is growing in strength, and will even have to make him stronger.

A *rapprochement* between Germany and Russia would not have a decisive influence on Britain's attitude either in making a concession to France or in searching for an ally. British policy is ruled by other more compelling motives than anxiety about some far-distant threat from a Russia made strong with the help of Germany. Later on a German politician may again have to choose between East and West, Russia and England. A much more immediate question is that of choosing between England and France. The answer to that will not be difficult for Germany, as it is dictated by the attitude of France as described above. . . . Germany's attitude towards Russia, however, cannot and need not be influenced by consideration of Britain. . . .

With Poland we come now to the core of the Eastern problem. The existence of Poland is intolerable and incompatible with Germany's vital interests. She must disappear and will do so through her own inner weakness and through Russia—with our help. Poland is more intolerable for Russia than ourselves; Russia can never tolerate Poland. With Poland collapses one of the strongest pillars of the Peace of Versailles, France's advance post of power. The attainment of this objective must be one of the firmest guiding principles of German policy, as it is capable of achievement—but only through Russia or with her help.

. . . The restoration of the frontier between Russia and Germany is a necessary condition before both sides can be strong. The 1914 frontier between Russia and Germany should be the basis of any understanding between the two countries.

This attitude to Poland on the part of Germany need be no anxiously guarded secret. As far as Russia is concerned its publication can only create confidence. . . . Above all, it is impossible to overestimate the advantage which would accrue to Germany if Poland knew that if she joined in a war of sanctions with France against Germany she would have Russia to contend with. . . . These matters must not be overlooked when considering a fresh strengthening of Russia with our assistance, and therefore at the same time a more active German policy.

Assuredly, he who only sees in an agreement with Russia the danger that we 'expose' ourselves to the British, and does not see that Russia needs us, rejecting every more active policy with the catch-phrase 'military experiment,' cannot arrive at a correct appreciation of the position, and still less can he exploit it logically. A man who suffers from a 'uniform complex' and has not yet understood that in the last resort all political and economic activity is based on power, will not pursue an active German policy. But he who sees in the Treaty of Rapallo mainly a political blunder, though perhaps fit to work in another place, would seem to be unfit for the post of German representative in Moscow.

In political life it is an old, but not a good, device to exaggerate the other side's intentions until they become absurd, and then to attack this absurdity. Who, then, has concluded a written military agreement, binding us unilaterally, or who intends at present to do so? Certainly not the responsible military authorities. Where, then, is this dreaded exposure of ourselves? That the Treaty of Rapallo has brought upon us the suspicion that we could have achieved this increase of power *without* binding ourselves is the main advantage, scarcely to be overestimated, of this agreement.

What, then, is our aim? What do we want from, in, and with Russia? Wherein lies the dreaded Eastern orientation?

We want two things. Firstly, a strong Russia, economically, politically, and therefore militarily, and thus indirectly a stronger Germany in as much as we would be strengthening a possible ally. We also want, cautiously and tentatively at first, a direct increase of strength for ourselves by helping to build up in Russia an armaments industry which, in case of need, would be of use to us. . . . Russian requests for further military assistance could . . . be met by supplying materials and personnel. . . . Details cannot be discussed here.

In all these measures, still largely in the initial phase, participation, and even official recognition, by the German Government would be absolutely out of the question. The detailed negotiations could only be conducted by military authorities. It should be taken for granted that the latter make no agreements binding on the Reich without the knowledge of the political authorities. . . . The German Embassy in Moscow is not the proper place in which to negotiate. It [the Embassy] should merely not work in opposition to the aims described. . . . The man who still lives in the days of Versailles, and maintains that Germany has permanently abjured all 'imperialist and military aims,' that is, stripped

E *

of its demagogic jargon, all policy of action, is not fit to represent German interests in Russia, nor perhaps anywhere else.

. . . It must be admitted that the spirit surrounding the Peace Delegation at Versailles has not yet disappeared, and that the stupid cry of 'No more war!' is widely echoed. It is echoed by many bourgeois-pacifist elements, but among the workers and also among the members of the official Social Democratic Party there are many who are not prepared to eat out of the hands of France and Poland. . . .

If it comes to war—and that seems to be already within measurable distance—it will *not* be the duty of our leading statesmen to keep Germany out of war—that would be either impossible or suicidal—but to come in on the right side with all possible strength.

Seeckt's principal aim in this compelling document was to discredit Brockdorff-Rantzau in the hope of upsetting his appointment to Moscow. Upon a cursory reading of the document Seeckt appears to be on the attack from the first sentence to the last, but closer scrutiny shows that he was also engaged in a defensive battle, skilfully protecting the vested interests of the Reichswehr. He scoffed at Brockdorff-Rantzau's charges, but felt compelled to reply to them. And the replies themselves, stripped of their vituperative embellishment, indicate that the two men were in closer agreement about German Foreign Policy than they believed themselves to be. There were significant differences of opinion about timing and how to approach problems, but these were only to be expected between a diplomat typical of the Edwardian era and a general descendant of Clausewitz and Moltke. Their objectives were the same. Both felt that Germany must redeem herself for the shame of Versailles.

But what is the right first step towards redemption? While Brockdorff-Rantzau believed that Germany must woo Britain to split her from France, Seeckt was certain that 'another historic conflict' between Britain and France was inevitable, and that Britain would therefore be compelled to woo Germany. Both men anticipated another Russo-Polish conflict in the near future, and both sought to insure that Germany would take advantage of the struggle. But while Brockdorff-Rantzau feared the immediate consequences of a war and wanted Germany to remain neutral, Seeckt, realizing that the military situation was not as disadvantageous to Germany as the Count imagined it to be, wanted to take part in the conflict on the 'right'—that is, on the Soviet—

side. Yet Brockdorff-Rantzau was not as completely ignorant of strategic matters as Seeckt made out. He had written that 'peace and reconstruction' must be the purpose of German-Russian relations, but he also specified that 'this does not exclude taking precautions in good time, and, in the event of compelling necessity, taking into account still other associations.' In other words, Brockdorff-Rantzau also looked for active Russian military support in the event Germany were threatened with invasion by France and Poland. But he thought that Russia's position in relation to Germany would force her to offer military support in the event of war, while Seeckt wanted a concrete assurance of this ahead of time.

Brockdorff-Rantzau's greatest anxiety was that the Bolsheviks would blackmail Germany if Seeckt and Wirth negotiated a military alliance with them. In a passage so acrimonious that the point of it is almost completely obscured, Seeckt dispelled this fear by explaining what the mutual interests and objectives of the military collaboration consisted of. There is no doubt that Brockdorff-Rantzau was relieved to hear that Seeckt's negotiations with the Russians did not extend to a plan of attack against the Allies. He continued to have reservations about the way Seeckt and Wirth had approached the Russians behind Ebert's back, but he never openly opposed the Reichswehr's collaboration with the Red Army. As a matter of fact, from the beginning of his time in Moscow he supported both the industrial rearmament programme and the training of German military personnel in Russia.

For all their acrimony, the exchange of memoranda between Seeckt and Brockdorff-Rantzau helped to overcome their respective fears of the other's policies. But the personal clash persisted. The Count continued to harbour suspicions about the interference of the military in the field of politics. He despised and feared 'political generals' and held Seeckt to be the most dangerous and aggravating of them all. He took immediate exception to Seeckt's remark, which was also a taunt, that certain 'detailed negotiations could only be conducted by military authorities.' Had Brockdorff-Rantzau let this slip by he would have given Seeckt an opening to do as he liked in Russia. Instead, the Count demanded assurances from Wirth, Gessler, also from Admiral Behnke, who was Chief of the Naval Command, and from Seeckt that all negotiations with the Russians—including military ones—would be carried on through the German Embassy in Moscow. Wirth complied: 'You may rest assured that all relations with Russia will be conducted through you.' To which Brockdorff-Rantzau added: 'Yes, or over my dead body.'[1]

Gessler and Behnke also gave assurances, but none of them, the Chancellor included, could speak for Seeckt, and he remained adamant.[2] On 22 September Brockdorff-Rantzau was officially named Ambassador to Moscow. Chicherin, with whom he had several interviews in Berlin even before the appointment was made public, urged him to depart for Moscow right away, but the Count would not leave until he was sure the military vendetta against him was crushed. He talked to members of the Reichstag, including Stresemann and Hoetzsch, in an effort to build up a cadre of support against Seeckt. Finally, Ebert prevailed on him to take up his post, and since Walter Simons had in the meantime intervened and persuaded Seeckt to give an assurance that he would not work against the Ambassador 'as long as he conducts or represents a policy which I consider to be in the interests of the Reich,' the Count relented and made ready to go.[3]

Many friends came to bid the Ambassador farewell at the railway station. As the train slowly pulled out Maltzan handed him a bottle of fine French cognac. In Moscow two days later Brockdorff-Rantzau was greeted by only a few officials of the German Embassy; no Soviet representative was there. Still fingering the cognac bottle, the Ambassador complained that he was being treated 'like a high-class bootlegger,' and that same night he warned Chicherin that he would not tolerate any further indignities. Two days later, on 4 November, when Brockdorff-Rantzau went to the Kremlin to present his credentials to Kalinin, he was greeted with as much pomp and ceremony as the Bolsheviks could muster, including a review of Red Army troops to the tune of his favourite German march.[4] For German-Russian relations the ceremony marked the beginning of the Brockdorff-Rantzau era.

[1] Helbig, op. cit., p. 340.

[2] Seeckt went to the extreme of sending Hasse to Moscow to persuade Chicherin to reverse the Soviet Government's decision to accept Brockdorff-Rantzau. But Chicherin refused to do this: ibid., p. 310.

[3] Heeresarchiv: Seeckt, Karton 15, Stück 214, and Helbig, op. cit., p. 311, n. 56, p. 312, n. 62. The first draft of Seeckt's letter still contains a number of new insults, but these were crossed out on second thought.

[4] Blücher, Deutschlands Weg nach Rapallo, p. 169; Hilger, Incompatible Allies, p. 97.

# CHAPTER VI

## NATIONALISM AND BOLSHEVISM

FROM Rapallo until the autumn of 1923 German-Russian relations were marked by a rapid and concurrent extension of political, economic, and military co-operation. Both countries remained outcasts from the respectable family of Western nations. Their *Schicksalsgemeinschaft*, as this common fate came to be called, was the basis of a partnership which was both symbolized and enhanced by the deep friendship that grew up between Chicherin and Brockdorff-Rantzau. These two men had much in common. Both were aristocrats and acutely aware of the irony of their positions as servants to, respectively, a nominally proletarian regime and a government based on popular support. The old world in which they had their roots had crumbled; they had become servants of governments of the common man which had unexpectedly happened upon the world as bastard children of war. Both men felt isolated in the convulsive mainstream of the new societies, and their loneliness induced a feeling of kinship between them.

Chicherin first encountered Brockdorff-Rantzau just before the latter's appointment to Moscow, on 23 June 1922. Chicherin was in Berlin consulting physicians about one of his numerous ailments. Brockdorff-Rantzau took the opportunity to go to see him, saying that he was being considered for the ambassadorship and wanting to know if it would be worth his while to accept the post if it were offered to him. He explained that he did not want to go to Moscow if the Soviet Government were bent on steering a revolutionary course to the detriment of friendly political relations. The Count's bluntness appears to have disarmed and delighted Chicherin. He assured Brockdorff-Rantzau that he would be welcome in Moscow and that he could serve a useful purpose there since the Soviet Government desired nothing more than to work together with Germany in accordance with the Rapallo treaty.[1]

---

[1] Helbig, 'Moskauer Mission Brockdorff-Rantzaus,' pp. 313-315; Stern-Rubarth, *Graf Brockdorff-Rantzau*, p. 124. Cf. Holborn, 'Diplomacy in the Early Weimar Republic' in *The Diplomats*, p. 171.

The relationship got off on the right foot. From the beginning, Chicherin and Brockdorff-Rantzau trusted and respected one another as skilled diplomats and, above all, as gentlemen. Only the bitter experience of the revolutionary outburst in Germany in the autumn of 1923 taught Brockdorff-Rantzau that Chicherin's pledges of good faith for the Soviet Government did not cover the activities of Comintern. But he blamed and castigated other Russian officials, not Chicherin. Their friendship endured and often served to minimize frictions and to bring about speedier solutions to disputes between the two countries.[1]

The signing of Russo-German military accords under the cover of economic negotiations has already been described in some detail.[2] *Bona fide* economic negotiations for trade and concessions on Russian soil were going on at the same time. As Soviet trade expanded so did the German share in it. In 1922 Russia took 32·7 per cent. of her imports from Germany, almost 6 per cent. more than in 1921, while Germany accounted for 18 per cent. of Russia's exports, an increase of over 10 per cent. over the preceding year.[3] At the end of 1922 Brockdorff-Rantzau and Krasin concluded an agreement whereby Germany imported thirty million gold marks' worth of grain during the following year, one-third of which was paid for in manufactured goods.[4] From 1921 to 1923 Germany took either first or second place as an importer of Russian exports; in 1924 third place. Britain's share in the Russian market steadily decreased during the same period. German firms also showed an intense interest in Soviet concessions. On 9 December 1922 Maltzan reported to the Reichstag's Foreign Affairs Committee that 20 German firms had secured concessions.[5] In these ways both countries helped one another to reconstruct vital industries and trade

[1] Chicherin's complete confidence in Brockdorff-Rantzau is illustrated by his frankness in talking about the difficulties of co-ordinating the policies of Narkomindel and Comintern (Hilger, *Incompatible Allies*, pp. 95 f., 101 f., 107, 143 f., and T. von Laue, 'Soviet Diplomacy: G. V. Chicherin' in *The Diplomats*, pp. 246 ff.). The *Brockdorff-Rantzau Nachlass* may contain more information about Brockdorff-Rantzau's conversations with Chicherin. The *Nachlass* is part of the German Foreign Ministry Archives in the possession of the Allied Governments, and not available for research purposes at this time.

[2] See above, pp. 92 ff., 124 f.

[3] Kuczynski and Wittkowski, *Die deutsch-russischen Handelsbeziehungen in den letzten 150 Jahren*, p. 5; *The Times*, 11 December 1922.

[4] Helbig, 'Moskauer Mission Brockdorff-Rantzaus,' p. 316.

[5] *Stresemann Nachlass*, 7113H/H145020/1, 7016H/H144244/6.

destroyed in the First World War, and, in the military field, conspired in the preparations for the mutual destruction which took place in the Second World War.

While the military and economic negotiations progressed without untoward incidents during the summer and autumn of 1922, important changes were also taking place on the political and the so-called ideological planes. Soviet policy towards Germany in 1922 was only partially defined by the Rapallo treaty. Subsequently a new line was developed which amplified the policies that had led to a treaty with the Germans, although the new line was called forth by factors of greater significance to the Bolsheviks than the signing of the treaty itself. One of these factors was Lenin's illness. The anticipation of widespread unrest within the country and uncertainty as to the succession in the event of Lenin's death caused the Soviet Government to follow a steady and safe path in relations with other countries. An equally important factor was the increasingly ominous threat of France—Soviet Russia's most relentless foe—to the Ruhr. These threats coupled with the fact that the world revolution had not materialized, influenced the amplification of Russian policy towards Germany and the simultaneous development of a new ideological line, for which Radek and Bukharin were the leading spokesmen.

In an address to the Fourth Congress of Comintern Radek said that the Rapallo treaty was based on Russia's eternal interests in Europe. According to Radek, 'the policy of throttling Germany, her destruction as an international factor,' implied the destruction of Russia as well. 'No matter how Russia is governed, it is always to her interest to see that Germany exists.' He said that there was no doubt that Russia could not have 'continued as a great power nor acquired the economic and technical means for her industrial reconstruction' if Germany had not been able to help counterbalance the supremacy of the Allies after the war. The subsequent Allied attempt to set Germany and Russia against one another by the inclusion of certain provisions in the Versailles treaty had failed, Radek continued. Instead, the Soviet Government had signed a treaty with the Germans which drove a wedge between Germany and the other capitalist powers, giving Russia an opportunity to play off one against the other. Radek was careful to note, however, that Rapallo did not make Russia dependent upon Germany; the treaty, he said, was not an exclusive arrangement and did not preclude negotiations between Russia and other Western powers. At Rapallo Russia gained a foothold in the West; she would have to gain a firmer position there in the future. Radek said that there was no longer a question whether or not a *modus vivendi* between capitalism and proletarian dictatorship were possible: a *modus vivendi* had already existed for five years in the form of an 'unstable equilibrium, which is characterized by a series of compromises.' The real question concerned the 'basis on which these compromises are effected,' and that depended on the rate of growth of the productive forces of the Soviet Republic, and on the development of its political power and the strengthening of the revolutionary parties. Russia had already made considerable headway in this direction, Radek concluded, because 'the Versailles treaty, as far as it relates to Russia, is wound-up.'[1]

The Communists were now firmly entrenched in power in Russia and faced concrete problems in relations with non-Communist governments; the Marxist-dialectic viewpoint had to undergo certain changes to keep up with the times. Radek's justification of the Soviet policies that followed the 'delay' in the world revolution was not enough; a new theoretical foundation had to be developed as well. It was left to Bukharin, an indefatigable theoretician, to expound the dogma of this newest station in the tortuous trek of Marxist-dialectic logic. In a speech delivered in November 1922 Bukharin elaborated on the ideological implications for Soviet policy in the event a French occupation of the Ruhr, rumours of which were then in the air, were actually to take place. 'May proletarian states,' he asked, 'on the basis of strategic expediency for the whole proletariat, conclude military alliances with bourgeois states?' Bukharin answered yes, and justified the answer with a clever rationalization: 'Here there is no difference in principle between a loan and a military alliance, and I maintain that we have already grown so strong that we may conclude a military alliance with the bourgeoisie of one country in order with its help to crush the bourgeoisie of another country.'[2] Thus, what had not been permissible now was. The new-found power of the Soviet Republic made the whole difference between the old view

---

[1] Radek, *The Winding-Up of the Versailles Treaty* (Hamburg, 1922), pp. 16, 22.
[2] *Fourth World Congress of the Communist International—Selected Reports, Speeches and Resolutions* (Moscow and Petrograd, 1923), pp. 195 f. See the discussion of Bukharin's speech in Kochan, *Russia and Weimar*, p. 66.

and the new. General von Seeckt was undoubtedly interested to hear this. But while Bukharin's revision of the theoretical basis of Soviet policy only confirmed what Seeckt had all along assumed to be possible, its significance for the world proletariat was new: they would have to accept the additional responsibilities of supporting any Soviet agreements or actions based on 'the strategic expediency for the whole proletariat,' no matter how unpalatable these turned out to be.

If a revolution were to break out in Germany [Bukharin wrote in *Izvestiya*] and Poland struck at Germany from the East, then revolutionary Russia would probably be obliged to attack Poland. And in this case the revolutionary workers of the whole world would be obliged to support both the German revolution and Russia's war against Poland.[1]

Looking back on Russo-German relations in 1922 and 1923 four years later, Bukharin said:

When Germany was crushed, was enslaved, when she was in the position of a semi-colony, and when in this capacity she offered a certain resistance to the victorious imperialism of the Entente, then even the highest organs of Soviet power in their manifestos, declarations and so on, expressed their own sympathy for her. . . . At the same time this was a period of maximum flirtation between the German bourgeoisie and a state alien to it in its social structure.[2]

By the time French forces occupied the Ruhr in January 1923, Bukharin had given the Marxist-dialectic a new twist which justified Russia's support for the oppressed German capitalists, who were then considered to be a part of the bourgeoisie playing a quasi-revolutionary role against French imperialism in defence of Soviet Russia. The interests of the Bolsheviks, in whose country alone Communist revolution had succeeded, were as much at stake in the Ruhr as the interests of the most reactionary German industrialists. Soviet policy towards Germany then had a certain inconsistent consistency. Once a line was preached there was no question of its authenticity. The Bolsheviks took a stand on the Ruhr crisis before it developed, and when the French invaded they

---

[1] *Izvestiya*, 11 January 1923.
[2] *XV Konferentsiya V.K.P.* (*b*) *Stenographicheski otchet* (Moscow and Leningrad, 1927), p. 30, quoted by Kochan, *op. cit.*, p. 67.

stuck by it. But the preparations for a revolution in Germany continued without let-up.

In spite of previous failures, the German Communists, and the most dangerous enemies of the Republic, the Right extremists, had good reason to believe that they would eventually be able to seize power. Even before the Ruhr occupation brought new turmoil there were mounting signs that the experiment with democracy had failed and that the Weimar constellation would soon be replaced by a different form of government. Effective government had failed and the society was disintegrating under the weight of reparations. Popular dissatisfaction with the Republic provoked new drives for separatism in a number of states; only a minority felt a strong allegiance to the national government. Because of its weakness the government continued to depend on the army for support, although the loyalty of the army to the Republic was, to say the least, dubious. Personal vendettas and political murders occurred all over Germany; courts were replaced by cults; judicial procedures gave way to vengeance: justice was replaced by the indiscriminate use of force.[1]

Walter Rathenau was assassinated by nationalist fanatics on 24 June 1922. The reasons given for the killing were that he was a Jew and that he signed the Rapallo treaty, which meant to Right-wing extremists that he was 'pro-Russian.'[2] Although this was only one of many acts of violence against leading German politicians of the time, it caused a great furore throughout the country. The killing of the Foreign Minister was deeply resented by large segments of the population, especially by members of the Left-wing parties and the trade unions. Mass protest meetings and street demonstrations were held, and Chancellor Wirth made a dramatic speech in the Reichstag in which he warned all those faithful to the Republic that 'the enemy is on the Right.'[3] But it was symptomatic of

---

[1] For the conditions in Germany at this time see A. Apfel, *Behind the Scenes of German Justice* (London, 1935), *passim*; Scheele, *The Weimar Republic*, pp. 57–65; Halperin, *Germany Tried Democracy*, pp. 232 f.; Waite, *Vanguard of Nazism*, pp. 212 ff.

[2] Hallgarten, 'Seeckt and Russia,' p. 33, n. 25. For some months before he was killed the nationalists and Fascists called Rathenau a 'traitor.' It is ironic that Rathenau himself—according to Heinrich Brüning—donated and raised funds totalling more than $5,000,000 for the support of the Free Corps during this time; see Waite, *op. cit.*, p. 220, n. 136.

[3] Wirth, *Reden während der Kanzlerschaft*, p. 406.

Weimar's decline that even the largest demonstrations and the most righteous speeches could not halt the drift to less and less effective government. When conspirators and murderers were not punished, dramatic appeals for justice, law, and order went for nought. As they discovered that no strong measures would be taken against them, the forces of anarchy and revolution grew bolder and intensified their attacks on the Republic. For their part, the German Communists took advantage of the turmoil following Rathenau's assassination to unleash a new propaganda drive against the Reichswehr. Their attacks were potent enough to worry Seeckt, who, ironically, was preoccupied by the negotiations with the Red Army at just that time. He issued an order of the day in which he admonished all officers to 'keep a sharp look-out for Communist agitation' and to 'prevent anything from happening that might be regarded as anti-Republican, which could therefore be used to instigate new political attacks against us.'[1] Despite these precautions the attacks on the army continued unabated. Although Rathenau's assassins and other Right-wing conspirators who resorted to violence against the Republic were not members of the army, the High Command had given the Right extremists every reason to believe that their efforts were supported by the military. The Communist slogan, 'Reichswehr: Enemy of the Republic,' was not misdirected. It is indeed ironic that the German Communists—whose co-conspirators in Moscow were collaborating with Seeckt—had a keener understanding of the political interests of the Reichswehr than the other Left-wing parties. They realized that the army's support of the national government during the prolonged political crisis of 1922-1923 was purely opportunistic; that it acted only to preserve itself and to maintain a unified German state. As long as Seeckt was its commander the army's political sympathies were with those on the Right who sought to re-establish a military-monarchical government which would ally itself with Soviet Russia against the West.

In November 1922 Germany took another important step away from the parliamentary Republic of 1919-1922. The Wirth cabinet, beset by reparations and inflation problems, fell owing to the refusal of the SPD to co-operate with it and was replaced by Cuno's 'non-partisan' government, comprising businessmen and

---

[1] *Heeresarchiv*: Seeckt, Karton 13, Stück 130. Seeckt issued a second order of the day to the same effect on 7 August 1922: *ibid*.

experts chosen from the parties of the Centre and the Right. Cuno's appeal to keep the government above party political strife was honoured by all the major parties, including the SPD, but not by the KPD, which was left as the only opposition group in the Reichstag. Soon after Cuno took office the Reichstag's Foreign Affairs Committee met in closed session to consider an agreement initialled by Maltzan and Krestinski at the beginning of November, which broadened the Rapallo treaty to include the Ukraine.[1] In the course of the discussion a dispute broke out about Germany's policies towards Russia. The substance of the dispute was publicized only because a news agency correspondent overheard it and *Vorwärts* managed to publish his dispatch before it could be officially censored. The portions of the dispatch that were censored in the accounts given by other newspapers dealt with a statement by Dr Breitscheid of the SPD against the new agreement, in the course of which he criticized the policy of friendship with Soviet Russia and said that the Rapallo treaty 'had come too early.' Referring to a report to the committee by Foreign Minister Dr von Rosenberg about Chicherin's attitude during his most recent visit to Berlin, Breitscheid exclaimed that it was 'the intention of Russian Foreign Policy to use Germany as a horse to hitch to their own wagon.' The Rapallo treaty, he insisted, would enable the Bolsheviks to exploit Germany for the cause of world revolution. A heated debate ensued. Wirth denied that Chicherin was insincere, and Hoetzsch of the DNVP joined Maltzan in making a spirited defence of the Rapallo treaty. An effort was made to strike Breitscheid's remarks from the record, but this was frustrated by *Vorwärt's* quick action in printing the uncensored report.[2] This incident serves to show how feeble the opposition to the Rapallo policies was in Germany. Apart from the Right extremists, only a handful of Social Democrats were against developing closer relations with the Soviet Republic. To the extent the government sought to publicize its Eastern policy the German people accepted it, while the military relations were carefully hidden from public view under Cuno's Government as they had been under Wirth's. In fact, Cuno was the only Weimar Chancellor whom Seeckt trusted completely. Immediately after Cuno took office Seeckt told him 'about his Eastern plans' without 'holding back' anything.

[1] *Stresemann Nachlass*, 7019H/H144690/5.
[2] *Ibid.*, 7113H/H145020/1; *Vorwärts*, 10 December 1922.

Cuno not only endorsed Seeckt's schemes but, like Wirth, helped to implement them.[1]

When the Reichstag extended Ebert's term of office at the end of November 1922, Seeckt decided to inform him, too, of the secret military connexions with Russia.[2] This was a dangerous step to take, for Seeckt knew from Wirth that the President had been inalterably opposed to any such arrangements. Yet Seeckt thought it necessary to inform Ebert, even at the risk of being dismissed from his post. He knew that Brockdorff-Rantzau would send his reports from Russia directly to the President, and that these might at any time mention the Reichswehr's activities there. Since Seeckt himself was not on speaking terms with Brockdorff-Rantzau, the only way he could prevent the Ambassador from bringing the military and rearmament activities in Russia under the control of the Moscow Embassy was to inform Ebert of these activities, win his support for them, and then persuade him that they should be under the jurisdiction of the army, not of the Embassy. Fortunately for Seeckt, Ebert approved the deals he had made with the Russians —or at least he did not vehemently object to them as he had earlier in 1922 when he heard rumours that such negotiations were going on. Exactly why Ebert reversed his position on this issue is not ascertainable. In spite of his socialist and predominantly anti-militarist leanings, Ebert's loss of faith in the party system, to which the appointment of the Cuno Government attests, may have made him more dependent on the army for the support of the Republic, and, hence, more susceptible to Seeckt's wishes. But for whatever reasons Ebert decided to approve German rearmament in Russia, it is most unlikely that he gave Seeckt a free hand to conduct these relations independently. More likely, Ebert's price for supporting these relations was that they had to be subjected to stringent political control through Brockdorff-Rantzau in Moscow.

Radek reappeared in Berlin in November 1922 and again met Seeckt. In the course of their talk, which was chiefly concerned with the rearmament ventures in Russia, Radek proposed that the two countries should try to create 'an organization of the most hetero-geneous elements of the whole world for the use of Russia and

---

[1] See Cuno's letter to Seeckt, dated Hamburg, 2 November 1926, in the *Heeresarchiv*: Seeckt, Karton 1, Stück 18; also Rabenau, *Seeckt*, vol. 2, p. 322; and Scheele, *The Weimar Republic*, p. 67.

[2] Rabenau, *op. cit.*, p. 319.

Germany.'[1] It is difficult to fathom exactly what Radek meant by this. He may have been thinking about a kind of international-nationalist revolution, or perhaps he was merely trying to persuade Seeckt that the objectives of Bolshevik policies were not incompatible with the goals of German nationalism. Radek certainly wanted to reassure Seeckt that Germany had nothing to fear from Russia. The Soviet leaders were convinced that a German Government of the Right was likely to offer the most effective resistance to the French. In so far as it did this and, simultaneously, followed the Rapallo policies and continued the military collaboration, a Right-wing government was also the most reliable ally Soviet Russia could have in Europe. But if Radek fed this line to Seeckt in his capacity as an agent of the Soviet Government, he had a second mission to perform in Berlin in his capacity as an agent of Comintern. To the leaders of the KPD Radek advocated a policy that was called the 'Schlageter line' when it was fully developed during the Ruhr crisis. The 'Schlageter line' was to create an alliance between the Communists and the Right-wing parties, and was therefore directly complementary to the National Bolshevism Radek preached to Seeckt.

Whether or not the Franco-Belgian occupation of the Ruhr was legally justified under the Treaty of Versailles is of minor importance when one considers the political unwisdom and the disastrous consequences of the move. By declaring Germany in default of reparations Poincaré found a debatable but sufficient pretext to occupy the entire Ruhr territory in January 1923. For weeks beforehand Poincaré had used the rumours of German rearmament and of a secret military protocol in the Rapallo treaty to whip up French fear and hatred of the Germans.[2] To what extent the French Government was actually convinced that Germany was carrying on secret relations with Soviet Russia is not clear. The French could not have taken the rumours and reports pointing to these relations less seriously than Ambassador D'Abernon, who not only convinced himself but Lloyd George as well that the evidence of secret German-Russian deals was all forged.[3] But if the French had obtained positive proof of Seeckt's plans and activities in Russia they would undoubtedly have published it to justify the drastic

[1] *Ibid.*
[2] Eyck, *Geschichte der Weimarer Republik*, pp. 308 f.
[3] D'Abernon, *Ambassador of Peace*, vol. 1, pp. 303 f., 311 f.

punitive steps they took. The German industrialist Arnold Rechberg, a notorious Russophobe who was later to become a charter
member of the Nazi Party, was often in Paris during this period
and pretended to know, and perhaps did know, how much the
French knew of Germany's relations with Soviet Russia. After the
French invasion in January 1923, Rechberg wrote to Stresemann
that 'German heavy industry's negotiations with Russia and most
particularly the Rapallo treaty provoked the French Government
to occupy the Ruhr.' The French, he wrote, look upon the treaty
as the start of 'a war of revenge by the Rapallo signatories' against
themselves and the Poles.[1]

At the start of the Ruhr crisis all the German parties—except the
KPD—renewed their pledges to support the Cuno Government.
The cabinet issued an appeal to the workers of the Ruhr to offer
'passive resistance' to the invaders. This was generally obeyed;
industry ceased to function.[2] But any attempt to freeze the French
out was doomed to failure, for in subsidizing the idleness of
Germany's arsenal and workshop in the Ruhr, the government
annihilated the nation's currency. As money dwindled in value
between morning and night the masses hungered because the notes
in which they were paid bought less bread every day. But the
spiralling inflation was not the most immediate nor the greatest
cause for concern. Berlin was gripped by the fear that the Ruhr
occupation would be followed by a Polish invasion in the East, and
that a major war would ensue. 'The French attack on us,' Stresemann wrote on 17 January, 'is a struggle of life and death. It is not
impossible that we shall be attacked from the East.'[3] The fear of a
Polish invasion continued throughout the winter and spring, and
was intensified by Marshal Foch's much celebrated visit to Warsaw
in May. The Germans reacted by mobilizing 50,000 to 80,000 men
—mostly from Right and extreme Right-wing organizations—
and creating para-military units to augment the 100,000 man army
to which they were restricted by the Versailles treaty.[4] In addition,

---

[1] *Stresemann Nachlass*, 7114H/H145292/7, 7116H/H145534/5.
[2] Stampfer, *Die vierzehn Jahre der ersten deutschen Republik*, p. 318.
[3] *Stresemann Nachlass*, 7113H/H145064.
[4] For the Seeckt-Severing accord, to which Ebert was a party, and the creation
of the Black Reichswehr see Wheeler-Bennett, *Nemesis of Power*, pp. 92 f.; Waite,
*Vanguard of Nazism*, pp. 240 ff. Cf. Papen, *Memoirs*, p. 120, for a typical rationalization of these illegal machinations.

Cuno asked the Soviet Government for assurance that it would support Germany in its battle for 'survival.'

'Nothing is more remarkable in the story of events in Germany in 1923,' writes E. H. Carr, 'than the lack of any apparent attempt to co-ordinate the policies of Comintern and of the Soviet Government, and the acceptance by the German Government of the distinction between them.'[1] In the Reichstag Paul Fröhlich, a member of the Left faction of the KPD, led the Communist protest against Cuno's 'passive resistance' policy in the Ruhr. 'The war in the Ruhr,' Fröhlich said, 'is the first international action of the Communists'—of the French and German Communists—against Poincaré and Cuno. He deprecated any attempt to confront the Communists with the dilemma 'either against Poincaré or against Cuno.'[2] No distinction between the two was to be made in the fight against imperialism. This first reaction of the KPD to the Ruhr crisis was not in line with the Comintern policies of marking time and of the 'united front.' And it stood in contrast to the reaction of the Soviet Government to the Ruhr invasion, which immediately gave the German Government strong diplomatic and propaganda support. On 13 January the Central Executive Committee published a resolution so passionately anti-French that the statements of German nationalists appear mild in comparison:

The imperialists of France have once again thrown the sword into the balance of history. . . . The sovereignty of the German people is infringed. The right of the German people to self-determination is trodden underfoot. Germany's disorganized economy has suffered a new and shattering blow. Cruel poverty and unprecedented oppression threaten the working masses of Germany, while all Europe will witness an increase in economic dislocation. The world is again thrown into a state of pre-war feverishness. Sparks are flying in the powder-cellar created by the Treaty of Versailles. . . . In these decisive days . . . Russia once again raises its voice in indignant protest against the senseless policy of imperialist France and its Allies. Again and with special vehemence it protests against the suppression of the German people's right to self-determination.[3]

The Soviet Government left no room for doubt that, in the circumstances, its interests could best be served by supporting the

[1] Carr, vol. 4, p. 157.
[2] *Internationale Presse-Korrespondenz*, No. 43, 9 March 1923, p. 319.
[3] Degras, *Soviet Documents*, vol. 1, pp. 368-370.

existing German Government. Chicherin wrote in *Izvestiya* that 'the Ruhr adventure has administered a shock to the political and economic life of all Europe, and thus brought great harm upon the Soviet republics which require economic relations with other countries.' He reassured Brockdorff-Rantzau that the main objective of Soviet Foreign Policy 'is to cultivate more cordial relations with Germany than with any other country.'[1] Steklov wrote in *Izvestiya* that 'Soviet Russia, *in her own vital interests*, cannot permit the final subjugation and destruction of Germany by an alliance of France and her vassals, of which Poland is the first.' He added a crucial sentence which made the Soviet position perfectly clear: 'A Polish attack on Germany at the present moment is a direct blow at Soviet Russia.'[2] Trotsky agreed completely with this analysis. He 'promised' Brockdorff-Rantzau that 'Russia would interfere' if the Poles tried to take advantage of the Ruhr crisis to seize East Prussia or Silesia.[3] Although Trotsky assumed that 'the hypothesis of a Polish attack on Germany will remain merely an hypothesis,' the threat of Soviet intervention certainly cut short any designs the Poles may have had to strike Germany in the back.[4] Brockdorff-Rantzau's earlier assumption that, in the event of an attack, Germany could count on Russia's military support without first signing a military alliance with her seemed to be vindicated.

Soviet Russia supported Germany against their common foes, France and Poland, because Germany was a source of industrial aid and also Russia's *point d'appui* in Europe. But why, it must be asked, did the Bolsheviks not greet the French invasion of the Ruhr as a revolutionary stimulus in Germany? When Trotsky was asked this question by a British correspondent in an interview at the end of February 1923, he gave a guarded and partially evasive answer. 'Certainly we are interested in the victory of the working class,' Trotsky started out, 'but it is not at all to our interest that the revolution should take place in a Europe exhausted and drained of blood. . . .' A war in Europe would lead to 'the bleeding and destruction primarily of those generations of the working class

[1] Hilger, *Incompatible Allies*, pp. 120, 121.

[2] *Izvestiya*, 24 January 1923, quoted by Kochan, *Russia and Weimar*, p. 68. Cf. Radek's article entitled 'Hands off Germany' in *Izvestiya*, 31 August 1923.

[3] Hilger, *op. cit.*, p. 120; Rabenau, *Seeckt*, vol. 2, p. 330. Cf. L. Fischer, *Soviets in World Affairs*, vol. 1, pp. 451 f.

[4] Degras, *Soviet Documents*, vol. 1, p. 376. Also see Carr, vol. 4, p. 166, and Hilger, *op. cit.*, p. 120.

which are the bearers of the future' and is therefore 'not the approach but, on the contrary, the postponement of revolutionary perspectives.'[1] This was a plausible reply, but not the real explanation. Radek gave a more complete and candid reply to the same question in a confidential chat with an official of the German Embassy in Moscow:

In case of radical upheavals in Germany, Russia will have to expect to see French troops on the shores of Berezina. Hence we Communists are interested in Germany's political and economic stability. Theoretically, a German Communist regime would be highly desirable, but it would at once be crushed by France.[2]

Not all of Radek's comrades in Germany were reconciled to his way of looking at their dilemma. At the beginning of 1923 the KPD had more than 200,000 members with 13 deputies in the Reichstag, but it was still split into factions: the Right, now led by Brandler and Thalheimer, and the Left, led by Maslow, Thälmann, and Ruth Fischer.[3] At Comintern's Fourth Congress in November 1922 a temporary truce was imposed on the KPD factions under the banner of the 'united front' tactics, but at the KPD's Leipzig Congress two months later the struggle between the factions was resumed over the interpretation of the new dogma. Brandler argued that the 'united front' tactics should lead to agreements with the leaders of the bourgeois Left parties, notably with the SPD, and that the Communists should try to form coalition 'workers' governments.' The Left faction disagreed. Their spokesmen argued that the SPD would always be 'the party of the bourgeoisie' and could not be won from revisionist policies. Unless the KPD concerned itself with the essential question, 'the question of power,' it would 'feed dangerous illusions to the masses.' 'We do not see any genuine possibility of workers' governments in the present situation,' Ruth Fischer asserted. The Left faction called for immediate revolutionary action.[4] Radek replied that—as at the Fourth Congress of Comintern—'the conquest of power as a practical task

[1] Degras, *loc. cit.*

[2] Hilger, *op. cit.*, p. 122. For Radek's activities in Berlin during the spring of 1923 see R. Fischer, *Stalin and German Communism*, p. 261.

[3] *Bericht über den 3. Parteitag der Kommunistischen Partei Deutschlands* (Berlin, 1923), p. 73. The membership may have risen to 400,000 during July and August 1923. See the table in Flechtheim, *Die KPD*, p. 235.

[4] *Bericht über den 3. Parteitag der Kommunistischen Partei Deutschlands*, p. 187.

of the moment is not on the agenda.' Even if the party managed to
seize power, he said, it would not be able to maintain itself. Therefore, Radek continued, the KPD would 'commit the greatest
blunder' if it allowed Germany to be beaten in the event of a
Franco-Polish attack. It was a mistake to oppose the Cuno Government and the 'passive resistance' campaign in the Ruhr. The
Communists 'must defend their country to the last breath.'[1] In
taking his stand with the Right, which was also the majority faction
at Leipzig, Radek was following prevailing Comintern policy, to
which even Zinoviev was reconciled. Brandler's interpretations of
the 'united front' tactics and of the slogan 'workers' governments'
were most nearly in line with the Soviet policy of supporting the
Cuno regime. The exigencies of Russia's national interests—which
the proletariat of the whole world were to defend—required
political and economic stability in Germany. Moscow wanted to
bolster the Cuno Government to strengthen it against the French,
and, therefore, Radek opposed the Left faction's bid to fight 'for
political power' which, in any event, was likely to lead to disaster.
The only reason Radek did not take an even stronger stand against
the Left at Leipzig is that Moscow wanted to keep the KPD unified
so that it would be prepared for the seizure of power at the right
moment.[2] To keep from splitting the party, the Ruhr crisis—the
most significant political fact of the time—was not officially an issue
on the agenda at Leipzig. The party did not take a definite stand in
the crisis and left the rank and file in doubt about what attitude
to adopt towards the Cuno Government.

The temperate 'united front' tactics of Brandler's faction did not
make headway. The SPD refused to form a national coalition
'workers' government' with the KPD. The Communists were
driven to a purely negative approach: 'As long as the Social-
Democratic workers do not fight together with us for a workers'
government, the KPD is indifferent as to whether another
bourgeois government replaces the present leaderless one.'[3] But in
contrast to the lukewarm leaders printed in the Rote Fahne, the

---

[1] Hilger, op. cit., p. 122.

[2] Flechtheim, Die KPD, pp. 85-87. Kochan (op. cit., pp. 74 f.), following Ruth
Fischer (op. cit., pp. 252 ff.), accuses Radek of bad faith in leading the KPD 'into
a blind alley.' Carr, on the other hand, minimizes the influence Radek had in
supporting Brandler against the Left faction at this time (vol. 4, p. 157).

[3] Rote Fahne, 27 May 1923.

Communists in the Ruhr, who were under the influence of the KPD's Left faction, took up arms against the French and, equally, against Cuno's bourgeois government. In the spring of 1923 they provoked disturbances and organized unsuccessful *putsches* which frightened Brandler and Radek with the galloping ghost of the 'March Action.'[1] To forestall a repetition of the March fiasco Comintern once again summoned representatives of both KPD factions to Moscow in order to reconcile the differences between them. Since it was anxious to keep the KPD unified, Comintern could not afford to support one faction against the other, but rather supported those policies of each faction of which it approved and also rebuked them in equal measure. The basic purpose of the conversations, however, was to restrain the Left faction from carrying its agitation to the brink of revolution, on the assumption that the attempt would almost certainly end in failure and bring the French deeper into Germany.[2]

Comintern restrained the KPD but gave it no positive line to follow in meeting the emergency of the Ruhr occupation. Under this influence, and because of the split in its ranks, the party wandered aimlessly until the end of May. By that time the crisis in Germany had become acute. Inflation was spiralling out of control and the masses were desperately seeking a way out of their dilemma. Violence was spreading; a general upheaval loomed on the horizon.[3] These were revolutionary potentialities and the Communists could not afford to continue ignoring them if they wanted to retain their support in the ranks of the workers. Comintern was finally forced to reconsider the German situation. The most significant change by the summer of 1923 was the rapid growth both in membership and power of the nationalist and Fascist organizations. In the absence of strong leadership from the KPD, which had no policy to meet the crisis, the Right extremists were able to monopolize the revolutionary cause and were threatening to seize power for themselves. Hitherto the Communists had simply labelled all Right extremist organizations Fascist. But now, in the midst of the crisis, as the membership rolls of these organizations

[1] R. Fischer, *op. cit.*, pp. 257-259; Carr, vol. 4, p. 162.

[2] Carr, vol. 4, pp. 162 f.

[3] Stampfer, *Die vierzehn Jahre der ersten deutschen Republik*, pp. 338 f. For the development of the German currency inflation see the table in K. Mielcke, *Geschichte der Weimarer Republik* (Braunschweig, 1954), pp. 135 ff.

swelled the Communists gave them serious consideration. What they had simply lumped together under the heading Fascist really comprised organizations of varying degrees of nationalistic fanaticism, with at least three distinct types among them: those who might be called the simple nationalists, most of whom belonged to the DNVP or to the DVP; Hitler's racists in the National Socialist Freedom Movement; and, finally, the former Free Corps soldiers who were unwilling or unable to find non-military employment, many of whom joined the Black Reichswehr. All these organizations were growing in numbers; their adherents constituted an immense reservoir of support for a revolution against Weimar. The Communists believed that the 'petty bourgeois,' who formed the bulk of the new members of all these organizations, had turned to extreme nationalism only under the threat of national and individual extinction, and they were intent on diverting them to broaden the support for their own revolution.

The new KPD tactics were proclaimed late in May and in June. Both factions of the party agreed that the proletarian masses had to be educated to understand that their suffering was due not only to French imperialism and capital but also to German capital, meaning Cuno, who was now described as 'Stinnes' prisoner.' Henceforth Poincaré and Cuno were equally to blame for the crisis and both had to be overthrown:

We have to go to the suffering, misled, infuriated masses of the proletarianized petty bourgeois to tell them the whole truth, to tell them that they can defend themselves and the future of Germany only when they have allied themselves with the proletariat for a struggle with the real bourgeois. The way to victory over Poincaré and Loucheur lies only through victory over Stinnes and Krupps.[1]

This KPD resolution, which was drafted by Radek in Berlin, is really the first clear enunciation of the 'Schlageter line,' but it was proclaimed almost a month before Radek's famous 'Schlageter speech' in Moscow. In telling the German masses that 'a workers' government and an alliance with Soviet Russia' were the only roads to salvation for them, the Communists were trying to divide the Right extremists, aligning the 'misled nationalistic petty bourgeois' with the KPD, and leaving those 'Fascists directly sold to capital'—in other words, those who refused to swing behind the

[1] *Rote Fahne*, 18 May 1923, quoted by Carr, vol. 4, p. 176.

KPD—isolated on the other extreme. Radek no longer rejected the label 'National Bolshevism' for this policy, but he made it clear that the policy was being introduced in circumstances entirely different from those which prevailed when Laufenberg and Wolfheim put forward their thesis under the same heading:

National Bolshevism meant in 1920 an alliance to save the generals, who would have wiped out the Communist Party immediately after victory. Today National Bolshevism means that everyone is penetrated with the feeling that salvation can be found only with the Communists. We are today the only way out. The strong emphasis on the nation in Germany is a revolutionary act, like the emphasis on the nation in the colonies.[1]

The KPD was strong enough, Radek said, to risk an alliance with certain nationalist elements. 'German nationalism is not only nationalism,' he explained to Comintern, 'but a broad national movement having a great revolutionary significance.' The idea was to channel this nationalist-revolutionary power in support of the KPD. On 19 June, four days after Radek addressed Comintern, Klara Zetkin, speaking to the same gathering, said she fully supported his ideas about what was to be done with the German nationalists and Fascists:

We must strive either to win them over to our side in the struggle, or at any rate to neutralize these social forces which have succumbed to the embraces of Fascism.[2]

Radek spoke again the next day. He said that when he listened to Zetkin's speech he had visions of 'the corpse of the German Fascist, our class enemy, condemned to death and shot by the lackeys of French imperialism.' Radek then pronounced a maudlin eulogy on Albert Leo Schlageter, a nationalist fanatic who had been shot by the French after being caught red-handed sabotaging railway lines in the Ruhr. Radek characterized Schlageter as the prototype of the 'honest, patriotic masses' in Germany whom he wanted to rally behind the KPD. Have the German nationalists really understood the significance of Schlageter's 'martyrdom'? Radek asked. Do they realize who their enemies are?

Against whom do the German nationalists want to fight: against Entente capital or the Russian people? With whom do they want to ally

[1] *Internationale Presse-Korrespondenz*, No. 103, 21 June 1923, p. 869.
[2] Quoted by Carr, vol. 4, pp. 178 f.

themselves? With the Russian workers and peasants to shake off together the yoke of Entente capital, or with Entente capital to enslave the German and Russian people?

Schlageter—and all the Schlageters—will have died in vain, Radek said, if the German nationalists do not align themselves with the Communists. The Communist Party, he insisted, 'is not the party merely of the struggle for the industrial workers' loaf of bread, but the party of struggling proletarians who fight for their freedom, for a freedom which is identical with the freedom of their whole people, with the freedom of all who work and suffer in Germany.'[1] This brilliant speech was the most audacious proclamation of the 'National Bolshevik' line. Since Radek made it with Zinoviev's assent, it can be assumed that the tactics had been officially adopted by Comintern.

Up to this point Comintern's tactics during the crisis were entirely consistent with the policies of the Soviet Government. For the Bolsheviks, including Radek, the 'Schlageter line' was never more than a change of tactics designed to split the burgeoning Right extremist movement in order to win the 'petty bourgeois' over to the Communist cause. There was no intention of changing KPD policy to one of following an active revolutionary course. The Soviet Government wanted to break up the powerful nationalist and Fascist front because it did not want the Right to overthrow the Cuno regime any more than it wanted the KPD to do so. In either event French troops would have advanced to the 'shores of Berezina' and endangered the Soviet Republic. The virtues of the 'Schlageter line' from the Bolsheviks' point of view were that it tended to curb the incipient Rightist revolution while combining various revolutionary forces in Germany for the purpose of forming 'a workers' government and an alliance with Soviet Russia.' The plan to link proletarian socialism with nationalism in Germany was entirely compatible with the best interests of Soviet security.[2]

When the 'Schlageter speech' was published in the *Rote Fahne* on 26 June there was a considerable stir in both nationalist and Communist circles. Several nationalist organizations expressed a willingness to co-operate with the KPD in a 'united front' of the

[1] K. Mielcke, *Dokumente zur Geschichte der Weimarer Republik* (Braunschweig, 1951), pp. 45-49.
[2] Cf. Carr, vol. 4, p. 157, and above, p. 150.

Right. Some joint meetings were held and the *Rote Fahne* offered space for articles by Count Reventlow and others of his ilk. But the new tactics were more of a curiosity than a success. Neither side enjoyed the incestuous relationship, and when they were equally embarrassed by what they were subscribing to, the experiment was dropped.[1]

As long as the 'Schlageter line' lasted, from May until early August, the KPD did, in fact, gain unprecedented mass influence. Its vote in local and state elections multiplied, and there were indications that it would continue to gain support as long as the national crisis persisted. Some writers on this period maintain that the KPD failed to take advantage of its 'mass influence' during the summer of 1923 to challenge the government's edicts against it and to start an insurrection.[2] These judgments cannot be upheld even with the benefit of hindsight, with which they were made. Until the Cuno Government fell at the beginning of August there were no conspicuous opportunities for the Communists to organize an insurrection which would have had a reasonable chance of succeeding. Although the party was gaining mass support, it was not following an overt revolutionary policy at the time, and it could therefore not depend on the masses—not even on a majority of those who voted Communist—to support an insurrection. The leaders of the KPD had no way of knowing that their influence had reached its peak during July and August. Brandler believed, and in the circumstances his judgment was sound, that the party did not yet have enough support for a successful revolution. He did not so much submit to Soviet policy as agree with it. Even if Brandler and the other leaders of the KPD had been able to prophesy during the summer that the party would never again enjoy as much support as it had then, they could not have persuaded the rank and file to co-operate with any segment of the nationalist-Fascist bloc in overthrowing Cuno and establishing a revolutionary government. The 'Schlageter line' was not really effective on that level;

[1] For details of the co-operation between the KPD and nationalist and Fascist organizations see Flechtheim, *Die KPD*, p. 89; F. Borkenau, *The Communist International* (London, 1938), pp. 245 ff.; Carr, vol. 4, pp. 181-183; R. Fischer, *Stalin and German Communism*, pp. 282-287. According to Georg Schwarz, Ruth Fischer was especially diligent in following the 'National Bolshevik' line (*Völker, höret die Zentrale: KPD bankerott* (Berlin, 1933), pp. 92 ff.), but Mrs Fischer denies this (*op. cit.*, p. 283, n. 1).

[2] Cf. Kochan, *op. cit.*, p. 80, and Flechtheim, *op. cit.*, pp. 90 f.

the most it achieved was a temporary truce and limited co-operation between the leadership of the extreme Right and the extreme Left, but not between their followers. The rank and file Communists continued to apply the label Fascist to the nationalists of the DNVP and to the nihilists of the Black Reichswehr as well as to the Nazis. This points to one of the gravest weaknesses of the 'Schlageter line,' for it required the mass of the Communists to think anew about 'Fascists,' and to distinguish among them in a way that, for all but the few subtler members of the party, bordered on duplicity. Radek had clearly outlined the essential dichotomy that had to be made, but not many workers could marshal their emotions behind precise intellectual distinctions as dexterously as he could. The workers were told that, on the one hand, it was their duty 'to struggle with arms in their hands against Fascist insurrection,' and that, on the other hand, they must 'do everything in order to convince the petty bourgeois elements of Fascism . . . that Communism is not their enemy but the star which shows them the way to victory.'[1] This was too much to ask of the workers. Throughout the Schlageter period they remained fiercely hostile to all 'Fascist' doctrine and policy.

By the end of July the Left faction of the KPD had grown impatient with the party's policy. They considered the 'Schlageter line' bankrupt. Ruth Fischer asserted that the time had come for the Communists to make an independent appeal to the masses to support 'the dictatorship of the proletariat.' Brandler and a majority of the KPD Central Committee held that the situation was not yet favourable for a seizure of power. From Moscow the party received contradictory advice. Zinoviev and Bukharin, who were on holiday and apparently out of touch with developments in Germany, encouraged the KPD to hold mass meetings and street demonstrations on 'Anti-Fascist Day'—29 July 1923—in defiance of police regulations against outdoor demonstrations. Radek feared a trap, suspecting that the Fascists and Social Democrats planned to crush the Communists in a street battle. Moreover, he did not want any unnecessary Communist demonstrations against any segment of the Right as long as the 'Schlageter line' was being applied. With the support of Stalin, who agreed that 'the Germans should be restrained,' Radek went over Zinoviev's head to save the situation. He sent a telegram informing the KPD Central Committee

---

[1] *Rote Fahne*, 7 July 1923, quoted by Carr, vol. 4, pp. 184 f.

that 'the presidium of Comintern advises the abandonment of street demonstrations on 29 July.' The KPD executive accepted Comintern's order as mandatory.[1] Anti-Fascist Day was marked by impressive mass meetings, but these were held in conformity with police regulations and there were no disorders.

Whether or not Radek was wise to restrain the KPD, the episode served to intensify the split in the party ranks. A meeting of the Central Committee on 5-6 August aired the same old dis-agreements between the factions without reaching any solutions. Ruth Fischer again attacked the policy of seeking to form coalitions with the bourgeois Left, and demanded that the party take direct action. But the majority followed Brandler, who maintained that 'the workers were not sufficiently prepared' and that everything should be done to prevent a showdown.[2] The workers may not have been ready to support a Communist revolution, but they were ready and willing to force Cuno to resign. On 10 August a Communist-inspired strike of the printers of currency notes led to a general strike in Berlin which quickly spread throughout the country. The nation was paralysed; Cuno's Government fell. The next four days, 11-14 August, were most propitious for a violent overthrow of the Weimar Republic, but the Fascists were un-prepared and the Communists were both unprepared and unwilling to take advantage of the crisis when it was at its worst. Having forced Cuno to resign, the strikers lacked the inspiration to create a new regime and went back to work.[3]

The only political leader who had the courage to take charge of a new government at this juncture was Gustav Stresemann. He took office on 13 August with a 'Great Coalition' of party support, ranging from the SPD on the Left to his own DVP on the Right, which left only the parties of the extreme Right and Left in opposition. During the Hundred Days of his chancellorship Strese-mann had to contend with the most chaotic conditions Germany had witnessed since 1918.[4] The currency was almost valueless; the

---

[1] Carr, vol. 4, p. 187; L. Trotsky, *Stalin* (London, 1947), pp. 368 f. Kochan makes the erroneous assertion that, 'In the actual event, the K.P.D. disregarded Radek's advice' (*op. cit.*, p. 81). Ruth Fischer virtually ignores the entire episode (*op. cit.*, p. 287).

[2] Carr, vol. 4, p. 188.

[3] Stampfer, *Die vierzehn Jahre der ersten deutschen Republik*, pp. 337 ff.; Eyck, *Geschichte der Weimarer Republik*, pp. 337 f.

[4] Scheele, *The Weimar Republic*, pp. 68-75.

nation was bankrupt. 'Passive resistance' in the Ruhr had given way to violence and to more repressive measures by the French. With great courage, and with the aid of Hjalmar Schacht's financial wizardry, Stresemann was soon making headway towards stabilizing the mark. Since the 'passive resistance' campaign had clearly failed to eject the superior power of France, Stresemann called the campaign off and shifted the battle against the occupation from the factories in the Ruhr to the embassies in London, Paris, and Berlin. It was Stresemann's way to cover long distances with short strides; he was flexible in negotiations, and usually chose the safest if not the most direct approach in solving problems. For the German masses Stresemann's methods were agonizingly slow, and his efforts were therefore menaced all along by the radical agitators of both extremes. During the Hundred Days riots were commonplace throughout the country, and at one time or another separatists tried to seize power in Aachen, Speier, Bonn, Coblenz, Crefeld, and in other cities. In October alone Stresemann had to repel three major attempts to overthrow his government: the Black Reichswehr *putsch* led by Major Buchrucker;[1] the abortive Hitler-Ludendorff *putsch*, which was further complicated by the simultaneous rebellion of Kahr and Lossow in Bavaria;[2] and the Communist uprising in Hamburg.[3] Equally dangerous problems had to be faced in Saxony and Thuringia, where the Communists formed coalition governments with bourgeois socialists and provoked the Bavarian Free Corps to mobilize for a march against them.[4] Crisis followed upon crisis: Germany was coming apart at the seams. Yet the Republic and the highest remaining German ideal, German unity, survived. In the hour of its most desperate need the Republic found two saviours: Stresemann and Seeckt.

[1] The best account of the Küstrin *putsch* is in Waite, *Vanguard of Nazism*, chap. 9, *passim*. Cf. E. J. Gumbel, *Verräter verfallen der Feme!* (Berlin, 1929), pp. 231-236. In regard to Buchrucker's later claim that Seeckt had pledged to co-operate with the Black Reichswehr against Stresemann's Government see the *Stresemann Nachlass*, 7336H/H163324/5.

[2] Wheeler-Bennett, *Nemesis of Power*, pp. 113-118, 167-176; Bullock, *Hitler*, pp. 83-101.

[3] See below, p. 181.

[4] Waite, *op. cit.*, p. 257.

# CHAPTER VII

## THE GERMAN CRISIS:
## SEECKT AND STRESEMANN

NO two men were more important in shaping the policies of the Weimar Republic than Stresemann and Seeckt. Their influence was so great that it seems in order to make some observations about the relations between them and their work, paying especially close attention to their roles in the crisis of 1923.

Stresemann once characterized his relationship with Seeckt as 'unhappy love.'[1] The two men were totally unlike in background and character. Seeckt was a Pomeranian of ancient and noble lineage, a slim, severe, and quiet man. Stresemann's origin, on the other hand, was strictly bourgeois. He was the son of a beer salesman, corpulent in build, free and genial in manner. Stresemann admired military men and remained, at heart, a monarchist, but Seeckt was not flattered by his attentions and often treated Stresemann, as other commoners, with contempt. Both were able men, but they possessed different special skills and abilities. Yet Germany needed both of them, and the goals they worked for were not at all dissimilar. Seeckt saved the Republic and Stresemann revived it. They worked together unwillingly and clashed more often than they saw eye to eye, but both believed in and laboured for the ascendancy and future greatness of Germany. A semblance of friendship grew up between them only after Seeckt was forced to resign from the command of the army in 1926. Thereafter both men could look back on years of collaboration with pride in mutual accomplishments, and with at least a grudging respect for the other's contributions.[2]

By the autumn of 1923, Seeckt, who had never respected the

[1] Gatzke, *Stresemann and the Rearmament of Germany*, p. 12. Stresemann's private secretary and friend Henry Bernhard has given a studiously one-sided account of the Stresemann-Seeckt relationship in an article, 'Seeckt und Stresemann,' *Deutsche Rundschau*, 79. Jhrg., Heft 5 (Darmstadt, May 1953), pp. 465-474. Also see Rabenau, *Seeckt*, vol. 2, pp. 355, 406.

[2] Stresemann hired Seeckt in May 1927 as an 'adviser on matters of general disarmament and other military-political questions' to the Foreign Ministry: Gatzke, *op. cit.*, p. 95.

Republic, was beginning to doubt if it were even useful as a façade behind which to rearm. The governments were weak and unstable. After Cuno the chancellors changed so frequently that it was difficult to take them seriously. Time and again Seeckt was tempted to assume dictatorial powers; he was confident that the army could overthrow the government at will. When Ebert appointed Stresemann to form a new government in August 1923, Seeckt contemplated withholding the support of the army, which was the one instrument the Republic had to defend itself against the revolutionaries of the Right and Left. But in the end he resolved not only to back up Stresemann but to crush all attempts to overthrow the government. Seeckt reasoned that the French would use a *putsch* as an excuse to occupy still more German territory, perhaps the entire country. That would have meant war. He looked forward to the day when Germany could revenge herself on France, but knew that the army was not yet strong enough to fight a full-scale war. Therefore, Seeckt refrained from attacking the Republic, even in the days when it was most vulnerable, for the same reason that the Soviet Government restrained the German Communists from revolutionary activity against the Cuno regime: both feared French reprisals. Furthermore, Seeckt realized that the army lacked mass support for a dictatorship, and he knew that without mass support he could not restore order and authority.[1] The anti-militarist Left would not let Seeckt seize power; he, in turn, was determined not to let the Communists or the forces of extreme reaction overthrow the government. Seeckt coldly refused to co-operate with the activist elements in the Black Reichswehr who tried to enlist his support for the Küstrin *putsch*. 'The time is not yet ripe,' he told them.[2] But the real reason why he wanted to prevent the Right extremists from seizing power was that their fanatic anti-Bolshevism would have interfered with his plans for co-operation with Soviet Russia. A shrewd analysis of the alternatives convinced Seeckt that the army should continue to prop up the Republic. When the army was prepared to avenge the country's defeat there

[1] Hallgarten, 'Seeckt and Russia,' pp. 33 f., n. 29.

[2] Gumbel, *Verräter verfallen der Feme!*, p. 198. Rabenau, writing in 1940, rationalizes Seeckt's reluctance to become dictator of Germany (*op. cit.*, p. 375). Walter Görlitz, writing with Rabenau's biography as the only evidence (according to a letter from Herr Görlitz to the present writer, dated 15 October 1953), says that Seeckt did not seize power because he believed 'dass die eigene Zeit abgelaufen war' (*Der Deutsche Generalstab*, p. 315).

would be time enough to revolutionize the form of government. Thus, in 1923, Seeckt turned a deaf ear to those who insisted that 'it was the duty of the Reichswehr to fight the [Weimar] system directly.'[1] Once his decision was made he stuck by it. When violence threatened in Saxony, Thuringia, and Bavaria, Seeckt, instead of helping to overthrow the Republic, undertook the most drastic powers that could be sanctioned by the Weimar Constitution—the emergency powers of Article 48—to protect it.[2] In this way Seeckt became a virtual dictator in Germany by legal means, not by force. He enjoyed playing the role of Protector of the Republic and did not abuse the powers with which Ebert entrusted him. It was not an empty boast he made to the President: 'There is only one man in Germany in a position to organize a *putsch*, and that is me. But the Reichswehr will not *putsch*!'[3]

Stresemann, like Seeckt, regarded the Left and Right radicals as the mortal enemies of the German State. He believed that the Communists were only waiting for the Fascists to start an insurrection so that they could take advantage of the resultant chaos to seize power for themselves. 'The Right extremists, on the other hand,' Stresemann wrote in July 1923, 'are waiting . . . for a Communist uprising somewhere, so that they have an excuse to take action.'[4] As he saw it, 'the only positive factor' in Germany was the army.[5] He needed its support even more than his predecessors had, for it held the key to the success of his government. Stresemann doubted Seeckt's proffered loyalty to the Republic:

Part of the Reichswehr is supposed to want to go along with the Right extremists. Gessler's faith in the Reichswehr's absolute reliability in its relations with the current State seems to me unwarranted optimism, considering the attitude of the Reichswehr officers and their men, about which I have some information.[6]

[1] Rabenau, *op. cit.*, p. 329. According to von Selchow's diary entry on 26 September 1923, 'again and again there was a demand from many circles that Seeckt should place himself at the head of the State': *Heeresarchiv*: Seeckt, Stück 289. Cf. G. F. W. Hallgarten, *Hitler—Reichswehr und Industrie* (Frankfurt/Main, 1955), pp. 35 ff., 58, 65 f.

[2] Ebert declared the *Ausnahmezustand*, which meant a state of siege and martial law, on 27 September 1923. See below, p. 178.

[3] Papen, *Memoirs*, pp. 120 f.

[4] *Stresemann Nachlass*, 7119H/H146064/9.

[5] Quoted by Gatzke, *Stresemann and Rearmament*, p. 11.

[6] *Stresemann Nachlass*, 7119H/H146064/9.

Although he was pessimistic about the outcome, Stresemann nevertheless made a strong bid for Seeckt's friendship and, along with that, the unswerving loyalty of the army. On the eve of his appointment, and again on his first day in office, the Chancellor had long discussions with Seeckt. The first discussion was held at Seeckt's villa, the second at the Chancellory. According to the report of these discussions given by von Selchow, Seeckt's personal adjutant, Stresemann outlined 'the criteria for the future course of the government's domestic policies.' At one point he 'pledged his complete and unreserved support for the national interests of the Reichswehr.' Seeckt said afterwards that he was 'satisfied' with the outcome of these talks, and, indeed, he had every reason to be.[1] When Stresemann was told about the secret rearmament activities in Russia, about which he had apparently been uninformed until this time, he immediately offered to take over from Cuno the responsibility for the secret funds in order to help continue the work.[2]

Several days after his discussions with Seeckt, Stresemann made another attempt to cement relations between the government and its army. He went to Döbernitz to review troops and addressed a large assembly of officers. Seeckt disapproved of Stresemann's informal conduct with the officers and was perturbed because he got along so well with them. Stresemann, said Seeckt, 'is a very agile and also a good politician,' but he does not know 'his place.' He brushed aside Stresemann's repeated overtures for friendlier relations: 'I have no close relations with him and shall not seek any.'[3] Stresemann was equally unsuccessful in trying to convert Seeckt to his own views on foreign policy. Seeckt refused to act as an 'accomplice' for a 'policy of fulfilment.' He considered the

[1] Quoted from von Selchow's diary: *Heeresarchiv*: Seeckt, Stück 289.

[2] One or two days before Scheidemann's speech in the Reichstag on 16 December 1926, which revealed the existence of Reichswehr-Red Army collaboration, Stresemann admitted to a small group of Reichstag deputies that when he was made Chancellor in 1923 he had taken over 'thirty million marks' from Cuno which were 'due [presumably to Russia] on the basis of earlier agreements' (*Stresemann Nachlass*, 7337H/H163462 ff. See below, pp. 204-205). With regard to Stresemann's involvement in the army's activities in Russia also see E. H. Carr, *German-Soviet Relations between the Two World Wars 1919-1939* (Baltimore, 1951), pp. 88 f.; Gatzke, *Stresemann and Rearmament*, pp. 82 ff. Cf. the spirited defence of Stresemann by his friend F. E. Hirsch, 'Stresemann in Historical Perspective,' *The Review of Politics*, vol. 15, No. 3 (Notre Dame, July 1953), pp. 360-377.

[3] Rabenau, *Seeckt*, vol. 2, pp. 335 f., 350.

revisionist approach to the Versailles treaty even more repugnant than the activist plans of the Right extremists. He disagreed with the radicals because their plans were misguided and their activities premature, but gave them credit for being staunchly patriotic. His disagreements with Stresemann, however, involved fundamentals. The Chancellor wanted to use slow and tortuous diplomatic means to achieve what Seeckt was preparing the army to do decisively, by force. 'We must regain our power, and as soon as we do, we shall naturally take back everything we lost.'[1] This was a naked statement of Seeckt's plan. The Ruhr occupation had intensified his already highly emotional and deep-rooted aversion to France; he wanted to crush both Poland and France by hitching Russia's masses to a German juggernaut.

Stresemann's approach to German Foreign Policy was completely different. He believed that some French fears of Germany and, consequently, France's oppressive policies, were due to the fervour of the 'German-Russian understanding.' Their fears had provoked the French to occupy the Ruhr, and Stresemann predicted that the French would go to even greater lengths to break up the Rapallo partnership in order 'to win Moscow for a Franco-Russian reconciliation.'[2] In his estimation, the only way to prevent a Franco-Russian *rapprochement*—which would be disastrous for Germany—was to disabuse the French of their fears of German-Russian collaboration. This was to be the underlying purpose of the 'policy of fulfilment.' Stresemann calculated that, as this policy was put into effect, Germany would gain concessions in the reparations questions and, slowly, achieve a general revision of the Versailles treaty.[3] But the 'policy of fulfilment' did not entail German acquiescence in the territorial awards to Poland. Stresemann had

[1] *Stresemann Nachlass*, 7129H/H147890.

[2] *Ibid.*, 7120H/H146305/11, Stresemann letter to Brockdorff-Rantzau, dated Berlin, 1 December 1923. Cf. Bretton, who finds in this letter a basis for writing that Stresemann 'considered an alliance with the Soviet Union' at this time (*Stresemann and the Revision of Versailles*, pp. 73 f.).

[3] The 'policy of fulfilment' is only considered here in so far as it had a bearing on Stresemann's policy towards the East. For more general accounts of Stresemann's foreign policy in non-biographical works see Scheele, *The Weimar Republic*, pp. 232 ff.; Wheeler-Bennett, *Nemesis of Power*, pp. 140-142; Bretton, *op. cit., passim*; Hirsch, 'Stresemann in Historical Perspective,' *passim*; Bernhard, 'Seeckt und Stresemann,' *passim*. Individually and collectively these works (and the biographies) do not do justice to Stresemann and his work. An authoritative account of his life and policies remains to be written.

no intention of recognizing Germany's Eastern frontiers of 1923 as the final boundary line, and, for this and other reasons, never even contemplated sacrificing Germany's good relations with Russia on the altar of friendly relations with the West. 'Russia,' he noted, 'also does not recognize her frontiers with Poland. Affairs in the East are by no means settled. As soon as Russia decides whether she is prepared to remain permanently within these frontiers or not . . . a new era will open up in European history.'[1] Stresemann realized that Germany's grievances in the East could not be rectified until the country had allayed French fears and removed the crushing force of the Allies in the West. Once the Allies' variegated fears of Germany were assuaged, when German soil was free of the invaders and after the Military Control Commission had ceased to function, then the government could turn its full attention to the Eastern questions. In other words, Stresemann was willing to postpone 'the readjustment of our Eastern frontiers—the recovery of Danzig, the Polish corridor and a correction of the frontier of Upper Silesia,' until his Western oriented 'policy of fulfilment' had gained Germany a *modus vivendi* with the Allies.[2] Thereafter Germany could afford to tighten her bonds with Soviet Russia—which Seeckt wanted to do right away —without fear of attack or occupation in the West.

To what extent Stresemann defined the principles of a long-range policy in the East, in which Germany's connexion with Russia could be utilized to recover her Eastern territories, is not to be gleaned from the papers which remain in his personal files.[3] It is possible, indeed likely, that he had no more than the basic tenets and goals of a long-range policy in mind when he became Chancellor in 1923. It is certain that Stresemann resisted Seeckt's insistent demands for an immediate and exclusive alliance with the Bolsheviks. In his judgment, such a policy would have led, in one way or another, to war. On the other hand, Stresemann 'was too much of a statesman . . . not to realize the importance of the Russian trump card in the German diplomatic game' even in the

[1] Stresemann, *Vermächtnis* (Berlin, 1932), vol. 2, p. 93.

[2] *Ibid.*, p. 554.

[3] Most of the diplomatic papers, including some of Stresemann's private papers, that have a bearing on German-Russian relations during Weimar are amongst the German Foreign Office files which the Allied editors have seen fit to withhold from research scholars. Cf. Klein, *Die diplomatischen Beziehungen Deutschlands zur Sowjetunion*, p. 7.

early stages of his foreign policy.[1] He saw no dangers in a policy based on correct and friendly relations with Soviet Russia under the Rapallo treaty, recognizing the intrinsic importance of Russia in relation to Germany's middle position in Europe. Stresemann did not shrink from using Germany's existing connexions with Russia and, whenever possible, the threat of forming new alliances with her, to cajole concessions out of the Western powers. He did not, however, agree with Seeckt that Germany's salvation lay in an alliance with the Russians. Stresemann considered 'the Bolshevik mentality' entirely alien to him, and was outraged by Moscow's attempts to undermine Germany's social structure. 'They will throw the rest of Germany to the French,' he exclaimed.[2]

Thus, Stresemann's foreign policy from the time he was Chancellor until Locarno was aimed at redressing Germany's bitterest grievances by loosening the shackles of Versailles, expelling the French from the Ruhr and driving the Military Control Commission out of the country—all by means of negotiations rather than war. Unlike Seeckt, who wanted to restore Germany's position in Europe by force, Stresemann favoured peaceful arbitration as a means of achieving his ends. Even if Stresemann envisaged using force to recover Germany's Eastern territories—which cannot be proven from the available sources—this would not gainsay his apparent preference for all means short of war. But this is not to say that Stresemann was a pacifist. 'We have nothing whatever to do,' he said on behalf of his party, 'with those pacifists who are proud to be disarmed. On the contrary, we are ashamed of the enforced disarmament.'[3] This thought, in practice, produced a large measure of agreement between Seeckt and Stresemann. Both men, regardless of their disputes in regard to German Foreign Policy, wanted a united and strong country. Stresemann's Republic needed the Reichswehr, and Seeckt's Reichswehr still needed the Republic. Stresemann's realism taught him that a nation must have a powerful army to force the settlement of political issues. On several occasions he went so far as to call the army 'the main factor in a

---

[1] The quotation is from Herbert von Dirksen's letter to Felix Hirsch in 'Stresemann in Historical Perspective,' p. 374.

[2] Stresemann, *Vermächtnis*, vol. 2, p. 554.

[3] Stresemann, *Reden und Schriften: Politik, Geschichte, Literatur 1897-1926* (Dresden, 1926), vol. 2, p. 167.

successful foreign policy.'[1] Furthermore, he believed that the army
was the only means of preserving order in the State, and he hoped
to use it to instil a new sense of national pride in the German
people. Therefore, while Stresemann objected to the unassailable
position Seeckt and the army cut out for themselves in the Republic
and feared that Seeckt would encroach on the government's prerogatives in conducting foreign relations, he was nevertheless
convinced that the country needed a stronger and larger army. To
build up the military establishment Stresemann readily conspired
with Seeckt against the armaments limitations prescribed at
Versailles, and was quite prepared to deceive Western statesmen
who enquired about the army's activities in Russia.[2] Seeckt's abuse
of Stresemann as an 'appeaser' was entirely unjustified; he simply
branded Stresemann for adopting a far-sighted and balanced
approach to foreign relations in opposition to his own principally
military one.[3]

The high-water mark of collaboration between Stresemann and
Seeckt was reached in September and October 1923 when the KPD
and Fascists became an active revolutionary threat to the Republic.
As was pointed out earlier, Communist preparations for a revolution in Germany did not cease with the proclamation of the 'united
front' tactics and the 'Schlageter line.'[4] Red Army intelligence
officers were active in Germany from the winter of 1922-1923 on,
organizing sabotage and terror units and an army of 'proletarian
(or Red) hundreds' in belated opposition to similar units established
by the extreme Right, and for the concomitant purpose of preparing the rank and file of the party for the seizure of power. Late
in the summer of 1923 the 'Red hundreds' were strengthened and
mobilized as a military cadre throughout Germany, with an
especially heavy concentration of them in Saxony and Thuringia,
the two Communist strongholds which were to serve as bases for
the revolutionary campaign.[5] Officials in Berlin were aware of the

[1] Quoted from the *Stresemann Nachlass* by Gatzke, *op. cit.*, p. 25.
[2] See above, p. 167, n. 2, and Hilger, *Incompatible Allies*, pp. 206, 207. Stresemann told Lord D'Abernon on 18 November 1923 that 'the talk about German
arms factories in Russia is nonsense': D'Abernon, *Ambassador of Peace*, vol. 2, p. 272.
[3] Gatzke, *loc. cit.*
[4] See above, p. 161.
[5] Details of the Communist underground fighting force in Germany are in
W. G. Krivitsky, *I was Stalin's Agent* (London, 1939), pp. 55 ff.; Carr, vol. 4,
pp. 209-212; R. Fischer, *Stalin and German Communism*, pp. 294-296, 326.

influx of Soviet emissaries into the country. The Moscow Embassy was anxiously instructed to keep track of Comintern's agents, especially of Radek's movements.[1] Radek, as usual, was to be found where the most crucial decisions were being taken; this time in Moscow.

The news of Cuno's resignation and of the formation of Stresemann's 'Great Coalition' Government caused a sensation in Russia. All the top Soviet leaders hurried back to Moscow from their vacation grounds. The excitement was caused by two distinct yet related aspects of the German situation. In the first place, the crisis appeared to be so acute that few people in Moscow (or anywhere else) thought Stresemann could save the country from complete chaos.[2] Some of the Bolsheviks were prone to overrate the revolutionary ferment in Germany at all times, and these now rushed to the conclusion that the great day was at hand: 'Revolution is knocking at the door in Germany and demanding admittance.'[3] What had failed to materialize in 1918-1919 and had misfired in 1921 was now going to come true, like a prophecy fulfilled. The second and equally sensational element in the news from Germany had the effect of reinforcing the new drive for revolutionary action. For at the very same time that the Bolsheviks' faith in the eventual triumph of the German revolution seemed to be vindicated, their interests in maintaining a stable German Government—those interests that had made them desist from revolutionary action while Cuno was in power—were dissolving. Stresemann, it seemed, was giving up the fight against the occupation, against 'Versailles.' He had called off the 'passive resistance' campaign and was making diplomatic overtures to London and Paris. Seen from Moscow, these manœuvres were leading Germany into a Western orientation and could only be interpreted as a reversal of the Rapallo policies. As far as the Bolsheviks could see, they were about to lose their *point d'appui* in Europe. Germany was going to stop fighting for the defence of Russia in the Ruhr, consequently the security of the Soviet Republic was impaired, even endangered. These two factors, the apparent reversal of the Rapallo policies and the

[1] Hilger, *Incompatible Allies*, p. 123.

[2] At the beginning of September $1 was worth 98,860,000 marks; by the beginning of October $1 was worth 25,260,208,000 marks.

[3] Quoted from Lozovsky's article in the September issue of the journal of Profintern by Carr, vol. 4, p. 203.

development of an acute revolutionary situation in Germany, caused the Bolsheviks to reconsider the relative importance of the component policies which made up the duality of Soviet relations with Germany. Since the last weeks of 1922 the active promotion of a proletarian revolution had been subordinated to the protection of the Soviet Government's immediate national interests—but only as a temporary expedient, as long as the Rapallo policies protected Russia's security more certainly than conditions in Europe favoured the expansion and triumph of the revolution. By September 1923 Moscow was convinced that the time to strike in Germany was at hand. *Izvestiya* trumpeted the new line:

We have never renounced our idea of furthering by all means the development of the international revolution, which will lead us to final victory. We are on the threshold of great events. . . .[1]

On the following day, 30 September, *Izvestiya* published an interview with Trotsky in which he said that the Soviets would give the German Communists all aid short of declaring war:

With all our souls we are on the side of the German working class in its struggle against exploitation internally and externally. And at the same time we are wholly for peace.[2]

In this way the Bolsheviks reversed the roles played by the component parts of their dual policy: 'victory of the revolution' now took precedence over Russian security.[3] But this did not mean that the protection of the Soviet State was excluded from active consideration. On the contrary, the triumph of the revolution would itself strengthen the Soviet Republic. By the same token the Bolsheviks were not going to co-operate with Stresemann in abrogating Rapallo, which they assumed was his intention. It was necessary for the Soviet Government to maintain the best possible relations with Berlin in order to bridge over the interval before the anticipated victory of the German proletariat, for the German Communists might fail if the Soviet Government did not take adequate measures to strengthen itself so that it could lend active support to the KPD. Moreover, the Bolsheviks had to provide for the contingency of the revolution collapsing, in which case Russia

---

[1] *Izvestiya*, 29 September 1923, quoted by Kochan, *Russia and Weimar*, p. 87.
[2] *Izvestiya*, 30 September 1923, quoted by Kochan, *op. cit.*, p. 88.
[3] R. Fischer, *Stalin and German Communism*, pp. 311 ff.; Flechtheim, *Die KPD*, p. 92; Carr, vol. 4, pp. 214 f.

would be left to fend for herself. These considerations must have been debated at great length in Moscow. Trotsky was profoundly convinced that the German proletariat would not fail again, but Chicherin, and possibly also Rykov and Kamenev, advised against pushing the revolution ahead at this time.[1] However, in the final analysis 'the decision of the Politburo to support the German revolution, if and when it broke out, was unequivocal.'[2]

Chicherin might have been faced by insuperable difficulties in maintaining good relations with the Stresemann Government at the same time that Comintern incited the German workers to overthrow the government. But, contrary to Chicherin's fears, Stresemann fully complemented the discrepancies in the policies of Comintern and the Soviet Government with equally anomalous ones of his own. He freely admitted that he was making every effort 'to draw a sharp line between the Russian Government and the Third International.'[3] The Rapallo policies were not reversed. Stresemann considered the treaty a 'correct' definition of Germany's policy towards Russia and upheld this view throughout the period that Comintern was actively engaged in overthrowing his government. He did not want to introduce the least uncertainty in regard to relations with the East while he had more than enough to contend with in the West. Even if Stresemann had wanted to adopt an active anti-Soviet stand because of Moscow's revolutionary policies he could not have done so, since this would have brought him into direct conflict with Seeckt on whom he had to depend for the support of the army. But regardless of the official policy, Stresemann's opinions about the nature of the Bolshevik regime had undergone some changes since the time in 1918 when he declared, with grand self-assurance, that it was 'at least not imperialistic under any circumstances.'[4] He gathered enough evidence in the autumn of 1923 to inform Brockdorff-Rantzau that the German 'Communist movement is financed with Russian gold' and to blame the Soviet Government for all the Left-wing subversive activity in Germany.[5] But although he knew that the

[1] Hilger, *Incompatible Allies*, pp. 122-123, n. 13. Also see Von Laue, 'Soviet Diplomacy' in *The Diplomats*, pp. 269-271.
[2] Carr, vol. 4, p. 204.
[3] *Stresemann Nachlass*, 7133H/H148765/79.
[4] See above, p. 27.
[5] *Stresemann Nachlass*, 7120H/H146305/11.

Bolsheviks inspired the KPD's activities, Stresemann lodged only the most perfunctory protests in Moscow. In exercising such notable self-control Stresemann proved himself to be a diplomat *par excellence*, for he evidently realized that even diplomacy has its limitations. Only the police and the army could deal effectively with Communist activities in Germany. It would not have profited the country if he had exacerbated the irritation of the Soviet leaders with the Western tendencies of his policy by lodging loud protests against Comintern's subversive activities. This is the principal reason why German diplomacy remained 'outwardly in-different not only to the most outspoken denunciations of the German Government by influential persons in Moscow, but to the incitement and active preparation of insurrection by agents of Comintern.'[1]

The details of the German uprising were debated for almost six weeks in Moscow. First Brandler and then the leaders of the Left faction, Maslow, Thälmann, and Ruth Fischer, were summoned from Berlin. The talks were prolonged because the KPD leaders could not agree on either the political issues or on the party's 'military strategy,' which was being discussed seriously for the first time. Brandler doubted that the KPD was sufficiently organized to seize and hold power. He wanted to hold off a final decision on the start of an insurrection until it was clear what the attitude of the workers would be to the new government, for Stresemann, unlike Cuno, had included the SPD in his coalition. Radek, who among the Soviet leaders was still the best informed about conditions in Germany, and apparently also Stalin, shared Brandler's pessimism. But they expressed these views only in private. In official declarations all three men seem to have agreed with the prevailing opinion that the seizure of power was now 'a fully practicable task.'[2] In describing the conditions in Germany to the Politburo Brandler apparently characterized his followers in Saxony and Thuringia as more revolutionary than the Communists in the Ruhr and else-where. This raised the ire of his enemies in the KPD. Ruth Fischer writes in her apologia that Brandler was motivated by cynicism to give a 'distorted' picture of revolutionary conditions in Germany. Although he was genuinely pessimistic about the success of an

---

[1] Carr, vol. 4, pp. 224 f.

[2] Brandler at a meeting of Profintern, quoted by Carr, vol. 4, p. 205. Cf. R. Fischer, *Stalin and German Communism*, p. 312.

insurrection, says Mrs Fischer, Brandler was 'driven by his temperament and his ambition' to make vast exaggerations of the revolutionary preparations that had been made in order to give the Politburo 'the impression that an armed nucleus existed in Germany that could be developed by energetic intervention from the outside.' But why should Brandler have tried to out-Herod Herod? Because, writes Mrs Fischer, his chief interest was to keep control of the KPD. He could not have retained control of the party if he had failed to go along with 'the about face of the Politburo,' which now espoused the revolutionary programme long advocated by the Left faction of the KPD. Pursuing her argument, Mrs Fischer recalls that the Left faction gave the Politburo a more 'sober survey' of conditions in Germany than Brandler's 'fanciful presentation' had led them to believe in. 'The Left wing,' she writes, 'was forced to be less "revolutionary"' than Brandler.[1] This last is the least plausible part of the argument, for there is no doubt that Ruth Fischer and the other leaders of the Left faction were as fervent in their advocacy of revolutionary action in the deliberations of September 1923 as they had always been before. Maslow, Thälmann, and Ruth Fischer were convinced that the German situation was ripe for a proletarian revolution, and no doubt they said so.

It is possible to agree with Mrs Fischer that Brandler wanted to prevent her and Maslow from taking control of the KPD without also subscribing to the notion that Brandler was motivated by dark and devious motives. If Brandler deliberately exaggerated the revolutionary fervour in Germany, he may have done so in order to retain the confidence of the majority in the Politburo, who were, it seems, determined to press for revolutionary action, so that he might save—or salvage, as it turned out—from the situation more than the KPD's Left faction could have done, since the latter were inclined to rush head-on into revolutionary action in accordance with the tactics advocated by Trotsky and Zinoviev, who, though 800 miles away, persisted in the fatal habit of 'transferring to the international sphere precedents drawn from Russian experience.'[2] The Left faction's real grievance in the Moscow discussions of September-October 1923 was one that Mrs Fischer only hints at in her book, namely that the revolution was to be centred in Saxony and Thuringia, where Brandler was in control, instead of in the

[1] R. Fischer, *op. cit.*, pp. 313 f. Cf. Carr, vol. 4, p. 204.
[2] Kochan, *Russia and Weimar*, p. 86.

Ruhr, where the 'Red hundreds' were then 'growing like mush-rooms, with tremendous speed,' and where the Left faction was in control.[1]

Fixing a date for the start of the insurrection proved to be the greatest stumbling-block in the discussions between the Politburo and the KPD. Trotsky made a fetish of Bolshevik precedents, and this led him to propose 7 November as the starting date; but Brandler would not let himself be tied down to a time-table. The talks dragged on and on, forcing the KPD leaders and the Russians who were to help direct the revolutionary action to remain in Moscow until 8 October, wasting time they should have devoted to preparations in Germany. These interminable wrangles about details seem all the more ludicrous in retrospect because they emanated from two completely false assumptions about the nature of German Social Democracy and the effects of the 'National Bolshevik' line. The Communists had obviously not learned from their previous failures that they were not only using the wrong tactics, but that their entire diagnosis of the conditions of the German working masses was fundamentally incorrect. They were still going on the assumption that if the misery of the German workers was great enough they would rise to a call for proletarian revolution behind Communist leadership on the Bolshevik model. Brandler's warning that the Communists should first gauge the working class support for Stresemann's coalition was disregarded by everyone—including, in the final analysis, Brandler. A closer examination of the situation in September would have shown that Stresemann had managed to separate the moderate constitutional wing of the Social Democrats from the extremists by taking the SPD into his coalition, so that a majority of the workers were, in fact, represented by the government. If Brandler, Maslow, and the others had remained in Germany, instead of wasting time debating details in Moscow, they would have had an opportunity to see for themselves that the KPD did not have enough support for a successful insurrection.[2]

The second basic and equally false assumption the Communists made concerned the Reichswehr, and this turned out to be the fatal flaw. Somehow the Communists convinced themselves that

[1] A. Thalheimer, *1923: Eine verpasste Revolution?* (-?-, n.d.), p. 19, quoted by R. Fischer, *op. cit.*, p. 314.

[2] Cf. Kochan, *op. cit.*, p. 80, and Flechtheim, *Die KPD*, pp. 90 f.

they could count on the complicity of a section of the army in fomenting a revolution. How they happened to entertain these fantastic hopes is not readily understandable. There was, it is true, some reason to believe that 'National Bolshevik' propaganda had infected groups in the army. Furthermore, because the High Command, notably Seeckt, wanted to collaborate with the Red Army, and since the Communists believed that this collaboration was being imperilled by Stresemann's policies, they may have deduced that the army would have no interest in protecting the Republic in the event of a proletarian uprising. But even this admixture of fact and fancy was an insufficient ground on which to base high hopes of army support for the revolution. Did Brandler, then, really tell wild stories in Moscow about 'Communist leadership of the Reichswehr opposition,' as Ruth Fischer asserts?[1] Perhaps he did, and Radek may also have contributed to the phantasmagoria by misrepresenting Seeckt's views about the future course of German-Russian relations. A few facts were enough to inspire the wildest dreams when the revolutionary spirit was running high in Moscow. Only two days before the ill-fated Hamburg uprising in October Trotsky was still supremely confident that there were 'working class elements' in the German Army 'which at a decisive moment will not defend the bourgeois very stoutly.'[2] It is obvious that Trotsky and other Communist leaders, apparently including Radek, did not really understand Seeckt. They failed, moreover, to appreciate the significance of the change that took place on 26 September when Ebert entrusted Seeckt with virtual dictatorial powers under the martial law provision of Article 48 of the Weimar Constitution. From that moment on the army became the Protector of the Republic; Seeckt stood ready to defend the government against insurrection from both Right and Left extremes. He could order troops to march against any formation, be they *Landtag* governments or Communists, whenever he deemed it necessary to do so for the protection of the German State. Thus, any attack against the Republic was also an attack on

[1] R. Fischer, *op. cit.*, pp. 314 f. See the different account by Carr (vol. 4, pp. 212 f.) which was written with the benefit of Heinrich Brandler's 'personal recollections of the events of 1923': *ibid.*, p. vi.

[2] *Izvestiya*, 21 October 1923, quoted by Carr, vol. 4, p. 212. According to Wheeler-Bennett, a higher percentage of officers in the Reichswehr of 1921 were members of the aristocracy than in the Imperial Army of 1913: *Nemesis of Power*, p. 99.

the Reichswehr. Seeckt had called the army the 'purest image' of the State. From September 1923 the army considered itself identical with the State.

But the Communists did not understand this; they completely misinterpreted the situation. All that mattered, they thought, was that the crisis had not diminished since the end of August: the prospects for a successful revolution were getting better and better every day. Indeed, Germany was still deep in the crisis. The Right extremists deplored the cessation of the 'passive resistance' campaign, which they called a 'capitulation' to the French, and stepped up their drive against Stresemann's Government.[1] The KPD kept pace by adjusting the familiar lines of the 'united front' to complement the Fascists' outcries against the government. The Communists protested against the 'capitulation of the Stresemann-Hilferding Government,' and Radek, still appealing to nationalist sentiments, asserted that 'the independence of the German nation' depended on proletarian leadership.[2] Meanwhile, in Saxony and Thuringia, where the KPD and SPD together had absolute majorities in the legislatures, negotiations between the two parties leading to the formation of coalition governments were progressing satisfactorily. However, when Zeigner's Government in Saxony agreed to let the KPD fill three cabinet posts, Brandler, who in theory favoured joining coalitions with the Social Democrats because he considered them 'the pivot of the situation,' reversed himself and asked for a respite of several weeks in which to campaign for greater mass support to back up the prospective coalition.[3] But Zinoviev, in Moscow, overruled him with a telegram to the KPD Central Committee in which he instructed the party to accept Zeigner's offer:

We interpret the situation in such a way that the decisive moment will come in four, five, or six weeks. Therefore we believe it is necessary to seize at once every position which can be directly utilized. . . . On the conditions that the Zeigner people are really prepared to defend Saxony against Bavaria and the Fascists we must enter. Carry out at once the arming of 50,000 to 60,000 men. Ignore General Müller. The same in Thuringia.[4]

---

[1] Waite, *Vanguard of Nazism*, p. 250.
[2] Carr, vol. 4, p. 220.
[3] Borkenau, *The Communist International*, p. 251.
[4] *Die Lehren der deutschen Ereignisse* (Hamburg, 1924), pp. 60 f.

The KPD entered the government of Saxony on 12 October and of Thuringia on 16 October. Following Zinoviev's orders Brandler tried to get hold of the arms of the Saxon police to equip '50,000 to 60,000 men,' but events moved too fast for him, with the result that only about 11,000 members of the Saxon 'Red hundreds' were armed.[1]

There were immediate repercussions in Berlin when the Communists acceded to power in Saxony and Thuringia. The government was faced at the same time by an insurrectionary movement in Bavaria where Erhardt's Free Corps were being massed on the Thuringian border ostensibly to protect Bavaria from the 'Red peril,' but actually to provoke the Communists in order to have a pretext for marching to the North—to Berlin.[2] Seeckt and Stresemann conferred in mid-October to decide how they were going to meet these threats and how to avoid a clash between the Free Corps and the 'Red hundreds.' They agreed to order General Müller, the regional commander (*Wehrkreis IV*), to dissolve the 'Red hundreds' in Saxony and Thuringia. No action was contemplated against the Bavarian Free Corps at this stage. When Müller demanded that the 'Red hundreds' be demobilized the Saxon Government followed Zinoviev's orders and gamely tried to ignore him. Zeigner himself made a public appeal for support against Stresemann and the army, asserting that the 'Red hundreds' were 'behaving in perfect accord with the law' and that the real threat to the Republic lay in Bavaria. 'Saxony,' he said, 'fights for the very existence of the German Republic, which can be smashed by the onslaught of the Bavarian reactionaries.' The rest of Zeigner's speech was taken up with a sharp attack on the Reichswehr, which he branded a stronghold of monarchism and reaction and accused of numerous breaches of the disarmament restrictions of the Versailles treaty.[3] Zeigner had dared more than either Stresemann or Seeckt were prepared to tolerate. They had to take decisive action to quash the threats to the Republic in Saxony and Bavaria, and after Zeigner's speech there was no longer any doubt where they would act first. For some of the same reasons both Stresemann and Seeckt decided that the greatest dangers lay in Saxony. Both were prepared to crush the Communists and their

---

[1] Borkenau, *op. cit.*, p. 252.

[2] Waite, *Vanguard of Nazism*, p. 257.

[3] Caro and Oehme, *Schleichers Aufstieg*, pp. 161 ff.

allies at any time, without any compunction. On the other hand, they were equally reluctant to use force against the Right extremists except in the very last resort, especially in Bavaria where there was the danger that loyal army units would have to fire on rebellious comrades in arms who had joined the Free Corps. Stresemann as much as Seeckt wanted to prevent the Reichswehr from being divided against itself. He was just as indignant as Seeckt about Zeigner's attacks on the High Command and equally determined to uphold the one instrument of national power at the government's disposal. As Stresemann and Seeckt saw it, the peril from the Left was so great that the strongest action had to be taken, or, as Arthur Rosenberg called it: 'an act of arbitrary brutality and an open breach of the law.'[1] On 20 October Seeckt, with Stresemann concurring, ordered Müller's troops to march into Saxony and Thuringia to depose the Leftist governments and arrest their leaders. With this order Stresemann and Seeckt forced the Communists to decide immediately whether to act or submit. They had either to start the insurrection or confess their impotence.

As General Müller's troops advanced, Brandler calmly expressed the conviction that the German workers 'will not allow the Saxon proletariat to be struck down.'[2] The KPD alerted its members to prepare for a showdown. The following day, 21 October, Brandler addressed a conference of workers' organizations in Chemnitz. He urged the workers, most of whom were Social Democrats, to call a general strike against the advancing army detachments. When Brandler finished there was 'an icy silence'; the last minute attempt to persuade the Left wing of the SPD to support a Communist uprising had failed.[3] There was nothing left for Brandler to do but to call off the projected insurrection. Couriers were sent from Chemnitz to Communist centres all over Germany with messages countermanding the orders to start the insurrection two days hence. Through some unexplained mischance the Hamburg Communists received the wrong message. Early in the morning of 23 October a few hundred of them started an uprising. They seized a section of Hamburg and held off the police for two days until troop

---

[1] *Geschichte der deutschen Republik*, p. 170. Wheeler-Bennett, on the other hand, calls the overthrow of Zeigner's Government a 'commendable display of forceful action . . .': *Nemesis of Power*, p. 113.

[2] R. Fischer, *Stalin and German Communism*, pp. 324-328.

[3] *Ibid.*, p. 336.

reinforcements were sent in to crush them. That was all there was to the Communist uprising of 1923; it never really got under way. Moscow was completely out of touch with the situation. A leader in *Pravda* on 24 October still hailed 'the October days in the centre of Europe.'

Müller's troops encountered almost no opposition in occupying Dresden and the rest of Saxony as well as Thuringia. Both governments were deposed and a commissioner installed in power without much bloodshed. By taking decisive action Stresemann and Seeckt had prevented the Bavarian Free Corps from intervening in Saxony and Thuringia, thereby staving off a possible civil war in the Reich. Stresemann was jubilant and gave credit where credit was due:

If we were able to march into Saxony and Thuringia without bloodshed, then perhaps the reason was that the Social Democrats were won over to support the invasion and that, therefore, the Communists stood alone against us.[1]

The Bavarian crisis came to a head several days later, at the beginning of November, when Hitler and Ludendorff staged their abortive *putsch*. Once again Stresemann and Seeckt took decisive action, on this occasion going to the extreme of ordering the Reichswehr to fire on Ludendorff.[2] By the middle of November order was restored throughout the country and the inflation had been curbed by the introduction of new currency. Seeckt earned the grateful thanks of Ebert and Stresemann for preserving the unity of the State and saving the Republic from disintegration.[3] Speaking at Halle on 11 November, Stresemann defended himself

[1] *Verhandlungen des Reichstags 1923* (Berlin, 1924), vol. 391, p. 8502.

[2] Shortly before the Hitler-Ludendorff *putsch* was crushed, Seeckt, fearing that the Reichswehr would have to fire on Reichswehr in Bavaria, told Stresemann that 'the conflict could still be resolved without bloodshed, if one were to establish a cabinet on a new basis' (Rabenau, *Seeckt*, vol. 2, pp. 367 f.). Seeckt meant by this that he himself should form a government and proposed this to Ebert. Ebert said 'he could not use him as a Chancellor because he could not spare him as Commander in Chief of the Reichswehr' (*ibid.*, p. 368). The details of this episode are now revealed by Hallgarten, *Hitler—Reichswehr und Industrie*, pp. 34 ff., who, however, overlooks the most significant fact, which was, as Stresemann put it, that 'there was never any question of Seeckt's refusing me the loyalty of the Reichswehr' (*Vermächtnis*, vol. 1, p. 200).

[3] *Stresemann Nachlass*, 7120H/H146211/4. Also see Wheeler-Bennett, *op. cit.*, p. 118.

against the charge that he had condoned unconstitutional military action against Saxony and Thuringia while showing excessive leniency towards the Bavarian racists and separatists. 'In the fight to maintain the unity of the Reich,' he said, 'it is, in my opinion, the duty of the German Government to adopt the means of peaceful understanding until the very last resort, *so long as it is a conflict in which there are Germans on both sides.*' Stresemann then showed himself to be in complete accord with Seeckt regarding the government's policies during the crisis and its mission in the future: 'I shall welcome the day when the hatchet is buried between Bavaria and the Reich. For what we need is a united front against the world, not dismemberment within.'[1]

[1] *Vermächtnis*, vol. 1, pp. 207-211.

## CHAPTER VIII

# THE ALLIANCE DISRUPTED:
# BROCKDORFF-RANTZAU

ALTHOUGH relations between Berlin and Moscow were not seriously disturbed during the autumn of 1923 while the German Communist revolution was being planned and, ultimately, frustrated, the Rapallo partnership did not go unscathed. The episode introduced a certain strain into relations between the two countries which was incompatible with the old *Schicksalsgemein-schaft.* An element of mistrust had been introduced which was never completely eliminated from the relationship.

The abortive Hamburg uprising had infuriated Brockdorff-Rantzau to the point of asking Stresemann to consider withdrawing him from Moscow.[1] The Ambassador remained at his post, however, and by the beginning of November had calmed down enough to make some shrewd observations about Russia's attitude towards Germany. Moscow's policy, he wrote to Maltzan at this time, would be determined by the struggle for supremacy between Comintern and the Soviet Government. The outcome of this struggle 'would depend chiefly on political developments in Germany. There has already been considerable disappointment here,' the Ambassador reported, 'especially about the events in Saxony and the failure of the Hamburg *putsch.*' If Germany were to recover from the crisis, then 'the policy represented by the Foreign Commissariat would be considerably strengthened.' But so far, Brockdorff-Rantzau concluded, 'the enthusiasts of the party leadership, among whom, as of recent times, there is in addition to Zinoviev and Bukharin also Stalin—although he remains in the background—still appear to have the upper hand.'[2]

The failure of the German insurrection caused an uproar in Moscow. Comintern meetings featured scenes of rancorous and recriminatory exchanges amongst the frustrated revolutionaries, each of whom tried to lay the blame for the failure of the revolt at somebody else's doorstep. Zinoviev accused Brandler and Radek,

[1] Helbig, 'Moskauer Mission Brockdorff-Rantzaus,' p. 341.
[2] *Ibid.*, pp. 341 f.

and also blamed Trotsky, for the 'October retreat.' Radek was subjected to especially harsh treatment. Zinoviev charged him with responsibility for the Politburo's 'incorrect assessment of the class forces in Germany.' Radek, he said, 'knew more than anyone about this movement and was supposed to be the greatest authority on it,' but in actual fact he had 'made more mistakes than anyone.' Radek's greatest blunder, according to Zinoviev, was to support Brandler's decision to call off the insurrection. Radek had held back the KPD 'by its coat-tails when it ought to have been summoned to battle.' He 'retreated without fighting,' and that was an unpardonable sin.[1] The feuds amongst the Bolshevik leaders inevitably embroiled foreign Communist parties as well, including the KPD. In February 1924 Brandler was replaced at the helm of the KPD by leaders of the Centre and Left factions. Following Brandler's demotion Radek lost his influence with the German party.[2]

Meanwhile, Stresemann's currency reform was leading to economic recovery and to a general strengthening of the Weimar Republic. When, at the end of November, British policy took on a marked German orientation, the Russians, as Brockdorff-Rantzau had predicted, tried to recapture the spirit of relations with Germany which had existed before October. The Bolsheviks realized now that they could not make another attempt to overthrow the Weimar Republic for a long time to come. Their hopes of engineering a successful revolt were dashed with the ruin of the KPD, which was outlawed, virtually without leadership, and rent by factionalism after the October fiasco.[3] The revolution in Germany had suffered another grave setback: the opportunity of tying Germany more securely to the Soviet Republic had vanished. Yet Soviet policy remained unchanged in all essentials. The Bolsheviks still wanted to keep Germany isolated except for the link forged at Rapallo. But their only chance of keeping this foothold in Europe now lay in the partnership with the German bourgeoisie. They therefore hurriedly returned to the old stand of

[1] Carr, vol. 4, pp. 235, 236, 239.

[2] *Bericht über die Verhandlungen des IX. Parteitags der Kommunistischen Partei Deutschlands* (Berlin, 1924), pp. 64 ff.

[3] Details of the upheavals in the KPD at this time are in Flechtheim, *Die KPD*, pp. 100 ff.; R. Fischer, *Stalin and German Communism*, pp. 348-383; Carr, vol. 4, pp. 226-242; E. H. Carr, *Studies in Revolution* (London, 1950), pp. 193-199.

professing a desire for only the best relations with the German Government. Starting in early December, Chicherin, Trotsky, and Radek made every effort to persuade the Germans that the Soviet Government was in no way responsible for the October *débâcle*; they wanted Berlin to forget the entire episode. For the Russians, Brockdorff-Rantzau's influence was the vital factor in maintaining the best possible relations with Berlin. They realized that without his support there was no chance of counterbalancing Stresemann's 'Western orientation.' Therefore, as early as the end of November 1923 the Russians were turning their charm on the Ambassador in order that he might take strong action on behalf of the Russo-German partnership. But Brockdorff-Rantzau was a vain individual; he did not forgive easily. He considered the Communist insurrection not only a stab in the back of the German Government, but a personal affront to himself. Earlier in 1923, in the days of the Ruhr invasion when the Soviet Government fully supported German resistance against the French, Brockdorff-Rantzau had come round to the idea of an exclusive Russo-German connexion. He despaired of gaining British support for Germany against France and Poland, and took the position, very close to Seeckt's, that the Rapallo partnership was the only means of redressing Germany's grievances. But the attempted Communist insurrection had aroused new doubts. Brockdorff-Rantzau feared that the Bolsheviks regarded Germany as merely a pawn in their revolutionary game; he doubted if the Soviet Government could really be depended upon. In consequence, the Ambassador told Chicherin that unless the Soviet Government openly denounced its revolutionary ambitions he could take no action to strengthen the Rapallo alliance. Nothing short of an open break between the Soviet Government and the Third International would satisfy him. This was an exorbitant price to charge for Germany's friendship, far more than the Russians were willing to pay. Chicherin was indeed greatly embarrassed by the revolutionary activities carried on by Comintern under the cover of—yet in opposition to—Narkomindel's policy of friendship with the German bourgeoisie, but he could not, of course, throw off Comintern's influence over the Foreign Commissariat. The Soviet Government could not be dissociated from the Third International. Nevertheless, functionaries of the Soviet State and foreign diplomats accredited to it had to work on the assumption that the Soviet Government and Comintern were distinct and unrelated, both in theory and in fact. Chicherin made strenuous efforts to force foreign diplomats to uphold this myth even as he had to uphold and shoulder the burden of it. 'Our government,' he said, 'is not responsible for the activities of Comintern and has nothing at all to do with it.'[1] This was a transparent lie, but it was Chicherin's only device for camouflaging Comintern's interference in the formation and implementation of Russia's foreign policies, and as such it was essential to the maintenance of tenable relations between the Soviet Government and all foreign powers. In demanding an open break between the Soviet Government and the Third International Brockdorff-Rantzau was violating the taboo at the heart of the whole Bolshevik system: he was demanding that the Communists' myth be relegated to the realm of mythology. This was unthinkable for the Russians. The interrelationship of Comintern and the Soviet Government could not be admitted any more than the myth of a separation between the two could be abandoned. Chicherin insisted that Brockdorff-Rantzau give up his demand for a break between the Soviet Government and Comintern and that he accept the separation of the two as an accomplished fact. This was a prerequisite for friendly relations between the two countries.

However, Brockdorff-Rantzau was not easily reconciled to duplicity. He had proof that the Soviet Government had sent hirelings and gold to the KPD for the October insurrection and he demanded an official explanation. He was particularly angry about the case of Michael Petrov, the alias of a French Communist, who had bought large quantities of weapons and ammunition from a German firm for the KPD. The transaction with the German firm had taken place 'in the quarters of the Soviet Embassy' in Berlin, apparently with Ambassador Krestinski's full knowledge.[2] Brockdorff-Rantzau was indignant about this episode when he confronted Trotsky at a meeting in mid-December. When Trotsky calmly admitted that he had personally attached Petrov to the Embassy in Berlin because he had counted on the imminence of a German revolution, the Ambassador could hardly control his rage. Trying to calm him down, Trotsky added that, had the French occupied the rest of Germany, Petrov's mission would have been to subvert the French authorities instead of the Weimar Govern-

---

[1] Hilger, *Incompatible Allies*, pp. 108 f.
[2] *Stresemann Nachlass*, 7120H/H146305/11.

ment. But Brockdorff-Rantzau was not pacified. Thereupon
Trotsky reminded him that the Soviet Government had been the
first to protest against the Ruhr invasion and that it had prevented
the Poles from attacking Germany's Eastern provinces by making
threatening declarations. The Ambassador assented, but only
grudgingly, and left the meeting without giving any assurances
about the attitude of his government.[1] However, the Bolsheviks
were not to be discouraged from trying to overcome Brockdorff-
Rantzau's bitterness towards them. They hoped to bring him
round by playing on his vanity. Not long after the interview with
Trotsky the Ambassador was invited to a luncheon with the
highest ranking officials of the Foreign Commissariat, together
with Radek and Krestinski, who had recently returned from
Germany. A splendid table was laid on and the Russians tried their
best to be convivial, but the Ambassador was in no mood to enjoy
pedantic conversation. As soon as the talk turned to political
matters he voiced his demand for an open break between the
Soviet Government and Comintern, emphasizing the dangers
threatening Russo-German relations if Soviet emissaries continued
to encourage subversive activity in Germany. The KPD,
Brockdorff-Rantzau added, is not fit to govern Germany in any
event, and if the Communists tried to seize power in Berlin the
French would immediately occupy the entire country. Had Radek
himself not said that the time was not ripe for revolution? The
challenge annoyed Radek. Before he could check himself he
answered back that 'the German Communists' unfitness to govern
had yet to be proved, whereas the bourgeois parties had already
demonstrated their political bankruptcy.' If he had to make a
choice between the two, Radek added impertinently, he would
resign from the Soviet Government in order to continue working
for the revolution with Comintern. The discussion might have
got out of hand at this point if Chicherin had not intervened. In
a conciliatory tone he drew a parallel which everyone present
found amusing. It was really pure chance, Chicherin said, that
Comintern's headquarters were in Moscow. Why should
Brockdorff-Rantzau blame the Soviet Government for that? After
all, King Leopold of Belgium had not been held responsible for the
Second International just because its headquarters were in Brussels!
Radek, who had regained his composure by this time, reminded

[1] Hilger, *op. cit.*, p. 124.

Brockdorff-Rantzau that Seeckt was perfectly willing to accept the myth of a separation between the Soviet Government and Comintern. According to Radek, Seeckt had said: 'We have to keep our fingers tight on the gullet of the Communists, but together with Soviet Russia.' The Soviet Government was content to work with Seeckt on this basis, Radek added, why could not the Ambassador take the same standpoint? 'Mussolini, you know very well, is our best friend,' Chicherin cracked in the same spirit.[1] These frantic attempts to patch up the German-Soviet alliance convinced Brockdorff-Rantzau that the Russians wanted and needed Germany's friendship. His fears that the Bolsheviks considered the German Government *quantité négligeable* which they could support or overthrow at will seemed to be unwarranted. He would, he said, try to reconcile himself to the continued coexistence of the Soviet Government and Comintern, and only hoped that Comintern would work together with the Foreign Commissariat in reviving the old spirit of Rapallo.

Although relations between the two countries improved during the winter of 1923-1924, the old spirit of the Rapallo days, the *Schicksalsgemeinschaft* that held the nations together, was never resuscitated. After 1923 both Germany and Russia ceased to be the pariahs of international politics. Relations between them were consequently taken out of the realm of political romanticism. Ostracism by the Western powers and exclusion from the respectable family of nations were the *raison d'être* of the strange feeling of community which made up the *Schicksalsgemeinschaft*. As the bitterness of the World War and the recriminations of its aftermath diminished, both Russia and Germany lost interest in maintaining an exclusive partnership. Other factors contributed to this process. Lenin's death in January 1924 increased the tempo of the struggle for supremacy in Moscow. The loss of their great leader soon after the failure of the German revolution and the growing crisis of the NEP combined to preoccupy the Bolsheviks with domestic matters. Because of the uncertainty in their own affairs the Russians were anxious to promote the tactics of friendly relations with foreign governments, to the detriment of pursuing their revolutionary ambitions. Most of the Western governments now recognized the Soviet regime and other steps were taken to normalize political and economic relations with the Bolsheviks. In con-

[1] *Ibid.*, p. 125.

sequence there was an improvement of relations between Soviet Russia and the bourgeois world as a whole. Germany's recovery from the crisis of 1923 and her emergence on the international political scene was even more dramatic. The war which had been carried on against her by political and economic means after the cessation of military hostilities was virtually terminated by the summer of 1924. The Weimar Republic was treated more and more as a partner instead of as an object of abuse in negotiations with the Allies. The London Conference during the summer of 1924 and the Dawes Plan headed Germany along the road of economic recovery and gave the Western nations a stake in the country's revival from war and occupation.[1] Sufficient order and stability had been restored within Germany by the middle of February to permit Ebert to end the state of national emergency. On 20 February Stresemann, who was now Foreign Minister in Chancellor Marx's cabinet, alluded to the possibility of a Rhineland security pact with the Western powers, a suggestion which was first put forward by Cuno in the dark days of December 1922 but which had not been treated seriously in London and Paris until this time.[2]

On the whole, the political atmosphere in Europe was calmer by the summer of 1924 than it had been at any time since 1914. Both Russia and Germany tried to gain the maximum advantages from the improved situation, and their respective efforts were often made at the expense of the mutual understanding which had brought them so close together during the bitter years from 1919 to 1923. Brockdorff-Rantzau did not want to adjust himself to the sober politics of the new era. He missed the turmoil and the dangers. 'All the old *charme* is gone out of our relations with Russia,' he complained with a curious touch of melancholy.[3] The Ambassador was worried, moreover, that Stresemann would jeopardize the Russian alliance in his eagerness to reach a *modus vivendi* with the West. The Russians had reacted strongly against Stresemann's overtures to London and Paris. Moscow as much as Berlin recognized Britain as a kingpin of the European political world, but the Russians were much more antagonistic to the British. Every

---

[1] Eyck, *Geschichte der Weimarer Republik*, pp. 403-410; G. M. Gathorne-Hardy, *A Short History of International Affairs 1920-1939* (Oxford, 1950), pp. 57 ff.

[2] Halperin, *Germany Tried Democracy*, p. 332.

[3] Hilger, *op. cit.*, p. 127.

German act of reconciliation with the West, and with Britain in particular, evoked a hostile response from the Soviet Government. The slightest gesture of goodwill prompted accusations implying that Germany was joining an anti-Soviet bourgeois coalition. Brockdorff-Rantzau loyally answered these *démarches* with assurances that Stresemann's policies were neither pro-British nor pro-Russian but simply pro-German, but his arguments did not seem to make any impression on the Russians. They adopted the line that 'those who are not for us are against us.'[1]

Brockdorff-Rantzau himself was not as convinced about Stresemann's intentions as he made out in conversations with the Russians. It seemed to him that the 'policy of fulfilment' was being pursued to the detriment of Germany's interests in the East. He felt that the gradual deterioration of relations with Russia could only be arrested if he travelled to Berlin to appraise Stresemann of the situation in Moscow. The trip took place at the beginning of February, and Brockdorff-Rantzau stayed in Berlin until April, but there is no indication that his visit had a marked effect on the government's policies. The Ambassador was reassured by both Maltzan, with whom he was closely befriended, and Stresemann that the government had no intention of sacrificing friendly relations with Russia in order to achieve its objectives in the West. But there was no question of allowing the Soviet Government to dictate Germany's relations with London and Paris. The Rapallo friendship would be upheld, but the treaty was not to be given the broad interpretation Moscow had adopted, which would have forced Germany to exclude the possibility of signing treaties with other countries.[2] That Brockdorff-Rantzau was not entirely satisfied with the results of his trip to Berlin is evidenced by the fact that, soon after he returned to Moscow at the beginning of April, Stresemann found it necessary to reassure him that the government considered the Ambassador's task in Moscow to be 'of historical importance' and was grateful to have him serve in a post where he could do 'an unending amount for the political future of Germany.'[3] One paragraph of Stresemann's letter refers to certain unspecified 'secret reports' he had received from the Ambassador and suggests that one of Brockdorff-Rantzau's tasks in Berlin had been to clear

[1] *Ibid.*, p. 131.
[2] See below, p. 214.
[3] *Stresemann Nachlass*, 7168H/H155566/8.

up problems concerning the Reichswehr-Red Army collaboration in which the Moscow Embassy was now taking an increasingly active part. 'It interested me especially,' Stresemann wrote, 'to hear more from you about the conversations with the gentlemen of the befriended firm. I take it from your report that you no longer object to the activities of the aforementioned gentleman [Seeckt?], since he has subordinated himself to your administration, and that this matter has been cleared up.'[1]

Throughout the spring of 1924 only Germany's military relations with Soviet Russia made real progress. There were no political discussions except the Soviet complaints [about] Stresemann's 'Western orientation,' and the negotiations for a trade treaty which commenced in the summer of 1923 and to which Brockdorff-Rantzau devoted most of his attention after returning from Berlin, were lagging. Chicherin no less than Brockdorff-Rantzau was dissatisfied with the prevailing state of affairs. Then at the beginning of May an incident took place that shook the very foundations of the Rapallo partnership. The incident itself was a minor one, but, as so often happens in international relations, it was blown up into a major dispute that raged for three months before it was settled.[2] The whole affair started on the morning of 3 May when a German Communist by the name of Bozenhard was arrested and escorted through the streets of Berlin by two detectives of the Württemberg criminal police. The policemen were unfamiliar with the environs of the capital city. Bozenhard took advantage of their ignorance and, it would seem, of their gullibility. He suggested that they enter a café for a cup of coffee but led them, instead, into the headquarters of the Soviet Trade Delegation, where he promptly made his escape. The detectives tried to recapture their prisoner but were unceremoniously ejected from the Soviet offices on the grounds that these enjoyed the privilege of extraterritoriality. Two hours later the Berlin police arrived in force, occupied the building and made a thorough search of the entire premises. While the police were still busy with this task Ambassador Krestinski invaded Stresemann's office loudly protesting that the action was a breach

[1] *Ibid.* Also see Appendix B.
[2] The following account of the trade delegation raid incident is taken chiefly from the Stresemann *Vermächtnis*, vol. 1, pp. 400-404. Kochan (*Russia and Weimar*, p. 95) and Hilger (*op. cit.*, pp. 179 ff.) summarize these events at the expense of accuracy.

of the extraterritoriality granted to the trade headquarters by the Provisional Agreement of 6 May 1921. Stresemann was taken by surprise. He apologized to Krestinski for the inconvenience caused the Russians by the zealous behaviour of the Berlin police, and although he said he doubted if the privilege of extraterritoriality extended to the trade headquarters he decided to call the Minister of Interior to request that the police be dislodged immediately. Krestinski was still very angry. He left Stresemann's office but telephoned back ten minutes later to complain that the police were still in the building and were now searching through all the desks and file cabinets—strange places to be looking for an escaped prisoner, even a Communist. Stresemann's secretary, Bernhard, asked the Ambassador to be patient; 'it was only a matter of time' until the police would clear out. But Krestinski was unwilling to wait; he was just as temperamental as his opposite number in Moscow. By nightfall he was on his way back to Russia, leaving Bratman-Brodowski in charge of the Embassy. In a matter of days all Russian orders to German firms were cancelled and all negotiations for concessions in Russia were suspended. The Soviet Government withdrew its exhibits from the industrial fairs in Cologne and Leipzig and closed the trade delegation branch offices in Hamburg and Leipzig.[1] Within a week Bozenhard's escape had become a major diplomatic incident.

Just before he left Berlin Krestinski sent a communiqué to Chicherin which gave a grossly exaggerated account of the incident that had taken place. The Ambassador made out that Bozenhard's escape and the subsequent police raid were parts of a carefully laid plot by the German Government to discredit the Soviet regime. This version of the incident was officially adopted by the Soviet Government.[2] At the Thirteenth Party Congress meeting in Moscow only a few days after the incident Zinoviev accused the Germans of a dastardly plot and Krasin charged them with a flagrant violation of the agreement of May 1921.[3] Other Soviet spokesmen alleged that Bozenhard was a tool of certain German capitalists who arranged his escape in order to give the police a pretext for an 'illegal search' of the trade premises.[4] On 31 May

---

[1] Kochan, op. cit., p. 95.          [2] Ibid. Also see below, pp. 194 f.
[3] XIII Syzed R.K.P. (b)—Stenographicheskii Otchet (Moscow, 1924), pp. 146-151, cited by Kochan, loc. cit. Also see below, p. 196.
[4] Ibid. Stresemann refuted these charges in an article in Die Zeit, 23 May 1924.

G

Chicherin sent a note to Berlin demanding an official apology and the punishment of the guilty police officials.[1]

There is no evidence to support the Soviet charge that Bozenhard's escape was contrived by the German Government. On the contrary, the Germans—including Stresemann—regretted the incident and wished to settle the dispute amicably as quickly as possible. In retrospect it is tempting to interpret the Soviet Government's vehement protests, which were out of all proportion to the injustice perpetrated against its officials in Berlin, as a clever plot to use the blunder committed by the police as an excuse for remonstrating against Stresemann's 'policy of fulfilment' and as a means of jarring Russo-German relations, especially the trade negotiations, out of their lethargy. But this interpretation does not stand up to a factual analysis of the dispute. Although Soviet officials might have foreseen that the German business community would suffer great losses as a result of the dispute and that considerable pressure would be put on Stresemann to follow a more amicable line with Moscow, the Russians must have realized at the same time that by breaking off commercial relations with Berlin they were also imposing severe hardships on themselves. If the Bolsheviks had intended to seize upon the incident to indict Stresemann's entire foreign policy they would have made sweeping generalizations about German policies in the course of the subsequent negotiations. But they did not do this. They took advantage of Stresemann's anxiety to settle the dispute only to the extent of demanding that their trade offices be recognized as an integral part of the Embassy, and hence as extraterritorial without limitations, which was more than the Provisional Agreement of May 1921 provided for.[2] The incident itself, however, was not contrived by either side; the dispute that followed was intensified and prolonged because the Russians insisted on full satisfaction for the wrong committed against them and the Germans refused to comply with the demands in the note of 31 May, which amounted to an ultimatum.

Most of the negotiations to settle the dispute took place in Moscow between Brockdorff-Rantzau and Chicherin. The fantasy that Bozenhard was a 'capitalist agent' and other wild stories about

---

[1] The date of the Russian note is established by Brockdorff-Rantzau's interview with Trotsky in June; see below, Appendix B.

[2] Hilger, *Incompatible Allies*, p. 180. And see above, p. 88 n. 2.

the police action embittered both sides. The negotiations dissolved into an ill-tempered debate. Brockdorff-Rantzau was exasperated and asked for an exit visa to leave Moscow.[1] Chicherin tried to dissuade the Ambassador from carrying out his threat of going back to Berlin by promising to arrange an interview for him with Trotsky. Brockdorff-Rantzau relented. On 9 June he and Trotsky discussed the whole range of German-Russian relations with special reference to the incident of 3 May and its repercussions on the Reichswehr-Red Army collaboration. The Ambassador gave a detailed account of the interview in a letter to Stresemann:[2]

When I had taken a seat I explained that the situation was so serious that I had to speak to Trotsky personally; I saw German-Russian friendship seriously endangered, and had to know if the relations with his department were also threatened. The lamentable incident has led to such untoward consequences that I, unhappily, had to assume as much. Of course, such a development would also have a decisive bearing on my own attitude.

At this point, according to Brockdorff-Rantzau's account, Trotsky interrupted in a highly animated fashion, saying:

'No, this is out of the question. This mess has to be cleaned up and does not have the remotest chance of influencing—in any way—the important military relations which have been fostered to our as well as your gratification. Rosenholz [Arkady Pavlovich Rosengolts, member of the Revolutionary Council and Chief of the Red Air Force] asked me on the first day that the incident became known what his attitude should be. I told him, that a change in our attitude was not even to be contemplated. The dispute has absolutely no bearing on this matter.'

'I responded [the Ambassador's report continues] that this explanation was very consoling; nevertheless I wanted to tell the Peoples' Commissar about a number of striking symptoms' which seemed to indicate that all was not well with the military co-operation. Brockdorff-Rantzau went on to complain that Junkers had not received contracts for aeroplane engines from the Soviet Government, although the company had been urged to begin its operations at Fili at the earliest possible time; that an American or British commission had been allowed to inspect a military factory at Tula

---

[1] *Ibid.*, p. 181.

[2] *Stresemann Nachlass*, 7414H/H175333/40. The complete report together with a letter Stresemann sent with a copy of it to Gessler will be found in Appendix B.

which was producing shells under German management; that two famous German pilots, Major Fischer and Captain Vogt, had been given a very cool reception by Rosengolts; and, finally, that he himself, the Ambassador, had been snubbed at an official function of the War Commissariat. When the Ambassador finished his catalogue of complaints Trotsky said he would inform himself about these matters; he 'understood completely,' he said, that Brockdorff-Rantzau could not treat these 'symptoms' as matters of secondary importance. A little later in the conversation the Ambassador found an opening to reassure Trotsky about Germany's Foreign Policy, using the military collaboration with the Soviet Government to achieve a political end:

I went on to say [Brockdorff-Rantzau wrote] that as far as my government is concerned the dispatch of the Messrs Fischer, Vogt, Arnold and Thomson is proof that we do not want to change our policy towards Russia. Trotsky remarked, he fully understands that the German police does not approve of a lot that is going on, but he never believed that we had the intention of re-orientating our policy. I explained that this very apt interpretation is unfortunately not being given [to the incident] in all quarters here.

Brockdorff-Rantzau complained that the dispute and the resultant crisis were due chiefly to the attitude that had been adopted in Moscow. Trotsky, he said, is 'the only statesman here who has been moderate about the incident in Berlin.' Ambassador Krestinski's 'outrageous communiqué' from Berlin had 'muddled the whole situation right from the start,' and Krasin's speech had further complicated the matter. Trotsky replied that he did not want to meddle in diplomatic negotiations because he did not understand them, but pointed out that 'Krasin is a notorious Germanophile' and had to attack Germany at the beginning of his speech 'in order to give special emphasis to the paragraphs calculated to mitigate the conflict.' Brockdorff-Rantzau retorted that he was sceptical of Krasin's friendship for Germany and added that he did not have to be told how public opinion is created. Apparently Trotsky let this slight pass without further comment. Brockdorff-Rantzau then led the conversation to its climax. He had given Germany's assurance that her policy towards Russia was unchanged; he wanted Trotsky to give a similar assurance on behalf of the Soviet Government. The Ambassador recalled first that in

December 1923 Trotsky had said that France was the common enemy of Russia and Germany; he then 'suggested that this conception may have changed since Poincaré's fall from power.' Trotsky retorted that this was far from the truth; 'neither the relations with France nor those with Britain could disrupt the German-Russian friendship. He was firmly convinced that this friendship would continue for years—he corrected himself—for decades to come.' Trotsky said that the Anglo-French demand for the repayment of the Czarist debts would prevent closer relations between Russia and either Britain or France. The Ambassador then asked Trotsky if he thought that the dispute between the two countries could be settled 'in the spirit of the Rapallo treaty' in order to re-establish 'the old friendly relations between Germany and Russia.' Trotsky replied without hesitation that he thought this could be done, whereupon Brockdorff-Rantzau added that, if the incident were settled with a protocol, as seemed likely, the protocol should state that 'the German and Russian governments have decided, in the spirit of the Rapallo treaty, to forget these misunderstandings and to work together in friendship in the future. We know what we mean to each other,' the Ambassador continued, 'but we should avoid giving our enemies the pleasure of witnessing an open break between us.' Trotsky agreed and ended the interview with a promise to use his authority to help settle the dispute.

If Trotsky exerted himself at all along the lines suggested to him by Brockdorff-Rantzau his efforts had remarkably little effect. The haggling went on for another two months before a protocol ending the dispute was finally signed. Gustav Hilger claims that he himself took the initiative that ended the dispute by appealing to Radek for help. Although Radek lost most of his previous political importance after the October fiasco in Germany and Lenin's death, in the summer of 1924 he still had an influential voice in Kremlin politics which he was able to use on behalf of the German-Russian relationship in which he remained deeply interested. According to Hilger, Radek offered to influence the Soviet Government to settle the dispute on the condition that Brockdorff-Rantzau agreed to retract his threat to leave Moscow.[1] The Ambassador complied, and thereafter the negotiations progressed smoothly. Litvinov ironed out some of the remaining difficulties in conversation with Stresemann

[1] Hilger, *op. cit.*, p. 181.

at the end of June,[1] and on 29 July, only a week before Stresemann went to London to sign the Dawes Plan, the German-Russian protocol was signed in Berlin.[2] But the protocol did not contain the elaborate professions of friendship and solidarity which Brockdorff-Rantzau suggested to Trotsky. It was, in fact, a rather one-sided agreement. The German Government repeated its earlier apologies for the incident and said that it had dismissed 'the leader of the police action' for infringing upon the extraterritorial privileges 'of officials of the Soviet Republic.' A compromise had been worked out whereby three-fifths of the trade delegation head-quarters were granted extraterritorial privileges. In the trade agreement of 12 October 1925 this privilege was extended to the entire premises of all Russian trade offices in Germany, granting them the rights previously restricted to foreign embassies. The precedent was an important one for the Russians, who later voiced demands for similar treatment from other nations, and is an example of how the Soviet Government used Germany as a *Vorspanne*—an involuntary pace-maker—in attaining certain international objectives.[3]

From the Soviet point of view, the incident of 3 May had the desirable consequence of enlivening Russo-German relations. It forced the German Government to pay attention to its Eastern policies, although the centre of international political activity remained in the West. The last clause of the protocol of 29 July affirmed the desire of both powers to resume the trade negotiations which had been suspended in May, and specified that a trade treaty was to be concluded within a year. As a matter of fact, however, the talks were not resumed until November. Even then they soon hit new snags. According to Hilger, who was one of the Germans charged with the unrewarding task of trying to reach concrete agreements with the Russians, the trade talks were prolonged because 'Moscow was primarily interested in demonstrating that an understanding of, and economic interchange with, the Soviet regime was possible, whatever the difference in social system.' Once

---

[1] *Stresemann Nachlass*, 7171H/H156139 and H156152/3. Kochan's assertion 'that Stresemann expressly delayed the settlement of the dispute' (*Russia and Weimar*, p. 95) is unsubstantiated and incorrect. Cf. H. W. Gatzke, 'Von Rapallo nach Berlin: Stresemann und die deutsche Russlandpolitik,' *Vierteljahrshefte für Zeitgeschichte*, 4. Jhrg., I. Heft (Stuttgart, January 1956), p. 6, n. 39.

[2] For the protocol see the Stresemann *Vermächtnis*, vol. I, p. 404.

[3] Hilger, *op. cit.*, p. 182.

again the Soviet Government was making use of the Germans, this time 'to arouse the competitive spirit of the capitalist world' and to attract the economic interests of other countries. For their part, the Germans were only interested in material results.[1] Instead of setting a good example, the Russians frustrated the Germans and dissuaded other countries from submitting themselves to economic negotiations with Moscow by procrastinating and employing other obstructionist tactics. They made such exorbitant demands for credits as a prerequisite to a trade agreement that the Germans even threatened to break off the talks. Finally, in October 1925, a trade treaty was signed. The Germans resigned themselves to meeting most of the Russian demands chiefly for political reasons, in order to maintain a balance in relations between East and West.[2]

In addition to the difficulties in the trade negotiations there were a number of incidents during the latter part of 1924 which disturbed the Rapallo partnership. German citizens working or touring in Russia were frequently arrested by the Soviet authorities, almost always without formal charges being preferred against them.[3] Usually on these occasions the German Embassy managed to have the victims released, often without demanding or receiving an official explanation of the arrests. One of these incidents took a much more serious turn, however. On the night of 27 October the GPU arrested two German students, Karl Kindermann and Theodor Wolscht, who were on their way to Central Asia to spend a holiday. The German consular staff made routine enquiries and took steps to have the adventurers released. The Foreign Commissariat seemed to be amenable at first, but then, probably under the influence of GPU, it suddenly took an unreasonably strong stand against freeing the prisoners. Chicherin himself told Brockdorff-Rantzau that Kindermann and Wolscht were not puerile youths, but 'hardened criminals who had entered the Soviet Union in order to do it serious harm.'[4] The Ambassador was startled. Neither he nor anyone on his staff seems to have connected the charges against the two students with the case that was then being prepared in

---

[1] *Ibid.*, pp. 182 f.

[2] See below, pp. 229 f. 233.

[3] Stampfer, *Die vierzehn Jahre der ersten deutschen Republik*, pp. 476-478.

[4] P. Scheffer, *Sieben Jahre Sowjetunion* (Leipzig, 1930), p. 439. Hilger was personally involved in this case and has given a detailed account of it: *Incompatible Allies*, pp. 137-145.

Leipzig against the Russian agent Skoblevsky, who was charged with organizing Communist terrorist gangs during the insurrection of October 1923. Only later in 1925, after the Soviet Government had officially charged Kindermann and Wolscht with plotting to poison Stalin and Trotsky with cyanide of potassium, did it become evident that the students were being held as hostages for Skoblevsky and his accomplices. But then the entire case was overshadowed by the major political battle in which the Russians strove desperately to prevent Stresemann from manifesting his 'Western orientation' in the Locarno Agreements and in German membership of the League of Nations.

# CHAPTER IX

# THE MILITARY COLLABORATION

IT is notable that the incidents which disturbed German-Russian political and economic relations, beginning with the insurrection of 1923 right up to and including the negotiations leading to the Locarno Agreements and German membership in the League of Nations in 1925 and 1926, had almost no repercussions on the secret military collaboration between the two powers. Even the sharp conflict which broke out following the police raid on the Soviet trade offices did not impinge upon the military tie. The 'symptoms' of trouble in the military sphere about which Brockdorff-Rantzau complained to Trotsky were all minor misunderstandings having little or nothing to do with the political crisis.[1] Personal relations between the two armies and between the men involved in the industrial rearmament projects were excellent. Differences in the countries' *Weltanschauung* neither interfered in the work nor in personal relations amongst the participants. The Russians were hospitable at all times to the Germans connected with the military collaboration, who never so much as brushed against an Iron Curtain.

The only friction in the entire military link between Moscow and Berlin was on the German side, between the War Ministry and the Foreign Ministry, and between Brockdorff-Rantzau, also Seeckt, and Stresemann. A number of disputes arose in these quarters, but at no time was the existence of the military programme made an issue. Seeckt had initiated the programme, Brockdorff-Rantzau supported it as soon as he arrived in Moscow, and Stresemann also co-operated from 1923 onwards. The issues which provoked constant disagreements concerned the jurisdiction of the civilian and military agencies in military negotiations with the Russians, and also the question of what demands were to be made of the Soviet Government in return for German aid.

When he took up his post in Moscow and had an opportunity to study the military agreements that Seeckt had negotiated with the Russians, Brockdorff-Rantzau complained—and apparently

---

[1] See above, pp. 195 f. and below, Appendix B.

never stopped complaining—that the Soviet Government had got the better part of the deal. In his opinion Seeckt had agreed to pay more and had committed the Reichswehr to give the Red Army much more aid than the Russians had undertaken to give in return. The Ambassador wanted 'concrete political advantages to be derived from the military agreements'; he insisted that, at the very least, the Soviet Government should give Germany 'an explicit guarantee against Poland.'[1] After the French invaded the Ruhr Brockdorff-Rantzau had, in fact, almost completely reversed his earlier stand against a military alliance with Russia, so that by the summer of 1923 his own ideas virtually conformed with Seeckt's policy.[2] Stresemann, however, did not want to negotiate a military alliance with the Bolsheviks and steadfastly refused to demand political advantages in return for the military agreements, despite the entreaties of both Brockdorff-Rantzau and Seeckt. The Foreign Minister was, it seems, afraid that the discovery of a Russo-German military alliance against Poland would prejudice Britain and France against Germany and prolong the Ruhr occupation. Stresemann apparently considered the rearmament collaboration with Russia, which, had it been discovered, would also have damaged Germany's relations with the West, a risk worth taking. Both Brockdorff-Rantzau and Seeckt, on the other hand, did not distinguish between the risks involved in the rearmament collaboration and in a potential military alliance with Russia. By the latter part of the summer of 1923 the Ambassador was entirely prepared to sign a treaty with Russia aimed at Poland, which is what Seeckt had been advocating for more than three years.[3] Brockdorff-Rantzau did not believe that Stresemann would be able to dislodge the French from the Ruhr by means of the 'policy of fulfilment,' and, moreover, blamed the Foreign Minister for disregarding Germany's interests in the East. But although Brockdorff-Rantzau agreed with Seeckt as against Stresemann, relations between the Ambassador and the army did not improve. As has been pointed out before, Brockdorff-Rantzau was almost instinctively suspicious of military men dabbling in politics. He fought a continuous battle with Seeckt over who should administer the military agreements with the Russians, the Moscow Embassy or Special Group R and GEFU. The

---

[1] Hilger, *Incompatible Allies*, p. 201.
[2] See above, p. 130.
[3] Cf. Hilger, *loc. cit.*

Ambassador 'bombarded his superiors in Berlin' with complaints that Seeckt, Hasse, Tschunke, and Niedermayer were running an independent side-show. In the summer of 1923 Cuno finally decided that the political and military authorities should establish a closer liaison and persuaded Seeckt to give the Moscow Embassy a say in the administration of the military agreements. Brockdorff-Rantzau was still dissatisfied, however. He wanted the cabinet to take direct responsibility for the military collaboration so that he would have official backing in his jurisdictional disputes with Seeckt. Late in the summer of 1923 the Ambassador seized upon Hasse's indiscretions in Moscow—Hasse had told the Russians that Germany would be prepared to fight a war of revenge against Poland and France in the near future—to convince Cuno that all secret military negotiations should henceforth be conducted in Berlin, under the direct supervision of the government. In this way the Ambassador compelled the cabinet to assume some responsibility for the military collaboration.[1] Subsequently the Moscow Central Office, Special Group R's branch office, was no longer allowed to frame its policies independently; it continued to be responsible to the War Ministry, but it was now also held accountable to the Moscow Embassy. Since Germany did not have a military attaché in Moscow at the time, Brockdorff-Rantzau himself assumed the responsibility of co-ordinating the policies of the Central Office with those of his Embassy. But he found himself unable to exercise as much control as he wanted. Niedermayer, head of the Central Office, was still in charge of the day-to-day negotiations with the Red Army and leaders of other branches of the Soviet Government, and, in practice, managed to follow a rather independent line, even to the point of making quasi-political and, on occasions, strictly political policy decisions.[2] In other words, the Ambassador not only failed to bring the operations of the military under his control, he was, at times, even unable to exercise the authority which had been vested in him. But in spite of the continuing frictions between the Embassy and the military, Brockdorff-Rantzau made several significant contributions towards the military collaboration, and on at least one occasion acted directly on Seeckt's behalf. During the interview with Trotsky in

[1] Ibid.
[2] Speidel, 'Reichswehr und Rote Armee,' pp. 19 f. Also see the diagram in Appendix C.

June 1924, Brockdorff-Rantzau warned the Soviet Government to stop negotiating with Colonel Bauer, Ludendorff's former aide, for the construction of a chemical factory. He explained that Seeckt had left no doubt in his mind when they conversed in Berlin in the spring that the Reichswehr did not have 'any intention of working together with Bauer' as long as he 'is in touch with General Ludendorff.' Trotsky said he was glad to know this since he did not want to do anything that might jeopardize the Soviet Government's relations with Seeckt.[1]

The liaison between the Foreign Ministry and the Reichswehr, specifically with Seeckt and Special Group R, in Berlin was better than that between the Moscow Embassy and the Central Office. Special Group R had to deal with all the 'basic questions of a political, economic, and military kind in general' which affected relations between the two armies and the industrial rearmament on Russian soil. 'The political problems were cleared up on consultation with the Foreign Ministry,' and the Ministry also helped to settle some of the details of the arrangements.[2] For example, although the Germans connected with the military relationship travelled to and from Russia under assumed names, the Foreign Ministry supplied them with genuine passports stamped with valid visas. Moreover, private as well as official mail between the bases in Russia and Germany was transmitted through the courier service of the Foreign Ministry.[3] Stresemann was, of course, fully aware of the extent to which his Ministry co-operated with the army in these secret and illegal activities. Most likely he personally authorized his officials to co-operate with the army in these ventures, although he probably did so in informal conversations rather than compromising himself with written instructions.[4] It is, however, impossible to determine how much Stresemann was directly involved. He undoubtedly tried to keep a safe distance from all the violations and breaches of the Versailles treaty in order to minimize the dangers to his foreign policy in the West in the event of a leak in

[1] *Stresemann Nachlass*, 7414H/H175334/40.
[2] Speidel, *op. cit.*, p. 19.
[3] *Ibid.*, pp. 33 f.
[4] See Gatzke, *Stresemann and Rearmament*, pp. 73 ff., 106 n. Cf. Hirsch, 'Stresemann in Historical Perspective,' p. 375, and Bretton, *Stresemann and Versailles*, pp. 145, 146, 149. Both Hirsch and Bretton admit that Stresemann knew of the secret rearmament, but both—in line with their general theses—try to minimize the importance of this fact.

the security system. But there is absolutely no doubt that Stresemann protected Seeckt and the Reichswehr's manifold rearmament activities, in Germany, Russia, and elsewhere, against those
who found out about them and tried to stop them. For example, in
January 1924 Professor Ludwig Quidde, the head of a reputable
German pacifist organization, wrote to Seeckt asking if it were true
that the army was engaged upon all manner of clandestine and
illegal rearmament ventures. In his reply Seeckt refused to answer
the question and threatened Quidde with an indictment 'for high
treason' if he dared to discuss the matter publicly. Quidde immediately forwarded copies of this exchange to Chancellor Marx
and to Stresemann.[1] There is no record of a direct reply by Stresemann, but it is entirely possible that Marx consulted with him
before replying to Quidde through State Secretary Bracht. Bracht's
letter told Quidde that the army's activities were none of his
concern and reiterated Seeckt's threat of prosecution for high
treason if the pacifist allegations were made in public. The record
of this altercation with Quidde—even taken by itself—is enough
evidence to give the lie to Stresemann's later assertion that he had
been uninformed about the Reichswehr's clandestine activities in
Russia until they were exposed in 1926. Stresemann tried so hard
to cover up his own tracks that he even accused Gessler of lying
after he told a Reichstag committee that 'nothing had been done
[by the Reichswehr in Russia] of which the Foreign Ministry was
not informed.'[2] If Stresemann ever really wanted to break up the
military collaboration with Russia he had a golden opportunity to
do so following Scheidemann's disclosures in the Reichstag in
December 1926. But since there was no adverse reaction to these
disclosures either in London or in Paris, Stresemann 'resolved not
only to continue as before with military co-operation, but to
intensify it. . . .'[3]

The first and most important of the Russo-German training
centres established under the military agreement of August 1923
was the air base at Lipezk. Work started there early in 1924. How-

[1] *Stresemann Nachlass*, 7166H/H155072/9. In March 1924 yet another German
pacifist, Professor Schücking, complained to Stresemann about the illegal
activities of the army (*ibid.*, 7167H/H155387/91). These papers confirm Wheeler-
Bennett's supposition that Stresemann was aware of the clandestine rearmament
(*Nemesis of Power*, p. 147).

[2] *Stresemann Nachlass*, 7337H/H163462 ff.

[3] Hilger, *Incompatible Allies*, p. 207. And see below, pp. 243 f.

ever, the first appropriation of 2 million marks, which was taken from the War Ministry's budget for 1923-1924, was not enough to defray the initial expenditures of building and equipping the aerodrome. Since the inflation had cut sharply into Special Group R's other funds, additional means had to be found for Lipezk.[1] Still, before the 'passive resistance' campaign was called off Special Group R was able to expropriate 10 million marks from the relief fund collected for the Ruhr workers. After the 'passive resistance' campaign was abandoned Special Group R got another slice of the remaining *Ruhrfond* to cover the rest of the initial expenses of Lipezk and to purchase 100 fighter planes from the Fokker Company of Holland.[2]

The basic training of the future Luftwaffe was undertaken in Germany itself, at schools that were ostensibly training sport and commercial pilots. But these schools were only useful up to the point where teaching and training 'assumed a military character.' Without Lipezk as a last step it would not have been possible to train a military air force.[3] The Fokker D-13 planes purchased in 1923 were used for training at Lipezk. In addition, the German air-craft industry built new and experimental craft which were first tested at the factories and then, under the auspices of the Reichs-wehr, at a secret field near Rechlin on Lake Müritz. But 'as soon as the military character of a plane could no longer be camouflaged, in other words, when weapons were fitted and technical-tactical testing had to be done in the air,' then the planes were flown to Lipezk.[4] From the German point of view, therefore, the two principal uses of Lipezk were to give pilots and other air personnel, such as navigators, their final training and to test and develop new war planes.

Of the three major combined training and testing bases estab-lished in Russia the one at Lipezk proved to be the most valuable, for the Russians as well as for the Germans. Much more informa-tion has come to light about Lipezk than about the gas warfare school at Saratov and the tank training centre at Kasan. It can be assumed, however, that the logistical problems involved in trans-

---

[1] Speidel, 'Reichswehr und Rote Armee,' pp. 22-24.

[2] *Ibid.* Also see Scheele, *The Weimar Republic*, p. 107, and Görlitz, *Der Deutsche Generalstab*, p. 365.

[3] Speidel, *op. cit.*, p. 21.

[4] *Ibid.*, pp. 21 f.

porting large numbers of men and tons of materials to Lipezk were also encountered in establishing and administering the Saratov and Kasan bases, and that they were solved in more or less the same manner as is indicated in the following account of the development of Lipezk.[1]

A number of dangerous frontiers lay between the two theatres of Reichswehr activity in Germany and Russia. Since the Russians only supplied the basic building materials, such as wood and stone, for the numerous hangars and facilities that had to be built at Lipezk, everything else, down to the last nail, had to be shipped from Germany. Neither men nor materials could be sent across Poland, which was the most direct route, for fear of detection. The safest railroad route was circuitous, via Königsberg-Kovno-Dünaburg-Smolensk and on to Moscow. However, even this trip involved six border and customs inspections all of which, not least of all the German ones, were best avoided. Overland rail transport was, therefore, normally restricted to goods that might be sent to Russia in the course of ordinary trade. Only the aeroplanes themselves and valuable precision instruments, such as bomb-sights, were flown to Russia, and then always without intermediate landings. Most of the materials were sent by sea, usually via the Free Port of Stettin to Leningrad. To escape watchful eyes at the ports all military articles were crated and carefully camouflaged. Ammunition and bombs, and other articles that could not be easily transported without detection, were sent across the Baltic Sea in small sail boats manned by German officers on their way to various bases in Russia. The bodies of pilots who crashed in Russia were smuggled home through Stettin in boxes labelled 'machine parts.' All sea and rail shipments of military articles were made under the mantle of two private commercial import-export organizations, *Derutra* and the Otto Wolff concern.

The German personnel travelled to the Russian bases in small groups, chiefly by rail on board the Paris-Berlin-Riga North-Express. In Dünaburg each party was met by representatives of the Soviet tourist organization *Intourist* who escorted the Germans through customs and on to their final destinations in Russia. As soon as they touched Russian soil all the Germans, regardless of whether they were instructors, technicians, pilots, or simply

---

[1] The following is chiefly based on *ibid.*, pp. 28-34, 39, and on information from reliable private sources.

labourers, fell under the jurisdiction of the Moscow Central Office of Special Group R. This office also arranged all mail and intercourse with the homeland for them in the reliable and efficient manner to which the Germans were accustomed. When they completed their tour of duty or work project in Russia the Germans were usually sent home in groups of a dozen or more on board Russian passenger and freight ships sailing from Leningrad to Stettin. Since a dozen Germans with a military bearing might have aroused suspicions when they passed through the customs and police controls at Stettin, some of the men were often landed unobserved at night on the dams of the Kaiser-Wilhelm Canal. The strictest secrecy was maintained on every level and at every stage of these operations. In view of the fact that Special Group R had to take numerous civilians into its confidence, including transport organizations, manufacturers, labourers, and other private individuals, it is simply astounding that these activities were successfully concealed from public awareness for so many years.

From 1924 on a total of 60 Germans were attached to Lipezk as a basic flight personnel. These were chiefly military and civilian pilots and flight instructors. During the summers, when flying conditions improved, the active flight group totalled upwards of 100. The composition of the personnel changed as men finished their six months' training course and were replaced by others who had graduated from the basic training schools in Germany. In addition to the flight personnel Lipezk's German colony also included in the neighbourhood of 75 to 100 technical experts and mechanics. The entire German outfit masqueraded under the title of the 4th 'Squadron' of the Red Air Force. This ruse was carried to the extreme of ditching a number of vintage Russian reconnaissance planes around the field. The administration and management of the entire concern was exclusively German. The aerodrome was guarded by Russian soldiers and no outsiders were permitted to enter. However, the Germans were allowed to move freely on and off the base.

According to General Speidel, who was active on the administrative side of Special Group R's work, Lipezk's most important contribution was the laying 'of the spiritual foundation for the future Luftwaffe in actual flying practice.'[1] Without underrating the importance of a military *esprit de corps*, the material accomplish-

[1] *Ibid.*, p. 28.

ments at Lipezk can still be adjudged to have been its most significant contribution to the Luftwaffe. At least 120 outstanding fighter pilots and another 450 flight personnel, including reconnaissance and dive bomber pilots, were thoroughly trained at Lipezk. As officers in later years these men were the core of Hitler's air force, which, for a time, was the finest in the world. Furthermore, Germany's aircraft industry took advantage of the opportunities at Lipezk to bridge the gap in technical thought and development which would otherwise have developed in the period from Versailles until Hitler started rearming in the open. At Lipezk the industry perfected fighter planes, invented and developed dive bombers, and also tested and standardized reconnaissance planes.[1] As a result of this work, Germany, which was prohibited from manufacturing any military aeroplanes under the Versailles treaty, developed prototypes of efficient all-metal war planes ready for mass production ten years before other major powers had them on their drawing boards.[2]

In the final stage of their training at Lipezk, German reconnaissance pilots were allowed to participate in manœuvres with Red Army troops and artillery. Air manœuvres with the Red Air Force were held only once; presumably the Russians felt that they could not meet the test of German machines and pilots. One Red Air Force officer explained apologetically to a German officer: 'We cannot put primitive people in complicated machines.'[3] But such self-deprivation was inapposite. The Russians also derived enormous benefits from the Lipezk base. Russian ground crew personnel were trained in courses given the year round by German mechanics and other specialists stationed at the base. Moreover, Red Air Force men were attached to the base at all times and were trained by the Germans in all the technical aspects of flying. Some of the Russian pilots were rated equal to the best German ones. Russian technicians were permitted to work with the Germans and had opportunities to examine and copy the latest developments in all the planes tested at Lipezk. *Zagi*, the Soviet institute of design and engineering, even sent specialists to help the Germans test their

---

[1] *Ibid.*, pp. 30 f., 37-39.
[2] Hauptmann Hermann, *The Rise and Fall of the Luftwaffe* (London, 1943), pp. 42 f. Also see General Edmund Wachenfeld, 'Die Luftwaffe nach dem Weltkriege' in *Die Deutsche Wehrmacht 1914-1939* (Berlin, 1939), pp. 529, 534.
[3] Speidel, 'Reichswehr und Rote Armee,' p. 38.

experimental planes. The net effect of these combined operations
was that every German technical accomplishment became a
starting-point for production by the Russians.[1]

In further compensation for the bases in Russia, Red Army and
Air Force officers—including members of the General Staff—were
permitted to participate in the secret training programmes for
German staff officers in Berlin. Among the Red officers who took
advantage of these opportunities were the later Chief of Staff
Tukachevsky and the later Marshal Zhukov.[2] During these courses
the Russians were able to see and study all directives, tactical and
operational studies, methods of recruitment and training, and even
the organizational plans of the illegal rearmament itself. Nothing
seems to have been withheld from them. No wonder, then, that
the Germans found the Soviet officers invariably more anxious
to learn than most of the German officer trainees.[3]

Starting in 1925, Red Army and Air Force officers were invited
to attend German war games, troop manoeuvres, and weapon
demonstrations. German Army officers were granted the same
privileges by the Red Army. To hide their identity when they
appeared at Red Army manoeuvres the German officers were clad
in mufti and introduced as a 'German Communist Workers'
Delegation'![4] In later years German officers were employed to
teach military history and strategy to Soviet officers. General Hans
Reinhardt and Field Marshal von Blomberg were among the most
notable of the German instructors.[5]

While the co-operation in military training and weapon experimentation at Lipezk, Saratov, and Kasan proved rewarding for
both partners, the armaments industries in Russia operating under
German auspices had anything but smooth sailing. The inflation of
1923 reduced GEFU's working capital to 75 million marks.[6]

---

[1] *Ibid.*

[2] *Ibid.*, pp. 35-37; Görlitz, *Der Deutsche Generalstab*, pp. 340 f.

[3] Speidel, *op. cit.*, p. 35.

[4] *Ibid.*, p. 36.

[5] Görlitz, *op. cit.*, p. 340. Blomberg's memoirs, which are written in several
notebooks that are now in possession of the U.S. Government at the Federal
Records Centre in Arlington, Virginia, apparently do not contain any recollections of Blomberg's experience in Russia. Cf. Gatzke, *Stresemann and Rearmament*, p. 120.

[6] See von Rabenau's marginal comment on Major Tschunke's letter: *Heeresarchiv* Seeckt, Karton 19, Stück 290.

General von Borries, the head of GEFU, seems to have been a very inept financier. Under his incompetent administration the company speculated itself out of existence in 1925 and had to be replaced by another organization, the *Wirtschaftskontor*, or WIKO.[1] Major Tschunke, who directed the activities of GEFU and later of WIKO from his office in Moscow, was notably unsuccessful. *Bersol*, a Russo-German company located at Trotsk for the manufacture of poison gases, failed owing to deficiencies in the process devised by Dr Hugo Stolzenberg.[2] The manufacture of ammunition in factories at Zlatoust, Tula, and Leningrad continued until December 1926, when the discovery by German pacifists of 300,000 grenades on board three chartered ships docking at Stettin led to Scheidemann's revelations in the Reichstag, which, Tschunke later complained, dealt 'a severe blow' to his work in Moscow.[3] The third and, originally, the most important of GEFU's and WIKO's undertakings, the manufacture of Junkers aeroplanes at Fili, was a complete failure. Junkers had not received a single Russian order to manufacture motors as late as the summer of 1924. Brockdorff-Rantzau warned Trotsky in June 1924 that Junkers would be faced with 'serious financial difficulties if they did not get Russian contracts'; their annual subsidy from the Reichswehr, the Ambassador said, did not amount to enough to keep the factory at Fili in operation.[4] In spite of these complaints, however, Russian contracts were not forthcoming. In 1925 the Reichswehr refused to authorize WIKO to pay Junkers another subsidy and the factory at Fili was consequently shut down. Since all the financial and political agreements between Junkers and both Special Group R and the Soviet negotiators had been concluded in secret, and were to remain secret, Junkers could not sue either the German or the Soviet Government for breach of contract and for the losses sustained by the company. Determined to make good its claims, Junkers issued a detailed memorandum about the matter and distributed copies of it to leading members of the Reichstag. However, one copy of the memorandum found its way to a correspondent of the *Manchester Guardian*, who subsequently published an article revealing some of the facts about the defunct Junkers project.[5] *Vorwärts* then

---

[1] Hilger, *Incompatible Allies*, p. 194.                    [2] *Ibid.*
[3] Tschunke's letter: *Heeresarchiv*: Seeckt, Karton 19, Stück 290.
[4] *Stresemann Nachlass*, 7414H/H175334/40.
[5] Melville, *The Russian Face of Germany*, pp. 68 ff.

took up the matter, and on 16 December Scheidemann gave it world publicity. Both *Pravda* and *Izvestiya* chose the day of Scheidemann's Reichstag speech to publish articles admitting the existence of German arms factories in Russia, but carefully omitted references to the military training of Germans on Russian soil, which Scheidemann had also failed to mention—presumably because he had not been informed of this.[1] The *Pravda* and *Izvestiya* articles remain, to this day, the only official statements made by the Russians about the military collaboration with Germany:

It appears that within the boundaries of our Union, by agreements between our military authorities and those of Germany, certain German firms several years ago erected three factories for the production of material necessary to our defence. In this material are included aeroplanes, gases, shells, etc. We are not initiated into the secrets of our military authorities and do not know whether these reports correspond to the facts.[2]

Radek, writing in *Izvestiya* on the same day, was, as usual, more candid and direct. 'The USSR,' he wrote, 'does not refuse the use of foreign technicians in order to strengthen its defences against foreign imperialists.'[3]

[1] Kochan assumes that it was 'a strange coincidence' that the Russian newspaper articles appeared the same day as Scheidemann spoke: *Russia and Weimar*, p. 122.

[2] *Pravda*, 16 December 1926, quoted *ibid*.

[3] *Izvestiya*, 16 December 1926, quoted *ibid*.

# CHAPTER X

## TO LOCARNO AND BERLIN

AT the Fifth Assembly meeting in Geneva during September 1924 Prime Minister Ramsay MacDonald earnestly proposed that Germany be invited to join the League of Nations. Herriot of France was less enthusiastic, but nevertheless endorsed the proposal. Although there was still strong opposition to League membership in Germany, especially among adherents of the Right-wing parties, a special session of Chancellor Marx's cabinet on 23 September, presided over by President Ebert, followed Stresemann's advice to accept the Allied offer in principle. One week later the German Government published a memorandum stipulating the conditions on which Germany was prepared to join the League. 'In view of its complete disarmament' and its 'geographic location' Germany felt justified in asking to be exempted from Article 16 of the Covenant, which required all member states to support the use of sanctions, including military sanctions, in accordance with League Council decisions against aggressor powers.[1] For almost a year thereafter, until the Locarno Conference of October 1925, this issue of sanctions was at the heart of Germany's negotiations with the Western powers. It was clear right from the start that Germany wanted to be exempted from sanctions obligations in order to safeguard her interests in the East. The government would not co-operate in any action that might be aimed at protecting Poland's boundaries, and, moreover, had no intention of committing Germany to a position in which she might be used as a bridge for an attack on Russia. Stresemann did not want to become embroiled in a Western crusade against the Bolsheviks any more than he would allow the Soviet Government to impose an exclusive alliance on Germany. The objectives of his policy, which was to lead to Locarno and then to League member-

---

[1] O. Meissner, *Staatssekretär unter Ebert–Hindenburg–Hitler* (Hamburg, 1950), p. 151. Article 17 of the League of Nations Covenant also related to sanctions. For the sake of convenience only Article 16 is referred to in the text of this chapter, but both articles were involved in the negotiations preceding Germany's entry into the League.

ship, were to revive German power and to gain an independent middle position in Europe. He would not commit Germany to either the East or the West; she would remain neutral in any struggle between Russia and the Allies. 'Our relations with Russia,' Stresemann wrote in 1924, 'will always have the greatest economic and political significance for us. Any action on the part of the League of Nations which is directed against Russia and involves us, would impose a much greater hardship on us than any other nation.'[1]

Throughout the period that the Locarno agreements were being negotiated, and then again while Germany's application for membership in the League was pending, the Russians were afraid that Germany would ally herself with the West against the Soviet regime. The Bolshevists argued that even if it were not Stresemann's intention to upset the Rapallo friendship, once Germany joined the League the Allies would force her to act against Russia. From Moscow's point of view Stresemann's overtures for better relations with France and Britain were incompatible with the Rapallo alliance, which the Russians interpreted as an exclusive alliance. The German cabinet's decision of 23 September to accept League membership in principle provoked immediate and vehement protests from the Russian side. As early as 26 September and again on 1 October Bratman-Brodowski, acting for Krestinski, who was in Moscow, accused Stresemann of 'inaugurating a new policy' which was irreconcilable with 'the spirit of Rapallo.' Stresemann retorted that Germany was not changing her policy and pointed out that League membership did not imply recognition of the disputed Eastern boundaries. On the contrary, Stresemann said, Germany wants to join the League 'just because Article 19 of the League Covenant gives us the opportunity' of revising the Versailles treaty and, with it, the Eastern boundary lines. Furthermore, Stresemann asked, was not the Soviet Republic itself planning to send an observer to Geneva? Bratman-Brodowski admitted that this was the case, but asserted that the Soviet Government 'has not changed its opinion about the League of Nations. Russia does not even contemplate joining the League of Nations,' he emphasized.[2]

In Moscow, too, loud protests were voiced against Germany's offer to join the League. Chicherin scorned Stresemann's assurances,

---

[1] *Vermächtnis*, vol. 1, pp. 314 f.    [2] *Ibid.*, pp. 586 f.

which were often repeated by Ambassador Brockdorff-Rantzau, that no fundamental changes in German Foreign Policy were taking place. As far as the Soviet Government was concerned a decisive change was taking place, for Germany, which until now had an exclusive partnership with Russia, was being reconciled with Britain and France. For the Bolsheviks Rapallo was a league against the League; Germany's drift towards the West was losing Russia her *point d'appui* in Europe and threatening her with isolation. And an even greater threat loomed: Germany might join the West's 'anti-Soviet bloc.' In a private letter to Professor Ludwig Stein which nevertheless—and surely not by accident—received wide publicity, Chicherin asserted that Germany's 'entry into the League would signify a capitulation.' No matter how many conditions Stresemann laid down for League membership, Chicherin wrote, the Covenant would still represent 'an international guarantee . . . of existing frontiers, the Versailles frontiers in particular.' By joining the League Germany would become 'part of an existing coalition. . . . Against her own will . . . Germany will, in this way, be drawn into combinations and actions that will lead her into conflict with us.'[1] Chicherin could not, of course, say outright that he wanted to keep Germany at odds with the Western powers and tied to Soviet Russia as its buffer and *Vorspanne*. He had to pretend that he believed it to be to Germany's interests as well as to Russia's for Germany to shun the League. His arguments were, therefore, highly emotional rather than reasonable; but that did not make them any less effective in those German circles which were adamantly opposed to Stresemann's policy of reconciliation with the West, notably the Fascists, the Reichswehr, and heavy industry. In Moscow, too, Chicherin's arguments were effective. He aimed one shaft after another at Brockdorff-Rantzau's Achilles' heel—the Treaty of Versailles—by repeatedly declaring that, if she joined the League, Germany would become part of 'the victors' club' and be forced to recognize as binding both the Versailles treaty and the boundary decisions on Upper Silesia, thereby condemning herself to the eternal shame of 'war guilt.'[2] Litvinov took up much the same line, arguing that Germany could play a much stronger role if she did not join the League and strengthened her alliance with Russia instead.

[1] L. Stein, *Aus dem Leben eines Optimisten* (Berlin, 1930), pp. 239 f.
[2] Hilger, *Incompatible Allies*, p. 131.

Brockdorff-Rantzau also felt that Stresemann's policies were endangering the Russo-German alliance, but he loyally followed the Foreign Minister's instructions to refute the Soviet protests by pointing out that Article 19 of the Covenant provided for the revision of the Versailles peace and for the adjustment of the Upper Silesian boundaries. The Ambassador also followed instructions to impress on the Russians that the Rapallo treaty would have to be given a more flexible interpretation in Moscow in order that it might still apply to the new conditions that were replacing the *Schicksalsgemeinschaft* of former years.[1]

Ambassador Krestinski conferred with Stresemann on 29 October. The Ambassador wanted to know if, as a consequence of Soviet protests, there had been any change in Germany's position regarding the League. Stresemann replied that his policy was unchanged; the chief problem was the apparent reluctance of the Allies to honour Germany's demand for exemption from the obligations of Article 16, which, he assured Krestinski, would not be withdrawn.[2] After this interview the Soviet Government must have realized that Stresemann could not be deterred from joining the League. Although Chicherin continued to oppose this move, it was, it seems, generally understood in Moscow that by far the greatest danger to Soviet security lay in the chance that Germany might enter into the League without being exempted from the provisions of Article 16. If Germany was determined to join the League, she must, Chicherin felt, at the very least, be prevented from doing so at the expense of Soviet security. He therefore started on a new tack, emphasizing the great danger that, as a member of the League, Germany would be obliged to participate in sanctions against Soviet Russia, at least to the extent of giving free passage to Western troops embarking on an anti-Soviet crusade. Poland, the Russians realized, would feel free to attack Russia if the French could march across Germany to support her:

The harmful and unacceptable aspect of the League of Nations consists just in the fact that during an international conflict it can force weaker states to comply with its sovereign will in the interests of a bandit or group of bandits.[3]

---

[1] *Ibid.*, p. 132.
[2] *Stresemann Nachlass*, 7125H/H147173/8.
[3] *Izvestiya*, 27 November 1925, quoted by Hilger, *loc. cit.*

Thus, Chicherin was in a dilemma. He was caught between wanting to prevent Germany from joining the League under any circumstances and wanting Stresemann to achieve a revision of Article 16 in the event Germany did join. Secretly Chicherin was hoping, of course, that both sides would stubbornly refuse to compromise over the issue of sanctions and that a deadlock would ensue which would keep Germany out of the League altogether. In order to encourage Germany's stand against the Allies, and hoping, at the very least, to counterbalance Stresemann's 'Western orientation,' Chicherin also proposed a renewal of the Rapallo treaty in the form of a neutrality pact. The first mention of this was made to Brockdorff-Rantzau in December 1924. Chicherin told the Ambassador that the Soviet Government wanted to negotiate a new treaty in which both countries would undertake to refrain from joining economic, political, or military combinations directed against the other. 'You keep away from England, and we'll keep away from France,' Chicherin said.[1] But Stresemann would not countenance a new treaty with the Soviet Government at this time. He knew that even a semblance of ambiguity in his policy would jeopardize the negotiations with the West and thus frustrate all efforts to end the Ruhr occupation and revise the Eastern boundaries. The French were bound to interpret any new political move in the direction of Moscow as a threat to their own security and, in consequence, prevent Germany from regaining her freedom of action and equality among nations. Stresemann did not, on the other hand, want to affront Chicherin with an outright rejection of his proposal for a neutrality treaty, so he did the next best thing: he simply did not reply to the proposal.[2] Brockdorff-Rantzau was seriously worried about the impression Stresemann's silence was giving the Soviet Government. He urged the Foreign Minister to accept the neutrality treaty proposal, at least in principle, and then, in January or February 1925, discussed with Chicherin the possibility of an even broader Russo-German treaty which was to be aimed at 'forcing Poland back within her ethnographic frontiers.' It cannot be determined in what context, or on whose initiative, this proposal was made, but it seems likely that Brockdorff-Rantzau was so concerned about the repercussions of Stresemann's

---

[1] Quoted by Hilger, op. cit., p. 138.

[2] H. W. Gatzke, 'Stresemann und die deutsche Russlandpolitik,' Vierteljahrshefte für Zeitgeschichte, 4. Jhrg., 1. Heft, pp. 8 f.

'Western orientation' on Russo-German relations that he decided to play 'the Polish card'—in the manner of Karl Radek—in the hope of allaying Chicherin's direst fears. How Chicherin reacted to this gambit is not known. But the proposal of an alliance against Poland at this time certainly did not stem from the German Foreign Ministry; in making the suggestion Brockdorff-Rantzau was operating entirely on his own initiative.[1] Even if Stresemann would have been prepared to consider a Russo-German alliance against Poland in the future, he realized that, in 1924 and 1925, such an alliance was neither a practical proposal nor essential for the maintenance of good relations with Soviet Russia. Stresemann did not have to make a strong bid for Moscow's friendship; he held a strong hand with the Russians and could afford to keep them waiting. Towards Britain and France, on the other hand, Stresemann was playing from a weaker position and for higher stakes and, therefore, had to be more complaisant.

Although his own reappointment to the Foreign Ministry was not in doubt throughout the political crisis that developed in Germany in December 1924, Stresemann could not make any major foreign policy moves in the West as long as the composition of the new government remained uncertain. In the elections of 7 December the SPD received the largest percentage of the votes and 131 seats, but the Right-wing parties held the balance of power in the new Reichstag. The DNVP won 103 seats, the Centre Party 69, and the DVP 51.[2] Ebert searched for more than a month before he found a candidate to form a government who could command the support of a majority of the deputies. The post of Chancellor finally went to Dr Luther, a former Minister of Finance who had little parliamentary experience and even less parliamentary skill. The new chancellor did not belong to any party, but his political opinions ranged him closest to Stresemann's DVP.

Luther took office on 15 January. Five days later, Stresemann, realizing that the Geneva Protocol was going to be rejected, revived the proposal of a Rhineland security pact as a substitute for the Protocol. He sent a note to London which repeated and elaborated on the idea of a security pact. On 9 February a similar note was sent to Paris. The seeds of Locarno were now firmly planted; but, since

[1] See the discussion in *ibid.*, pp. 9, 15; Hilger, *Incompatible Allies*, p. 154; and see below, p. 232.
[2] Mielcke, *Geschichte der Weimarer Republik*, p. 127.

the notes were dispatched in deepest secrecy, Moscow was entirely in the dark about the proposal.[1] However, a week before Austen Chamberlain announced that Stresemann's proposal had the provisional support of the British Government, sometime between the 4th and 7th of March, Stresemann instructed Brockdorff-Rantzau to inform the Soviet Government that negotiations for a Rhineland security pact had begun. The Russians were taken completely by surprise and became angry to the point of bitterness.[2] Only just a day or two before this startling announcement was made to him, Chicherin had tried to lessen the fears of Stresemann's policies among his colleagues. In an address to the Central Executive Committee of the Communist Party on 4 March he said he was sure that 'whatever vacillations have been apparent in German policy—and there were, are, and will be such vacillations—in the final analysis Germany will not break with us.'[3] That was a reasonable analysis and a fair prediction, but as soon as they heard that Western security pact negotiations had started Chicherin and Litvinov joined in an angry chorus to denounce Germany for having made up her mind to go with Britain and France and having faced Russia with a *fait accompli*. Brockdorff-Rantzau tried desperately to calm their fears, and in Berlin Stresemann multiplied his interviews with Krestinski, assuring him that the prospective security agreement had not yet been discussed in detail and that, in any event, it would have nothing to do with the Eastern boundaries disputes.[4] But the Russians were not appeased, and when a few days later, on 14 March, the League Council rejected Germany's first application for membership on the grounds that her status under Article 16 could only be discussed after her unconditional acceptance of the Covenant, Russo-German relations reached a crisis. Chicherin now had to face the worst: Stresemann, he feared, might yield to the Council's demand to join the League without exemption from Article 16; he saw the spectre of Germany 'as a *place d'armes* for future attacks against the Soviet Union.'[5]

[1] J. W. Wheeler-Bennett, *Hindenburg: The Wooden Titan* (London, 1936), p. 249.

[2] Hilger, *Incompatible Allies*, p. 134.

[3] Degras, *Soviet Documents*, vol. 2, p. 17.

[4] *Vermächtnis*, vol. 2, pp. 511 f.

[5] *Izvestiya*, 12 June 1925, quoted by Kochan, *Russia and Weimar*, p. 99.

But, contrary to the Russians' fears, Stresemann had no intention of yielding over Article 16. He instructed Brockdorff-Rantzau to impress this point on Chicherin. The Ambassador subsequently gave Chicherin and Litvinov a detailed briefing on Germany's policies towards the East and West, and reaffirmed the conditions which would have to be met before Germany would enter into the League. 'If the Soviet Government is interested in strengthening German-Russian relations,' Brockdorff-Rantzau said, 'then it must, at the same time, be interested in Germany's overcoming her political weakness and in her regaining a position in European politics as a factor worthy of attention. That can only be accomplished by freeing Germany from the French occupation.' Germany's policy towards the West, Brockdorff-Rantzau continued, has no other purpose than to thwart 'French imperialism, which is an imminent threat to the very existence of Germany.' The Ambassador pointed out that, whether or not Germany joined the League, the preponderant military strength of the Western powers ruled 'any active steps against Poland' out of practical consideration in the foreseeable future. Meanwhile, however, Germany would not enter into any 'agreement regarding security matters' which, in the government's estimation, could 'ever be understood as an agreement which recognizes or guarantees in any form Germany's Eastern boundaries.' No fundamental change of policy was being contemplated, the Ambassador said. Chicherin and Litvinov should see, he continued, that 'as a member of the League of Nations Germany could counteract all anti-Russian tendencies' in that body. If the Soviet Government were to look at Germany's policy in the light of this fact, then, the Ambassador was certain, 'a clarification of the questions, if and in what way a positive understanding regarding common political goals were possible, would also follow.'[1] But even after this explanation was given to them Chicherin and Litvinov remained adamant, perhaps because Brockdorff-Rantzau was not very persuasive. He was not really convinced of his own arguments. He disapproved of Stresemann's policies; they were endangering relations with Moscow. On 10 April the Ambassador travelled to Berlin 'to argue his point of view personally.' He stayed in the German capital for three months, believing that in this way he could best influence the decisions that were being taken affecting relations with Russia, for he did not

[1] *Stresemann Nachlass*, 7415H/H175570/9.

trust the Foreign Ministry to keep him informed and to consult him if he returned to Moscow.[1]

Stresemann wrote in his diary for 15 April that, 'while Count Brockdorff-Rantzau negotiates about German-Russian relations [with Under-Secretary von Schubert] in the next room, Krestinski talks with me along the same lines and suggests that we should sign a security pact with Russia too.' The Soviet Government, Krestinski told Stresemann, 'does not doubt the good intentions' of the German Government to keep the Western security agreements from developing into 'some kind of alignment against Russia.' But the prevailing view in Moscow was 'that in the course of events Germany would be forced into such a position . . . and this would give rise to an anti-Russian orientation.' Stresemann replied that the time was not ripe to conclude a new Russo-German treaty:

Under the present circumstances we do not want to sign a secret treaty with Russia before the conclusion of the security pact. With every treaty . . . one must assume that it will become public despite every precaution. It does not please us either that the start of negotiations with Russia is held up so long, but that is not our fault, rather that of the Western powers, who cannot agree on an answer to Germany.[2]

This meant, in other words, that Germany would not sign a treaty with Russia until the Western security agreements were concluded. To help Krestinski swallow this bitter medicine Stresemann added that, 'in spite of the pressure exerted on her to join the League of Nations unconditionally,' Germany would hold out for exemption from the obligations of Article 16. Countering Krestinski's rejoinder that, regardless of the conditions of her entry, Germany 'would be forced by the Entente powers to go against Russia' when she joined the League, Stresemann said that the Soviet Government need have no fear that Germany would ever 'go with Poland against Russia.' The aim of his policy, Stresemann continued, was 'to create a stable situation in the West while keeping a weather eye on developments in the East . . . and preserving our freedom of action there. . . . Russia would have to

[1] Helbig, 'Moskauer Mission Brockdorff-Rantzaus,' p. 319; Hilger, *op. cit.*, p. 135.

[2] *Stresemann Nachlass*, 7129H/H147779/80. Cf. *Vermächtnis*, vol. 2, p. 513, where it is incorrectly stated that Stresemann's conversation with Krestinski on 15 April was held 'still before Count Brockdorff-Rantzau's arrival in Berlin.'

realize, however, that we cannot, after all, base our policy solely on co-operation with her.' At the end of the discussion Krestinski still maintained that Russo-German treaty negotiations should at least parallel the negotiations for a Western security pact. Brockdorff-Rantzau also insisted that a treaty designed to confirm and elaborate Rapallo should be worked out right away.[1]

On 25 April Krestinski had another interview with Stresemann. The Ambassador had been given a lengthy document drafted by the legal staff of the German Foreign Ministry which was intended to prove that Russia would benefit from Germany's entry into the League. Although the document warns that, 'as a member of the League, Germany could never simply start a military offensive against Poland,' it goes on to say that, if Germany is exempted from fulfilling the obligations under Article 16, she could never be forced to brand Russia the aggressor in the event of another Russo-Polish conflict. This meant, as Stresemann pointedly explained to Krestinski, that Germany 'could prevent military sanctions from being invoked.' But the Ambassador was not favourably impressed. He said it was obvious that Germany had already fully decided to join the League and would not listen to Russia's arguments. Stresemann objected: no final decisions had been made, he said; Germany's conditions for League membership had neither been met nor altered. There were internal political questions as well as legal ones that had still to be settled. Stresemann confessed that there was still considerable opposition to League membership in the Reichstag, but he was confident, he said, that this could be overcome as soon as the Allies met the government's conditions.[2]

The deadlock in Russo-German relations was now virtually complete. Since December 1924 the Russians had been trying un-successfully to divert Stresemann from negotiating a Western security pact and joining the League, and they had also failed to start negotiations for a treaty to amplify Rapallo. On 27 April Krestinski returned to Moscow for further consultations with Chicherin. All that the Ambassador had managed to get out of Stresemann by the spring of 1925 was an assurance—oft repeated—that Germany would not join the League unless she were granted at least *de facto* exemption from Article 16. But this did not satisfy the Russians; moreover, they did not trust Stresemann. An

[1] *Ibid.*
[2] *Stresemann Nachlass*, 7133H/H148697/H148707, 7129H/H147795.

*Izvestiya* leader in May 1925, which was most likely written or dictated by Chicherin, clearly defined Russia's position towards Germany and revealed deep doubts about the future course of relations between the two countries:

> The logic of things is stronger than any subjective intentions, and there can be no doubt that after entering the League of Nations, that is, after submitting to the command of the Western imperialist powers, Germany will sooner or later—probably sooner—become a helpless plaything in their hands. . . . It goes without saying that for the Soviet Union Germany's choice of a definitely Western orientation and entry into the League of Nations can objectively lead only to the deterioration of relations between Germany and the Soviet Republic.[1]

When Krestinski returned to Moscow Schubert hinted to Brockdorff-Rantzau that he, too, should go back to his post since his services were needed in Moscow. But the Count refused to leave Berlin. He was waiting, as the entire European political world waited at this time, for France's reply to Germany's note of 9 February, and used the time to drum up support against Stresemann's 'Western orientation.' By the end of May Russo-German trade negotiations, which had been going on sporadically in Moscow since they were revived in November 1924, reached an impasse—largely due to Russian intransigence. The stalemate in relations between the two powers was now complete.

At the beginning of June Chicherin registered another formal protest against German policies. The new *démarche* took the form of a note to Stresemann purporting to be a reply to Brockdorff-Rantzau's declaration of policy in Moscow on 7 April.[2] The note summarized the inconclusive talks since the beginning of April, condemned the League, and reiterated that Germany's entry into the League would be 'an important step towards the complete destruction of the Treaty of Rapallo.' There was nothing new in these protests. However, one paragraph of the note implied a modification of the views previously expressed by the Soviet Government. After repeating that Germany, regardless of her intentions, would be forced into 'the combination of Entente powers against the U.S.S.R.,' the note continued:

> The correctness of this analysis of the objective tendencies of German Foreign Policy is partly substantiated by the fact that the German

---

[1] Hilger, *Incompatible Allies*, p. 134.          [2] See above, p. 220.

Government is negotiating with the Entente powers regarding the conclusion of written treaties, . . . while, towards the U.S.S.R., it restricts itself to friendly verbal assurances and postpones the start of negotiations for the proclamation of these assurances in a binding agreement of both powers.[1]

The Soviet Government, the note continued, could not be satisfied with an exchange of friendly words; there was, therefore, a distinct possibility 'that the Soviet Union may be forced to seek other ways' of gaining sufficient guarantees for herself, although 'she has no such intentions or desires at the present time.' Chicherin was clearly making a new bid for treaty negotiations paralleling those leading to Locarno. He objected to the Western negotiations only in so far as these seemed to be leading to German membership in the League, a step he condemned yet again in the concluding paragraph:

Germany's . . . entry into the League of Nations will indubitably . . . strain the friendly political and economic relations between the U.S.S.R. and Germany, the basis of which was laid at Rapallo, if they are not, in fact, made impossible.[2]

Stresemann had to take Chicherin's threat to 'seek other ways,' meaning agreements with Poland and possibly also with France, seriously. The Soviet Government was still sharply divided from both of these powers, and also from Britain, but the very chance that Chicherin might seek a reconciliation with them was an implied threat to Germany's interests in the East which might also seriously complicate and endanger her negotiations with the Allies.[3] On 10 June, eight days after Chicherin's note was delivered, Stresemann called Krestinski to him.[4] The Russian Ambassador began with a short statement about his visit to Moscow in which he emphasized the chief purpose of the note of 2 June. He said he was 'glad to say that there was a very strong desire in Moscow for a German-Russian understanding'; the Soviet Government 'was anxious to reach a settlement.' Stresemann replied that he, too, wanted a German-Russian understanding. The Soviet Govern-

---

[1] *Stresemann Nachlass*, 7415H/H175580/7.

[2] *Ibid.*

[3] Cf. Gatzke, 'Stresemann und die deutsche Russlandpolitik,' p. 11.

[4] A 'Memorandum regarding Future Political Negotiations with Russia' was prepared in the Foreign Ministry immediately following the receipt of Chicherin's note of 2 June: *Stresemann Nachlass*, 7415H/H175588/95.

ment should know, he continued, that whether or not Germany was formally released from fulfilling the obligations of Article 16 when she joined the League, 'in all foreseeable circumstances that may arise' the German Government would be 'in a position not only to refuse to participate in sanctions against Russia, but actually to make such sanctions impossible.' Referring to the Soviet note of 2 June, Stresemann said the assertion that he did not want to negotiate with Russia as long as negotiations were going on in the West was based on a 'misunderstanding.' Recalling his conversation with Krestinski on 15 April the Foreign Minister said:

> I did not say that we could not negotiate with Russia, but I did say that I would not care to conclude a treaty with Russia as long as our political situation in the other direction was not cleared up, because I want to be able to answer the question whether we have a treaty with Russia in the negative.[1]

In other words, Stresemann was now ready to negotiate with the Soviet Government, which he had refused to do since December 1924 and had only implied as a possibility in April 1925. But he would not go further than that. Germany would start to negotiate, Stresemann said, but until the Locarno agreements were signed and Germany joined the League the talks with Russia could not be formally concluded—in other words, they might continue *ad infinitum*. Moreover, the Foreign Minister gave Krestinski no reason to believe that Germany would negotiate a neutrality treaty, as Chicherin had suggested in December 1924. As a matter of fact, he envisaged no more than a declaration of friendship which was to be incorporated in a preamble to the pending trade treaty. Then, if Germany joined the League without formal exemption from sanctions obligations, the Soviet Government might be given additional verbal assurances. Krestinski was, of course, still dissatisfied. He told Stresemann that his government could understand Germany's reasons for negotiating security agreements in the West but it remained irrevocably opposed to her joining the League.[2] Two days later, on 13 June, Litvinov arrived in Berlin and reiterated all the Russian fears of Germany's 'Western orientation' to Stresemann. Although Russia preferred to sign a new treaty with Germany, Litvinov added, the Soviet Government might be forced to seek closer relations with Poland and France. He pointed

---

[1] *Ibid.*, 7129H/H147845/7. Cf. above, p. 221.           [2] *Ibid.*

H

to the 'uncompromising position' adopted by Germany's trade delegation in Moscow as further evidence of Berlin's unfriendly attitude. The conclusion of a trade treaty would gratify the Soviet Government, Litvinov said, because it would be looked upon as 'a political act' in other capitals. Stresemann denied that German obstinacy was responsible for the failure of the trade negotiations. He admitted, however, that some of the difficulties in the negotiations were due to the disagreements between the German Government and certain businessmen and politicians in Berlin. 'We are not in the fortunate position of dealing with these in the dictatorial manner in which one can do so in Russia,' Stresemann added sarcastically.[1]

On 16 June the French Government finally replied to Germany's proposals for a security pact in the West. Although they were favourably disposed to the proposals, the French demanded that Germany agree to join the League unconditionally. German exemption from sanctions obligations was unacceptable to them. Furthermore, the French proposed a link between the Western security agreements and a guarantee of Germany's Eastern boundaries in order to safeguard Poland. Stresemann refused to bow to these demands. In closed sessions of the Foreign Affairs Committee and in off the record interviews with representatives of the press he said that the French amendments to the security pact proposals were inconsistent with his own policies. For Stresemann the 'security pacts were above all an instrument to achieve a revision of the Eastern boundaries'; he would not allow the French to misuse his proposals to reaffirm the very decisions which were the source of German grievances.[2]

Although the French note had made Stresemann's task much more difficult, he was not discouraged from seeking the kind of agreements he wanted. But he was now confronted by the dual task of extracting concessions from the Allies, from France in particular, and, at the same time, checking the outbursts against the prospective Locarno agreements and League membership which the French note provoked on the domestic political scene. Both the 'pro-Russian Right' and the 'anti-Russian Right' were agitating against the government's policies; the DNVP especially, which had three places in Luther's cabinet, was becoming

[1] *Ibid.*, 7129H/H147855/65.
[2] Stampfer, *Die vierzehn Jahre der ersten deutschen Republik*, pp. 459 f.

increasingly critical of Stresemann.[1] Moreover, Seeckt and the Reichswehr were unalterably opposed to the 'Western orientation,' and to the Locarno agreements in particular. Seeckt left no doubt about his position when he spoke in a cabinet meeting on 25 June. According to Stresemann's notes taken at the meeting, Seeckt brushed aside the arguments regarding Article 16. The whole idea that Germany's boundaries, East or West, might be limited or guaranteed was entirely reprehensible as far as Seeckt was concerned. 'Whether or not the right to march through [Germany] should be granted is not a practical question,' Seeckt said. 'We will not tolerate such an invasion [Durchmarsch] nor make the railroads available for it. We shall only be able to make alliances again when we regain our power, and as soon as we do, we shall naturally take back everything we lost.'[2]

Just when the opposition to the 'Western orientation' in Germany was asserting itself with new vigour, Ambassador Brockdorff-Rantzau, who had still not returned to Moscow, threatened the government with his resignation. He complained that Schubert had 'insulted' him with critical remarks about the fact that he was still in Berlin. The Ambassador also felt hurt because Stresemann refused to heed his advice and continued to pursue Western policies at the expense of Germany's Russian connexion. In Brockdorff-Rantzau's estimation the preamble that Stresemann wanted to negotiate with Chicherin was 'worthless'; he was quite sure that the Soviet Government would not accept it as a substitute for the proposal of a neutrality treaty. In the course of a long discussion on 21 June, Stresemann persuaded Brockdorff-Rantzau that Schubert had intended no offence; he had merely stated what everyone else felt, namely that it was unfortunate to be deprived of the Ambassador's valuable services in Moscow at such a crucial juncture. Brockdorff-Rantzau insisted that, if he returned to Moscow at all, Dirksen, who had replaced the Count's trusted friend Maltzan at the head of the Eastern Department of the Foreign Ministry when the latter became Ambassador to Washington,

[1] Eyck, *Geschichte der Weimarer Republik*, pp. 422 ff. See also the interview with Count Reventlow in the *Bergisch-Märkische Zeitung*, 20 June 1925.

[2] *Stresemann Nachlass*, 7133H/H148824/5. On Seeckt's opposition to Stresemann's policies and the Locarno Pacts also see *ibid.*, 7129H/H147935. At a dinner party in Munich Seeckt sat by Sphinx-like when his wife asserted to the assembled company: 'Nothing will come of Locarno, my husband won't tolerate it': *ibid.*, 7140H/H149755/6.

would have to accompany him. He himself would not confront Chicherin with Germany's half-hearted offer to negotiate a political preamble to the trade treaty, the Ambassador said; that would have to be done by Dirksen. Stresemann consented to let Dirksen go to Moscow, and, in the further course of the conversation, mollified Brockdorff-Rantzau with assurances that the government considered its relations with Russia to be just as important as its policy towards the West. The Foreign Minister said he was 'very disturbed about the present state of German-Russian relations.' Brockdorff-Rantzau himself had said, Stresemann went on, 'that the Russians are now—despite their predilections—fully capable of rushing ahead into signing an agreement with Poland that will guarantee Poland's boundaries.' This threat made it all the more important to have Brockdorff-Rantzau in Moscow at the earliest time. He depended on him, Stresemann said, to reverse the trend of events in the East—'would it be possible for him to leave next week?'[1]

Anti-German sentiment was running high in the Russian capital when Brockdorff-Rantzau and Dirksen arrived there at the end of June. On 19 June the Soviet press had published the government's charges against the two students, Kindermann and Wolscht, alleging that they were members of the Fascist underground organization that had plotted the murder of Walter Rathenau— who had signed the Rapallo treaty for Germany—and that their mission in Moscow was to poison Stalin and Trotsky. German Government circles were accused of conniving at the plot, and Hilger of the Moscow Embassy was specifically accused of giving 'assistance and advice' to the two students. The entire case against Kindermann and Wolscht was, of course, a frame-up in retaliation for the trial of the Soviet agent Skoblevsky in Leipzig, against whom evidence had been presented that implicated the Soviet Embassy in the organization of KPD terror units in 1923. The timing of the trial of Kindermann and Wolscht was most probably also an expression of Russia's general dissatisfaction with Germany's policies. The trial started on 24 June, and on 3 July both the accused were found guilty and sentenced to death. As far as the Russians were concerned this ended the matter; they were confident that, sooner or later, Kindermann and Wolscht would

[1] L. Fischer, *Soviets in World Affairs*, vol. 2, p. 606; Stern-Rubarth, *Graf Brockdorff-Rantzau*, pp. 143 f.; *Stresemann Nachlass*, 7129H/H147876/81.

be exchanged for Skoblevsky and his men.[1] But Brockdorff-Rantzau refused to let the matter rest. He surprised Chicherin with a sharp demand that the verdict against the two students be rescinded and that the Embassy, Hilger in particular, be exonerated. Chicherin was bitter. He protested that the German Government had refused to delete the references to the Soviet Embassy from the charges against Skoblevsky and had condemned him to death—why should the Soviet Government now accede to Germany's demands? In the end Chicherin agreed to clear Hilger's name and to exchange Kindermann and Wolscht for Skoblevsky on the conditions that the trade negotiations and the discussions of a political agreement, which had been interrupted by the trial, be resumed.[2] Both of these conditions were met. But by the middle of July the leaders of the German trade delegation, von Koerner and now also Dirksen, proposed to Stresemann that the negotiations be suspended in view of the unsatisfactory course they were taking. The Russians, it seems, were making excessive demands. They wanted upwards of 100 million marks credit and a German undertaking not to compete with Russia in China.[3] Although some of the Russian demands were beyond the pale, Stresemann would not consent to halt the negotiations. Moscow was already suspicious of Germany's policies and would regard an adjournment of the trade talks as positive proof that German Foreign Policy was turning away from friendship with Russia. Moreover, German industry needed Soviet trade, and Stresemann did not want to give the opponents of his 'Western orientation' more ammunition to use against him. Subsequently the German trade negotiators, presumably acting under orders from Stresemann, abandoned some of their earlier demands and agreed to most of the Russian ones. From the end of July on the negotiations went smoothly. A treaty which, in general, favoured Russia more than Germany was completed and

[1] Hilger, *Incompatible Allies*, pp. 140 f. Kochan supports the Soviet assertion that Kindermann and Wolscht 'belonged to the same organization as had the killers of Rathenau,' but he presents no evidence to substantiate the charge: *Russia and Weimar*, p. 107.

[2] Hilger, *op. cit.*, pp. 144 f. Hilger was vindicated by *Izvestiya* on 8 August 1925. Kindermann and Wolscht were exchanged for Skoblevsky and his accomplices in 1926.

[3] *Stresemann Nachlass*, 7129H/H147885/8. The best detailed accounts of the trade negotiations are in Hilger, *op. cit.*, pp. 182 ff., and Helbig, 'Moskauer Mission Brockdorff-Rantzaus,' pp. 318-320.

ready to be signed by the end of September. The timing of Stresemann's consent for the signing, and also the date of the actual ceremony, were both dictated by political considerations.[1]

The negotiations of a preamble to the trade treaty, which went on simultaneously with the trade talks, do not appear to have been taken very seriously by either side. For Stresemann the proposal was a means of keeping the Russians at arm's length without impelling them into agreements with Poland and France during the time that the Western security agreements were being negotiated. Chicherin, on the other hand, tried to turn the proposed political preamble into an instrument to keep Germany from joining the League.

Dirksen handed Chicherin the German draft of a preamble at the beginning of July.[2] On 18 July Chicherin countered with a Russian draft. His version contained clauses which outstripped anything normally found in the preamble of a treaty. It was, as a matter of fact, a neutrality treaty in disguise, incorporating Chicherin's proposals of December 1924 which Stresemann had rejected. It also included a sentence which would have prevented Germany from joining the League without the express consent of the Soviet Government. Chicherin must have known that his draft was entirely unacceptable to Stresemann. Even after it was formally rejected Chicherin wanted to publish it, presumably to create the impression in the West that Germany did not really want to join the League.[3] In the end Brockdorff-Rantzau managed to dissuade Chicherin from publishing the Russian draft. But the Soviet campaign to impede Germany's reconciliation with Britain and France and to retain a monopoly of friendly relations with her continued unabated throughout the summer of 1925. Stresemann nevertheless stubbornly refused to opt for either the East or the West and 'was very disappointed that Moscow did not understand his position.'[4] It did not help Stresemann during the crucial weeks

[1] See below, pp. 231, 233. Cf. Dirksen, *Moskau-Tokio-London*, p. 75; cf. Kochan, *op. cit.*, p. 107, who alleges that Stresemann made 'the conclusion of the [trade] talks dependent on prior agreement over the Western Pact'; and Helbig, *op. cit.*, p. 320, who gives Brockdorff-Rantzau too much credit for the eventual success of the trade talks.

[2] The text of the German draft of the preamble is to be found in the *Stresemann Nachlass*, 7415H/H175588/95, and has been published by Gatzke, 'Stresemann und die deutsche Russlandpolitik,' p. 11, n. 57. Dirksen, *op. cit.*, p. 69.

[3] Hilger, *op. cit.*, p. 145.　　　　[4] *Ibid.*, p. 146.

immediately preceding the Locarno Conference that Brockdorff-Rantzau spent ever more time and energy representing the Russian position to Berlin and less and less time reassuring the Soviet Government of Germany's goodwill.

On 15 September the invitations were issued for the Locarno Conference, which was to begin on 5 October. On 25 September Chicherin left Moscow for what was said to be a private visit to German health resorts. The trip was highly publicized and timed in such a way that considerable political significance was rightly ascribed to it. Instead of going directly to Berlin, as he usually did, Chicherin made a stopover in Warsaw, where he was given a cordial reception. This was a blatant attempt to scare Stresemann with the threat of a Russo-Polish *détente*. Chicherin made the most of it by repeatedly speaking of Russia's desire for closer political and economic relations with Poland: but, in actual fact, no agreements were reached.[1] In any event, Stresemann was not intimidated by the threat and undeterred from pursuing his Locarno plans. He did, however, choose the day of Chicherin's arrival in Warsaw—26 September—to tell Litvinov that he would allow the Russo-German trade treaty to be signed early in October.[2]

Chicherin arrived in Berlin on 30 September with a flourish. The visit to health resorts was entirely forgotten: Chicherin devoted all his time to disrupting Germany's plans of entering into the League through agreements with the Allies at Locarno. 'Germany is becoming a pawn in the anti-Soviet diplomacy of Britain,' he announced as he stepped off the train. 'By means of Article 16 Britain is forcing Germany to act against Russia.' 'Russia,' Chicherin said on another occasion, 'would never join the League.'[3] The Soviet Foreign Commissar even turned the official reception given him by President Hindenburg and Chancellor Luther's luncheon in his honour into political demonstrations.[4] Since he could no longer prevent the Locarno Conference from taking place, Chicherin's attacks were aimed chiefly at German membership in the League, particularly at the provisions of Article 16 from which the Allied powers had not yet freed the German Govern-

[1] *Izvestiya*, 27 September, 30 September, and 4 October 1925.

[2] Kochan, *Russia and Weimar*, p. 108.

[3] *Berliner Tageblatt*, 2 October 1925; *Deutsche Allgemeine Zeitung*, 3 October 1925.

[4] Meissner, *Staatssekretär*, p. 156.

ment. But public outbursts were not the most powerful weapon
Chicherin carried in his diplomatic arsenal; he still had an ace up
his sleeve. He probably travelled to Berlin chiefly to play a single
card which he, and apparently Brockdorff-Rantzau too, relied
upon to trump any bid made to Stresemann by the Western
governments. If Stresemann anticipated a last desperate manœuvre
by Chicherin he did not have to wait long for it. Chicherin, as it
turned out, had indeed been far from signing an alliance with
Poland when he visited Warsaw, for in a conversation with Stresemann on the same night he arrived in Berlin he played an entirely
different 'Polish card.' What, Chicherin asked Stresemann
pointedly, had become of Brockdorff-Rantzau's proposal of
December 1924 'for an alliance between Russia and Germany
against Poland [to] force Poland back into her ethnographic
frontiers?' The Soviet Government interpreted this proposal to
mean that Germany was prepared to form 'a military alliance
against Poland, in order to smash the current Polish State.' Stresemann obviously did not want to play this game. According to his
own notes of the discussion, Stresemann declared that he was
'astounded' and 'overcome' to hear that any move had been made
towards an 'alliance with Russia for the partition of Poland.'
Although it was after midnight, Stresemann—right then and there
—called Schubert and Gaus, the legal counsellor of the Foreign
Ministry, to ask if either one of them knew anything about such a
proposal. Both denied having any knowledge of it. Stresemann
relayed this information to Chicherin and then tried to end the
discussion of this topic; he had clearly refused to take the bait.
Chicherin was furious. His *démarche* had completely failed. In a
sudden outburst of temper he said that Dirksen had stated in
Moscow that Germany would join the League of Nations under
any conditions: he demanded to be told if this was Stresemann's
intention. It really seemed to be the case, he said. Stresemann hotly
denied that Germany would join the League unconditionally and
said he doubted if Dirksen had ever said so. In the further course of
this stormy exchange Chicherin managed to extract a definite
statement—though not a promise—from Stresemann that he would
not conclude agreements at Locarno nor enter into the League
without at least *de facto* exemption from Article 16. Apparently
Chicherin considered this a major achievement, although it did not
involve the slightest change in official German policy. Gradually

a calmer atmosphere returned to the discussion. Stresemann said he wanted to conclude the trade treaty as soon as possible 'in order to counteract the talk of a Western orientation.' Then both Foreign Ministers recalled that, only recently, officers of their respective armies had been the only foreigners present at each other's field manœuvres and agreed that this was a positive sign of friendship between the two countries. Since it was now two o'clock in the morning, and because Krestinski, who had sat by in silence during the stormier parts of the session, had fallen asleep, the discussion came to an end.[1]

Two days later, when he entrained for Locarno, on 2 October, Stresemann made public the announcement that a Russo-German trade treaty would be signed in the immediate future. The actual ceremony took place in Moscow on 12 October.[2] The announcement went a long way to calm Russia's fears of Locarno. In an interview with *Izvestiya* on 4 October Chicherin hailed the trade treaty as 'a clearly expressed demonstration in favour of the Rapallo line' which eliminated the possibility of an Anglo-German trade boycott of Soviet Russia after Locarno.[3] But Chicherin wanted still more assurances from Stresemann on the eve of Locarno. Until an hour before he left Berlin, Stresemann was closeted with both Chicherin and Krestinski. Once again the Russians pressed for the conclusion of an immediate Russo-German neutrality alliance, only to be rebuffed by the German Foreign Minister. Stresemann reiterated that neither Brockdorff-Rantzau's supposed offer of an anti-Polish pact nor Dirksen's alleged statement that Germany would join the League unconditionally—if these were made at all—had followed from instructions sent out by the Foreign Ministry. Just as Rathenau had refused to confront the Allies with a Russo-German *fait accompli* at the Genoa Conference, Stresemann now refused to conclude any agreement with the Soviet Government just before the Locarno Conference. When the Russians suggested that a neutrality treaty might be signed in secret in order to forestall Western protests, Stresemann

[1] *Stresemann Nachlass*, 7129H/H147979/91. Chicherin exaggerated when he told Louis Fischer that Stresemann had *promised* him not to sign the Locarno Pacts nor to join the League unless Article 16 was revised: Fischer, *Soviets in World Affairs*, vol. 2, p. 606.

[2] Helbig, 'Moskauer Mission Brockdorff-Rantzaus,' p. 320; Hilger, *Incompatible Allies*, p. 183.

[3] Degras, *Soviet Documents*, vol. 2, pp. 57 f.

retorted that he was equally opposed to signing a 'secret agreement' as a public one, because in either case the Allies would, sooner or later, conjecture—as they did after Rapallo—that there 'are huge secret German military rearmament' schemes behind the agreement, and then Germany would be made to suffer 'on the Western frontier.' Although he did not give in to any of Chicherin's demands, Stresemann seems to have convinced him that Russia had nothing to fear from the Locarno discussions—Germany would not join the League at the expense of Soviet security.[1]

But Chicherin was taking no chances. On the first day of the Locarno Conference he held a press conference in Berlin and resumed his attacks on the Western governments in general, and on British policy and Article 16 in particular. When he was asked if his talks with Stresemann had not allayed his fears of Germany's stand on Article 16, Chicherin replied that 'this question had been thoroughly discussed . . . but one could not know yet what the outcome of the Locarno Conference would be.'[2] Chicherin's remarks did not fall on deaf ears at Locarno. Stresemann made a direct reference to his talks with Chicherin when he said on 4 October: 'For us there is no option between an Eastern and a Western policy. We want to live on good terms with both sides.'[3]

The German delegation at Locarno made good use of their Russian connexions and of Chicherin's relentless campaign in Berlin. 'It does seem,' America's Ambassador Schurman cabled to Washington during the Locarno Conference, 'that Chicherin is by all odds the best bargaining card the Germans hold, and I gather that Luther and Stresemann mean to play it for all it is worth.'[4] This is precisely what the Germans did. They managed to secure a modification of Article 16 which, in Stresemann's words, gave Germany 'the right of deciding as to the extent to which [she] would join in taking action against a disturber of the peace, even when a state was obviously and unmistakably in the wrong.'[5] The reinterpretation of Article 16, to which all the Locarno powers subscribed, read as follows:

[1] *Stresemann Nachlass*, 7129H/H147992/8.

[2] *Vermächtnis*, vol. 2, p. 527. Chicherin held press conferences in Berlin on 2, 3, and 4 October 1925.

[3] *Ibid.*, p. 528.

[4] From an unpublished telegram of 12 October 1925, quoted by Hirsch, 'Stresemann in Historical Perspective,' p. 374.

[5] Stresemann, *Essays and Speeches on Various Subjects* (London, 1930), p. 237.

Each state member of the League is bound to co-operate loyally and effectively in support of the Covenant and in resistance to any act of aggression to an extent which is compatible with its military situation and takes its geographical location into account.[1]

In other words, Germany could now join the League without any binding sanctions obligations whatsoever. The Russians were satisfied; Stresemann had not gone back on his pledges to the Soviet Government. Article 16, Chicherin noted, 'was really emasculated.'[2]

The German delegation also used their connexions with Russia to good advantage over the issue of France's alliances with Poland and Czechoslovakia. When Briand insisted that these alliances be incorporated in the Locarno Pacts in order to reaffirm Germany's Eastern boundaries, Stresemann—ever the resourceful diplomat—threatened to invite Chicherin to the conference.[3] The prospect of having the Soviet Foreign Commissar participating in the Locarno discussions was enough of a threat to convince Briand to withdraw his demand.

The Locarno Pacts were a signal success for Stresemann. The pacts were initialled on 16 October and signed in London at the beginning of December. The pacts were not to come into force until Germany entered into the League, but the negotiations themselves convinced Chicherin that Germany would no longer rely exclusively on her friendship with the Soviet Union. The heyday of Rapallo had long since passed; the Russo-German alliance was now simply one in a network of many.

But Germany had not been granted neutrality at Locarno; Stresemann had not bargained for that. According to the reinterpretation of Article 16 Germany was committed to resist international aggression in support of the Covenant 'to an extent which is compatible' with her military situation and geographic position. As long as Germany was virtually disarmed—at least officially disarmed—the government could easily justify a decision not to participate in sanctions against an aggressor; but the military situation might have changed—for example, the Allies could have permitted Germany to increase the size of her army to 500,000. In that event a German government could not simply have pleaded

---

[1] L. Fischer, *Soviets in World Affairs*, vol. 2, p. 603.

[2] *Ibid.*, p. 604.

[3] A. Erusalimski, *Germaniya Antanta i S.S.S.R.* (Moscow, 1928), p. 150, cited by Kochan, *Russia and Weimar*, p. 111.

military impotence in the event it was called upon to participate in sanctions against Russia or any other aggressor nation. In order to reassure Russia of Germany's friendship for the foreseeable future as well as in the current situation, Chicherin was still anxious to negotiate a new political treaty with Stresemann which would guarantee Germany's neutrality, regardless of her military situation, in the event of an act of aggression involving Russia. Almost as soon as Stresemann returned to Berlin from Locarno, Krestinski pressed him to resume the political discussions with the Soviet Government.[1] But Stresemann felt that the trade treaty of 12 October had taken the Eastward sting out of Locarno and that another agreement with Moscow would be superfluous. He proceeded to stall. No further talks were held until the middle of December. During this interval, however, Stresemann used his speeches and news conferences to reassure the Soviet Government, and also the increasing number of Reichstag deputies who were anxious lest Locarno disrupt Germany's relations with Russia, that Germany would not join 'a bloc against Russia.'[2] In spite of these assurances, however, the Locarno Conference produced considerable apprehension in Moscow. The favourable propaganda surrounding the conference, more than the agreements that were reached, aroused the suspicion that a united European capitalist movement had been formed which would try to isolate the Soviet Union. But no member of the Soviet Government, not even Chicherin, reacted as sharply as Brockdorff-Rantzau. He lodged the strongest protests against Locarno. His objections were not so much criticisms of the substance of the security pacts as the product of hurt feelings because he had not been consulted nor informed about the agreements before they were concluded. The Ambassador was aware that the Locarno agreements had been hailed in all the Western countries as a great victory for the cause of European peace and stability. He felt that this new atmosphere would prevent Germany from making good her territorial grievances in the East and lead to constant friction between Berlin and Moscow. Resorting to the special privilege Ebert had granted to him at the time of his appointment, Brockdorff-Rantzau went over Stresemann's head and wrote an angry letter to President

[1] *Stresemann Nachlass*, 7129H/H148010/2.

[2] For example, see Stresemann's speech in Karlsruhe on 23 October 1925 in the *Vermächtnis*, vol. 2, pp. 528 f.

Hindenburg in which he denounced the Locarno Pacts. The Ambassador also protested that the preliminary negotiations for Germany's entry into the League had been completed without his having had an opportunity to voice his objections. Brockdorff-Rantzau wrote that he was unalterably opposed to joining the 'French League' because this would break Germany's tie with Russia, which he personally was holding together. This time the Ambassador not only threatened to resign, he actually tendered his resignation.[1]

Stresemann was furious. Brockdorff-Rantzau had not only by-passed the authority of the Foreign Minister, he had given Hindenburg the impression, which Stresemann knew to be entirely incorrect, that Germany's relations with Russia were in serious danger because of Locarno. Stresemann had every reason to believe that the Russians were not only still friendly to Germany, but that he could negotiate a treaty amplifying Rapallo whenever he chose to do so. As a matter of fact, the most serious threat to Russo-German relations was the resignation of Brockdorff-Rantzau himself, which seemed to have been prompted by nothing other than excessive vainglory. Everyone, including Brockdorff-Rantzau, realized that his resignation would give the Russians to believe that fundamental changes in German policy really had taken place at Locarno. The task at hand for every German who was truly interested in maintaining good relations with the Soviet Government was, clearly, to reassure the Russians that Stresemann's policy was in no way anti-Soviet. Yet the Ambassador, who could fulfil this task best, not only refused to do so, but, just at this crucial juncture, left Moscow and resigned.

Brockdorff-Rantzau arrived in Berlin on 4 November and immediately went to see Hindenburg. The President agreed that the government should not, under any circumstances, jeopardize its connexions with Soviet Russia, but he did not—as the Ambassador undoubtedly hoped he would—take a stand against Locarno and German entry into the League. Instead, Hindenburg persuaded Brockdorff-Rantzau to withdraw his resignation and to return to his post, giving him an assurance that, in future times, Luther and Stresemann would remain in closer consultation with the Moscow Embassy.[2] In spite of his anger about Brockdorff-

[1] Helbig, 'Moskauer Mission Brockdorff-Rantzaus,' pp. 320 f.
[2] *Ibid.*, p. 322.

Rantzau's high-handed dealings, Stresemann also besought him to retain his post—in the interests of Germany's good relations with Russia.[1] Brockdorff-Rantzau remained truculent for several weeks and stubbornly refused to return to Moscow, but then, as everyone knew he would, the Ambassador changed his mind.

Meanwhile, on 11 December, Stresemann and Schubert had received Krestinski and Bratman-Brodowski to discuss the possibilities of a Russo-German political agreement. The Russians still insisted on a formal treaty of neutrality, while Stresemann thought it was enough to exchange notes stating that the Rapallo treaty remained the basis of German-Russian relations and that both countries recognized and approved the conditions on which Germany was applying for membership in the League. Krestinski recalled that Chicherin had dubbed the German proposal a mere 'toast' and insisted on the Russian version. Stresemann replied 'that toasts often have much greater political significance than treaties. At Locarno, the Foreign Minister continued, the German Government had repeatedly declared 'that Germany would not, under any circumstances, join in a war against Russia, and that Germany would, in all circumstances, try to live in peace with Russia.' There was, therefore, no need for an Eastern neutrality treaty, Stresemann continued, but 'there cannot be any doubt that Germany wants to come to an agreement with Russia.'[2]

The negotiations were now suspended for almost two weeks until Chicherin returned to Berlin from Paris. Stresemann welcomed even a short respite at this time because he was preoccupied with the defence of his policies against the Right-wing parties in the Reichstag. The Locarno Pacts had been ratified by 291 votes to 174 after a bitter parliamentary fight against them led by the DNVP and the NSDAP, with Stresemann's own DVP and also the KPD contributing many of the negative votes. But the attacks on Locarno and on League membership did not cease even after the pacts were ratified. The nationalists and Fascists appealed to Hindenburg not to sign the instrument of ratification.[3] In defending himself against the Right Stresemann gave increasingly narrower and more nationalistic interpretations to the Locarno Pacts. On one occasion he wrote:

[1] *Stresemann Nachlass*, 7129H/H148095/H148100.
[2] *Ibid.*, 7129H/H148073/94.
[3] Meissner, *Staatssekretär*, pp. 156 f.

The Locarno Pacts were not concluded for the benefit or disadvantage of any foreign state or people, but rather in the full understanding of the interests of the German nation and the German people. With these [Locarno Pacts] a policy shall be inaugurated that will serve German interests exclusively.[1]

To help him stem the tide of criticism Stresemann appealed for 'a package announcement by the Allies about relief in the occupied areas.' He wanted Paris and London to consider ordering an immediate withdrawal of the occupation forces in the Ruhr. But these appeals were not answered. The continued silence across the Rhine played havoc with Stresemann's position at home. The nationalists charged that the Foreign Minister had played into the hands of the Western powers while spurning Germany's only real friend, Soviet Russia.[2] As the attacks on his policy mounted, Stresemann became aware that the Reichswehr, which had opposed his Locarno policies from the start, was tapping the ministry's telephone and intercepting its cablegrams. There were, moreover, reports that Seeckt and his closest political adviser, von Schleicher, were hatching a plot to persuade Hindenburg to appoint the pliable Gessler as Chancellor in order to reconstitute the government and adopt 'an entirely new foreign policy . . . which will be chiefly orientated towards the East.' According to the reports reaching Stresemann, the Reichswehr 'wanted to make use . . . of its countless ties . . . with Soviet Russia' where Seeckt saw 'the enormous reservoir of manpower for a war.'[3] The pressures on Stresemann reached unprecedented intensity just as Chicherin arrived in Berlin towards the end of December 1925 to continue the negotiations for a political agreement. Chicherin had come directly from conversations with Briand. In Paris Chicherin had played the French half of the Franco-Polish card against Germany. He told a press conference that he thought 'the present general situation most propitious for the development of stable friendly relations between the Soviet Federation and France.'[4] No Franco-Russian agreement was signed, but Chicherin did conclude a treaty with the Turkish Ambassador in which both countries pledged their neutrality in the

[1] *Stresemann Nachlass*, 7415H, undated notes, but apparently November-December 1925.
[2] Cf. Bretton, *Stresemann and Versailles*, p. 95.
[3] *Stresemann Nachlass*, 7138H/H149451/9, 7138H/H149466/9, 7414H/H175350.
[4] Degras, *Soviet Documents*, vol. 2, pp. 66-68.

event of military action by or against the other, and agreed not to participate in any political, economic, or financial combinations, military conventions, or hostile acts of any other kind directed against the other country. Chicherin indicated to Stresemann that he wanted to negotiate a Russo-German treaty paralleling the Russo-Turkish one. Stresemann rejected this proposal out of hand. Such a treaty would have given Chicherin a veto over Germany's decision to join the League, and that was intolerable. Stresemann then read aloud to Chicherin the text of a German counter-proposal—now also in the form of a treaty instead of a preamble or an exchange of notes—which the Soviet minister 'seemed to like very much.' The German draft declared that the country would remain neutral in the event of an attack on Russia and stated that there was no chance of Germany being drawn into a conflict pro-voked by the Soviet Government since this 'was a purely theoretical contingency without any real political significance.' At the end of their discussion Chicherin and Stresemann agreed that the negotia-tions should continue on the basis of the German draft in Moscow as soon as both Brockdorff-Rantzau and the Soviet Foreign Com-missar arrived there in January. Stresemann added, however, that, regardless of how quickly a final agreement was reached, Germany would not sign a new treaty with Russia until the question of her membership in the League was decided at Geneva.[1]

The prolonged 'Christmas crisis' in Germany's domestic politics ended on 19 January 1926 when Luther managed to form a second cabinet. The SPD, the party with the most seats in the Reichstag, was again not represented in the coalition government, which was disbalanced to the conservative and nationalist side. On 28 February Germany submitted her second application for admission to the League. But already, four days earlier, on 24 February, Luther's Government, which was now under constant intense pressure not only from the Soviet Government but also from a majority of the Reichstag and many powerful constituents—especially business-men—had authorized Stresemann to conclude a formal treaty of neutrality with Russia. Stresemann apparently concurred in this decision, which reversed his previous official stand against a

[1] Gatzke, 'Stresemann und die deutsche Russlandpolitik,' p. 21. The shortened account of these negotiations in the *Vermächtnis* (vol. 2, pp. 535 f.) apparently misled Kochan to conclude that 'by the end of December 1925 all was in order'—the treaty was ready to be signed (*Russia and Weimar*, p. 115).

neutrality treaty.[1] He did not, however, abandon the principle of not signing with the Russians until Germany had been admitted to the League.

At the end of February Stresemann sent Brockdorff-Rantzau four short draft paragraphs of a treaty with an appended protocol which the Ambassador was to present to Chicherin with the verbal stipulation that Germany would not sign the treaty until after the League admitted her to membership in March. The German draft was, in essence, the same one Stresemann had read to Chicherin in December 1925.[2] According to Article 1 the Treaty of Rapallo remained the basis of Russo-German relations and both governments undertook 'to promote an understanding with regard to all political and economic questions jointly affecting their countries.' Article 2 called for neutrality in the event of unprovoked aggression against either country by a third power, and Article 3 pledged both countries not to take part in any economic or financial boycott of the other. Article 4 prescribed that the treaty would remain in force for five years and governed its ratification. The appended protocol, which in the published version took the form of an exchange of notes between Stresemann and Krestinski, stated that both governments considered the treaty to be an essential contribution to world peace and that both governments had discussed Germany's plan to join the League and were convinced that this step would not disrupt relations between them. Furthermore, it was agreed that if the League developed anti-Soviet tendencies 'Germany would most energetically oppose such efforts.' Since the League would only invoke sanctions against Russia in the event she was adjudged the aggressor against a third power, and since Germany, as a member of the League Council, would be able to decide for herself whether or not Russia was, in any given instance, the aggressor, Germany, the protocol declared, could never be obligated to take part in any measures against Russia instituted under the authority of Article 16. The protocol did not go any further than this; there were no secret agreements.

Chicherin agreed to the entire treaty and protocol except for one word. He objected to the clause in Article 2 which provided for neutrality in the event of 'unprovoked' aggression against one of the partners by a third power. Chicherin resented the implication

[1] *Stresemann Nachlass*, 7326H/H161386; Hilger, *op. cit.*, p. 146.
[2] Hilger, *op. cit.*, pp. 146 f., and see above, p. 270.

that Russia might provoke a third power to attack her. Moreover, he wanted to 'widen the conception of neutrality to include any attack.'[1] Indeed, a version of the protocol had been drafted by a junior official of the German Foreign Ministry which provided for mutual neutrality in the event of any conflict involving either power, even if one of them were guilty of wanton aggression against a third power. However, this version was not approved by Stresemann and was not sent on to Moscow for consideration.[2] Gaus, the legal expert of the ministry, left no doubt that such a broad conception of neutrality was incompatible with Germany's obligations to the League Covenant as envisaged by the reinterpretation of Article 16 at Locarno. Stresemann was determined to uphold the Locarno Pacts.[3] After lengthy negotiations in Moscow, which were interrupted in March by the arrest of several German civilians and by other minor incidents against which Brockdorff-Rantzau protested to the Soviet Government, it was finally decided to replace the objectionable word in Article 2 with the phrase 'in spite of a peaceful attitude.'[4]

The treaty and protocol were ready to be signed in mid-April. By that time, contrary to world-wide expectations, a deadlock had developed at Geneva over the issue of Germany's entry into the League Council. The entire question of German membership in the League was consequently postponed until the Council's next session in September.[5] This episode greatly embarrassed Stresemann and weakened his position in Berlin. He still wanted to delay signing the treaty until Germany joined the League. But Chicherin now insisted that the treaty should be concluded at once. Stresemann was forced to yield. The renewed intense criticism of the government by the Right wing, which was fed by the rebuff suffered at Geneva, made it incumbent on Stresemann to gain some public and concrete reassurance of Russia's friendship. He had to prove

[1] *Ibid.*, p. 150; L. Fischer, *Soviets in World Affairs*, vol. 2, p. 608.
[2] *Stresemann Nachlass*, 7415H/H175553/61. Cf. Gatzke, 'Stresemann und die deutsche Russlandpolitik,' pp. 23 f., 29. Gatzke suggests that the version of the protocol providing for total neutrality was sent on to Moscow as a basis of negotiations.
[3] *Stresemann Nachlass*, 7129H/H148128; Hilger, *loc. cit.*
[4] Hilger, *op. cit.*, pp. 148-150. The Treaty of Berlin may be found in 'The Development of Soviet Foreign Policy in Europe 1917-1942,' *International Conciliation* (New York, January 1943), pp. 61 f.
[5] Gathorne-Hardy, *Short History of International Affairs*, pp. 200-202.

that Germany was no longer obliged to choose between Britain and Russia, between East and West; he wanted to show that his policies had succeeded in giving Germany a new freedom of action and an assurance of eventual ascendancy.[1]

The problem now was how to break the news of a treaty with Moscow to Germany's Locarno partners in such a way that it would not arouse alarm. Stresemann solved this problem by giving London and Paris 'confidential information' about the treaty, in the hope that the Quai d'Orsay would, as it had on so many previous occasions, leak the story to the press.[2] In actual fact, however, it was the London *Times* which broke the news on 14 April. The treaty was then signed on 24 April, not, as Brockdorff-Rantzau wished, by himself and Chicherin in Moscow, but by Stresemann and Krestinski in Berlin. What Brockdorff-Rantzau wanted to be called the 'Rantzau Treaty' came to be known as the Treaty of Berlin.[3]

The first reaction to the news of the treaty in London was stoic compared to the minor tempest it raised in Paris, where it was interpreted as a victory for Soviet diplomacy. But when the treaty was published *in extenso* on 27 April, even the French quickly reconciled themselves to it. For all intents and purposes, the agreement seemed to have contributed nothing new except a more precise re-definition of the presuppositions of Rapallo. Briand informed Stresemann that the treaty would 'not deter him from his line up to now' with regard to Germany's entry into the League.[4]

In some Western circles, especially in the press, it was suspected that a secret military protocol had been appended to the treaty. In a prepared statement to the press Stresemann calmly denied these allegations:

There is talk . . . of the possibility that there are secret agreements between Germany and the Soviet Union. That has been denied often

[1] The record of the negotiations leading to the Treaty of Berlin disproves Lord D'Abernon's rationalization (repeated by Kochan, *Russia and Weimar*, pp. 115 f.) that the treaty was concluded because of Germany's rejection at Geneva (*Ambassador of Peace*, vol. 3, p. 245). But there can be no doubt that the *débâcle* at Geneva in March hastened the final agreement. Cf. Hilger, *op. cit.*, p. 148; cf. Gatzke, 'Stresemann und die deutsche Russlandpolitik,' p. 24.
[2] Dirksen, *Moskau-Tokio-London*, p. 78.        [3] Hilger, *op. cit.*, p. 150.
[4] *Stresemann Nachlass*, 7415H/H175547/50. Seeckt negotiated with Russian military leaders and others, including Ambassador Krestinski, less than a month before the Treaty of Berlin was signed: Rabenau, *Seeckt*, vol. 2, p. 430.

enough already, but one will probably have to deny it again to satiety. If one repeats such insinuations today, then I can no longer believe them to be well-intentioned.

Germany, Stresemann continued, has to conduct foreign policies towards both the East and the West; but this does not mean, he concluded, that her 'two-sided policy' is a 'double-dealing policy.'[1] Few people doubted the sincerity of Stresemann's pronouncement. Those who did were not listened to, for the warm summer days of Locarno had ushered in a new era—an Era of Good Feelings.

[1] *Stresemann Nachlass*, 7415H/H175562.

# CHAPTER XI

# CONCLUSION

SPEAKING about his Locarno policies to a private audience in January 1927, Stresemann said: 'I never thought more about the East than during the time I was looking for an understanding in the West.'[1] Indeed, there was no choice between East and West for Stresemann, as there cannot be for any German foreign minister who tries to serve the interests of his country. It is unrealistic to speak of a 'Western orientation' or an 'Eastern orientation' in German policy during the Weimar period. There was only one German Foreign Policy with both Western and Eastern aspects.

From the Bolshevik seizure of power until the Armistice of November 1918 the determining factor in Russo-German relations was the demands of the military situation. To inflict a decisive defeat on the Allies in the West, Ludendorff needed Russian resources and had to prevent a resumption of the fighting in the East. The Bolsheviks, during the same period, had as their main objectives to halt the advance of foreign troops on Russian soil and to establish their own authority in the country. Lenin signed the Brest-Litovsk terms in order to save the revolution in Russia; he was convinced that the continuation of the war in the West would hasten the spread of the revolution over the rest of Europe. When the Allies intervened in Russia in order to overthrow the Bolsheviks and to reactivate the Eastern Front against Germany, the one-sided peace of Brest-Litovsk was transformed into a virtual Russo-German alliance against the West. But this proved to be an abortive alliance, cut short by the sudden collapse of the German armies in France.

After the Armistice of November 1918 the Allies tried to create a *cordon sanitaire* between Germany and Russia, but they only succeeded in driving the two countries closer together and arousing their hatred of Poland and the other countries established in the East to keep them apart. As long as the Germans had hopes of

---

[1] *Stresemann Nachlass*, 3167H/H163659 ff., quoted by H. W. Gatzke, 'The Stresemann Papers,' *The Journal of Modern History*, vol. XXVI, No. 1 (Chicago, March 1954), p. 58.

modifying the peace terms they resisted Soviet overtures for an alliance against the Versailles powers, but when the Allies remained obdurate Germany verged towards the East. The sensational element of the Treaty of Rapallo was the timing of the agreement; it came as a shock to the entire diplomatic world. The real significance of the treaty is not to be found in any of its provisions, but rather in the very fact that Russia and Germany, the two outcasts from Western society, dared to defy the Allied powers by signing it. Rapallo was, therefore, not, as Chicherin later called it, 'chiefly an economic treaty.'[1] It was, above all, a political declaration in which Germany and Russia pitted themselves against the system of alliances that had grown up in Europe since the war and, by implication, affirmed their mutual hostility to Poland.

Russian trade was indeed important for Germany throughout the Weimar period. In the Treaty of Brest-Litovsk the Germans tried to insure a steady flow of Russian resources to replenish their stockpiles of grains and fuels which were being rapidly depleted because of the deadly effectiveness of the Allied blockade. After Versailles German industry had to regain its Russian markets in order to help stabilize Germany's economy and to pay her war debts. For the Bolsheviks, too, German capital, trade, and, above all, technology were vital to the tasks of reconstructing war-torn industries and building a highly industrialized society. Both the Provisional Agreement of May 1921 and the Rapallo treaty provided for the resumption of commercial relations, but it was not until after the agreement of October 1925 was signed that trade between Germany and Russia started to expand on the larger scale that had been envisaged for it on both sides in preceding years.[2]

Seeckt had already started the negotiations with the Soviet Government when the Rapallo treaty was signed. The treaty did not touch on military matters, but there is no doubt that when it was concluded the Reichswehr was encouraged to reach agreements of its own with the Russians in order to speed its rearmament. The significance of the Reichswehr-Red Army collaboration has been consistently misjudged and its importance has just as frequently been underrated. Because the entire operation was carried on in secrecy not much has been revealed about it, even to this day. This lack of information has, in turn, contributed to the

---

[1] *Stresemann Nachlass*, 7129H/H147979/91.
[2] Hilger, *Incompatible Allies*, pp. 183 ff.

air of mystery that surrounds the entire affair. On the face of it the collaboration seems to have been simply a convenient arrangement allowing the Germans to manufacture weapons and to train men while giving the Russians the benefit of Germany's technological advances. The Germans were determined to subvert the narrow armaments restrictions imposed on them at Versailles and Spa. The Russians allowed them to use facilities for this purpose in order to benefit in the development of their own military establishment. It is not unusual for current writers, especially German historians, to limit the discussions of the military collaboration to just these elementary facts about it, completely obscuring those aspects which give it a far greater significance.[1] Gustav Hilger, for example, although he is justified in ridiculing some authors for their 'tone of righteous indignation over the sinister dealings between Prussian generals and Red dictators,' completely fails to elucidate those aspects of the collaboration which are really noteworthy.[2] Among these are the fact that, on both sides, not only military figures, but the highest placed political leaders were involved and, in some cases, in the forefront of the clandestine rearmament; and the fact that the collaboration not only had political ramifications, but was interwoven with political and economic relations between Soviet Russia and Weimar Germany almost from the start. It should not be forgotten, moreover, that in the minds of some of the German leaders, notably in Seeckt's, the Russo-German rearmament was to lead both countries into a war of revenge against Poland and the West.

Stresemann's motives in co-operating in these illegal machinations are still a matter of conjecture.[3] It would be unreasonable, on any account, to accuse him of preparing the way for Hitler. But regardless of the policies Stresemann would have followed had he lived long enough to effect a revision of the Eastern boundaries— either by armed force or by diplomacy—it is essential to any realistic appraisal of this man and his policies to be aware of the extent to which he co-operated with Seeckt and the Russians in the interests of German rearmament. One cannot simply ignore the fact that Germany's rearmament during the Weimar period

[1] For example, cf. K. D. Bracher, *Die Auflösung der Weimarer Republik* (Stuttgart and Düsseldorf, 1955), pp. 272, 274-275 and n. 165.

[2] Hilger, *op. cit.*, p. 189, n. 1, and chap. VII *passim*.

[3] Gatzke, 'Stresemann und die deutsche Russlandpolitik,' pp. 27 ff.

prepared the army and the Luftwaffe for rapid mobilization and, finally, for war under Hitler. Was Stresemann a patriot or a statesman? How much, after all, is foresight a part of statesmanship?

One theory of Russo-German relations during the Weimar period which has been widely accepted, although it remains unproven, holds that Russia had a defensive aim in the Rapallo partnership while Germany considered her alliances with Russia to be of primarily offensive significance.[1] Like most speculation about history and international relations, this theory is based on an arbitrary selection of facts and the convenient dismissal of those facts which do not support it. The Rapallo treaty was indeed defensive from Moscow's standpoint in so far as it gave the Bolsheviks a foothold in Europe and enabled them to escape from the isolation to which Western ostracism had condemned them. In 1925 the Treaty of Berlin reassured the Bolsheviks that in times of strategic retreat, when their revolutionary and aggressive policies were perforce subordinated to the other arm of Soviet policy, the strengthening of the Russian State by conventional means, Germany would stand between them and the hostile West. However, the Bolsheviks used Germany not merely as a shield or buffer —'a vast belt of neutralized territory,' as one recent writer put it— between themselves and the capitalist states, but also as a horse to lead their revolutionary cart.[2] Russia exploited Germany's battle against Versailles. The Rapallo partnership intensified the disunity and created discord in the ranks of the capitalist powers, and for the Bolsheviks dissension of any kind was a fertile ground for the advancement of their revolutionary ambitions. The German Communist movement, moreover, was at all times the key to Moscow's plans for the 'ultimate victory' of the world revolution. The KPD was both the largest and best organized Communist party outside Russia; the Soviet leaders were confident that the crisis conditions in Germany after 1918 would give the German Communists an opportunity to seize power. For Russia, therefore, Germany served as a buffer, but also as a *Vorspanne*—an involuntary pacemaker; Germany was a foothold in the outside world, but it was also the pivot of the Communist revolution.

For Germany, on the other hand, the alliance with Russia was

[1] This theory was most recently put forward by Lionel Kochan in *Russia and the Weimar Republic*, pp. vi ff.

[2] *Ibid.*, p. vii.

not merely a weapon with which to cajole, threaten, and bribe the Western powers into modifying the peace terms and withdrawing their occupation forces from the Rhineland, but also, as we have seen, an integral part of the policy of balancing East and West in order to strengthen her own middle position in Europe and in European politics. Those Germans, like Seeckt, who advocated maintaining an exclusive alliance with Russia, wanted to lead the country into a war of revenge against Poland and the West. For them, and for the Soviet Government, which also wanted to keep Germany divided from Britain and France, the heyday of Rapallo only lasted from 1922 until the winter of 1924.[1] Throughout this period the essential *Schicksalsgemeinschaft* bound the two outcasts together in an exclusive alliance, although relations between them were severely strained at times by various incidents, notably the abortive KPD uprising in 1923 and the raid on the Berlin trade delegation headquarters in May 1924. But then, when Stresemann's overtures for a reconciliation with the West were favourably received in Paris and London, the Rapallo treaty immediately lost its greatest attraction. It was reduced from an exclusive alliance to simply one agreement in a network of many. The Locarno Conference and Germany's entry into the League of Nations vitiated the value of Germany's connexion with Russia from the point of view of the Soviet Government and the 'Easterners' in Germany. Stresemann regained Germany's independence and freedom of action; thereafter she was no longer dependent upon Russia for support. For Stresemann the Treaty of Berlin was no more than a public reaffirmation of his policy of steering a middle course between East and West in order to reassert Germany's power in Europe.

Weimar Germany had to have relations with Soviet Russia. They were neighbours but for the Poles, whom the Western powers were committed to protect, but whose territory was coveted by both Russians and Germans, not excluding Stresemann. The intensity of Russo-German relations during the Weimar period depended, on the one hand, on the extent to which Britain, France, and America made it possible for Germany to serve her own best interests by maintaining a balance between East and

[1] Cf. *ibid.*, chap. VII *passim*; cf. Carr, *German-Soviet Relations Between the Two World Wars*, p. 91; cf. Gatzke, 'Stresemann und die deutsche Russlandpolitik,' pp. 24 f.

West, and, on the other hand, on the tactics employed by the Soviets in realizing their own ambitions. When the Russians sought to strengthen their position in Europe by conventional political and economic means they found willing partners in Germany; but when they followed aggressive revolutionary tactics relations between Moscow and Berlin suffered.

The inherent dynamic of relations between Germany and Russia, which prevents the judicious historian from introducing any facile themes or theories into his account of these relations, was that each power served, at least potentially, several equally important functions for the other. This dynamic—the complexity, diversity, and flexibility of Russian and German policies—has subjected relations between them to sudden, and sometimes sweeping, reversals. Yet it is on this relationship that the balance of power and, hence, the peace of Europe depends.

# APPENDIX A

TELEGRAM FROM FOREIGN MINISTER VON HINTZE TO LEGATION COUNCILLOR
LERSNER AT HIGH COMMAND HEADQUARTERS,
DATED BERLIN, 6 AUGUST 1918.[1]

Tel. Hughes—IMMEDIATELY—

General Ludendorff has wired to me:

'To 1843

For the personal orientation of Your Excellency: concerning the
forces that are available to us at the present time for use against Russia,
I am able to inform you that we can advance towards Petrograd at any
time with six or seven divisions. Regarding those forces which the
Eastern Command can bring to bear on the Rostov-Voronezh railroad
line, I shall not commit myself at this time. There, too, it will be a
matter of several divisions which can be deployed against Russia, in the
event Krasnov guards our flank on the Volga. This represents a force
with which we can, as far as I can see, support a new government in
Russia, one that has the people behind it.

Nr. 34712 p. 1.'

Please transmit the following reply:

'Until yesterday Your Excellency had mentioned four divisions as
being available against Russia, but now Your Excellency has hopes of a
larger number of troops for this purpose. I welcome this as a new state
of affairs and as a great boon to our policy. Your Excellency says that,
with the troops that are now available, we could support a government
in Russia *that has the people behind it*. This is a highly restricting stipulation; for a government that has the people behind it does not need our
support, at least not in its internal affairs. There is still the possibility of
using the newly available troops against the Entente in the North and
against the Czecho-Slovaks in the East and South, regardless which
regime is at the helm or accedes to power. The Bolshevik Government
has asked for such intervention against our enemies; any other government—we have to be perfectly clear about this—is either immediately
or within a short time a friend and ally of the Entente. We do not have
any friends worth mentioning in Russia; whoever informs Your
Excellency to the contrary is deceiving himself. The proof whether
or not a new government has the people behind it will come to light
when it asserts its power with the help of the people. The Bolsheviks

[1] *Verhältnis Deutschlands zu Russland,* St. A. Nr. 85

have certainly been weakened, but so far we do *not* hear of mutinies in the Red Guard or of revolts in the Russian villages, which are full of armed ex-soldiers. If the new government does not have the people behind it, then, as Your Excellency admits, the available divisions will not suffice to support it. Therefore, I am still in favour of waiting for the beginning of the Bolsheviks' downfall and of holding ourselves in readiness so that in the event of a change we can quickly come to terms with the victor. Now as before, the material and intellectual preparations should be made for this purpose. . . . In the meantime we have no reason to wish or to provoke a rapid end to the Bolsheviks' regime. The Bolsheviks are an evil and most antipathetic people; but that did not prevent us from forcing the peace of Brest-Litovsk on them and, bit by bit, taking even more of their territory and possessions from them. We have milked them for all they are worth; our quest of victory requires us to continue doing so as long as they remain in power. Whether or not we like the idea of working with them is unimportant as long as it is useful to do so. History shows that to introduce feelings into politics is a costly luxury. To allow ourselves to indulge in such luxury in our position would be irresponsible. Anyone who works with the Bolsheviks as the de facto rulers and yet complains about what bad company they are is harmless; but if one would lose the advantages of working with the Bolsheviks because one is disinclined to bear the odium of having any-thing to do with the Bolsheviks, then one is stepping on dangerous ground. To this day and for a long time to come, politics are utilitarian; in the conversations with Your Excellency I was able to ascertain that Your Excellency is fully convinced of this elementary thesis. There are certain signs that the Bolsheviks are nearing the end of their rope; their downfall could take place tomorrow or could be postponed for months. Instability is a characteristic of Russia. Chicherin's cry for help and the attempted expulsion of the English and French consuls are more reliable signs of the approaching collapse than rumours are. On the other hand, our revolutionary and so far undetected confidant reports that the Social-Revolutionaries have split and have for the most part renounced terrorism and inclined towards the Bolsheviks. Only the rather small group of Kamkov and Spiridonova is said to be still holding out. The bourgeoisie are divided into a number of heterogeneous groups whose unification for a common purpose could only be brought about by a Russian and a genius. *This* genius has not yet come forward. All these groups, with the exception of some individuals, have one thing in common: hatred of Germany. The Siberians, who were recommended to us as allies, have, according to newspaper reports, declared *war* on us. What, after all, do we want in the East?

The military paralysis of Russia. The Bolsheviks are doing a better and more thorough job of this than any other Russian party, and without our devoting a single man or one mark to the task. We cannot expect them or other Russians to love us for milking their country dry. Let us rather be content with Russia's impotence.

The Bolsheviks are the only Russian party who have taken sides against the Entente. That is daily becoming more evident, and it is our duty to intensify this conflict, as we have been doing of late. The Bolsheviks are the only ones in Russia who stand for the Brest peace. According to Excellenz Helfferich co-operation with other parties is *only possible under the condition* of a modification of the Brest peace; above all, the Ukraine would have to be given back to Russia. Here we have heard of much more far-reaching demands: namely the restoration of Russia's borders quo ante bellum. Are we to sacrifice the fruits of four years of battle and triumph in order to absolve ourselves of the odium of having used the Bolsheviks? Because that is what we are doing: we are not working with them, we are exploiting them. That is both politic and politics.

I should welcome Your Excellency's answer to the following question:

Is the High Command prepared and does it consider it useful and practicable to carry out a revision of the Brest treaty at this time which involves giving up the Baltic Provinces, Lithuania and the Ukraine? Not to mention the Crimea, Taurius, the Donets-Basin, which will most certainly be demanded back immediately.

The Brest treaty bears the signature of our Most Gracious Sovereign, it was concluded by us together with our Allies, it divides Austria from Russia through the establishment of the Ukraine; it has been submitted to the Reichstag.

Permit me to summarize:

It is good policy to exploit the Bolsheviks as long as they have something to give. If they fall, we can observe the chaos which may result with calm detachment, until we think the country is weak enough for us to restore order without great loss to ourselves. If no chaos develops, but a new party takes over right away, then we have to move in under the heading: no war with Russia nor with the Russian people, no conquests, rather order and protection for the weak against their being ill-used by our enemies. The lattermost alternative forces us to act without foreseeable advantages, therefore I prefer the other two.'

Please also submit General Ludendorff's telegram and my reply to both the R.K. and to His Majesty.

(Signed) HINTZE.

# APPENDIX B

I. A LETTER FROM FOREIGN MINISTER STRESEMANN TO REICHSWEHR-
MINISTER GESSLER, DATED 18 JUNE 1924, REGARDING NOTES OF
A DISCUSSION BETWEEN AMBASSADOR BROCKDORFF-RANTZAU AND
PEOPLES' COMMISSAR TROTSKY IN MOSCOW ON 9 JUNE 1924.[1]

Berlin, 18 June 1924.

Most worthy colleague!

I have received from our Ambassador in Moscow, Count Brockdorff-
Rantzau, a record of a conversation with Peoples' Commissar Trotsky
held on 9 June. I am taking the liberty of transmitting to you a copy of
those sections of the discussion which deal with military questions with
the request that they be treated as secret, and have also enclosed another
copy which is intended for General von Seeckt.

With highest esteem,

I am yours very respectfully,

(signed) STRESEMANN.

To the Reichswehrminister, Dr Gessler,
here.

2. NOTES OF A DISCUSSION BETWEEN THE AMBASSADOR IN MOSCOW,
COUNT BROCKDORFF-RANTZAU, AND PEOPLES' COMMISSAR TROTSKY ON
9 JUNE 1924.[2]

*Strictly Secret!*

*Notes:*

I had an hour-long discussion with Trotsky yesterday. He received me
at 9.30 p.m., not at the Kremlin, but rather in the offices of the Commissariat of War. I started the discussion by saying that I was glad to see him
recovered—he really looked very well—and added that it was a source
of satisfaction for me to know that he is back in Moscow. At the time
of our last conversation he had given me permission to approach him
directly in the event serious incidents occurred. For formality's sake I
remarked that I assumed Mr Chicherin was informed that I had come to
talk to him [Trotsky]; I did not have the opportunity to discuss this at
the Foreign Commissariat. Trotsky replied that, of course, Chicherin

---

[1] *Stresemann Nachlass,* 7414H/H175333.
[2] *Stresemann Nachlass,* 7414H/H175334/40.

was informed; he himself [Trotsky] had asked him [Chicherin] to tell me that he [Trotsky] regretted not being able to receive me two days ago when I asked to see him; he had been in the country (it is noteworthy that Chicherin did not tell me a word of this).

When I had taken a seat I explained that the situation was so serious that I had to speak to Trotsky personally; I saw German-Russian friendship seriously endangered and had to know if the relations with his department were also threatened. The lamentable incident has led to such untoward consequences that I, unhappily, had to assume as much. Of course, such a development would also have a decisive bearing on my own attitude.

Trotsky interrupted me very animatedly saying: 'No, this is out of the question. This mess has to be cleaned up and does not have the remotest chance of influencing—in any way—the important military relations which have been fostered to our as well as your gratification. Rosengolts asked me on the first day that the incident became known what his attitude should be. I told him, that a change in our attitude was not even to be contemplated. The dispute has absolutely no bearing on this matter.' I responded that this explanation was very consoling; nevertheless I wanted to tell the Peoples' Commissar about a number of striking symptoms.

In the first place, the reception given Major Fischer and Captain Vogt by Mr Rosenholz about four weeks ago was noticeably cool; moreover, on the 8th of this month permission for the participation of a Junkers Company plane in the parade was suddenly withdrawn, although the plane had already arrived at the starting line. In addition, I heard today just by chance that all the ambassadors except me took part in the parade. Frankly, I will not allow myself, as German Ambassador, to be treated like a naughty child whose sweet is taken away because one does not see eye-to-eye here with the policies of my Government. Trotsky laughed, but said very seriously he would make immediate enquiries and understood completely that I could not treat these 'symptoms' as matters of secondary importance. With regard to the refusal of permission for the participation of the German aeroplane, this was done by the G.P.U. as a safety precaution: the aerodrome was overcrowded and therefore the number of planes that could participate had to be restricted. As a matter of fact, a woman was actually killed out there.

I then asked the Peoples' Commissar in detail about the position of the Commissariat of War regarding the Junkers Company, saying that they had not received any Russian orders, that they are prepared to manufacture motors, but that they would have to contend with serious financial difficulties if they did not get contracts in Russia, although, as he knows, they had recently received a considerable subsidy from the German side. Trotsky declared, and it was undoubtedly not an excuse, that he is not informed about the details, but would make enquiries right away.

I went on to say that as far as my Government is concerned the dispatch of Messrs. Fischer, Vogt, Arnold, and Thomsen is proof that we do not want to change our policy towards Russia. Trotsky remarked, he fully understands that the German police does not approve of a lot that is going on, but he never believed that we had the intention of reorientating our policy. I explained that this very apt interpretation is unfortunately not being given [to the incident] in all quarters here. In regard to the dispatch of Messrs Fischer, Vogt, and others, I wanted it to be known that the famous Colonel Thomsen had now arrived, and that I will not, under any circumstances, allow him to be badly treated here. I have therefore advised him not to get in touch with Mr Rosenholz before our discussion today. Trotsky asked me excitedly when Colonel Thomsen arrived in Moscow and declared, after I replied, already a week ago, that he will certainly contact Rosenholz immediately and personally arrange a meeting between them. I remarked, Colonel Thomsen also intends to negotiate with Rosenholz about the hiring of 10 German officer pilots. Although these men are our best pilots, all sorts of unexpected objections were raised against 6 or 7 of them which has prevented their employment here.

It was also a shock that, as I heard from a reliable source, at the arms factories in Tula, which operate under German management, a foreign, either an English or an American, commission was received about two weeks ago. Trotsky said he will enquire about this immediately; the report was undoubtedly false.

I then asked abruptly if one were still negotiating with Colonel Bauer here. Trotsky replied that there is the intention of resuming the negotiations regarding the chemical factories in the near future; there was, after all, also German capital behind Bauer. I retorted that this seemed to be the case; nevertheless I wanted to inform the Peoples' Commissar that in Berlin there was not any intention of working together with Bauer. General von Seeckt has given me a categorical assurance to this effect. It is known that Bauer is in touch with General Ludendorff; co-operation between him and the Reichswehrministerium is out of the question. Trotsky said that this information was invaluable; he naturally did not want to jeopardize the working relationship with the Reichswehrministerium under any circumstances.

When this question was dealt with, I directed the conversation to the international situation and said, Mr Trotsky is the only statesman here who has been moderate about the incident in Berlin. Krasin's speech had made my work here much more difficult for me. Moreover, I could not justify in any way the position adopted by Ambassador Krestinski. His outrageous communiqué had muddled the whole situation right from the start. Trotsky said he did not want to talk about diplomatic negotiations because he does not understand anything about them. I retorted that the issue is not one of 'diplomacy,' but rather Mr Krestinski's conception of his job as Ambassador, with which I do not agree. With regard to Krasin, Trotsky declared—after I said that Mr Krasin began his speech by saying that Mr Zinoviev had not exhausted the subject of the incident in his speech—that Krasin is a notorious Germanophile and had to begin with this introduction in view of the excited state of all public opinion, in order to give special emphasis to the paragraphs calculated to mitigate the conflict. I took the remark regarding Krasin's friendship for Germany sceptically and remarked that one knows, after all, how public opinion is created.

In the further course of the discussion I reminded Trotsky of his statement to me in December last year with regard to relations with France. At that time he had said that France was the common enemy of Russia and Germany. I suggested that this conception may have changed since Poincaré's fall from power. Trotsky replied with great emphasis that this was not the case at all; neither relations with France nor those with Britain could disrupt the German-Russian friendship. He was firmly convinced that this friendship would continue for years—he corrected himself—for decades to come. The present cabinet in France has the unique assignment of burying first Millerand and then itself. If Herriot accedes to the helm he will probably orientate himself somewhat to the Left; but the change of governments in France will not have a decisive influence on relations with Russia. If de facto recognition were to follow, the French would immediately 'present their big bill,' just as the English are doing now, and this big bill is the obstacle to a real improvement in relations. At this juncture Trotsky said he is very sceptical about the negotiations in London. It is noteworthy, however, that he remarked that he does not think it impossible that America will take a commercial interest in Russia; but he added in this connexion, and then repeated himself, that this is his personal opinion.

When I took my leave after about an hour I thanked Trotsky for his trust and candour and asked him to use his great authority to see to it that this incident is finally completely settled. I asked him directly if he thought that, in spite of this lamentable conflict, the old friendly relations between Germany and Russia might be restored. He answered affirmatively without any hesitation; whereupon I said my job here should be made easier for me and one should not forget that I want to work with the Soviet Government. The Russian note of 31 May is a virtual ultimatum; the repressive measures that have been taken here have done incalculable harm. Because of the new economic policy that was adopted here about six months ago it will, in any case, be very difficult for me to interest German financial and commercial circles to

I

do any further work in Russia; I therefore wanted to suggest to Mr Trotsky, as I have already advised Mr Chicherin in a conversation, that if the incident is settled with a protocol, as seems likely, the protocol should state that the German and Russian Governments have decided, in the spirit of the Rapallo treaty, to forget the misunderstandings of the last years and to work together in friendship in the future. We know what we mean to one another, I added, but we should on no account give our adversaries the pleasure of seeing an open break between us.

Trotsky indicated that he understood completely and promised me his support.

(Signed) BROCKDORFF-RANTZAU.

Moscow, 10 June 1924

# APPENDIX C

### Organization of German Military Training Establishments in Russia[1]

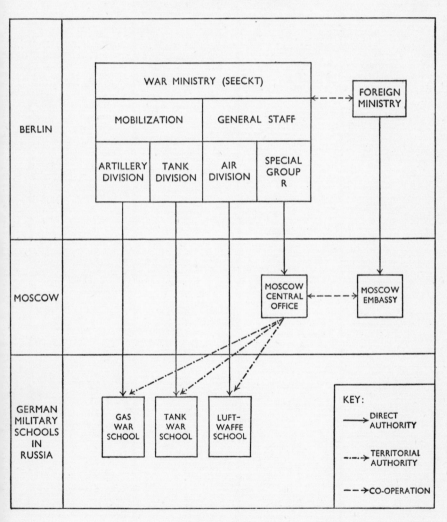

[1] After Speidel, 'Reichswehr und Rote Armee,' p. 43.

I *

# BIBLIOGRAPHY

## UNPUBLISHED DOCUMENTS

*Akten betreffend: Karl Radek* (St Antony's College, Oxford).

*Akten der Kaiserlich Deutschen Gesandtschaft in Kopenhagen betreffend Helphand 1915-1916* (Public Record Office, London).

*Allgemeine Angelegenheiten der Ukraine* (St Antony's College, Oxford).

*Das Verhältnis Deutschlands zu Russland* (St Antony's College, Oxford).

*Die Waffenstillstands- und Friedensverhandlungen von Brest Litowsk* (Archives of the United States of America, Washington).

*Friedensverhandlungen mit Russland in Brest Litowsk* (Public Record Office, London).

*Heeresarchiv:* Wilhelm Groener (Archives of the United States of America, Washington).

*Heeresarchiv:* Hans Friederich Leopold von Seeckt (Archives of the United States of America, Washington).

*Nachlass des Reichsministers Dr Gustav Stresemann* (Public Record Office, London).

*Waffenstillstands Verhandlungen mit Russland* (St Antony's College, Oxford).

## PUBLISHED DOCUMENTS

### 1. KPD:

*Bericht über den Gründungsparteitag der Kommunistischen Partei Deutschlands (Spartakusbund)* (Berlin, n.d.).

*Bericht über den 2. Parteitag der Kommunistischen Partei Deutschlands (Spartakusbund)* (Berlin, 1919).

*Bericht über den 3. Parteitag der Kommunistischen Partei Deutschlands (Spartakusbund)* (Berlin, 1923).

*Bericht über die Verhandlungen des IX. Parteitags der Kommunistischen Partei Deutschlands* (Berlin, 1924).

*Die Lehren der deutschen Ereignisse* (Hamburg, 1924).

*Zur Geschichte der Kommunistischen Partei Deutschlands* ([East] Berlin, 1955).

### 2. COMINTERN:

*Aufrufe des Exekutivkomitees der Kommunistischen Internationale zur polnischen Frage* (Berlin, 1920).

*Der I. Kongress der Kommunistischen Internationale* (Hamburg, 1921).

*Der II. Kongress der Kommunistischen Internationale* (Hamburg, 1921).

*Protokoll des III. Kongresses der Kommunistischen Internationale* (Hamburg, 1921).

*Fourth World Congress of the Communist International: Selected Reports, Speeches and Resolutions* (Moscow and Petrograd, 1923).

*Resolutions and Theses of the Fourth Congress of the Communist International* (Moscow, n.d.).

*Fifth Congress of the Communist International* (abridged) (Moscow, n.d.).

3. OTHER:

*Documents on British Foreign Policy*, ed. E. L. Woodward and R. D. Butler, First Series, Vol. 2 (London, 1948); First Series, Vol. 3 (London, 1949).

*Dokumente der deutschen Politik und Geschichte von 1848 bis zur Gegenwart*, ed. J. Hohlfeld, Vol. 3 (Berlin, 1952).

*Foreign Relations of the United States: The Paris Peace Conference 1919*, Vol. 3 (Washington, 1943).

Hale, R., *Report of the Mission to Finland, Latvia, Lithuania and Esthonia on the Situation in the Baltic Provinces* (Washington, 1919).

Laserson, M. M., 'The Development of Soviet Foreign Policy in Europe 1917-1942,' *International Conciliation*, No. 386 (New York, January 1943).

*Parliamentary Debates: Official Report, House of Commons*, Vol. 118, 5th Session (London, 1919).

*Proceedings of the Brest-Litovsk Conference* (Washington, 1918).

*Reichs-Gesetzblatt*, Nr. 130 (Berlin, 1920); Nr. 75 (Berlin, 1921).

*Report of Court Proceedings in the Case of the Anti-Soviet Trotskyite Centre* (Moscow, 1937).

*Report of Court Proceedings in the Case of the Anti-Soviet 'Bloc of Rights and Trotskyites'* (Moscow, 1938).

*Resolutions Adopted by the Supreme Council at Cannes, January 1922, as the Basis of the Genoa Conference* (London, 1922).

*Soviet Documents on Foreign Policy*, ed. J. Degras, Vols. 1 and 2 (Oxford, 1951-1952).

*Texts of the Russian 'Peace'* (Washington, 1918).

*Trials of War Criminals: The Krupp Case*, Vol. 9 (Washington, 1950).

*Verhandlungen des Reichstags*, Bänder 330, 332, 341, 344-346, 349, 352, 388, 391 (Berlin, 1920-1926).

## AUTOBIOGRAPHIES, BIOGRAPHIES, DIARIES, AND MEMOIRS

Apfel, A., *Behind the Scenes of German Justice* (London, 1935).

Awaloff, General Fürst, *Im Kampf gegen den Bolschewismus* (Glückstadt/ Hamburg, 1925).

Berndorff, H. R., *General zwischen Ost und West* (Hamburg, 1951).

Bessedovsky, G., *Revelations of a Soviet Diplomat* (London, 1931).

Blücher, W. von, *Deutschlands Weg nach Rapallo* (Wiesbaden, 1951).

Bothmer, K. von, *Mit Graf Mirbach in Moskau* (Tübingen, 1922).

Brockdorff-Rantzau, Graf U., *Dokumente* (Charlottenburg, 1920).

Buchrucker, Major B. E., *Im Schatten Seeckts: Die Geschichte der Schwarzen Reichswehr* (Berlin, 1928).

Bullock, A., *Hitler: A Study in Tyranny* (London, 1952).

Caro, K., and Oehme, W., *Schleichers Aufstieg: Ein Beitrag zur Geschichte der Gegenrevolution* (Berlin, 1933).

D'Abernon, Lord, *An Ambassador of Peace*, 3 Vols. (London, 1929-1930).

D'Abernon, Lord, *Portraits and Appreciations* (London, 1931).

Deutscher, I., *The Prophet Armed* (London, 1954).

Dirksen, H. von, *Moskau-Tokio-London* (Stuttgart, 1949).

Ebert, F., *Schriften, Aufzeichnungen, Reden*, 2 Vols. (Dresden, 1926).

Erzberger, M., *Erlebnisse im Weltkrieg* (Stuttgart, 1949).

Fischer, R., *Stalin and German Communism* (Cambridge, U.S.A., 1948).

Fröhlich, P., *Rosa Luxemburg*, trl. E. Fitzgerald (London, 1940).

Goltz, General Graf von der, *Meine Sendung in Finnland und im Baltikum* (Leipzig, 1920).

Groener-Geyer, D., *General Groener: Soldat und Staatsmann* (Frankfurt/Main, 1954).

Gumbel, E. J., *Verräter verfallen der Feme!* (Berlin, 1929).

Hoffmann, Major-General M., *War Diaries*, trl. E. Sutton, 2 Vols. (London, 1929).

Kabisch, E., *Groener: Männer und Mächte* (Leipzig, 1932).

Kessler, Count H., *Walter Rathenau* (London, 1929).

Krassin, L., *Leonid Krassin* (London, 1929).

Krivitsky, L., *I was Stalin's Agent* (London, 1939).

Laue, T. von, 'Soviet Diplomacy: G. B. Chicherin, Peoples' Commissar for Foreign Affairs, 1918-1930,' *The Diplomats 1919-1939*, ed. G. A. Craig and F. Gilbert (Princeton, 1953).

Löwenstein, H. Prinz zu, *Stresemann: Das deutsche Schicksal im Spiegel seines Lebens* (Frankfurt/Main, 1952).

Meissner, O., *Staatssekretär unter Ebert, Hindenburg, Hitler* (Hamburg, 1950).

Morgan, Brigadier-General J. H., *Assize of Arms* (London, 1945).

Noske, G., *Von Kiel bis Kapp* (Berlin, 1920).

Okay, C., *Enver Pasha: der grosse Freund Deutschlands* (Leipzig, 1935).

Papen, F. von, *Memoirs* (New York, 1953).

Pope, A. U., *Maxim Litvinoff* (New York, 1943).

Price, M. P., *My Reminiscences of the Russian Revolution* (London, 1921).

Rabenau, General F. von, *Seeckt: Aus seinem Leben 1918-1936*, Vol. 2 (Leipzig, 1940).

Rathenau, W., *Briefe*, 2 Vols. (Dresden, 1926).

I * *

Rathenau, W., *Cannes und Genua* (Dresden, 1922).

Rathenau, W., *Ein Preussischer Europäer* (letters) (Berlin, 1955).

Scheffer, P., *Sieben Jahre Sowjetunion* (Leipzig, 1930).

Scheidemann, P., *The Makings of New Germany*, trl. J. Mitchell, Vol. 2 (New York, 1929).

Schmidt-Pauli, E. von, *General von Seeckt: Lebensbild eines deutschen Soldaten* (Berlin, 1937).

Seymour, C. (ed.), *The Intimate Papers of Colonel House*, Vol. 4 (London, 1926).

Stein, L., *Aus dem Leben eines Optimisten* (Berlin, 1930).

Stern-Rubarth, E., *Graf Brockdorff-Rantzau* (Berlin, 1929).

Stresemann, C., *Essays and Speeches on Various Subjects* (London, 1930).

Stresemann, G., *Reden und Schriften: Politik, Geschichte, Literatur, 1897–1926*, Vol. 2 (Dresden, 1926).

Stresemann, G., *Vermächtnis*, 3 Vols., ed. H. Bernhard and others (Berlin, 1932–1933).

Trotsky, L., *Stalin* (London, 1947).

Vallentin, A., *Stresemann*, trl. E. Sutton (London, 1931).

Waleszewski, K., *Peter the Great*, trl. Lady Mary Loyd (London, 1898).

Wheeler-Bennett, J. W., *Hindenburg: The Wooden Titan* (London, 1936).

Wirth, J., *Reden während der Kanzlerschaft* (Berlin, 1925).

Zetkin, C., *Lenin* (Moscow, 1925).

## ARTICLES, ESSAYS, PAMPHLETS, AND SPEECHES

Bernhard, H., 'Seeckt und Stresemann,' *Deutsche Rundschau*, 79. Jhrg., Heft 5 (Darmstadt, Mai 1953).

Boveri, M., 'Rapallo. Geheimnis—Wunschtraum—Gespenst,' *Merkur*, September 1952.

Craig, G., 'Germany between the East and the West,' An Address before the *Academy of Political Science* (New York, 1949).

Craig, G., 'Reichswehr and National Socialism: The Policy of Wilhelm Groener, 1928–1932,' *Political Science Quarterly*, Vol. 43, No. 2 (New York, June 1948).

Epstein, J., 'Der Seeckt Plan,' *Der Monat*, 1. Jhrg., Nr. 2 (Berlin, November 1948).

Fraenkel, E., 'German-Russian Relations in Soviet Diplomacy since 1918,' *Review of Politics*, Vol. 2, No. 1 (Notre Dame, January 1940).

Gatzke, H. W., 'The Stresemann Papers,' *Journal of Modern History*, Vol. 26, No. 1 (Chicago, March 1954).

Gatzke, H. W., 'Deutsch-Russische Beziehungen im Sommer 1918,' *Vierteljahrshefte für Zeitgeschichte*, 3. Jhrg., Heft 1 (Stuttgart, Januar 1955).

Gatzke, H. W., 'Von Rapallo nach Berlin: Stresemann und die deutsche Russlandpolitik,' *Vierteljahrshefte für Zeitgeschichte*, 4. Jhrg., Heft 1 (Stuttgart, Januar 1956).

——, 'Generale in der deutschen Republik: Groener, Schleicher, Seeckt' (Berlin, 1932).

Görlitz, W., 'Wallensteins Lager 1920-1938,' *Frankfurter Hefte* (Frankfurt/Main, Mai 1948).

Hallgarten, G. F. W., 'General Hans von Seeckt and Russia, 1920-1922,' *Journal of Modern History*, Vol. 21, No. 1 (Chicago, March 1949).

Helbig, H., 'Die Moskauer Mission des Grafen Brockdorff-Rantzau,' *Forschungen zur Osteuropäischen Geschichte*, 2. Band (Berlin, 1955).

Henn, R., 'Deutschland-Russland in Vergangenheit, Gegenwart und Zukunft' (Hamburg, 1920).

Hirsch, F. E., 'Stresemann in Historical Perspective,' *Review of Politics*, Vol. 15, No. 3 (Notre Dame, July 1953).

Katkov, G., 'German Foreign Office Documents on Financial Support to the Bolsheviks in 1917,' *International Affairs*, Vol. 32, No. 2 (London, April 1956).

Klemperer, K. von, 'Towards a Fourth Reich? The History of National Bolshevism in Germany,' *Review of Politics*, Vol. 13 (Notre Dame, 1951).

Kochan, L., 'The Russian Road to Rapallo,' *Soviet Studies*, Vol. 2, No. 2 (Oxford, October 1950).

Kochan, L., 'General von Seeckt,' *Contemporary Review* (London, July 1950).

Kollman, E. C., 'Walter Rathenau and German Foreign Policy,' *Journal of Modern History*, Vol. 24, No. 2 (Chicago, June 1952).

Luckau, A., 'Kapp Putsch: Success or Failure?' *Journal of Central European Affairs*, Vol. 7, No. 4 (New York, January 1948).

Morgan, Brigadier-General J. H., 'The Present State of Germany,' A Lecture delivered at the University of London (London, 1924).

Niedermayer, Captain Professor R. von, 'Sowjet-Russland, ein wehrpolitisches Bild,' *Militärwissenschaftliche Rundschau* (Berlin, Dezember 1939).

——, 'The Nemesis of Power,' an anonymous review, *The Times Literary Supplement*, 53rd Year, No. 2,710 (London, 8 January 1954).

Palmer, A. W., 'The German Army and Politics from the Armistice to the Kapp Putsch,' unpublished paper (Oriel College, Oxford, November 1951).

Phelps, R. H., 'Aus den Groener-Dokumenten,' *Deutsche Rundschau*, 76. and 77. Jhrg. (Darmstadt, 1950-1951): 'Groener, Ebert und Hindenburg,' Juli 1950; 'Die Aussenpolitik der O.H.L. bis zum Friedensvertrag,' Aug. 1950; 'Bayern und Reich,' Sept. 1950; 'Das

Baltikum 1919,' Oct. 1950; 'Der Fall Scheringer-Ludin-Wendt,' Nov. 1950; 'Die Briefe an Alarich von Gleich 1930-1932,' Dez. 1950; 'Das SA-Verbot und der Sturz des Kabinetts Brüning,' Jan. 1951.

Phelps, R. H., 'Aus den Seeckt-Dokumenten,' Deutsche Rundschau, 78. Jhrg., Hefte 9-10 (Darmstadt, September-Oktober 1952).

Pollmüller, I. H., 'Die Reichswehr in der Republik,' Frankfurter Hefte (Frankfurt/Main, Dezember 1946).

Pollmüller, I. H., 'Die Rolle der Reichswehr von 1918-1933,' Frankfurter Hefte (Frankfurt/Main, November 1946).

Radek, K., 'Die auswärtige Politik des Deutschen Kommunismus und der Hamburger Nationale Bolschewismus,' Die Internationale, 1. Jhrg., Heft 17/18, 20 (Berlin, Dezember 1919).

Radek, K., 'Deutschland und Russland: Ein in der Moabiter Schutzhaft geschriebener Artikel für "Richtiggehende" Bourgeois,' Zukunft, No. 19 (Berlin, 7 Februar 1920).

Radek, K., 'Genua, die Einheitsfront der Proletariats und die Kommunistische Internationale' (pamphlet) (Hamburg, 1922).

Radek, K., 'The Winding-Up of the Versailles Treaty' (pamphlet) (Hamburg, 1922).

Radek, K., 'Zur Taktik des Kommunismus: Ein Schreiben an den Oktober-Parteitag der KPD' (pamphlet) (Hamburg, 1919).

Rheinbaben, W. Freiherr von, 'Deutsche Ostpolitik in Locarno,' Aussenpolitik, 4. Jhrg., Heft 1 (Stuttgart, Januar 1953).

Rosinski, H., 'Rebuilding the Reichswehr,' Atlantic Monthly, Vol. 173, No. 2 (New York, February 1944).

Russbueldt, O. L., 'The Reichswehr' (pamphlet) (-?-, n.d.).

——, 'Russian Documents,' Soviet Studies, Vol. 3, No. 2 (Oxford, October 1951).

——, 'Russland und Wir: Betrachtungen über Russland und den Bolschewismus' (pamphlet) (Stuttgart, 1951).

Scheffer, P., 'Die Lehren von Rapallo,' Merkur, April 1953.

Schoenaich, General Freiherr von, 'The What and Why of German Militarism,' The Living Age (London, 1 November 1924).

Speidel, H., 'Reichswehr und Rote Armee,' Vierteljahrshefte für Zeitgeschichte, 1. Jhrg., Heft 1 (Stuttgart, Januar 1953).

Wheeler-Bennett, J. W., 'Twenty Years of Russo-German Relations, 1919-1939,' Foreign Affairs (New York, October 1946).

## NEWSPAPERS

American: Chicago Daily News; New York Evening Post; New York Times; New York Tribune; San Francisco Chronicle.

British: *Daily Mail; Daily Telegraph; Manchester Guardian; The Times; Yorkshire Evening News.*
German: *Bergisch-Märkische Zeitung; Berliner Tageblatt; Deutsche Allgemeine Zeitung; Hamburger Allgemeine Zeitung; Kreuz-Zeitung; Münchner Post; Norddeutsche Allgemeine Zeitung; Völkischer Beobachter; Vorwärts; Vossische Zeitung; Die Weltbühne.*
Russian: *Izvestiya; Pravda.*


## HISTORIES OF WEIMAR GERMANY AND SOVIET RUSSIA, AND OTHER WORKS

Antonelli, F., *Bolshevist Russia*, trl. A. S. Lipschitz (London, 1920).

Barker, E. K., *Reflections on Government* (Oxford, 1942).

Basseches, N., *The Unknown Army: The Nature and History of the Russian Military Forces* (London, 1943).

Baykov, A., *Soviet Foreign Trade* (Princeton, 1946).

Beloff, M., *The Foreign Policy of Soviet Russia 1929-1936*, Vol. 1 (Oxford, 1947).

Bischoff, Major A. D., *Die letzte Front: Geschichte der Eisernen Division im Baltikum 1919* (Berlin, 1935).

Borkenau, F., *The Communist International* (London, 1938).

Bracher, K. D., *Die Auflösung der Weimarer Republik* (Stuttgart and Düsseldorf, 1955).

Bretton, H. L., *Stresemann and the Revision of Versailles* (Stanford, 1953).

Bruck, M. von der, *Das Recht der jungen Völker*, ed. H. Schwarz (Berlin, 1932).

Butler, R. D., *The Roots of National Socialism* (London, 1942).

Carr, E. H., *The Bolshevik Revolution 1917-1923* (London, 1953).

Carr, E. H., *German-Soviet Relations Between the Two World Wars, 1919-1939* (Baltimore, 1951).

Carr, E. H., *The Interregnum 1923-1924* (London, 1954).

Carr, E. H., *Studies in Revolution* (London, 1950).

Churchill, W. S., *The Gathering Storm* (London, 1948).

Clark, R. T., *The Fall of the German Republic* (London, 1935).

Craig, G. A., *The Politics of the Prussian Army 1640-1945* (Oxford, 1945).

Cumming, C. K., and Pettit, W. W., ed., *Russian-American Relations March 1917-March 1920* (New York, 1920).

Daniels, H. G., *The Rise of the German Republic* (London, 1927).

Dennis, A. L. P., *The Foreign Policies of Soviet Russia* (New York, 1924).

Eyck, E., *Geschichte der Weimarer Republik 1918-1925* (Erlenbach-Zurich, 1954).

Fischer, L., *Men and Politics* (New York, 1941).

Fischer, L., *The Soviets in World Affairs*, 2 Vols. (London, 1930).

Flechtheim, O. K., *Die Kommunistische Partei Deutschlands in der Weimarer Republik* (Offenbach, 1948).

Fraser, L., *Germany Between Two Wars: A Study of Propaganda and War Guilt* (Oxford, 1944).

Fried, H. E., *The Guilt of the German Army* (New York, 1942).

Gathorne-Hardy, G. M., *A Short History of International Affairs 1920–1939*, 4th Edition (Oxford, 1950).

Gatzke, H. W., *Stresemann and the Rearmament of Germany* (Baltimore, 1954).

Grzesinski, A. C., *Inside Germany* (New York, 1939).

Hallgarten, G. F. W., *Hitler—Reichswehr und Industrie* (Frankfurt/Main, 1955).

Halperin, S. W., *Germany Tried Democracy* (New York, 1946).

Hartlieb, W. W., *Das politische Vertragssystem der Sowjetunion 1920–1935* (Leipzig, 1936).

Hermann, Hauptmann, *The Rise and Fall of the Luftwaffe* (London, 1943).

Hilger, G., and Meyer, A. G., *The Incompatible Allies* (New York, 1953).

Hoffmann, General-Major M., *Auf allen Enden Moskau* (Berlin, 1925).

Hohlfeld, A., *Versailles und die Russische Frage 1918–1919* (Hamburg, 1940).

Holborn, H., 'Diplomats and Diplomacy in the Early Weimar Republic,' *The Diplomats*, ed. G. A. Craig and F. Gilbert (Princeton, 1953).

Kautsky, K., *Das Weitertreiben der Revolution* (Berlin, 1919).

Klein, F., *Die diplomatischen Beziehungen Deutschlands zur Sowjetunion 1917–1932* ([East] Berlin, 1952).

Klotz, H., *Germany's Secret Armaments*, trl. H. J. Stennings (London, 1934).

Knight-Patterson, W. M., *Germany from Defeat to Conquest, 1918–1933* (London, 1946).

Kuczynski, J., and Wittkowski, G., *Die deutsch-russischen Handelsbeziehungen in den letzten 150 Jahren* (Berlin, 1945).

Lenin, V. I., '*Left-Wing*' *Communism, an Infantile Disorder* (New York, 1940).

Lutz, R. H., ed., *The Fall of the German Empire 1914–1918*, 2 Vols. (Stanford, 1932).

Luxemburg, R., *Die russische Revolution*, ed. P. Levi (Berlin, 1922).

Macartney, C. A., and others, *Survey of International Affairs 1925*, Vol. 2 (London, 1928).

Melville, C. F., *The Russian Face of Germany* (London, 1932).

Mielcke, K., *Dokumente zur Geschichte der Weimarer Republik* (Braunschweig, 1951).

Mielcke, K., *Geschichte der Weimarer Republik* (Braunschweig, 1954).

Mikolajizyk, S., *The Rape of Poland* (New York, 1948).

Oertzen, F. W. von, *Die Deutsche Freikorps 1918-1923* (München, 1936).

Ovseyenko, A., *Der Aufbau der Roten Armee in der Revolution* (Hamburg, 1923).

Radek, K., *Die auswärtige Politik Sowjet-Russlands* (Hamburg, 1921).

Radek, K., *Portraits and Pamphlets*, ed. A. J. Cummings (London, 1935).

Radek, K., *Die russische und die deutsche Revolution und die Weltlage* (Berlin, 1919).

Rosenberg, A., *Geschichte der Deutschen Republik* (Karlsbad, 1935).

Rosinski, H., *The German Army* (London, 1939).

Rudin, H. R., *Armistice 1918* (New Haven, 1944).

Scheele, G., *The Weimar Republic: Overture to the Third Reich* (London, 1945).

Schüddekopf, O. E., *Heer und Republik* (Hannover and Frankfurt/Main, 1955).

Schwarz, G., *Völker, höret die Zentrale: KPD bankerott* (Berlin, 1933).

Seeckt, General H. von, *The Future of the German Empire*, trl. O. Williams (London, 1930).

Seeckt, General H. von, *Die Reichswehr* (Leipzig, 1933).

Seeckt, General H. von, *Thoughts of a Soldier*, trl. General Sir I. Hamilton (London, 1930).

Seeckt, General H. von, *Wege deutscher Aussenpolitik* (Leipzig, 1931).

Shotwell and Laserson, *Russia and Poland 1919-1945* (New York, 1945).

Stampfer, F., *Die vierzehn Jahre der ersten deutschen Republik* (Karlsbad, 1936).

Taylor, A. J. P., *The Course of German History* (London, 1951).

Taylor, Brigadier-General T., *Sword and Swastika* (New York, 1952).

Toynbee, A. J., *Survey of International Affairs 1920-1923* (London, 1927).

Treitschke, H. von, *Politics*, trl. B. Dugdale and T. de Bille, 2 Vols. (London, 1916).

Troeltsch, E., *Spektator-Briefe: Aufsätze über die deutsche Revolution und die Weltpolitik 1918-1922* (Tübingen, 1924).

Trotsky, L., *History of the Russian Revolution to Brest-Litovsk* (London, 1919).

Volkmann, E. O., *Revolution über Deutschland* (Oldenburg, 1930).

Wachenfeld, General E., 'Die Luftwaffe nach dem Weltkriege,' *Die Deutsche Wehrmacht 1914-1939* (Berlin, 1939).

Waite, R. G. L., *Vanguard of Nazism* (Cambridge, U.S.A., 1952).

Wheeler-Bennett, J. W., *Brest-Litovsk: The Forgotten Peace, March 1918* (London, 1938).

Wheeler-Bennett, J. W., *The Nemesis of Power* (London, 1953).

Wheeler-Bennett, J. W., *The Treaty of Brest-Litovsk and Germany's Eastern Policy* (New York, 1939).

Winnig, A., *Das Reich als Republik 1918-1928* (Stuttgart/Berlin, 1928).

Wollenberg, E., *The Red Army* (London, 1938).

Zinoviev, G., *All Power to the Workers: Four Speeches delivered at the Tenth Congress, Russian Communist Party (Bolshevists), 1921* (Petrograd, n.d.).

# INDEX

## Date Due

| MAY 22 '59 | | |
|---|---|---|
| MAY 22 '64 | | |
| | | |
| | | |
| | | |
| | | |
| | | |
| | | |
| | | |
| | | |
| | | |
| | | |
| | | |
| | | |
| | | |
| | PRINTED IN U. S. A. | |